Robert Fletcher
Easter 1999

The Rule of Law under Siege

Weimar and Now: German Cultural Criticism

Martin Jay and Anton Kaes, General Editors

1. *Heritage of Our Times,* by Ernst Bloch
2. *The Nietzsche Legacy in Germany, 1890–1990,* by Steven E. Aschheim
3. *The Weimar Republic Sourcebook,* edited by Anton Kaes, Martin Jay, and Edward Dimendberg
4. *Batteries of Life: On the History of Things and Their Perception in Modernity,* by Christoph Asendorf
5. *Profane Illumination: Walter Benjamin and the Paris of Surrealist Revolution,* by Margaret Cohen
6. *Hollywood in Berlin: American Cinema and Weimar Germany,* by Thomas J. Saunders
7. *Walter Benjamin: An Aesthetic of Redemption,* by Richard Wolin
8. *The New Typography,* by Jan Tschichold, translated by Ruari McLean
9. *The Rule of Law under Siege: Selected Essays of Franz L. Neumann and Otto Kirchheimer,* edited by William E. Scheuerman

The Rule of Law under Siege

Selected Essays of Franz L. Neumann
and Otto Kirchheimer

EDITED BY
William E. Scheuerman

UNIVERSITY OF CALIFORNIA PRESS
Berkeley   Los Angeles   London

University of California Press
Berkeley and Los Angeles, California

University of California Press
London, England

Copyright © 1996 by
The Regents of the University of California

Library of Congress Cataloging-in-Publication Data
Scheuerman, William E.
 The rule of law under siege: selected essays of Franz L. Neumann and Otto Kirchheimer / edited by William E. Scheuerman.
  p. cm.
 Includes bibliographical references and index.
 ISBN 0-520-20379-8 (alk. paper)
 1. Rule of law—Germany. 2. Legitimacy of government—Germany.
3. Rule of law. I. Scheuerman, William E., 1965-   .
KK4426.R85   1996
340'.11—dc20   96-2157
                                              CIP

Printed in the United States of America

1 2 3 4 5 6 7 8 9

The paper used in this publication meets the minimum requirements of American National Standard for Information Sciences—Permanence of Paper for Printed Library Materials, ANSI Z39.48-1984 ∞

CONTENTS

ACKNOWLEDGMENTS / *vii*
INTRODUCTION
William E. Scheuerman / *1*

PART I • THE DESTRUCTION OF WEIMAR DEMOCRACY AND THE DEBATE ON LEGALITY AND LEGITIMACY

1. The Decay of German Democracy (1933)
   Franz L. Neumann / *29*

2. Legality and Legitimacy (1932)
   Otto Kirchheimer / *44*

3. Remarks on Carl Schmitt's *Legality and Legitimacy* (1933)
   Otto Kirchheimer / *64*

PART II • LAW AND POLITICS IN THE AUTHORITARIAN STATE

4. The Change in the Function of Law in Modern Society (1937)
   Franz L. Neumann / *101*

5. State Structure and Law in the Third Reich (1935)
   Otto Kirchheimer / *142*

6. Criminal Law in National Socialist Germany (1940)
   Otto Kirchheimer / *172*

PART III • TOWARD A CRITICAL DEMOCRATIC THEORY

7. The Concept of Political Freedom (1953)
   Franz L. Neumann / 195

8. Labor Law in Modern Society (1951)
   Franz L. Neumann / 231

9. The *Rechtsstaat* as Magic Wall (1967)
   Otto Kirchheimer / 243

INDEX / *265*

ACKNOWLEDGMENTS

Many people have helped in the preparation of this volume, but special thanks go to Mrs. Anne Kirchheimer and Professor Michael Neumann for making it possible in the first place. Ed Dimendberg of the University of California Press has been unfailing in his support. Martin Jay made a number of characteristically insightful criticisms on an earlier version of the introduction. My cotranslator, Anke Grosskopf, saved me from committing many embarrassing mistakes, and I am very grateful for the superb job that she has done. Peter Breil also helped by checking earlier drafts of the translations. Finally, the competent and gracious staff at the Bremen *Staats- und Universitätsbibliothek* patiently serviced my many requests for old books from dusty basement shelves.

I would also like to thank Julia Roos for many reasons, not the least of which is the courage she demonstrated when trying, almost single-handedly, to ward off an attack by an East German gang of neo-Nazis on a pair of East European street gamblers in the summer of 1991. While working on this volume, I have often found myself thinking about that horrible afternoon in the town of Warnemünde, in part because I am now less sure than I was at the time of the attack that such things are impossible on American streets. Finally, let me thank my parents, Bill and Louise, for making sure that not only Jerry Lee Lewis and Little Richard were household names when I was growing up, but C. Wright Mills and Herbert Marcuse as well.

Chapter 1 is reprinted with the permission of *The Political Quarterly*. Chapters 2, 3, and 5 originally appeared in German and are translated here by permission of the Suhrkamp Verlag in Frankfurt. Chapters 4 and 7 are reprinted with the permission of the Free Press, Chapter 9 with permission of the Beacon Press, and Chapter 8 by permission of the German labor law journal *Recht der Arbeit*.

Introduction

William E. Scheuerman

For nearly twenty-five years now, radical scholars in the American legal academy have subjected the ideal of the rule of law to a scathing critique. Whereas classical liberal democratic jurisprudence has demanded that law take a clear and cogent form in order to render state action as predictable as possible, contemporary authors associated with the Critical Legal Studies movement (CLS) have countered with the thesis that

> it is impossible to imagine any central or local legal institutions advocating a coherent, noncontradictory body of rules. *All* rules will contain within them deeply embedded, structural premises that clearly enable decision makers to resolve particular controversies in opposite ways.... [A]ll law seems simultaneously either to demand or at least allow internally contradictory steps.[1]

Allegedly, the traditional quest for determinate legal rules is illusory; a profound and unavoidable indeterminacy necessarily lies at the core of all legal experience. From Jeremy Bentham to John Rawls, a rich tradition of liberal political thought has emphasized the virtues of the rule of law for democratic politics. Some recent scholars instead prefer to highlight its purportedly privatistic and antiegalitarian elements. Roberto Unger goes so far, at least at one juncture, to endorse its dismantlement: since "the experience that supports the rule of law is one of antagonism among private wills," he suggests that a communal, solidaristic, political and social system very well might be able to do without it. If classical law depends on illegitimate forms of inequality, why not just discard the rule of law? A system of indwelling communal values, based on odd moralistic standards (such as "in good faith," "in the public interest") that have taken on ever greater significance in contemporary law, purportedly could make up the core of an alternative to it.[2] Why worry about a panoply of signs that suggest the ongoing decay of the rule of law?

The essays collected in this volume serve to introduce an alternative tradition of "critical legal studies" to an audience that has long been denied access to it. Franz L. Neumann (1900–1954) and Otto Kirchheimer (1905–1965)—the resident legal and political scholars of the pathbreaking and rightly famous neo-Marxist Institute for Social Research—were hardly oblivious to the ways in which liberal legal forms are implicated in the manifest inequalities and injustices of contemporary society.[3] Yet in dramatic contrast to much of contemporary radical American legal scholarship, the Frankfurt School theorists Neumann and Kirchheimer expressed substantial sympathy for a number of traditional components of the ideal of the rule of law. Unlike some currents within contemporary Critical Legal Studies, their analysis and critique of the rule of law ideal never succumbed to the temptations of a one-sided "deconstruction" of the modern legal tradition. Of course, the concerns of Neumann and Kirchheimer are oftentimes analytically and temporally distinct from contemporary Critical Legal Studies; we obviously cannot expect a decisive intellectual response to contemporary CLS from two intellectual offspring of Weimar Germany. By the same token, Neumann and Kirchheimer present an impressive challenge to the knee-jerk hostility to liberal legalism widespread in contemporary critical legal scholarship. Witnesses to the tragic destruction of the Weimar Republic and the rise of Nazism, Neumann and Kirchheimer argued early on that crucial components of the rule of law are threatened in the twentieth century by a series of unprecedented political and social transformations. In the most general terms, the transition from classical liberal parliamentarism to a form of bureaucratized mass democracy and the evolution of traditional competitive capitalism into a increasingly "organized capitalism" dependent on extensive state intervention threaten to undermine the rule of law by destroying many of its original institutional presuppositions. Whereas many contemporary radical legal scholars suggest that we should welcome this trend, Neumann and Kirchheimer powerfully argue that we very much need to acknowledge its ambivalent and in many ways truly worrisome implications.

Like their colleagues at the Institute for Social Research, Neumann and Kirchheimer were often obsessed with the significance of the Nazi experience for understanding contemporary legal development; they, too, at times undoubtedly overstated the centrality of fascism when formulating their dramatic views about the (alleged) ongoing disintegration of the rule of law. In some distinction to Max Horkheimer, Theodor Adorno, and Herbert Marcuse, however, the experience of fascism simultaneously cemented Neumann's and Kirchheimer's appreciation for a series of liberal legal and political institutions. The Frankfurt School's political and legal scholars thus ultimately proved able to integrate the traditional concerns of liberal legal and political theory into their theorizing in a manner that none of their colleagues was able to rival. This also helps explain the real tensions that existed between Neumann and Kirchheimer and theorists such as Horkheimer and Adorno. Within the Institute for Social Research, Neumann and Kirchheimer were, unquestionably, "outsiders"; their nuanced interpretation of the achievements of the modern legal tradition conflicted with the increasingly apocalyptic theorizing of the Frankfurt School's main representatives during the late 1930s and early '40s. A real divide separates the careful, empirically minded—but nonetheless socially critical—essays collected in this volume from the brilliant but excessively one-sided view of Western modernity articulated, for example, in Horkheimer and Adorno's famous *Dialectic of Enlightenment*.[4]

Neumann and Kirchheimer also engaged in a life-long intellectual dialogue with Carl Schmitt, twentieth-century Germany's foremost right-wing authoritarian political and legal theorist (and an object of growing interest among scholars today).[5] In light of contemporary debates among jurists and political scientists, their intense exchange with Schmitt takes on renewed significance.[6] In Germany in the 1930s, it was Carl Schmitt who led a chorus of voices that was busily occupied with the task of demonstrating the alleged incoherence of liberal legal and political ideals. In contrast to contemporary theoretical constellations, representatives of the authoritarian right argued that liberal ideals of determinate law were a mere myth: "the sovereignty of law means only the sovereignty of men who draw up and administer law."[7] Fascist antilegalists proceeded to draw at least one possible conclusion from this position and began to emphasize the role of the sovereign, normatively unregulated *will* or *power decision* within law. For them, the emerging Nazi legal order was superior to its liberal democratic rivals in part because fascist Germany's heavy reliance on vague, open-ended *indeterminate* legal provisos alone allegedly gave full expression to the centrality of an arbitrary *willfulness* that was thought to constitute the unavoidable essence of all legal experience. In the 1930s, right-wing authoritarians insisted that liberal legalism's attempt to delineate between law and morality was incoherent; many of them helped make sure that the new legal order of the German "folk community" would build on amorphous, moralistic legal standards in order to subject it to reactionary, antipluralistic moral ideas.[8] Right-wing authors like Schmitt enthusiastically proclaimed the death of the basic tenets of universalistic liberal jurisprudence, and he and his allies then relied on this claim to help justify the situation-oriented, highly arbitrary structure of Nazi law.

The essays collected in this volume should encourage contemporary students of the rule of law to reconsider many of the political and intellectual divisions characteristic of contemporary debates within political and legal theory: an easy "deconstruction" of the rule of law may very well prove to have far more *indeterminate* political implications than many contemporary scholars are willing to recognize. Neumann's and Kirchheimer's essays also demand that we try to answer a question that remains as crucial today as it was in the 1930s and '40s: if left unchecked, might not the apparent decay of some facets of the rule of law—now widely documented by a diverse group of scholars[9]—leave us with a troubling, highly discretionary system of law very much incompatible with democratic politics?

Although the world of the early Frankfurt School is undoubtedly very different from our own, we surely would do well not to make the mistake of naively assuming that the political catastrophes of the 1930s and '40s are unrelated to the fate of contemporary democracy.

THE DESTRUCTION OF WEIMAR DEMOCRACY AND THE DEBATE ON LEGALITY AND LEGITIMACY

Franz Neumann and Otto Kirchheimer reached intellectual maturity during the Weimar Republic's final, crisis-ridden years, and their Weimar-era experiences decisively shaped the structure of their intellectual interests. Both labor lawyers, activists in the Social Democratic Party, and prolific contributors to a wide variety of legal and political journals, Neumann and Kirchheimer spent much of their time during Weimar's final years doing battle with those trends that culminated in a process in which—as Neumann describes it in "The Decay of German Democracy" (1933)—"German democracy committed suicide and was murdered at one and the same time."[10] Written for the British journal *The Political Quarterly* immediately following the Nazi takeover, this early essay not only anticipates elements of the neo-Marxist account of German fascism provided by Neumann's classic *Behemoth: The Structure and Practice of National Socialism*,[11] but also offers a preliminary analysis of those features of Weimar's demise that he and Kirchheimer came to consider of more general significance for understanding legal and political processes in the twentieth century: the potential fragility of welfare state–type constitutional systems based on uneasy compromises among antagonistic social groups, growing evidence that privileged social blocs are increasingly hostile to traditional liberal democratic institutions, the decline of parliament whereby "the state is no more a liberal one but which interferes with nearly all aspects of human life,"[12] the growth of judicial discretion and its potential perils to democracy, and the blurring of any meaningful distinction between parliamentary law and administrative decree and the concomitant transformation of the bureaucratic apparatus into the central decision-making body of the contemporary state. The essays that appear in this volume deal with one or more aspects of these vital issues.

As Neumann notes in "The Decay of Weimar Democracy," the Weimar Constitution represented an unprecedented attempt to synthesize traditional liberal institutions with new forms of direct democracy, socialist conceptions of economic democracy, and ambitious programmatic constitutional rights and standards—some of which, like Article 162's announcement that "the federal government shall endeavour to secure international regulation of the legal status of workers to the end that the entire working class of the world may enjoy a universal minimum of social rights," possessed a distinctly radical character.[13] Undertaking their task in the immediate aftermath of the Soviet Revolution and then Germany's own revolution in 1918, the Constitution's architects—jurists and politicians like Hugo Preuss and Friedrich Naumann—believed that the special conditions of political and social existence in postrevolutionary Germany necessitated undertaking a series of legal innovations if the new republic were to gain a measure of stability. In order to do justice to the breathtaking ideological pluralism of postwar Germany, the Constitution seemed to abolish, as Neumann points out, any transcendental justification of government. In contrast to many previous democratic constitutions, it supplemented a first, rather traditional section that outlined basic organizational and formal decision-making procedures with a second, highly detailed section dedicated to an ambitious set of "basic rights and duties of the German people." Aiming to bring together Germany's heterogeneous social and political groups *and* simultaneously provide meaningful opportunities for substantial political and social evolution by means of constitutionally circumscribed paths, these "basic rights and duties" included provisions for classical liberal democratic rights as well as a rather diverse set of so-called material clauses: Article 119, for example, declared that marriage constituted "the foundation of family life" and hence should enjoy "special protections," Article 151 required that the economy should be organized in conformity with "the principles of justice," and Article 165 anticipated the possibility of restructuring economic production along democratic socialist lines.

Unsurprisingly, Weimar's constitutional agenda proved controversial in the explosive political and social atmosphere of Germany in the 1920s and '30s. Both left- and right-wing radicals belittled its idiosyncratic aspiration to codify a political and social order situated "between capitalism and socialism."[14] Even today, attempts to update traditional liberal constitutionalism by attributing special constitutional status to the welfare state and so-called *social rights* (to a job, health care, or a guaranteed income) remain the object of heated disputes among jurists and political scientists.[15] The Weimar Constitution clearly represents an early example of the ongoing and very much unfinished quest to fashion *posttraditional* constitutions—that is, constitutions combining traditional liberal democratic political mechanisms and rights with new forms of direct democracy and, typically, a constitutional acknowledgment of the emergence of the welfare state.[16] Consequently, the fate of the Weimar Constitution raises a series of questions of great importance for the evolution of contemporary constitutionalism.

Otto Kirchheimer's "Legality and Legitimacy" (1932) and his "Remarks on Carl Schmitt's *Legality and Legitimacy*" (coauthored with Nathan Leites in 1933) provide an introduction to the fascinating debate that took place in response to the decay of constitutional government during Weimar's final years. Kirchheimer's essays offer a powerful corrective to first, misleading contemporary analyses of the legal roots of Weimar's demise, and second, apologetic interpretations of Carl Schmitt's political and legal theory.[17]

In *Economy and Society,* Max Weber famously argued that "rational legal authority" constitutes a characteristically modern answer to the problem of generating belief in the rightness of the political order. In a morally disenchanted world, the belief in enacted rules provides the most effective means for guaranteeing political obedience. The question of legitimacy in the contemporary world is a problem of legality; modern law guarantees its own legitimacy.[18] In "Legality and Legitimacy," Kirchheimer builds on Weber's claim in order to demonstrate that German legal and administrative practices in the early 1930s constitute a blatant surrender of Weber's rational legality—which Kirchheimer, in some contrast to Weber, interprets in a democratic fashion[19]—in favor of a premodern, morally substantial, and potentially authoritarian concept of *legitimacy,* not unlike that which Weber believed necessarily lacked an adequate normative grounding in modern times. In Kirchheimer's account, administrative elites in post-1930 Germany take advantage of some elements of the Weimar Constitution, especially the emergency clauses of Article 48, in order to establish a system of "supra-legality" that is dependent on suspect, premodern legal standards that allegedly possess eternal validity and indisputable rectitude. Traditional liberal guarantees of formal equality before the law are jettisoned, and bureaucratic elites undertake openly discriminatory action against those (chiefly left-wing) groups whose social and political views are interpreted as constituting a potential threat to the reactionary political agenda of the administrative elite and its allies among the socially privileged. In short, the Weimar Constitution is robbed of its flexible, open-ended character, and an executive-centered conception of rule by administrative decree—justified by reference to the plebiscitary personage of the federal president—results in the effective abandonment of political liberalism, which in Kirchheimer's account represents a practical organizational principle for modern, socially divided Germany.

Kirchheimer's "Legality and Legitimacy" never denies that deep divisions within the German Parliament after 1930 impaired the functioning of traditional parliamentary democracy. In contrast to many accounts of this period, however, he is reluctant to conclude the story there. As Hans Boldt has similarly argued, the Weimar executive after 1930 "did not try to find a majority in Parliament at all, and the inability of Parliament to pass resolutions had been largely brought about by the government itself, which dissolved the *Reichstag* again and again."[20] Weimar's profound political and social splits contributed to the political system's ills. But a complete analysis of Weimar's demise also needs to focus on the conscious attempt by traditional elites within the governmental apparatus—in particular, in the judiciary and state bureaucracy—to destroy Germany's first experiment in democratic government. As Kirchheimer argues, they appealed to some components of the Weimar Constitution while distorting its underlying spirit; as we will see, this was precisely the strategy pursued by Carl Schmitt.

Kirchheimer's essay thus challenges a widely held interpretation of the sources of Weimar's ills. For decades, jurists have argued that Weimar's instability stemmed in part from the (alleged) pervasiveness of legal positivism among German jurists in the Weimar period. Because legal positivism insisted on a clear distinction between the spheres of morality and legality, its followers—so the argument goes—refused to concern themselves adequately with the moral character of the legal order. In turn, this rendered them impotent in the face of Nazism: unable to confront the moral ills of fascist legal and political trends, German jurists marched in line with fascist legal commands during the 1930s and '40s just as they allegedly had done during the democratic Weimar period.[21] As Kirchheimer argues here, however, administrative and judicial elites were happy to abandon formalistic characteristics of the Weimar constitutional agenda—for example, its emphasis on the need for equal treatment of different political groups—in favor of a concept of legitimacy based on a set of traditional, antipluralistic moral standards. Weimar did not collapse because its jurists were afraid to distinguish between "friends and foes," as Schmitt and his compatriots have argued, but because administrative and judicial actors hostile to democracy were all too willing to instrumentalize legal institutions in order to squelch their political opponents. Positivism was hardly an unchallenged, hegemonic theoretical orientation among German jurists during the early '30s. Instead, the belief that law should immediately serve nationalistic and belligerently bourgeois ends inspired many jurists and then led them to condone and ultimately embrace the rise of fascism.

Although "Legality and Legitimacy" emphasizes the role of Article 48 in Weimar's disintegration, Kirchheimer simultaneously hints in the essay that the amorphous material-legal standards of the second part of the Weimar Constitution might also provide a constitutional starting point for attempts within the administration and judiciary to undermine the lawmaking authority of the democratic Parliament. In Kirchheimer's analysis, such clauses permit political interests to appeal to open-ended constitutional standards (for example, Article 119's emphasis on the sanctity of the family) in juxtaposition to parliamentary legislation, and this accordingly might generate a system of "dual legality" in which judicial and administrative decision makers are outfitted with special authority that the Constitution never intended them to possess.[22] Carl Schmitt's extremely influential *Legality and Legitimacy*, which appeared in 1932 shortly after Kirchheimer's essay, seizes upon this insight but radicalizes it in order to serve altogether different political purposes. Whereas Kirchheimer points to the potential dangers of such clauses in order to warn his fellow citizens of the spectre of authoritarianism, Schmitt focuses on them with the aim of demonstrating the inherent incoherence of the Weimar Constitution—and, by implication, *any* post-traditional democratic constitution that tries to undertake a synthesis of divergent political and social ideals.

In *Legality and Legitimacy*, Schmitt depreciatively dubs the provisions in the Weimar Constitution for parliamentary lawmaking "functionalistic" and "value-free."[23] By promising to provide an "equal chance" to every political party to make up a political majority, such procedures appear to presuppose some minimal standard of justice. According to Schmitt, however, mere equal chance remains an inadequate and ineffective normative standard. Especially in crisis situations, it is unlikely that governments will assure an equal chance to their opponents. At the same time, certain material components of the Constitution's second section on "basic rights and duties" point to the outlines of a political system based on an appeal to a substantial, value-laden concept of legitimacy. Precisely this feature of the Weimar Constitution had worried Kirchheimer; in Schmitt's alternative gloss, it offers a starting point for an improved "second constitution" and thus "deserves to be freed from all internal contradictions and bad compromises and developed in a consistent manner."[24] In other words, the multifaceted democratic Weimar constitutional order should be jettisoned for a new system based on *select* elements of "the basic duties and rights" described in the latter portion of the Weimar Constitution.

Which elements did Schmitt have in mind? For the most part, his answer to this question remains vague. Nonetheless, he clearly does not aspire to salvage the Weimar Constitution's liberal democratic core, let alone its provocative social democratic elements. Much of the central argument of *Legality and Legitimacy* is devoted to trying to demonstrate the anachronistic and incoherent character of (traditional, parliamentary-based lawmaking or) *legality* and the virtues of an alternative system of political *legitimacy*. In Schmitt's view, although parliamentarism and the rule of law matches the imperatives of an early bourgeois state/society constellation, an authoritarian plebiscitary system proves better suited to the tasks of government in an era requiring extensive state intervention in social and economic affairs. As he openly announces, "the administrative state which manifests itself in the praxis of 'measures'"—in other words, a system of case-oriented, situational law like that supposedly required by the complexities of the contemporary interventionist state—"is more likely appropriate to a 'dictatorship' than the classical parliamentary state."[25] A plebiscitary dictatorship, based on an appeal either to charisma or "the authoritarian residues of a predemocratic era,"[26] accords more closely with contemporary political and social needs.

The existence of a value-laden constitutional basis for this alternative "second constitution" generates a series of immediate political difficulties for Weimar. How can a constitution be both formal and material, value-free and value-laden? Such underlying contradictions not only inevitably manifest themselves in a series of irrationalities that plague the decision-making procedures outlined in the Constitution, but a series of concrete, *empirical* dysfunctionalities result as well. Without risking a host of concrete problems, how could any constitutional order possibly institutionalize material protective clauses (for religion, for example, or marriage) that function to hinder the legislative regulation of some spheres of political existence while simultaneously endorsing a formalistic concept of parliamentary legality, according to which any conceivable political group should have an equal chance to gain majority status? For Schmitt, the fragility of Weimar democracy is preprogrammed into the Republic's own founding document.

Kirchheimer's "Remarks on Carl Schmitt's *Legality and Legitimacy*" offers an impressive critical discussion of Schmitt's most important work from the early 1930s. Here I can point only to its most provocative features.

Kirchheimer begins by criticizing both Schmitt's *normative* argument for the necessity of homogeneity in democracy and Schmitt's related *empirical* claim that democracy ultimately cannot survive without homogeneity. Relying on Hans Kelsen, Kirchheimer accomplishes this by resisting Schmitt's reductive interpretation of the ideal of democracy to the ideal of a far-reaching, substantial form of equality or "sameness." As Kirchheimer rightly points out, the struggle for democracy has always involved the attempt to realize *both* equality *and* autonomy. Only a democratic theory that acknowledges both principles can even begin to make sense of classical democratic decision-making devices such as majority rule; in contradistinction to Schmitt's attempt to ground majority rule in an illiberal interpretation of the concept of equality, Kirchheimer insists that majority rule has to be seen as aspiring to guarantee autonomy "for as many people as possible," that substantial empirical evidence suggests that heterogeneity is compatible with democratic stability, and that new sources of democratic stability, ignored by Schmitt's dramatic account of inevitable liberal democratic disintegration, may be emerging. Kirchheimer offers a tentative assessment of both the merits and demerits of an "instrumental" relationship to the political system that he considers increasingly widespread among political actors and movements in the twentieth century. But if heterogeneity is inevitable in contemporary democracy, this also implies the problematic character of Schmitt's insistence on the incoherent nature of any attempt to synthesize formal democratic rule-making procedures with special material constitutional clauses. For Kirchheimer, the Weimar Constitution does not demand that we opt *either* for its (purportedly) value-free *or* value-laden elements. Instead, it represents a sensible attempt at a compromise between decision-making procedures whose neutral character is *unimpeded* and those whose neutrality is relatively *impeded*. There is no a priori reason why "compromises between the value of democratic forms and the value of definite objective values" necessarily imperil democracy. Furthermore, "heterogeneity always implies the necessity of protection" like that provided by material constitutional clauses. In some situations, special constitutional protective clauses in fact may *reduce* political friction and thus contribute to democratic stability. Particular groups (labor unions supportive of a constitution's endorsement of economic democracy, for example, or religious dignitaries attracted by its acknowledgment of religious freedom) thus may be brought into a positive relationship to democracy. In short, the overall story—readers interested in the ongoing debate about posttraditional constitutionalism will want to pay special attention to this section of the analysis—is more complicated than Schmitt suggests: according to Kirchheimer, the integrative character of material protective clauses depends on many different factors. *Contra* Schmitt, posttraditional constitutionalism is *not* inevitably destined for the trash can of political history.[27]

Whereas Schmitt devotes much of his energy in *Legality and Legitimacy* to an analysis of the alleged irrationalities of the democratic ideal of an "equal chance," Kirchheimer shows that existing democracy, even with all of its well-known flaws, does a far better job of realizing this principle than Schmitt admits or his *own* authoritarian alternative could possibly achieve. A reformed democracy—namely one restructured in accordance with the young Kirchheimer's brand of democratic socialism—could allegedly do even better. Notwithstanding his claims to the contrary, Schmitt's proposed plebiscitary replacement for Weimar cannot be considered democratic, in part because his call for the destruction of parliamentary democracy's organizational core would fail to guarantee a "necessary minimum of freedom and equality." Democracy clearly has to involve more than a system in which, as Kirchheimer comments elsewhere,

> the people can only say "yes" or "no," it cannot counsel, deliberate, or discuss. It cannot govern or administer, nor can it posit norms; it can only sanction by its "yes" the draft norms presented to it. Nor, above all, can it put a question, but only answer by "yes" or "no" a question put to it.[28]

The real aim of Schmitt's *Legality and Legitimacy* is not to "save" the Weimar Republic, but to rob Weimar of its most elementary democratic elements by relying on a limited portion of the Weimar Constitution.

LAW AND POLITICS IN THE AUTHORITARIAN STATE

Soon after the Nazi takeover, Franz Neumann and Otto Kirchheimer joined the ranks of thousands of refugees who sought—tragically, and so often without success—asylum abroad. Neumann was able to gain a scholarship and complete a second dissertation in political theory[29] at the London School of Economics before joining the Institute for Social Research in New York in 1936. Kirchheimer first fled to Paris, but was able to become an affiliate of the Institute and join Neumann in New York in 1937.

Unsurprisingly, Neumann and Kirchheimer devoted their talents during this period to an analysis of the legal origins and structure of the National Socialist regime. The horrors of Nazism energized both thinkers intellectually; their most creative contributions to political and legal analysis stem from their attempts to come to grips with German fascism and its concrete assault on the mainstream of modern political and legal thought. Neumann's "The Change in the Function of Law in Modern Society" (1937), which appeared in the Institute's *Zeitschrift für Sozialforschung*, represents the centerpiece of this project. Kirchheimer's "State Structure and Law in the Third Reich" (1935) and "Criminal Law in National Socialist Germany" (1940) elaborate on many of the themes developed in Neumann's classic essay.

For Neumann, the most striking facet of legal development in the West was the struggle for the codification of law. For centuries, political and legal thinkers had argued that law could only secure a set of protective functions if it were *general* and relatively *unambiguous* in character. Inspired by Max Weber's account of Western legal history, Neumann endorses this view: whereas open-ended legal clauses provide extensive room for discretionary and potentially arbitrary exercises of state authority, cogent general norms bind state actors and thus provide a measure of legal security. In contrast to amorphous legal forms, general law works to regulate and thereby tame the exercise of state sovereignty. Neumann acknowledges the claim that the distinction between general norms and (discretionary) particular measures is often overstated, and that "[t]hose legal theorists who accept as legitimate only those concepts that lend themselves to a logically unambiguous formulation . . . will also reject the distinction between general norms and particular measures."[30] Nonetheless, he believes that jurists should hesitate before throwing the baby out with the bath water. However idealized, the traditional emphasis on the clarity and generality of the legal norm remains essential to the ideal of the rule of law. In his view, mean attacks on it in the twentieth century—Neumann has Carl Schmitt and his complicity in the ills of Nazi law in mind—have helped generate an increasingly *decisionist* system of law based on arbitrary "individual power commands" effectively unregulated by a coherent set of legal norms.

Although "The Change in the Function of Law in Modern Society" attributes a number of distinct functions to general law in both modern jurisprudence and real-life legal history, the marxist structure of Neumann's argument encourages him to emphasize the economic roots of the rise and subsequent disintegration of general law. Indeed, many scholars have rightly criticized the economistic core of Neumann's account of how the transition from "competitive" to "monopoly" capitalism results in the inevitable decay of the centerpiece of the rule of law, the general legal norm.[31] It would be naive to think that his underlying argument is defensible in the form presented here; indeed, Neumann himself concedes this point in the subsequent "The Concept of Political Freedom." At the same time, it would be a mistake to ignore the creativity of Neumann's 1937 essay—or the fact that a substantial body of empirical evidence buttresses at least some of Neumann's anxieties about the present fragility of classical liberal law.[32]

Neumann builds on Weber's famous argument for the interdependence of general law and capitalism, but he undertakes a crucial revision of his liberal predecessor's view. For Neumann, Weber was right to see an "elective affinity" between general law and capitalism, yet he obscured the fact that this relationship only obtains for a relatively early stage of capitalist development, when capitalism is still characterized by relatively competitive markets and the existence of proprietors roughly equal in size.[33] In contemporary capitalism, this "elective affinity" no longer exists. In Neumann's own bluntly marxist formulation,

> [i]n a monopolistically organized system the general law cannot be supreme. If the state is confronted only by a monopoly, it is pointless to regulate this monopoly by general law. In such a case the individual measure is the only appropriate expression of the sovereign power.[34]

Thus general law is anachronistic in light of the necessity of regulating massive individual firms. Not only does Neumann thereby suggest, in opposition to Weber and much of contemporary liberal jurisprudence, that capitalism and the rule of law increasingly *contradict* one another, but he starts to provide a provocative response to Weber's account of so-called antiformal legal trends as well.

Like many analysts of modern law, Weber had worried about growing evidence that legal evolution in the twentieth century tends to conflict with the traditional insistence on the ideal of a gapless system of cogent, general norms. Although liberal jurists classically sought to drive ambiguous standards (*Generalklauseln*, or "general principles," in Neumann's terminology) from the legal order, blanket clauses ("in good faith," "unconscionable," "in the public interest") undergo a renaissance with the emergence of modern forms of state intervention in social and economic life. Weber's account of this trend placed primary responsibility for it on the doorsteps of the

INTRODUCTION 13

political left. Allegedly, the real threat to classical legal forms came from "irrational" antimodern social movements intent on establishing a system of welfare state–type legislation dependent on profoundly complex forms of governmental action unlikely to take a classical legal form.[35] In contrast, Neumann's restatement of Weber allows him to shift the blame for this alarming trend to those social and political forces which, in his view, show a willingness to defend contemporary capitalism at any cost, even if it means surrendering liberal democracy. According to Neumann, substantial empirical evidence from Germany and elsewhere suggests that

> legal standards of conduct [blanket clauses] serve the monopolist. . . . Not only is rational law unnecessary for him, it is often a fetter upon the full development of his productive forces, or more frequently, upon the limitations that he may desire; rational law, after all, serves also to protect the weak.[36]

The fact that fascist Germany, in Neumann's view, was aggressively defensive of capitalist privilege *and* ruthlessly bent on obliterating the most minimal remnants of the liberal legal tradition simply reinforced his suspicions about the basically deleterious qualities of nonclassical law: not only did Nazi law rest on a set of profoundly open-ended, amorphous legal forms, but, as he noted, "the antagonisms of capitalism are operating in Germany on a higher and, therefore, a more dangerous level."[37] In the context of such evidence, it made sense for Neumann to conclude his analysis of contemporary legal development by valorizing general law's protective functions. With the fate of the rule of law very much undecided in 1937, "The Change in the Function of Law in Modern Society" defends the claim that the rule of law plays a role that goes well beyond its services to classical capitalism, for "if the sovereign is permitted to decree individual measures, to arrest this man or that one, to confiscate this or that piece of property,"[38] then legal security is irresistibly undermined, and even the most basic measure of freedom is threatened. Despite Neumann's reliance on a series of traditional marxist claims, the Frankfurt School jurist thus reaches a very non-marxian conclusion: the rule of law possesses a historically transcendent "ethical" function.

Kirchheimer's "State Structure and Law in the Third Reich" and "Criminal Law in National Socialist Germany" (which appeared in the *Zeitschrift für Sozialforschung* in 1940 but has never been reprinted in English) similarly make the transition from competitive to monopoly capitalism the starting point of an analysis of National Socialist legal development. Kirchheimer, however, applies this global thesis to a far broader range of specific legal spheres than Neumann was ever able to achieve. He also shows its relevance for an area of the law that was of great significance for understanding Nazi law but of little interest to Neumann—criminal law. Kirchheimer chronicles in great detail the manner in which the Nazis either abandon or transform traditional liberal democratic legal institutions so that they no longer perform protective functions. In their quest to jettison "vacuous" formalistic democratic law for the "material justice" of the nationalistic *Volksgemeinschaft,* new and rather ominous possibilities for analogous legal reasoning are tolerated, traditional legal ideals ("where there is no law, there can be no crime") are simply tossed to the wayside, amorphous standards ("healthy popular sentiment") proliferate, and other traditional categories are expanded and redefined in a manner giving judges and administrators far-reaching discretionary powers. Whereas liberal criminal law traditionally had tried to make an ascertainment of visible features of an offence central to the criminal law, Nazi criminal lawyers downplay such relatively objective factors in the criminal trial in favor of an emphasis on the underlying "will" or "innate character" of the criminal; Kirchheimer's essays provide an excellent account of the development of these ideas within Nazi legal theory and practice. Perhaps most dramatically, Nazi law undergoes "the disappearance of a unified system of criminal law behind innumerable special competences (departmentalization)."[39] The growing indeterminacy of law not only blurs any meaningful distinction between administrative and judicial decision making, but the Nazis' surrender of the most minimal elements of a liberal universalistic perspective, positing the basic equality of all human beings, results in an unprecedented *particularism* within the institutional core of the legal order. New types of courts (*Sondergerichte* and *Volksgerichte*) and an array of novel administrative units (the SS, Nazi Party, Labor Service) compete with the traditional court system, and action undertaken within their confines is often exempted from the scrutiny of the traditional courts. This not only results in a curtailment of the traditional judiciary's authority, but it subjects the populace as a whole to unmediated forms of political and social power to an extent impossible in liberal democracy.[40]

Somewhat paradoxically, Neumann argues in "The Change in the Function of Law in Modern Society" that the ongoing renaissance of moralistic standards in contemporary law *undermines* modern law's "ethical function." In a morally disenchanted world "there can be no unanimity on whether a given action, in a concrete case, is immoral or unreasonable, or whether a certain punishment corresponds to or runs counter to 'healthy popular sentiment,'"[41] and hence vague standards of this sort represent nothing but a mask for arbitrary action. They may have possessed moral substance when natural–law-ideals remained defensible, but in contemporary society they inevitably have been robbed of such substance.[42] Kirchheimer appears to have something similar in mind when he unfavorably contrasts Nazism's fusion of morality and legality to liberalism's "restriction of law to an ethical minimum," but the conclusion of "Criminal Law in National Socialist Germany" appears to leave open the possibility that a future legal order might be able to bring legality and morality into a more intimate relationship without necessarily succumbing to the manifest ills that result from a subjection of law to crude antimodern moral categories like that undertaken by the Nazis. In Nazism, "[t]he attempt of the legislator and of the judiciary to use the criminal law to raise the moral standards of the community appears, when measured by the results achieved, as *a premature excursion by fascism into a field reserved for a better form of society*" (emphasis added).[43] Here Kirchheimer may intend more than the modest "ethical function" described by Neumann. Reminiscent of the theorizing of many of his colleagues at the Institute for Social Research, Kirchheimer finds himself highlighting liberalism's positive qualities in the face of Nazi horrors. He still seems to hope that a future political and social order might be able to overcome one of the central components of modern liberal jurisprudence—the view that morality and legality need to be distinguished.[44] But Kirchheimer—again, like his colleagues at the Institute—is able to say little here about the precise form that this supersession of liberal jurisprudence might take.

The figure of Carl Schmitt continues to play a pivotal role in the writings of the Frankfurt School jurists from this period. For Neumann and Kirchheimer this is justified by the fact that increasingly the "legal theory and legal practice of bourgeois society are, as Carl Schmitt put it, *Situationsjurisprudenz*," according to which, "law is a mere technique for the conquest and maintenance of power."[45] In other words, trends in contemporary capitalist society that suggest the ongoing replacement of a norm-guided system of liberal law by a discretionary, situational legal system *correspond* to Carl Schmitt's theoretical endorsement of a system of arbitrary law based on the exigencies of the "exception" and "individual situation." Because Schmitt's theory thus captures real and quite worrisome tendencies in contemporary law, the political battle against the decline of the rule of law simultaneously needs to take the form of an intellectual assault on Carl Schmitt's political and legal theory.

Nothing better demonstrates this facet of Neumann's and Kirchheimer's agenda than the origins of "State Structure and Law in the Third Reich," which here appears for the first time in English. Smuggled into Germany in 1935 in the form of a pamphlet written under the pseudonym of Hermann Seitz, the essay seems to have had two central purposes. Kirchheimer hoped to awaken interest among the German people in the barbarities of the emerging Nazi legal order (thus the essay's sarcastic and polemical style) *and* bring an awareness of these ills to criminologists, like those attending the Eleventh International Penal and Prison Congress in Berlin in 1935. The pamphlet served a further purpose as well. As "Leader" of the Nazi law professors' guild and State Councillor for Prussia, Carl Schmitt belonged to the most influential circles of Nazi jurists during this period, and Kirchheimer's brochure was cleverly structured so as to embarrass Schmitt; its format suggested that it was volume twelve in a Nazi-inspired series on "the new contemporary German state" that Schmitt was editor of, and its title was more than slightly similar to a study by Schmitt that had recently appeared in the same series.[46] Unsurprisingly, Schmitt responded in kind. The *Deutsche Juristen Zeitung*, which Schmitt edited, immediately published in its pages a nasty response in which Kirchheimer was accused of belonging to an "international clique" obsessed with misrepresenting Nazism's unambiguously peaceful intentions.[47]

TOWARD A CRITICAL DEMOCRATIC THEORY

The postwar writings of Franz Neumann and Otto Kirchheimer reveal a degree of theoretical and political sobriety that some of their earlier contributions lacked. The horrors of Nazism undeniably had provided an immediate incentive even for the marxist-oriented Neumann and Kirchheimer to reconsider the status of key liberal legal and political categories. In the aftermath of the defeat of Nazism, Neumann and Kirchheimer *systematically* integrate the concerns of political liberalism into their increasingly eclectic political and legal theorizing. Commentators have rightly associated Neumann and Kirchheimer with a rich tradition (which commenced with Lukacs's classic *History and Class Consciousness*) that attempted syntheses of Marx and Weber. One qualification of this categorization is probably in order here: Neumann's and Kirchheimer's pre-1950 writings surely tend toward the marxist end of this spectrum, whereas their subsequent contributions suggest at least a gradual movement toward its Weberian side. However one chooses to evaluate the migration of their theory from the world of Frankfurt School neo-Marxism to somewhere "between Marxism and liberal democracy,"[48] there is no doubt that the postwar writings of Neumann and Kirchheimer continue to pose questions of surprising relevance for contemporary intellectual and political disputes.

Not only do the Frankfurt School jurists distance themselves from some features of classical Marxism but they also offer a more modest assessment of the tasks of the rule of law in modern democratic societies. Although remaining adamant defenders of the ideal of the rule of law, they now seem to doubt that it alone is capable of preserving the relatively extensive degree of freedom that many classical liberal jurists believed possible. Yet in contrast to those who seize upon the limits of the rule of law in order to belittle its achievements, the Frankfurt School writers instead focus their efforts in many of their writings from this period on the problem of *supplementing* an analysis of the rule of law with an adequate understanding of the workings of democratic politics.[49] This, they seem to believe, might allow us to begin to compensate for some of the limitations inherent in legal protections in contemporary society.

Neumann's 1953 "The Concept of Political Freedom," which can be read as a democratic antipode to Carl Schmitt's protofascistic *The Concept of the Political*,[50] is crucial for grasping the intellectual contours of this intellectual sea change. Although his previous writings had pointed to the outlines of the problem, Neumann now openly concedes that the traditional demand for cogent, general legal rules necessarily has limited applicability in the contemporary world, where there is a clear necessity for substantial state activity in social and economic affairs. In contrast to free-market critics of totalitarianism like Friedrich Hayek, Neumann does not believe that a return to laissez-faire capitalism constitutes a reasonable response to Nazism and its legal ills;[51] in contemporary organized capitalism, Neumann argues, free-market thinking constitutes nothing but an ideological mask for the most powerful, entrenched economic interests. At the same time, Neumann is forced to admit that increased state intervention raises difficult questions for defenders of the rule of law: as democracy is forced to regulate "power concentrations" in the interest of the public good, the rule of law is inevitably replaced "by clandestine individual measures." Complex state activity requires equally complex forms of nontraditional law. Monopoly capitalism may still lie at the root of the problem, but there is no guarantee that democratic socialism can automatically resolve the basic dilemma at hand—even if, as Neumann writes in "Labor Law in Modern Society," "socialization solves many problems."[52] Neumann then tries to skirt the potentially dreary implications of this concession by insisting that legal freedom should be seen as constituting only one part of a broader set of elements that go into the makeup of political freedom. Even if legal security is irresistibly undermined to some extent in contemporary society, democracy can still hope to realize "cognitive freedom," which in Neumann's view helps provide us with intellectual mastery over natural and historical processes as well as "volitional freedom," which allows active participation in the decision-making process. *Legal rationality* may have to remain incomplete in modern society, but a broader democratic system that strives for a *rational system of self-government* may be able to compensate for some of the ills stemming from this loss.

At the analytical level, Neumann thus clearly believes that the deepening of democracy can help make up for a decline in legal security. But he remains unsure about the actual institutional structure that democratic reforms should take. As a result, Neumann's "The Concept of Political Freedom" leaves the reader with a series of questions that remain unanswered even today. The most important of these is: can we be so sure that new forms of interest-based corporatist representation, like those that have become widespread in the welfare state, contribute to the responsiveness and openness of the democratic process? As Neumann points out, such reforms often have resulted in situations where governmental bodies have simply been captured by narrow interest groups. At other times they have robbed political movements of their independence and helped transform them into little more than stultified bureaucratic structures. Neumann had earlier argued that the Weimar labor movement had succumbed to this fate. What protections are there against such dangers today? Further, the institutionalization of social rights does not provide an easy answer to the enigmas of contemporary democracy. Neumann does not share Schmitt's suggestion in *Legality and Legitimacy* that such rights inevitably undermine liberal democracy; at the same time, he is more skeptical about demands for legally based social rights than either he or Kirchheimer had been in some of their Weimar-era essays. Neumann now openly concedes that "it is extremely doubtful whether it is wise to designate as civil rights positive demands upon the state." Such demands risk overburdening governmental authorities, and they serve only social utility and thus do not constitute "the very essence of a democratic political system." In the process, their institutionalization inadvertently might lead to a degradation of classical civil liberties, which government is more likely to be able to protect effectively. Too often their defenders ignore such potential perils.[53] At some junctures "The Concept of Political Freedom" seems to endorse a traditional model of parliamentary democracy in which a conventional bureaucratic apparatus would be responsible to elected legislators outfitted with the task of overseeing administrative activities. But Neumann hesitates before openly endorsing a model along these lines: he is well aware of the fact that legislative authority has disintegrated substantially in many contemporary liberal democracies, and he seems to believe that the possibilities for reversing them often appear quite limited.

Although concerned with a distinct set of issues of immediate concern, Kirchheimer's "The *Rechtsstaat* as Magic Wall" echoes many of the basic themes of Neumann's final essays from the early 1950s. Kirchheimer is reluctant to concede that complex welfare state–type regulatory activities inevitably necessitate the demise of the rule of law. He writes that "it is not intelligible why social security rules cannot be as carefully framed, and the community burdens as well calculated, as rules concerning damage claims,"[54] and he struggles to offer a response to free-market critics of welfare state law like Friedrich Hayek and Bruno Leoni.[55] Readers should pay special attention to this facet of Kirchheimer's essay: in 1966, such free-market arguments appeared to Kirchheimer to be little more than "rearguard skirmishes," but in recent years they have gained a substantial number of followers. Kirchheimer worries that the mere availability of possibilities for legal redress cannot alone guarantee a humane political order; in Neumann's terms, guarantees of legal security fail to exhaust the agenda of political freedom. To make his point, Kirchheimer recounts the sad story of postwar Germany's failure to prosecute Nazi war criminals. Despite a universe of juridical and bureaucratic remedies available for the prosecution of former Nazis, legal action was undertaken against them only on occasion, and judicial, administrative, and elected officials were far too ready simply to ignore the fact that legal remedies were rarely exploited. For Kirchheimer, "this whole episode shows that the *Rechtsstaat* concept can be honored by scrupulous observation of all prescribed forms and proceedings while its spirit is constantly violated."[56] Although "The *Rechtsstaat* as Magic Wall" says little about how we might successfully overcome this problem, Kirchheimer clearly believes that political freedom in contemporary society rightfully consists of more than the existence of a potpourri of possibilities for legal appeal or even a mass of judges and administrators given the job of looking after them. Elsewhere, he at least hints at an answer to this question that is not altogether unlike Neumann's: political apathy stems from a "missing link between high-level decision and individual fate."[57] Moreover,

> while the technical and, though to a somewhat smaller degree, the social forms of human existence in the West have undergone immense changes in the last half-century, our political arsenal has been refurbished mainly with new dimensions and techniques of domination and manipulation rather than with—what is admittedly more difficult—new means of participation. . . . Political innovations that could remedy this imbalance have been rare everywhere.[58]

An adequate response to the limited nature of legal security in our epoch seems to require an expansion of democratic politics and new possibilities for participation and political self-education. The nature of the institutional innovations required in order to bring about this change, however, remain murky.

Like so many others addressed by Neumann and Kirchheimer, this problem remains surprisingly contemporary. Of course, Neumann and Kirchheimer fail to provide a complete answer to it—or to many of a host of related questions posed by their work. Yet they formulate many of the most important questions within contemporary political and legal thought with refreshing clarity. Ultimately, it is this feature of their work that makes it so relevant even today.

NOTES

1. Mark Kelman, *A Guide to Critical Legal Studies* (Cambridge: Harvard University Press, 1987), pp. 59–61, 258.
2. Roberto M. Unger, *Law in Modern Society* (New York: Free Press, 1976), pp.

221–222, 238–242; also, Duncan Kennedy, "Legal Formality," *The Journal of Legal Studies* 2 (June 1973): 351–398. Critical Legal Studies is a diverse and provocative movement; I only can raise tentative questions about *some* of its argumentative strategies here. For a sympathetic, well-grounded criticism of CLS see Andrew Altman, *Critical Legal Studies: A Liberal Critique* (Princeton: Princeton University Press, 1990).

3. There is a growing literature, especially in German, on Neumann and Kirchheimer. See Alfons Söllner, *Franz Neumann zur Einführung* (Hannover: SOAK, 1982); Alfons Söllner, *Geschichte und Herrschaft* (Frankfurt: Suhrkamp, 1979); Joachim Perels, ed., *Recht, Demokratie, und Kapitalismus. Aktualität und Probleme der Theorie Franz L. Neumanns* (Baden-Baden: Nomos, 1984); Rainer Erd, ed., *Resignation und Reform, Gespräche über Franz L. Neumann* (Frankfurt: Suhrkamp, 1985). In English see William E. Scheuerman *Between the Norm and the Exception: The Frankfurt School and the Rule of Law* (Cambridge: MIT Press, 1994); H. Stuart Hughes, "Franz Neumann: Between Marxism and Liberal Democracy," in *The Intellectual Migration: Europe and America, 1930–1960*, ed. Donald Fleming and Bernard Bailyn (Cambridge: Harvard University Press, 1969). Jürgen Habermas's recent contributions to legal theory parallel at least some of the themes of his predecessors at the Institute for Social Research. See Habermas, *Between Facts and Norms: A Democratic Theory of the Rule of Law* (Cambridge: MIT Press, 1996). For a discussion of the relationship between Neumann and Habermas, my "Neumann v. Habermas: The Frankfurt School and the Rule of Law," *Praxis International* 13 (1993): 50-67.

4. For discussions of the role of Neumann and Kirchheimer in Frankfurt critical theory see Martin Jay, *The Dialectical Imagination* (Boston: Little, Brown & Co., 1973), esp. ch. 5; Rolf Wiggershaus, *The Frankfurt School: Its History, Theories, and Political Significance* (Cambridge: MIT Press, 1994), esp. ch. 4; William E. Scheuerman, *Between the Norm and the Exception: The Frankfurt School and the Rule of Law* (Cambridge: MIT Press, 1994), pp. 149–164.

5. Joseph Bendersky, *Carl Schmitt: Theorist for the Reich* (Princeton: Princeton University Press, 1983); George Schwab, *The Challenge of the Exception: An Introduction to the Ideas of Carl Schmitt* (New York: Greenwood, 1989). In a series of thoughtful essays, Richard Wolin has criticized much of the ongoing Schmitt renaissance in North America: "Carl Schmitt—The Conservative Revolutionary: Habitus and Aesthetics of Horror," *Political Theory* 20, no. 3 (1992): 424–447, and "Carl Schmitt, Political Existentialism, and the Total State," *Theory and Society* 19, no. 4 (1990): 389–416. I should add that scholarship on Schmitt (and Weimar political thought in general) has improved dramatically in recent years: scholars like David Dyzenhaus, Renato Cristi, Paul Caldwell, Stanley L. Paulson, and John McCormick are in the process of revolutionizing our understanding of Weimar political and legal thought.

6. Schmitt was Kirchheimer's doctoral dissertation advisor, and many of Kirchheimer's earliest essays clearly were influenced by Schmitt. Neumann's early work was also influenced, although far more modestly, by Schmitt. See Scheuerman, *Between the Norm and the Exception*, pp. 13–63; and, as well, the essays by Ellen Kennedy, Martin Jay, Ulrich Preuß, and Alfons Söllner in *Telos*, no. 71 (Spring 1987).

7. Carl Schmitt, *The Concept of the Political*, trans. George Schwab (New Brunswick, N.J.: Rutgers, 1976), p. 67.

8. Martin Jay has suggested to me that it was *more* the belief in an unregulated,

irrational sovereign *will* that constituted the core of fascist law than the *indeterminacy* of law per se. Jay's point is well taken. But Schmitt and many fascist legal scholars saw these two facets of fascist law as *inextricably* linked: in their view, vague legal standards permitted the greatest possible leeway for acts of unregulated, irrational sovereignty. In contrast, determinate liberal law shackled the sovereign will in a manner incompatible with the unlimited "power decisions" romanticized by fascist thought. The key text here is Carl Schmitt, *Über die drei Arten des rechtswissenschaftlichen Denkens* (Hamburg: Hanseatische Verlagsanstalt, 1934), where Schmitt argues for a revalorization of amorphous legal stands (for example, "good faith") in order to help bring about thorough Nazi domination of the legal system. Schmitt also authored innumerable short polemical pieces during this period. Especially revealing are "Nationalsozialismus und Rechtsstaat," *Juristische Wochenschrift* 63, nos. 12–13 (March 24/31, 1934), and "Nationalsozialistisches Rechtsdenken," *Deutsches Recht* 4, no. 10 (May 25, 1934). There is a massive literature in German on Schmitt's relationship to Nazi law. A helpful introduction is provided by Bernd Rüthers, *Entartes Recht, Rechtslehren und Kronjuristen im Dritten Reich* (Munich: C. H. Beck, 1988).

9. For an argument along these lines inspired by Neumann and Kirchheimer see Ingeborg Maus, *Rechtstheorie und politische Theorie im Industriekapitalismus* (Munich: Wilhelm Fink, 1986). On the alleged disintegration of classical law in the United States see Theodore Lowi, *The End of Liberalism* (New York: Norton, 1979). For the free-market liberal view of these trends see Friedrich Hayek, *Law, Liberty, and Legislation*, vols. 1–3 (London: Routledge & Kegan, 1976).

10. This volume, p. 41.

11. Franz L. Neumann, *Behemoth: The Structure and Practice of National Socialism* (New York: Harper & Row, 1944).

12. This volume, p. 41.

13. I am following the translation provided in Howard L. McBain and Lindsay Rogers, *The New Constitutions of Europe* (New York: Doubleday, 1923). At times I have altered it when I felt that this was necessary. On the Weimar Constitution see Hermann Potthoff, "Das Weimarer Verfassungswerk und die deutsche Linke," *Archiv für Sozialgeschichte* 12 (1972).

14. Otto Kirchheimer originally belonged to this group of critics. See "Weimar—and What Then?" in *Politics, Law, and Social Change: Selected Essays of Otto Kirchheimer*, ed. Frederic S. Burin and Kurt Shell (New York: Columbia University Press, 1969), pp. 33–74.

15. For an overview of the recent German debate on these issues see Bernd Guggenberger and Tine Stein, ed., *Die Verfassungsdiskussion im Jahre der deutschen Einheit* (Munich: Carl Hanser Verlag, 1991).

16. See S. L. Elkin and K. E. Soltan, eds., *A New Constitutionalism: Designing Political Institutions for a Good Society* (Chicago: University of Chicago, 1993); Ulrich K. Preuß, ed., *Zum Begriff der Verfassung* (Frankfurt: Fischer, 1994).

17. These essays have also been very influential in left-wing jurisprudence in the Federal Republic of Germany. Ulrich Preuß, for example, relied on Kirchheimer's account here in order to provide a critical analysis of the practices of the German Constitutional Court. Ulrich Preuß, *Legalität und Pluralismus. Beiträge zum Verfassungsrecht der Bundesrepublik Deutschland* (Frankfurt: Suhrkamp, 1973).

18. At times, Weber gave his famous account of the three basic types of legitimacy—traditional charismatic, and legal-rational—an evolutionary gloss: legal rationality was seen as constituting the most advanced form of legitimacy. Kirchheimer builds upon this evolutionary strand in Weber's thought in order to discredit tradition and charisma-based appeals to legitimacy in Weimar's final years. Max Weber, *Economy and Society* (Berkeley: University of California, 1979), pp. 212–299.

19. Kirchheimer notes that the concept of legality emerged out of a "rationalization" of the right to resistance. Because he emphasizes the democratic features of rational legal authority, Kirchheimer seems to believe that his reliance on this aspect of Weber's theory does not require him to subscribe to Weber's own rather problematic brand of value-relativism. This becomes even more clear in "Remarks on Carl Schmitt's *Legality and Legitimacy*," where Kirchheimer provides a normative justification for democracy and also argues that both parliamentary and direct-democratic, plebiscitary forms of decision making represent forms of *democratic legitimacy*. This is a crucial point: Schmitt and his defenders have repeatedly claimed that arguments like those developed by Kirchheimer here were morally nihilistic and thus incapable of proving a normative justification for democracy. To a great extent, this is a myth. The Frankfurt political theorist, Ingeborg Maus, has demonstrated this quite effectively: see Ingeborg Maus, *Bürgerliche Rechtstheorie und Faschismus. Zur sozialen Funktion und aktuellen Wirkung der Theorie Carl Schmitts* (Munich: Wilhelm Funk, 1980); Ingeborg Maus, "'Gesetzbindung' der Justiz und der Struktur der nationalsozialistischen Rechtsnormen," in *Recht und Justiz im 'Dritten Reich'*, ed. Ralf Dreier and Wolfgang Sellert (Frankfurt: Suhrkamp, 1989).

20. Hans Boldt, "Article 48 of the Weimar Constitution, Its Historical and Political Implications," in *German Democracy and the Triumph of Hitler*, ed. Anthony Nicholls and Erich Matthias (London: George Allen & Unwin, 1971), p. 93. For an excellent survey of Weimar's demise and the debate on it see Gotthard Jasper, *Die gescheiterte Zähmung. Wege zur Machtergreifung Hitlers, 1930–1934* (Frankfurt: Suhrkamp, 1986).

21. For a fine critical discussion of this argument see Manfred Walther, "Hat der juristische Positivismus die deutschen Juristen im 'Dritten Reich' wehrlos gemacht?" in *Recht und Justiz im 'Dritten Reich,'* ed. Ralf Dreier and Wolfgang Sellert. For a short, popular account of this debate see Ingo Müller, *Hitler's Justice: The Courts of the Third Reich* (Cambridge: Harvard University Press, 1991).

22. It is important to point out that the Weimar Constitution provides no place for a constitutional court outfitted with the authority to determine the constitutionality of parliamentary law. Weimar progressives like Neumann and Kirchheimer were skeptical of attempts to develop such a court in Weimar Germany because they feared, not unjustly, that it would serve as an additional political instrument for antidemocratic elites in the judiciary.

23. Schmitt places these procedures under the rubric of parliamentary *legality*.

24. Carl Schmitt, *Legalität und Legitimität* (Munich: Duncker & Humblot, 1932), pp. 41, 98.

25. Schmitt, *Legalität und Legitimität*, p. 87.

26. Schmitt, *Legalität und Legitimität*, p. 94.

27. But this should *not* suggest that either Kirchheimer or Neumann had an altogether uncritical attitude toward the emergence of new constitutionally based so-

cial rights. As we will see, their postwar writings offer a refreshingly sober assessment of social rights.

28. Schmitt, cited in Otto Kirchheimer, "Constitutional Reaction in 1932," in his *Politics, Law, and Social Change*, p. 78.

29. Written under the guidance of Harold Laski and Karl Mannheim, it has recently appeared under the title *The Rule of Law: Political Theory and the Legal System in Modern Society* (Leamington Spa: Berg, 1986).

30. This volume, p. 106.

31. See Matthias Ruete's foreword, "Post-Weimar Legal Theory in Exile," to Neumann, *The Rule of Law*. The limitations of Neumann's Marxism are most evident in his *Behemoth*. However powerful in other respects, Neumann's marxist analysis of German fascism leaves little room for an analysis of Nazism as a mass-based popular movement, or for an account of Nazi antisemitism that adequately acknowledges its central role. For Neumann, Nazism is primarily a *counterrevolutionary* movement in the interests of German monopoly capital and directed against the German working class; this basic position never seems to permit him to grasp the relatively autonomous dynamics of Nazi anti-Semitism. For a discussion of this issue see Martin Jay, "The Jews and the Frankfurt School: Critical Theory's Analysis of Anti-Semitism," in his *Permanent Exiles: Essays on the Intellectual Migration from Germany to America* (New York: Columbia University Press, 1986).

32. Maus, *Rechtstheorie und politische Theorie im Industriekapitalismus*; Lowi, *End of Liberalism*; Dieter Grimm, *Die Zukunft der Verfassung* (Frankfurt: Suhrkamp, 1991), pp. 159–175.

33. For example, a law setting the length of the working day at ten hours for some firms and eight hours for others contradicts the principle of the equality of competitors essential to classical capitalism.

34. This volume, p. 126.

35. Weber, *Economy and Society*, pp. 880–895. Radical jurists today often try to adduce evidence for the purportedly indeterminate character of the rule of law by focusing on such open-ended legal clauses. Stanley Fish, for example, focuses on the clause "usage of trade" in order to attack liberal legal ideas; see Stanley Fish, *There's No Such Thing As Free Speech and It's a Good Thing, Too* (New York: Oxford University, 1994), pp. 148–151, 169. But Weber's argument here already suggests why this is at least somewhat misleading: liberals themselves were very concerned about such standards, and they long fought to minimize their role in the legal order. To take them as *prima facie* evidence for the incoherence of the ideal of the rule of law obscures how its defenders (including Montesquieu, Locke, Beccaria, Rousseau, Kant, Hegel, and Bentham) emphasized the necessity of *codifying* the legal order in as clear and concise a manner as possible.

36. Neumann, *Behemoth*, pp. 446–447.

37. Neumann, *Behemoth*, p. 227.

38. This volume, p. 118.

39. This volume, pp. 178–179.

40. Much of this account of Nazi law has inspired subsequent scholarship in Germany. See Dreier and Sellert, *Recht und Justiz im 'Dritten Reich'*; Hubert Rottleuthner, ed., *Recht, Rechtsphilosophie und Nationalsozialismus* (Wiesbaden: Franz Steiner, 1983);

Ernst-Wolfgang Böckenförde, ed., *Staatsrecht und Staatsrechtslehre im Dritten Reich* (Heidelberg: C. F. Müller Juristischer Verlag, 1983); Bernard Diestelkamp and Michael Stolleis, eds. *Justizalltag im Dritten Reich* (Frankfurt: Fischer, 1988). The English-language literature on Nazi law remains paltry, but Ernst Fraenkel's classic study remains reliable: *The Dual State* (Chicago: University of Chicago, 1941).

41. This volume, p. 107.

42. Franz Neumann, "Natural Law," in Franz Neumann, *The Democratic and Authoritarian State* (New York: The Free Press, 1957).

43. This volume, p. 186.

44. Recall Adorno's rather defensive portrayal of the artistic achievements of classic modernity, as well as the reservations expressed in his famous quarrel with Walter Benjamin about a politicization of aesthetic experience.

In contemporary jurisprudence, Ronald Dworkin has argued that the border between the spheres of legality and morality needs to be made much more permeable than traditional liberalism permits. Dworkin, in turn, is building on the arguments of natural law theorists like Lon Fuller who attacked legal positivists (including Dworkin's own favorite target, H. L. Hart) in the '50s and '60s. In these debates, differing interpretations of the Nazi legal experience played a crucial role. Antipositivists like Fuller tried to make positivism complicit in the Nazi disaster; unsurprisingly, positivists disputed this view. For an excellent recent account of the origins of this debate see Stanley L. Paulson, "Lon L. Fuller, Gustav Radbruch, and the 'Positivist' Theses," *Law and Philosophy* 13 (1994): 313–334.

45. Neumann, *The Rule of Law*, p. 6. Neumann's concerns here about Schmitt's radically decisionistic conception of law—that is, the idea that law at its base is nothing but an expression of arbitrary power—are again quite relevant in light of recent debates within political and legal theory. In a provocative recent essay, Stanley Fish has gone so far as to criticize contemporary Critical Legal Studies for its inadequately radical intellectual aspirations. Fish believes that CLS authors are right to focus on the unavoidable indeterminacy of all legal experience. In his view, however, too many CLS authors implicitly accept liberal legal ideals by seeing law's ad hoc character as constituting a failing or weakness. For Fish, law's willful or ad hoc core is not to be lamented or regretted. Rather, it should be seen as essential to the workings of law and, it seems, something that we might even celebrate. In demanding that we valorize law's (alleged) roots in pure acts of will, Fish's position at times becomes disturbingly reminiscent of Schmitt's decisionism. Of course, Fish offers no discussion of the potential dangers of this type of position in his analysis: he seems uninterested in anything as mundane as the history of fascist law or, for that matter, the ongoing disintegration of formal law and the possible threats it poses for the weak and socially oppressed. Fish, *There's No Such Thing as Free Speech*, pp. 141–179. Fish's valorization of law's inherently arbitrary, willful nature is increasingly common among authors influenced by French poststructuralism. For a powerful analysis of these trends see Seyla Benhabib, "Democracy and Difference: Reflections on the Metapolitics of Lyotard and Derrida," *The Journal of Political Philosophy* 2, no. 1 (1994): 1–23.

46. Carl Schmitt, *Staatsgefüge und Zusammenbruch des zweiten Reiches* (Hamburg: Hanseatische Verlagsanstalt, 1934).

47. *Deutsche Juristen-Zeitung* 40 (September 15, 1935): 1104. For a full account of this moment in the history of the early Frankfurt School see Wolfgang Luthardt, "Einleitung zu Otto Kirchheimer, *Staatsgefüge und Recht des Dritten Reichs*," *Kritische Justiz* 9 (1976).

48. Hughes, "Franz Neumann."

49. For Otto Kirchheimer this task is primarily empirical. Much of his postwar writing is devoted to an analysis of the roots of a purported "decline of political opposition"—in other words, a free-wheeling public space—in welfare state capitalist democracies. Many of these essays have been collected in Kirchheimer, *Politics, Law, and Social Change*.

50. This becomes most clear in the essay's concluding paragraphs, where the "integrative" element of fascism is identified with "the existence of an enemy whom one must be willing to exterminate physically." This integrative element is contrasted with democracy's political freedom, which is the object of Neumann's piece.

51. Friedrich Hayek, *The Road to Serfdom* (Chicago: University of Chicago, 1944). I should add that Hayek borrows from Schmitt both in this text and in many others. See my "The Unholy Alliance of Carl Schmitt and Friedrich Hayek," *Constellations: An International Journal of Critical and Democratic Theory* 3 (1996), as well as Renato Cristi's extremely thoughtful "Hayek and Schmitt on the Rule of Law," *Canadian Journal of Political Science* 17, no. 3 (1984): 521–536.

52. This volume, p. 232.

53. Neumann's postwar critique of social rights probably focuses less on limits posed to their institutionalization by specifically *economic* factors (for example, the possibility that a "right to work" may be unachievable in a capitalist market economy) than on *their direct dangers to legal security itself*: an inflationary view of civil liberties may lead us to obscure vital differences between rights that can be effectively protected by traditional judicial devices and those which cannot. For a critical discussion of the "right to work" from a political perspective not unlike the elder Neumann's see Jon Elster, "Is There (or Should There Be) a Right to Work," in *Democracy and the Welfare State*, ed. Amy Gutmann (Princeton: Princeton University, 1988).

54. This volume, p. 247.

55. Hayek, *Law, Legislation, and Liberty*, and *The Road to Serfdom*.

56. This volume, p. 254.

57. Otto Kirchheimer, "Private Man and Society," in *Politics, Law, and Social Change*, p. 462.

58. Otto Kirchheimer, "Germany Democracy in the 1950s," in *World Politics* 13 (1961): 265.

PART I

The Destruction of Weimar Democracy and the Debate on Legality and Legitimacy

ONE

The Decay of German Democracy

Franz L. Neumann

Germany was never a united nation—and never a democracy. She was always divided. Pierre Vienot, in his famous book, *Incertitudes Allemandes*, has described it in an illuminating way:

Besides the Germany of Potsdam and the Germany of Weimar there exists an industrial and an agrarian Germany, a proletarian Germany and a Germany of the propertied classes, a Catholic and a Lutheran Germany, a Germany of the federal states and a Germany of the Reich, a Germany of youth and one of old age. There is above all a democratic and an antidemocratic Germany. This division began in the Reformation, which was never completed either in regard to space or in regard to its fundamental conception. The Reformation did not emancipate the German people, but converted Germany from a community of slaves of the Church to a community of slaves of the prince. It is true "that the absolute state was the child and the heir of the Reformation" and that "divine right . . . was a defensive weapon against militant Catholicism."[1] But in all other countries absolutism created a united state. Not so in Germany. In all other countries the ideas of popular sovereignty and of the consent of the people were emerging. Not so in Germany. At no time had Germany a liberal middle class. Very early the bourgeoisie made its peace with the monarchy and the nobility. The nobility retained control of home and foreign politics and of the active army, the bourgeoisie furnished the reserve of officers and retained liberty to earn money. Freedom was betrayed for money.

At no time has Germany fought for the ideas of liberty and democracy. Universal suffrage came from above without fighting. Democracy arose out of the breakdown of the monarchy in 1918.

Editor's Note: Originally appeared in *The Political Quarterly* 4, no. 1 (1933).

The predominant philosophy of Germany was that of German idealism. Meanwhile, the state availed itself of Hegel's philosophy and the bourgeoisie found its justification in Kant. Indeed, it was the easiest thing in the world to abuse that philosophy which, on the one hand, acquiesced in transcendental ideas that could be translated into whatever concrete demands might be desired and which, on the other hand, declared that only property and education were the bases for exercising political rights whilst condemning the right of resistance and revolution.

The thesis of this article is that the National Socialist revolution is a counterrevolution of monopolized industry and the big landowners against democracy and social progress, that this revolution was only successful because the structure and practice of the Weimar Constitution facilitated it, that the revolution was largely due to the creation of an antistate which the democratic state tolerated though it was born to destroy democracy, that the Social Democratic Party and the German free trade unions which were the sole defenders of parliamentary democracy were too weak to fight against National Socialism, that their weakness was due both to fate and guilt.

I. THE DOMINANT IDEAS OF THE WEIMAR CONSTITUTION

The so-called revolution of November 1918 was no real revolution but only the collapse of the monarchy, of the personal dictatorship of General Ludendorff, and of all those forces that supported the Prussian monarchy. But at the very moment when those forces broke down the process of restoration began.

Immediately after the revolution, an agreement was reached between General Wilhelm Gröner and Friedrich Ebert, the Socialist leader and later president of the Reich, with the object of suppressing Communism and safeguarding the Constitutional Assembly. General Groener himself, when giving evidence in a law case brought by the editor of a socialist paper against Professor Cossmann, admitted this fact and also the fact that a direct telephone line existed between him and Ebert.[2] Leaving aside the question whether this agreement was necessary or not, whether it was good or bad, it was in any case more important than any later decision in the making of the Republic. It anticipated the settlement of this major issue: whether Germany should become a socialist and democratic republic. It was unthinkable that a republic guaranteed by a military caste would be willing to comply with socialist and democratic demands. It was inconceivable that a socialist democracy could be erected with the help of an army composed of the remnants of the old military caste and the corps of volunteers who were dominated by reactionary and nationalist ideas.

The second decisive step in the making of the Republic was the agreement between the trade unions and the big employers' organizations in November 1918, the Stinnes-Legien covenant. By this agreement the employers granted equality of status to the trade unions in the regulation of wages and labor conditions. So far as the trade unions were satisfied by mere equality, they renounced their claim to unlimited dominion of the working class: that is to say, they renounced socialism.

The third fatal decision was the acceptance of the Treaty of Versailles. It is probable that acceptance was a necessity, but the political consequences in Germany were disastrous. Though the Social Democrats were responsible neither for the war nor for the defeat, and though the minority in the Constitutional Assembly which rejected the Treaty acknowledged the sincerity of the motives of the majority in the Assembly, there was no doubt that the Social Democratic Party was compelled to assume responsibility for the peace treaty and its results.

In common with many continental constitutions the German Constitution of 1919 was divided into two parts, the first dealing with the organization of the Reich, the second with the constitutional rights of the individual in regard to the purposes of the state. Germany had become a democracy on the basis of freedom and equality with identity of rulers and ruled. Every kind of transcendental justification of government was abolished; the justification was only an immanent one. The functions of the state were divided into legislation, administration, and justice, and following Montesquieu, the Weimar Constitution "emphasized legislation as the main mechanism of social change."[3] According to the intention of the Constitution, political power should have been concentrated exclusively in Parliament. It had the monopoly of legislation. The referendum and the initiative were of no importance. The Upper House (Reichsrat) was not a second chamber, for it had no right of veto, though it was able to hamper legislation.

The cabinet was a kind of parliamentary committee, responsible to Parliament. Thus, Parliament was the central administrative authority as well. Through the medium of ministerial responsibility it was able to control all aspects of the Reich government. And the same was true in the separate states of the federation. Only the administration of justice was outside the scope of Parliament and was exercised by independent judges subject to the law alone.

The problem in every industrial democracy with a strong and developed labor movement is how to anchor Parliament in the people. The problem in every state wherein the state has to deal with nearly all social and economic affairs is how to enable Parliament to perform its tasks.

There existed different powers for these purposes.

First of all there were the parties. German parties were—apart from one unimportant exception—based on a totalitarian philosophy (*Weltanschaungs-*

Parteien). They laid claim to the whole of the individual. They were totalitarian parties. Literally from the cradle to the grave the party dominated the life of its members. Organizations for children and youth, for sport and for singing, for welfare work and for the care of the sick, for the provision of literature and arts, for jurists, doctors, and teachers and—last, but not least—private armies, were included in the sphere of party competence. In spite of their enormous social importance, parties are not mentioned—or only mentioned in a hole and corner way and negatively—in the Constitution which otherwise deals with every body and every form of organization. The political power of the parties was based upon the proportional electoral system, which on the one hand guaranteed each party mathematical equality in Parliament and on the other hand strengthened the influence of the bureaucracy of the parties. This system of the domination of the party could not work well, because in the first place totalitarian parties do not suit parliamentary democracy and in the second place the radical totalitarian parties did not recognize the rules of the parliamentary game.

The Constitution tried to root parliamentarism and to relieve Parliament by means of self-government, local as well as industrial. Local self-government in Germany is not the same thing as it is in England. For in England "the truth is that there is no antithesis between central and local government,"[4] though since the appearance of the Labour Party in politics some conflicts have arisen between central and local government. In Germany, municipal democracy could only support and relieve parliamentary democracy if local government and Parliament pursued the same political ends.

The German Constitution added a new form of self-government to be exercised by trade unions and the organizations of the employers. Trade unions are recognized in Article 165. They have the task of cooperating in the development of productive industry on an equal footing with the employers. The actual wording is "the organization of both sides and their agreements are recognized." By virtue of that constitutional maxim, the unions acquired the right of having representatives in a large number of state organizations. The members of labor courts included in all three instances representatives of the trade unions and, of course, representatives in equal numbers of the employers' organizations. Delegates of the trade unions were appointed to the social insurance boards, to the arbitration boards, to the National Coal and Potash Councils, to the National Economic Council, etc. All those representatives were not elected by the working class, but delegated by the trade unions, so that it is permissible to speak of a new form of democracy, a collectivist democracy, by means of which political democracy was to be rooted in the masses of the people. This collectivist democracy did not create a corporative state as it did in Italy, because the whole of political power was concentrated in the Reichstag, and the trade unions were legally independent of the influence of the state. The National Economic Council had no part in legislation.

The second part of the Constitution contains the fundamental rights. It defines the relations between state and subject and deals with the tasks of the Reich.

What was the decisive object of the Reich? A negative one, as we have already seen: to ward off bolshevism. To define its positive object is very difficult. Many authors, therefore, hold the German Constitution to be without a main guiding principle.[5]

Four groups of constitutional rights have to be distinguished: the rights of personal freedom—freedom of dwelling and of person, of political freedom—freedom of speech and of assembly, of capitalist freedom—freedom of property, contract and trade, and of socialist freedom—all those rights that guarantee the emancipation of the working class. The three first groups are well known. They appear in nearly every modern constitution. Political freedom together with equality of rights constitute democracy, for political freedom renders the creation of the will of the state possible. Without political freedom there is no democracy.

The fourth group, however, is a completely new one. Article 159 protects freedom of association for economic purposes; Article 165 recognizes the trade unions and their collective agreements. Article 165 gives the power to socialize industries. Article 162 recognizes the constitutional obligation of the state to provide social insurance of all kinds, etc. The difference in the legal protection accorded to the fourth group, as compared with that of the three other groups, is astonishing. Whereas the first three groups only restrict state action and do not curtail the acts of private individuals (except in regard to freedom of speech in Article 118) the fourth group also applies to individual restrictions within the scope of private law. An agreement whereby a worker agrees not to belong to any union is constitutionally null and void. Another point: whereas the first three groups may be suspended by an emergency decree of the president (Article 48), the fourth group is exempt from emergency power. The fourth group was intended to create a "social democracy" but not a socialist democracy, that is to say, a democracy based not only upon freedom of property but also upon economic freedom of the working class. A compromise between capitalism and socialism was intended. The Constitution saw clearly that private property involves power, power over men and over things, that the worker is separated from the means of production, that he has only one means of production, his labor, but that he can only utilize his power in conjunction with this means of production. Thus, private ownership has an attractive effect on him. He is forced into a chain of relations outside his sphere and must enter into contracts with his employer who is his master. The German Constitution created a body of rules dealing with direct intervention by the state or by organized society in the relations between master and servant so as to make the servant the real equal partner of his master.

II. THE SOCIAL STRUCTURE OF THE WEIMAR CONSTITUTION

This system somewhere between socialism and capitalism could exist only as long as no economic crisis intervened. During the boom years 1924–1928 the development of the social services in Germany was enormous. "The illusion of security" was a perfect one. The standard of living increased for everybody, even the unemployed.

But capitalism, the real owner of power in every nonsocialist state, could only make social concessions up to a certain point, to the point where profit ceases. This limit being reached, capitalism will do everything to prevent organized labor from securing control over the state and exercising power in favor of social progress. In regard to Germany it must be added that it was not enough to stop social progress in order to make the state safe for capitalism. A retrograde movement was necessary, and, in addition, all the forces of the state had to be used to save capitalism. The total expenditure on social services even in 1931 was as follows:

Social insurance	RM	4,040,000,000
Unemployment insurance	RM	2,318,000,000
Victims of war	RM	1,300,000,000
Public reliefs	RM	2,000,000,000
Total	RM	9,658,000,000
	(£480,000,000)	

State intervention in one form or the other is always necessary if free competition no longer exists, if the economic doctrines of laissez faire have been superseded by the structure of monopolization. Capitalism knew that a state in the hands of a Socialist government would and must use its power to create a new distribution of wealth either by taxes or by socialization. It knew "that the rise of a new class to political power is always, sooner or later, synonymous with a social revolution; and the essential characteristic of a social revolution is always the redistribution of economic power."[6] Therefore, the efforts of all reactionary parties were concentrated on one single point: to destroy parliamentary democracy, the constitutional platform for the emancipation of labor.

And they succeeded. They succeeded because the framework and the practice of the Constitution facilitated it and because the Social Democratic Party and the trade unions, the sole defenders of the Weimar system, were weakened.

After the election of Hindenburg the whole of the bourgeoisie including the Catholics adhered unanimously to the slogan "all powers to the president."

It cannot be doubted that the Parliament and the parliamentary groups are responsible for the decay of parliamentary democracy.

Parliament was never anxious to retain its authority. Little by little it lost power, authority, and dignity. It may be true that "it is not a paradox to argue that a legislative assembly is unfitted by its very nature directly to legislate."[7] It is true that in a state that is no more a liberal one but one which interferes with nearly all aspects of human life, Parliament is unfitted to perform its legislative tasks. But if that is so, Parliament has a duty to create other organs of legislation and to be satisfied with discussing the main principles of home and foreign politics. But it means the destruction of the sovereignty of Parliament if dozens of private and public organizations deprive it of legislative power while it still pretends to be the real sovereign. Since 1923, the German Parliament has more than once given emergency powers to the cabinet (*Ermächtigungsgesetze*). A large number of very important statutes are the creatures not of the Reichstag but of the ministers. In addition to that, Parliament was satisfied with laying down general principles and leaving their application to the ministers (*Blankettgesetze*) so that parliamentary legislation very often consisted of two or three sections while the very important bylaws for the introduction of the acts issued by the ministries had hundreds of clauses. In the end, from 1930 onward, parliamentary legislation was replaced by that of the president (Article 48). According to the original meaning of the Constitution, the president had no emergency power of legislation. He was only entitled to execute individual administrative acts in defence of public security and order. His power was only a military and police power. But in September 1930 he became the real and sole legislator. These three facts destroyed the authority of Parliament.

The same development placed the bureaucracy in power, especially the ministerial bureaucracy. In Germany, it is not true that the main object of the officials in the ministries is "to save their chief from disaster."[8] Gustav Radbruch, professor of the philosophy of law and former socialist Minister for Justice has stated: "Ministers come and go but under-secretaries of state always remain." It must be borne in mind that after fourteen years of the Republic only about a dozen high officials out of many hundreds in the ministries of the Reich were members of the Social Democratic Party. The main object of the ministerial bureaucracy was to minimize social progress, to weaken the break with the militarist, capitalist, and reactionary tradition.

Thus, because Parliament was unable to control the ministers and their bureaucracy, an antistate was created within the framework of the democracy. There were three main causes for this. The most important means of controlling administration is the declaration of nonconfidence whereby a minister is forced to resign. But the creation of a German cabinet was such a difficult task, everyone was so glad if the parties succeeded in reconciling conflicting opinions, that no one dared endanger the life of a cabinet by a vote of censure. This important means of asserting parliamentary sovereignty was thus never successfully used in Germany. Moreover, the very nature of a coalition cabinet makes parliamentary control unsuccessful because the cabinet has no antagonist in opposition. The opposition in the German Parliament was at no time a parliamentary one obeying the rules of the game. Their criticism was therefore disregarded and the coalition parties dared not criticize their own ministers. Finally, the task of each minister was a burden that increased every day. The cabinet was—as in every modern state—overwhelmed with business so that permanent control became technically impossible.

The result of this whole development was the increasing power of an uncontrolled bureaucracy which legislated and governed against democracy and social progress.

Not only high officials and civil servants, but the judges, too, were an organized power in the state on the opposing side, a part of the antistate. Judges in England are neither civil servants nor agents of the crown, a judge "is not employed in the sense that a civil servant is employed."[9] Not so in Germany. It is true that in Germany judges are formally independent. But in fact they are only civil servants, and they depend not so much upon their individual convictions as upon their "social mind," their political, religious, and social associations—that is to say on all those groups that hate social progress and the "well-paid" laborer and the emancipation of the working class. According to the liberal ideology, the judge is only the mouthpiece of the law (*la bouche de la loi*), judgment only a matter of reason, and the judge has nothing to do but to apply a body of strict rules to the actual facts of a case.[10] But German justice was always a matter of politics.

German justice has, since 1919, suffered two important changes. At first the theory of the free discretion of the judge became dominant. The judges have on the ground of their free discretion practically abolished a large number of rules in the civil code without "breaking the law," especially those rules which were favourable to the working class.[11] But apart from that, German judges after 1919 constituted themselves into a kind of Upper House, in addition to the Reichstag, by assuming the power of judicial control. Each law enacted by the Parliament could be reviewed by every judge on the ground of its compatibility with the Constitution, though under the Bismarkian Constitution no judge would have dared do so. A large number of laws interfering with property and freedom of contract were held unconstitutional so that German justice approached the American system and constitutional rights played the role of "due process of law" in the Constitution of the United States of America.[12]

But in addition to the new status of the bureaucracy, the system of municipal and industrial self-government, which had been intended to neutralize the influence of the bureaucracy, to root Parliament in the masses of the people and to relieve Parliament, was destroyed. I have already pointed out that local government in Germany was always the antithesis of central government. Municipal bureaucracy always tried to create municipal socialism. But in Parliament, the influence of the Social Democrats was at no time definitive. Therefore, municipal and central government were in permanent conflict with one another, and central government, of course, got the better of the struggle by reason of the power of the purse.

On the other hand, the municipalities destroyed self-government by divorcing the most important administrative services (gas, water, power, and transport undertakings) from the jurisdiction of the municipal councils. Every town took a pride in creating private limited companies to which the public institutions were transferred. The most important services, not only in the towns, but also in the Reich and in the federal states, became more or less private and free from political influence. Johannes Popitz, now Prussian Minister of Finance, has called this development "polycracy."[13]

Industrial self-government failed. It is impossible to describe here all the mistakes of the trade unions. The main point is that the trade unions lost their freedom and independence. Legally, they were completely independent of the state (Articles 159 and 165). But in fact they were on the one hand dependent upon the state, and on the other hand they lost their original functions. Trade unions are in the main, organizations of a cartel character designed to raise wages. They are, in addition, cooperative organizations for affording mutual relief and, finally, guild organizations to represent the working class in relation to the state. They lost their first function little by little. Free collective agreements for regulating wages disappeared. The state itself fixed them. Strikes disappeared. In 1931 practically no offensive strike took place. Only 146,000 members of the free trade unions were out in strikes and lockouts. The expenditure for all kinds of labor disputes in 1930 was RM 9,887,000 out of a total income of RM 231,655,000, and in 1931 RM 10,595,000 out of a total income of RM 184,306,000. The measure of relief accorded to members decreased as the economic crisis increased.

Thus trade unions became almost entirely guild organizations, representing the working class in hundreds and thousands of state organizations. They lost their freedom to an increasing extent as Germany became a fascist state. Toward the end they tried to abandon their relations with the Social

Democratic Party and to form a new, half-fascist ideology in the hope of avoiding capture by the National Socialist Party.

III. THE BREAKDOWN OF THE GERMAN DEMOCRACY

From 1931, the power of the Reich disintegrated. Germany was ripe for a dictatorship.

The following forces existed:

>The army with the president and the police
>The civil servants and the high bureaucracy
>Industry and the big landed property
>The churches and the federal states
>The Social Democratic Party and the trade unions
>The Communists
>The National Socialist Party, its private army and its affiliated organizations

The economic crisis was disastrous. The number of unemployed increased every day. In 1929, 13.3 percent; in 1931, 34.7 percent; and in the months of February and March, 1932, 45 percent of the members of the free trade unions were out of work, and a large number of the remaining members working part-time. At the end of 1932, 96 percent of the members of the building trade unions were out of work.

Even the years 1928 and 1929 brought wage increases, in 1928 6.9 percent, in 1929 3.8 percent. In 1930 wages and labor conditions were unchanged. But in 1931 wages were cut by 17 percent, and 1932 brought new and important reductions.

German industry is monopolized to an enormous extent. Nearly 50 percent of the industry of the country is organized in cartels and trusts. The economic doctrines of laissez faire had lost influence. The process of rationalization on a colossal scale resulted in the investment of enormous sums which required amortization and profit. Industry could only exist with the aid of the state. Tariffs, subsidies, guarantees for export (to Russia), and maintenance of the cartel system supplied this assistance. The peasants once again came into debt although the inflation of 1923 had freed them of debt. The big estate owners could only exist with state subsidies which were granted to them on an enormous scale (*Osthilfe*).

The middle classes, demolished during the inflation, had recovered in the period from 1924 to 1929. But during the economic crisis, with the consequent reduction of purchasing power, they feared a new breakdown.

Students were without hope. Their number increased every day, but the number of jobs available for them decreased. Many of the positions in the

Prussian administration, formerly a privilege of the bourgeoisie, were filled by men of the working class, Social Democrats and trade unionists.

The efforts of Brüning, von Papen, and Schleicher to govern have been described elsewhere. The Social Democrats were weakened. Although their membership, it is true, was constant at nearly 1,000,000, continuous elections had weakened their financial power. The policy of the "lesser evil," the policy of toleration, from September 14, 1930, had changed the party from a tolerating into a tolerated party. The coup d'état of July 20, 1932, has disappointed the masses and destroyed their confidence in the "Iron Front" (*eiserne Front*), the holding organization of the Social Democratic Party, the trade unions, and the Labour Sporting organizations. The masses felt instinctively that Brüning abused them for his own obscure purposes. They were right. The trial of the conservative commissar, Dr. Gereke, revealed the perfidious policy of Brüning. His close friend, former minister Treviranus, admitted as a witness that Brüning's aim was to win the aid of the Social Democrats for the election of Hindenburg as president, then to clear away all internal and foreign political difficulties (reduction of wages, reparations, rearmament) with the help of the Social Democrats, and then afterwards to form a coalition with the National Socialists. For a time he succeeded. With the aid of the Social Democrats he reduced social expenditure, lowered wages, operated a nationalist policy—and then Hitler came to power.

The socialist trade unions were still strong in number (1931: 4,417,000 members), but unemployment, disappointment, and their bureaucracy, which had very much to lose in case of resistance, and the hundreds and thousands of positions they had acquired in the state, had deprived them of freedom, independence, and strength. Their great mistake was to believe that economic democracy was possible without political democracy.

The disastrous role of the Communist Party is well known. They hoped to create a revolutionary situation by destroying parliamentary democracy and then creating a bolshevist dictatorship. In fact, they were the allies of the National Socialists in their struggle against the "Social Fascists," in other words Social Democrats and trade unions. It is a fact that half the votes of censure against the Prussian cabinet of Otto Braun were moved by Communists and supported by Nationalists, and the other half moved by Nationalists and supported by Communists. They joined the Nationalists in the referendum for the dissolution of the Prussian Diet; together with the National Socialist cells they organized strikes against the trade unions and cities with Socialist municipal boards; and they even took over the nationalist slogans of the National Socialists for the loosing of the chains of Versailles and the liberation of suppressed German minorities abroad.

The National Socialist Party, the development of which cannot here be described, united the industrialists who hated trade unions, Social Democrats, and parliamentarism as the constitutional basis of social progress; the white-collar workers who did not want to become proletarians and whose numbers increased with the progress of rationalization; the middle classes who believed the sole causes of their economic plight to be finance, department stores, cooperatives, and Jews, and who formed the important "fighting league of middle-class traders"; the peasants who regarded with hate and envy the high wages of workmen and unemployment insurance; the students who hated democracy and Parliament as "Ungerman" and Social Democrats and trade unions as the makers of Versailles, the Dawes Scheme, and the Young Plan; the impoverished *déclassés* which had nothing to lose.

The cabinet of von Schleicher was dismissed because Schleicher had dared to investigate the subsidies for the relief of the big estate owners in East Prussia (*Osthilfe*). Hitler, together with von Papen and Hugenberg, became his successor.

Resistance was impossible. The only forces who resisted were Social Democrats, trade unions, and Communists. The Lutheran churches were always nationalistic and reactionary. The Catholic Church had no political convictions of its own. It was, it is true, associated with the Centre Party, but not to the extent that the Centre Party was officially recognized by the Church. Everyone in Germany knew that the Catholic Church would make its peace with any government that would allow it to retain its religious freedom and its property.

But why did not the southern federal states offer resistance? The reason is that their strength was always overrated. They could successfully resist a weak democracy, as in 1923 when they successfully opposed the weakness of President Ebert, but they could not resist a strong attack. Even large numbers of Social Democrats were not willing to fight against National Socialism for the sake of the Bavarian People's Party, the crown pretender Rupprecht, and the separation of the south of Germany from the north.

The universities were not willing to resist. On the contrary, they had worked to a great extent for the destruction of the idea of parliamentary democracy in the minds of the students. Professors of constitutional law were in the main implacable opponents of parliamentary democracy. The enormous influence of Professor Carl Schmitt, who served uninterruptedly as an expert under Ebert, Brüning, von Papen, Schleicher, and now Hitler, and who took only an aesthetic view of the Constitution, did much to bring into contempt liberty, Parliament, and so-called Western democracy.

Labor's only available weapon was a general strike. But as a weapon it was inexpedient at a time when unemployment stood at 8 million. Moreover, a general strike would have led to civil war, the issue being between socialism and capitalism. In practice, no Socialist would have gone into a civil war in defence of the Weimar Constitution; his participation in such a struggle would only have been secured in order to achieve socialism. But in this case, the army, the police, the brown-shirts, the black-shirts, the steel-helmets, the whole of the bourgeoisie, the federal states, the churches—all would have fought against labor. It is not my task to answer the question whether in spite of this labor should not have fought, whether a heroic death would not have helped the cause of democracy and socialism more than their collapse without any resistance. But there is no doubt that the fate of liberty and democracy was decided after two years of a policy of the lesser evil in addition to an enormous economic crisis.

German democracy committed suicide and was murdered at one and the same time. A democracy without democrats found its end with the appointment of Hitler as chancellor on January 30, 1933.

IV. THE SOCIAL SIGNIFICANCE OF NATIONAL SOCIALISM

The thesis that the national socialist revolution is a counterrevolution by monopolized industry and the big estate owners must now be proven. Since the appointment of Hitler we can distinguish three stages:

1. Until February 28, the date of the Reichstag arson.
2. Until the dismissal of Hugenberg.
3. The stabilization of power and the revelation of the social and economic aims of the Hitler government.

The first stage had no striking features. The key change took place on February 28 when the Reichstag was burned down. On the evening of the same day the Communist Party was suppressed, and all socialist papers were banned. By an emergency decree of the president, all fundamental constitutional liberties were set aside. Hundreds and thousands of Communists were sent to concentration camps. Nevertheless, the election of March 5 brought no National Socialist majority. But as the Communists' votes were cancelled, a qualified majority of National Socialists and nationalists and Catholics gave Hitler power to legislate without Parliament, even to alter the Constitution, dispensing with the necessity of the president's consent to legislation. The cabinet thus became the sole legislator.

The only person to be feared within the cabinet was Dr. Hugenberg. He was the sole member with real political and economic power of his own, a private army, a large number of newspapers, and nearly the whole of the production of talkies. During the second period National Socialism strengthened its position. By the process of coordination (*Gleichschaltung*), nearly all mass organizations were recruited to consolidate their power. Commissars were appointed in hundreds and thousands of firms and organizations to strengthen the Nazis' power. These appointments caused insecurity and disorder in the economic system, and Hugenberg was blamed for this. On

May 2 the trade unions were taken over. It is true that no agreement existed in the cabinet as to the settlement of the trade union question. Hugenberg advocated their prohibition and the recognition solely of the yellow company-unions. As no law was passed, owing to disagreement, a revolutionary path was adopted and the trade unions were taken over. The importance of the capture lies in its support for the power of the National Socialist Party, a step towards the totalitarian state dominated by a totalitarian party. Then, the Socialist Party was banned, its properties seized, the Centre Party dissolved itself, the other parties followed, and finally, by a July 14th law prohibiting the creation of new parties, only the National Socialist Party was allowed to exist.

The process of coordination came to an end with the dismissal of Hugenberg. It would be a mistake to believe that his dismissal was due to differences in the cabinet on the economic policy of Germany, although this was the reason provided. Hugenberg's policy of self-sufficiency was even more suited to the program of the National Socialist Party than that of his successor Dr. Kurt Schmitt. At the very moment of his downfall, the real social and economic aims of Hitler were revealed. His famous Berchtesgaden speech put an end to the revolution. The newly created National Economic Council is composed only of industrialists, the sole representative of labor being Dr. Robert Ley, the leader of the German Workers' Front, who cannot be considered a real representative of labor. The institution of thirteen "Trustees of Labor" by the decrees of May 19 and June 13 deprived trade unions of the power to make collective agreements.[14] The "Trustees of Labor" who, with one or two exceptions, were all legal advisers to employers' organizations, determine wages and labor conditions. According to a statement by Dr. Ley, the only task of German trade unions is the education of their members. The Works Councils, which are now purged of all Socialists, Communists, and trade unionists, and which formerly limited in various respects the social power of the entrepreneur, are to be reformed. They will now be composed of workers, employees, and the employer—who is to become chairman of the council.

The "Fighting League of Middle-Class Traders" had been dissolved by Dr. Ley because "it lost its raison d'être when a National Socialist minister of economics was appointed."[15] All commissars, even to Jewish firms, have been withdrawn since the appointment of Dr. Schmitt. An order of Rudolf Hess, Hitler's representative, prohibits all interference with economic affairs.[16] The new minister has even stopped the guild organization of German industry. The "Trustees of Labor" have prohibited all strikes. Dr. Richard Darré, the new Minister of Agriculture, has officially stated that no big landed property, however substantial it may be, will be touched. The district leaders of the Party for Rhineland and Westphalia have placed the whole of economic power in the hands of Fritz Thyssen. No appeal against his economic decisions in the most important industrial districts of Germany is allowed.

The new Cartel Law of July 15 shows the true economic convictions of National Socialism. The minister of economics now has the power to create compulsory cartels and to prohibit the creation of new undertakings or the enlargement of existing enterprises.

German National Socialism is nothing but the dictatorship of monopolized industry and of the big estate owners, the nakedness of which is covered by the mask of a corporative state.[17]

NOTES

1. G. P. Gooch, *Political Thought in England from Bacon to Halifax* (London, 1946), pp. 7, 20.
2. *Der Dolchstossprozess in München* (Munich, 1925), p. 294.
3. Harold J. Laski, *Political Thought in England from Locke to Bentham* (London, 1949), p. 127.
4. Ivor Jennings, *Principles of Local Government Law* (London, 1928), p. 28.
5. Editor's Note: This was the interpretation of the Weimar Constitution provided by the young Otto Kirchheimer in "Weimar—and What Then?" in *Politics, Law and Social Change: Selected Essays of Otto Kirchheimer*, ed. Frederic S. Burin and Kurt Shell (New York: Columbia University Press, 1969).
6. Harold J. Laski, *Democracy in Crisis* (London, 1935), p. 54.
7. Laski, *Democracy in Crisis*, p. 81.
8. Laski, *Democracy in Crisis*, p. 102.
9. William A. Robson, *Justice and Administrative Law* (London, 1928), p. 44.
10. The technical possibilities for a judge to change the parent meaning of a law into its opposite cannot be dealt with here.
11. Franz L. Neumann, *Die politische und soziale arbeitsgerichtlichen Rechtsprechung* (Berlin, 1928).
12. For Germany, see Franz L. Neumann, "Gegen ein Gesetz zur Nachprüfung der Verfassungsmäßigkeit von Reichsgesetzen," *Die Gesellschaft* 6 (1929). For the USA see W. I. Heyting, *The Anglo-American Conception of Due Process Law* (1932).
13. Editor's Note: The reference is to Johannes Popitz, 1884–1945. His analysis of the "polycratic" nature of the Weimar Republic was extremely influential among right-wing intellectuals in Weimar's final years—including Carl Schmitt. See Carl Schmitt, *Der Hüter der Verfassung* (Tübingen: Mohr, 1931).
14. Editor's Note: For a more detailed analysis of Nazi labor law, see Kirchheimer's "State Structure and Law in the Third Reich" and Neumann's "Labor Law in Modern Society," both reprinted below.
15. *Frankfurter Zeitung*, no. 582–584 (August 8, 1933).
16. *Frankfurter Zeitung*, no. 585–587 (August 9, 1933).
17. Editor's Note: Fortunately, Neumann later modified this extremely economistic view of the nature of the Nazi power elite. See *Behemoth: The Structure and Practice of National Socialism* (New York: Harper & Row, 1944), pp. 365–399. There, he broadens his analysis of the Nazi "ruling classes" to include political groups.

TWO

Legality and Legitimacy

Otto Kirchheimer

I

Every social system possesses a need for a certain legitimization and strives, as Max Weber expressed it in *Economy and Society*, to transform itself from a set of factual relations of power into a cosmos of acquired rights. The immanent yearning of every social order for legal stabilization is not the topic of this essay, for the social order's need for legitimization and the operating legal order do not contradict one another; on the contrary, the legitimation of the given system of social power is achieved through the forms of the existing legal order. It belongs precisely to the essence of a legal order that has become rational—and is no longer feudal or bound to tradition—that it provides opponents of the existing social system with a certain opportunity of at least formally equal treatment by the law, so that existing law is applied without regard to individual persons in a nondiscriminatory manner. In order to guarantee this opportunity, the separation of the legislative and executive authorities—as it was more or less completely implemented throughout Europe in the nineteenth century—is a necessary precondition. At the juncture when this division is nullified for a period of time having an indeterminate duration, as is now the case in Germany, this opportunity for formal equality vanishes. As the government—which now fuses legislative and executive authority—attempts to obtain for itself a legitimization transcending the formal consensus of Parliament, it does so by trying to make up for its loss of an indubitable legal basis by strengthening its ties to the people as a whole. In order to achieve this, it invokes its own authority and, in particular, that of the federal president; in its goals and basic orientation this authority is then taken to be binding on all segments of the people. Such a demand for authority based on a principle of legitimacy was

Editor's Note: Originally appeared in *Die Gesellschaft* 2, no. 7 (1932).

already formulated at the beginning of the last century as absolutism reacted to the revolutionary bourgeoisie. An anonymous French journalist, writing in 1814 in the period of the Congress of Vienna, gave expression to the distinct characteristics of this principle even better than Talleyrand was able to do: "A lucky general who by chance controls an army is not for that reason—even with the best possible conduct—a real power, while a legitimate king remains a power to be reckoned with even if he is in exile or in shackles."[1] Having sacred origins beyond the pale of discussion, this form of power possesses an eternal legal character. But since the monarchical principle of legitimacy made way for parliamentary monarchy, legitimacy has been transformed into a mere symbol for the national and social order represented by parliamentary government.

Today, however, the rule of a new form of legitimate power is emerging in Germany. In the face of the impotence of the contemporary legislative state, the problems of a class-divided democracy have made the professional bureaucracy *the* key power bloc. What is more natural than that the bureaucracy try to take advantage of the opportunities presented by the present situation? The bureaucracy is striving to make its supposed position "beyond class" independent of the interplay of class relations and to establish itself as the unmediated representative of the national order, independent of all social and political constellations. The bureaucracy seeks the legitimation for this power position in the special relationship between the civil service and the state; allegedly, one thereby can do without the mediation of a democratic concept of popular sovereignty. We do not believe that this unparalleled situation, in which the relative impotence of social mass organizations coincides with the growth and usurpation of state activities by the administrative apparatus, can in the long run prepare the way for the domination of some type of "bureaucratic aristocracy." Just as little as the legitimate monarchy was spared the choice between the position of head of state in a seignorial aristocracy and its diminished functions in liberal constitutionalism, so too shall a bureaucracy that has become independent prove unable to consolidate its socially neutral position between the bourgeoisie and proletariat in the form of a lasting, free-standing system of political rule. The certainty that we are dealing only with a passing phenomenon still does not free us from the duty of analyzing the ongoing decay of the legislative state[2] or the question of how the intermediate stage of rule by an all-embracing administrative bureaucracy can consolidate itself—if only provisionally.

II

Nineteenth-century political theory does not acknowledge the right to resistance anymore, even though it had dominated the structure of oppositional political discourse under absolutism. Along with constitutional practice, the absorptive power of democratic ideology contributed to the elimination of the right to resistance; it was the product of a social order that had not yet been fully rationalized. Indeed, one can go so far as to identify the distinguishing mark of the modern state with its degradation of the right to resistance to a catalog of constitutional rights. The rationalized concept of law stepped into the place of an indeterminate right to resistance, whose strength lay exclusively in being anchored in popular consciousness—that is to say, in its substantially unlimited character.

It is by no means superfluous today to recall that both the origins and significance of the concept of legality, which presently appears to be undergoing a process of decay, emptying it of its original meaning, is intimately indebted to the nineteenth-century concept of law. The concept of legality has a certain safeguarding function; it is not supposed to perpetuate the right to resistance, but instead make it superfluous. The expressions *légalité constitutionelle* (in the constitutional language of the Continent) and *rule of law* (in Anglo-Saxon legal circles) refer to the necessity of an agreement between every governmental or administrative act and the laws of the country in question. The rationalization of the concept of law corresponds to the formalization of the concept of legality. This, in turn, secures a more effective system of control over the administration than the competing German concept of the *Rechtsstaat*, which always tries to rework historical events that have already taken place.

It is no accident that it is precisely in France that the concept of legality, in the context of the recent and altogether unambiguous rejection of an independent "empire" of administrative bodies, has been determined by tracing it back to legal norms that are supposed to lie at the basis of administrative action.[3] Since they contain only organizational norms but no laws of a material nature, the constitutional laws of France, the so-called *lois organiques* of 1875, clearly have promoted the process of formalization; this process constitutes the basis of the concept of legality. These laws placed limits on the jurisdiction of the sovereignty of the democratic parliament but no material restraints on it. In those settings where appeals to the constitution can be juxtaposed to a particular law—and thus the problem of a system of "dual legality" emerges—this is likely to lead the bureaucracy to develop its own concept of legality based on its own particular interpretation of the constitution. But in France, the maxim that law must be in accordance with the constitution—found alongside the maxim that administrative action must agree with the law—is not permitted to take on any special significance because of the purely formal character of constitutional laws there. Quite consistently, French legal praxis never permitted courts to test the constitutionality of the law, thus harnessing the concept of legality to the framework of the statute. In the process, the French secured a broader sphere of applicability for the concept of legality than has often been realized in Germany. Indeed, the second part of the Weimar Constitution contains a rich variety of material-legal standards open to an infinite number of interpretations. In a country characterized by the intensive cultivation of so many different political interests, this inevitably leads to frequent attempts to appeal to the constitution against the legislature. In the hands of the judicial bureaucracy, the precision of the individual technical law is neglected in favor of the interpretable structural framework of the Constitution. Well before the appearance of the present system of rule by emergency decree, the judicial bureaucracy had in many cases already become the guardian of a system of dual legality that hindered the formalization and operationalization of the concept of legality in Germany.[4] Still, no "pluralism of concepts of legality," as Carl Schmitt describes it,[5] has emerged yet, because here, too, the concept of legality is aligned with the statute. This is true even though the confrontation between the statute and the Constitution gives significant leeway to the judiciary's cravings to usurp power.

The determination of the legality of an administrative body's activities presupposes, in any event, that the standard for evaluating such activities is neither indirectly nor directly furnished by the discretion of the very same administrative body. Legal transfers of special power (*Spezialermächtigungen*) to the administration do not affect the question of legality. The legislative body is allowed to transfer its authority as long as it determines the exact extent and scope of that transfer. Article 48 of the Weimar Constitution itself provides provisions for such a transfer of authority. More precisely, the constitution not only prescribes but anticipates it in a special case and only refers to the possibility of parliamentary intervention in a subsequent phase of the procedures. In the case of a significant disturbance of the peace and threat to the political order, the Constitution transfers exceptional powers to the federal president.[6] Only the character of this transfer of exceptional power guarantees that the system of legality as a whole is not suspended; only in particular cases to be determined by the discretion of the federal president (who is to exercise his power in accordance with the duties of his office), is legality partially suspended. In this case, legality consists of the existence of a legal norm that covers administrative practices; the determination of legality of action in the case of Article 48 is restricted to ascertaining that in the replacement of a legal norm by the federal president's special powers the delineated boundaries of that article have not been transgressed. According to judicial practice, the necessity of individual measures remains up to the discretion of the federal president. In order to preserve the essential character of such an exceptional grant of legal authority, however, it is necessary that the temporary (*Einstweiligkeit*) nature of the measures in question be strictly preserved. As soon as emergency lawmaking transgresses this characteristic—as soon as its provisional character is abandoned in favor of "an indeterminate time period probably of a lengthy duration"[7]—then governmental practice can no longer be described in terms of the traditional concept of legality.

One cannot respond by claiming that a clear and practically relevant difference exists between "an indeterminate time period probably of a lengthy duration" and an unlimited period of time. Some of the decrees undertaken under the auspices of the emergency legal powers (such as the budget and bank guarantees) are provisional, but this is attributable more to their very nature than the will of the federal president. In other cases (involving, for example, alterations in judicial practices and procedures) no evidence whatsoever justifies the expectation that we are dealing with decrees having a temporary character. In contrast to what is often falsely assumed, the power of Parliament to suspend such decrees after they have been issued does not imply that the failure to use it constitutes a retroactive legalization. For the moment, we do not need to consider to what extent parliamentary failure to demand the suspension of such decrees is significant for their constitutionality, nor do we need to determine whether Article 48 of the Constitution should pertain to budgetary laws in the first place. For, the question of their constitutional status is losing any immediate significance: administrative bodies subordinate to the federal president are complying with the administrative decrees because they are orders of their superiors, and the courts regularly accept the constitutionality of this practice. Of course, such administrative and judicial practices cannot hide the fact that the concept of legality is undergoing a structural transformation. In any event, the replacement of the legislative functions of Parliament with the federal president's emergency decree–based rule means that the concept of legality has been robbed of its previous meaning. We are not dealing here with a set of passing incidents. Rather, rule by emergency decree—and thus the fusion of legislative and executive authority—has taken on a permanent character in such a manner so as to leave no room for the core element of the principle of legality, the scrutiny of the administration against the yardstick of the law. So when there is talk today about the legality of government action as a way of contrasting its actions to those of "illegal" oppositional groups, obviously an altered version of the traditional conceptualization of legality is inherent in this discourse. The so-called legality of the executive organs focuses on the fact that they did not obtain their positions of power in antagonism to the Constitution, but along constitutionally ordained paths. Reference is made to the constitutionally based popular election of the federal president—who, after all, is given emergency powers by Article 48—and to the fact that the cabinet has yet to receive a vote of no confidence. It is then easy to draw a parallel to the relationship of the people to Parliament: since the people have no direct influence over the content of laws passed by Parliament, there is no qualitative difference in relationship to the federal president's system of authoritarian rule by decree. But whoever draws this parallel is simply missing a profound distinction: the difference between parliamentary democracy and dictatorship. The legislative state, parliamentary democracy, knows no form of legitimacy beyond that of its origins. Since any legislative resolution of a majority of the people constitutes a law, the legitimacy of this form of government consists simply in its legality. The emergency regime, secured by the plebiscitary personage of the federal president and executed by the administrative authorities, is not characterized by legality but by legitimacy, an appeal to the indisputable correctness of its actions and goals. Essential to the concept of legality is not simply the fact that power has been acquired by legal means, but, more important, that it be exercised in a legal fashion. Nothing makes the shift in accent from a political system based on legality to one based on an appeal to legitimacy more clear than Chancellor Brüning's now famous comment: "If you gained power by legal means but then declared that you intended to disregard legal boundaries, that cannot be considered legality."

The legal path to power here again refers to law-based origins, but what does "legal boundary" mean in this context? Since legislative and administrative functions have been unified in the hands of the government, legal boundaries—according to the juristic meaning of the word legality—are only to be located in those sections of Article 48 of the Weimar Constitution that cannot be suspended. It is apparent that Chancellor Brüning envisaged something other than those minimal features of the Constitution that cannot be suspended by Article 48; in the face of resolute government action, these do not amount to very much—just think of the abrogation of property rights or of the right to free assembly, or the substantial interventions into the autonomy of regional and municipal governments that are permissible according to contemporary judicial practice.[8] Apparently, legal boundaries are being equated with the legitimacy of the regime's goals. Which of those goals are legitimate, though, is determined solely by the ruling cabinet. An instructive essay published in the journal *Tat*[9] refers to a "concept of legality of the ruling cabinet" that does not allow it to take responsibility for ceding the government to a politically catastrophic majority coalition. One can only agree with the author when he concludes on the basis of this claim that "it (that is to say, the refusal to hand over the governmental apparatus to such a majority) will unleash a domestic struggle for the legality, i.e. the legitimacy, of power." One only needs to add that we do not have to await the refusal to hand over power to a "catastrophic" political majority before a battle for the legitimacy of power is unleashed. The transition from majority-based parliamentary lawmaking—the sanctioned abridgment of social power struggles—to a system of rule by emergency decree that supersedes the law really constitutes the decisive stage in the struggle for the legitimacy of power: by claiming that its goals are universally binding, a government unregulated by law is trying to bestow upon itself a broad consensus that it lacks in everyday political reality.

III

The same transformation observable within the federal government on the basis of its extensive use of Article 48 has been partially achieved in regional governments through the establishment of a series of temporary governments. Until now, the federal legislature has not withdrawn its confidence in the federal government, but in the states of Saxony, Hesse, and Hamburg this has been the case. The respective state constitutions contain provisions calling for governments that have been toppled by the legislature to stay in power as a caretaker government until a new government is appointed by the legislature. Such governments are only supposed to fulfill a temporary replacement function. The constitutions refer explicitly to the provisional character of these caretaker governments by stating that only the authority to pursue "ongoing business" is to be conferred on them. In Prussia, this term has been discussed on previous occasions; to be sure, there it was still a question of a temporary government that was replaced by a parliamentary cabinet after a relatively short period of time. Hence, problems that emerge when governments limited to "ongoing business" take on a permanent character were never fully played out. At least there is widespread agreement that "ongoing business" does not refer to all business underway at that particular moment when a government loses power.[10] The distinction between ongoing transactions and political decisions, however, remains questionable. Perhaps this distinction is practically meaningful for a caretaker government in power for a reasonable period of time. But because the concept of a political decision cannot be delineated a priori in light of the fact that the degree of intensity of a particular governmental act can vary according to the historical situation (just think of Hitler's appointment to the governmental council in Brunswick), the distinction lacks theoretical clarity. Since it is impossible to determine an objective limit on the forms of activities appropriate to a caretaker government, it can undertake all the same types of actions as a regular government. Thus, a peculiar situation emerges. The caretaker government, which the state legislature cannot topple, possesses substantial political autonomy and is not responsible to the legislature. As a consolation it is often mentioned that there is a possibility of indicting government ministers. Apart from the practical meaninglessness of this leftover from early southwest German constitutionalism—it does not lead to the removal of the minister from office, but at the most to a ruling that specific actions are irreconcilable with existing constitutional law—it remains questionable whether a governmental minister can be indicted on the basis of acts undertaken during the temporary government's term of office.[11]

One can deny the constitutionality of permanent caretaker governments by referring to Article 17 of the federal Constitution, which prescribes a parliamentary form of government for the individual states as well. On the basis of this, one might conclude that the federal government has the authority, by means of the second paragraph of Article 48, to suspend such governments and then replace them with a federal commissioner.[12] But the obscure nature of this solution should be evident enough. If the continued reliance on a device provided by the Constitution as a mere makeshift has to be seen as implying an amendment of the Constitution, repeated encroachments against the sovereignty of state governments by means of Article 48 have to be seen as entailing a dictatorial alteration of the Constitution. Essential for this discussion is merely the insight that a shift in the basis of the existence of the state governments has actually occurred. But if the state legislatures have gotten on the wrong track because they can no longer control their respective governments, those governments themselves have, by the same token, simply traded in their old masters for new ones. Even though the state governments no longer possess a legal basis for their activities, their survival is secured as long as their activity is seen by the national government as being in agreement with its own—in other words, as long as it accords with the national government's concept of legitimacy.

IV

As of late, the problem of the legality of political parties has gained substantial public attention. This issue raises no special questions for the concept of legality. As long as legislative and executive instances were separate, the so-called legality of a party was identical with the lawfulness of its actions. The lawfulness of party activity was determined primarily according to general laws valid for all citizens; the scope of the criminal law was especially significant for disputes of this sort. In addition, it was always left up to the sovereign decision of democratic parliaments to fight specific political groups in a more or less hostile fashion. Parliament could do that by making certain political actions or convictions punishable beyond the scope of the common penal laws. One only needs to recall the notorious example of the laws passed on the 23 Ventôse and 22 Prairial of Year II by the revolutionary French National Convention, which effectively declared all of the political enemies of the convention majority traitors to the fatherland and enemies of the people.[13] In Germany, neither the constitutional assembly nor the legislature ever decided to subject specific political groups to exceptional criminal laws on account of their political aims or convictions. At best, one can find a tentative starting point for this type of practice in paragraph 4 of the Defense of the Republic Act, which threatens a prison sentence of no less than three months to anyone who takes part in a secret or subversive organization aspiring to overthrow the constitutionally established republican form of government at either the state or the federal level. The real meaning of this law can only be correctly appreciated by taking into consideration its references to paragraphs 128 and 129 of the criminal code and to the idea of a constitutionally established form of government. Both references involve an attempt at formalizing this law with the aim of realizing a more effective legal defense of the Constitution without subjecting particular political groups to a set of exceptional laws. The notion of a party "hostile to the political order" was defined in reference to the Constitution and a set of general laws valid for everyone; no attempt was made to defame a specific set of political views by legal means. So if the government wanted to persecute certain political groups on account of their activities (which was common enough given the intensity and depth of divisions among political parties in Germany), it was necessary to rely on the fiction that they were not being persecuted on the basis of their convictions but as organizations "hostile to the political order." In short, the government had to try to prove that concrete offences against provisions of the criminal law had taken place. Even this method of persecution was limited: its employment was impermissible against the organizational core of the political party, its parliamentary representatives. This organizational core was considered unassailable from the perspective of the law even when, as occasionally happened, an entire political party was declared an illegal organization and thus an attempt was made to prevent it from engaging in effective political work. Legislatures have never undertaken to develop legal distinctions between parties by referring to the contents of their worldviews and actions. For example, the December 1927 Prussian law that regulates the organization of local government expressly determines that "an elected representative cannot be denied his seat on the basis of membership in a particular political party." The constitutional right of every political party to participate in Parliament—along with all of its auxiliary rights, the most important of which is the right to wage a political campaign—was always preserved. As long as Parliament still functioned in a regular manner, the only thing that mattered for determining the legality of a party was whether it relied on illegal methods to gain political power. Since no constitutional or other type of legal norm insisted on the universally binding character of a set of specific social views, the ultimate political or social goals of a party were irrelevant in the determination of the legality of a party. Even the administration was generally required to respect these limits when pursuing political opponents. The federal courts occasionally failed to exercise these supervisory functions effectively, but such transgressions only took place oc-

LEGALITY AND LEGITIMACY 53

casionally against the Communist Party (KPD), and even then, quite typically, courts avoided the formulation of new legal principles. Instead, they preferred to rely on an extremely extensive interpretation of the category of treason that clearly overstepped the boundaries of the law.

Such trends seemed alien to the spirit of an otherwise uniform system as law—as long as there was no opportunity to supplement the concept of legality by means of the legal standard of a "revolutionary party." Recently, Otto Koellreutter has undertaken precisely this task.[14] He wants a principled distinction within the legal order between revolutionary parties and those capable of exercising governmental authority. All those parties that can be seen as representatives of the existing political order belong to the latter; they can be seen as parts of a unified people, since they possess a conscious will for political unity which, in turn, constitutes the basis of national unity. Such parties extend from the National Socialists to Social Democrats, and though one cannot eliminate the possibility that they might opt at some juncture to undertake a putsch, they are to enjoy all the advantages of the official presumption of legality. Since they seem to deserve a presumption of legality on their behalf, the burden of proof to the contrary lies with their opponents. However, Koellreutter seems to have overlooked the fact that revolutionary parties historically have proven themselves to be the most dependable source of a "national will." Thus, it has been correctly argued against him that his conceptual innovations can discredit no one but the anarchists.[15]

In reality, the question of social structure lurks behind the concept of a national "life order." At another juncture in his exposition, Koellreutter concretizes—in fact, reduces—the concept of national unity to a belief in the sanctity of private property, marriage, and religion. If we disregard marriage for a moment (which, as far as I can tell, no one wants to abolish), the question of the transformation of private property is really what must be of concern to Koellreutter—the structure of which, by the way, is already undergoing a functional transformation much more profound than that achieved by many revolutionary transformations,[16] even though no constitutional changes in the organization of property have been undertaken. The exclusion of a revolutionary party from the framework of the existing constitutional order would presuppose that German constitutional law had developed a category in accordance with the French idea of "supra-legal constitutionality." But "supra-legal constitutionality" means nothing more than the acknowledgment of the legitimacy of a specific set of cultural values.[17] Whether the juristic legitimacy of a supra-positive individualistic legal order, standing above constitutional and legal texts, exists in France, it certainly does not in Germany. The second part of the Weimar Constitution provides possibilities for too many different types of legal appeals to justify the claim that its structure is exclusively individualistic in character.[18] But, by implication, this also eliminates the possibility of a material criterion, existing alongside the principle of legality, according to which one could evaluate party activity. Since Koellreutter himself admits that a party lacking a revolutionary character could act illegally, there really does not seem to be a need for the category of a revolutionary party. As long as a revolutionary acts in a legal fashion, it is irrelevant from the perspective of the legal order whether his present legality rests on revolutionary objectives or on "legal cretinism." Yet if the revolutionary acts in an illegal fashion, he inevitably comes into conflict with the existing legal order. This holds true whether his illegal activities are based on revolutionary considerations or merely on the "romance of illegality."[19]

The legal order does not reproach the revolutionary for relativizing the concepts of legality and illegality. Instead, he is reproached because his thought process sometimes leads him into the sphere of illegality that brings him into conflict with the legal order. It is equally irrelevant for the existing legal order whether a party happens to belong to the circle of "good parties" if, while on its path to power, that party conceives the idea of ignoring criminal laws. We dare not be so presumptuous as to claim the ability to anticipate what only the historian is entitled to: the highly relative distinction between revolutionary and "good" parties.

We need to ask to what extent the contemporary system of rule by decree, as well as the administrative and judicial practices associated with it, has abandoned the formal character of the principle of legality and a certain type of liberalism. Although its opponents prefer to overlook this, this liberalism has less to do with a fundamental commitment to liberal ideals than to the fact that it proved to be a practical organizational principle for a class-divided country. The system of emergency decrees, which has caused problems for almost every party because of the indeterminacy of its constantly changing regulations (just think of the manner in which uniforms and political insignia have been banned), has not resorted to declaring specific parties *hors de la loi*, that is, beyond the scope of the law. This has not happened in particular because an unwelcome discrepancy in relation to the principle of the equal treatment of all parties, which is still considered a component of valid parliamentary law, would thereby have become apparent. But, undoubtedly, the indeterminate legal structure of rule by emergency decree (the reference to "vital life interests" in the emergency decree of August 10, 1931, for example, or the extensive blanket powers given the administration in the regulation of some of the most basic civil rights) has allowed administrative bodies to discriminate against those parties whose legal character remains a matter of dispute. The extent to which parties are able to act autonomously is now determined by administrative decisions. These often stand beyond the scope of effective legal scrutiny either because they cannot be appealed or because of a lapse of time. The question of whether a specific meeting or poster is acceptable is no longer determined by general rules but by specific conceptions of public order held by the police. The manner in which administrative bodies make use of this discretionary authority is determined in accordance with the general character of the party in question. In other words, evidence for the legality of political action in a particular case loses significance in relation to the general presumption of legality. In turn, whether such a presumption of legality can be made is primarily determined by the orders of central administrative bodies; to a lesser degree, it is determined by court decisions. In deciding whether a party can be presumed to possess a legal character, the key administrative units ultimately find it very difficult to separate the question of the legality of particular acts from the question of the legitimacy of a particular set of political goals. Through equal treatment of the National Socialist and Communist parties, the Prussian decrees guarantee a certain formal approach by emphasizing the role of violence as a political instrument.[20] But, typically, even there reference is made to violent subversion as a goal and not a means.

The recent decree of Defense Minister Groener constitutes a deviation from the dominant administrative practices to the extent that it is not concerned with the question of illegality, but rather with issuing a certificate of good behavior to the NSDAP valid throughout Groener's jurisdiction.[21] On the basis of the decree's general context and its political objectives, one can conclude that the belief in the legality of the National Socialists no longer depends chiefly on the behavior of the party members, but rather on their acknowledgment of a set of so-called "national aims."

The position of the courts (understood here as every independent institution having the power to settle individual cases authoritatively) in a political system with a separation between the executive and legislature is shaped most fundamentally by their power to verify administrative acts according to the law. Courts undergo a functional transformation when there is no longer a legislature distinct from the administration. Previously, the courts were only occasionally able to utilize their usurped power of testing the constitutionality of laws. But now they possess the authority to make sure that every emergency decree is in accordance with the limits to emergency power outlined in Article 48. It is only the failure to make use of this veto power that ensures the undisturbed functioning of the system of emergency rule over subordinate administrative bodies and the citizenry. The courts have continually shielded and sanctioned the practice of rule by emergency decree. The caution they exercised by focusing on individual cases stemmed from the judiciary's aspiration not to lose its acquired share in the exercise of political power by establishing legal precedents, but to preserve it. Once the courts sanctioned the emergency decrees, they were in fact bound to their contents. But as far as the question of the legality of parties was concerned, their judgment was not binding since the relevant decrees of the administration lacked a legal character. In contrast to subordinate administrative bodies for which the decisions of superior administrative bodies on the presumption of legality or illegality were binding, even the lowest disciplinary court could make decisions on a case-by-case basis without having to refer to anything but paragraphs 128 and 129 of the criminal code or paragraph 4 of the Defense of the Republic Act.[22]

To the extent that unanimity was found in the administration (in other words, in the case of the Communist Party), the courts have considered the presumption of illegality to be the determining factor. They went a step further and eliminated the very possibility of proving the opposite. The Higher Administrative Court of Thüringen ruled that dissident Communists (KPO)[23] at the present time are not pursuing armed rebellion, but the court then proceeded to deny any significance to this concession. The reason given for this is that "they differ from the Communist Party (KPD) only in their political tactics and in their view of the present political situation. In contrast to the Communist Party (KPD), they do not believe that the possibility of seizing power is imminent. However, this changes nothing as far as their revolutionary goals are concerned."[24] In the face of the court's presumption of illegality, even its own well-considered acknowledgment of evidence suggesting the legality of the actions of the KPO at the present time is rendered inconsequential; the only thing that really counts is the KPO's illegitimate goal, its "revolutionary objectives." As far as the case of the National Socialists is concerned, there is as little unanimity within the judiciary as within administrative bodies. Most of the decisions, mainly those from Prussian higher disciplinary courts,[25] focus on the illegality of the political means employed by the National Socialists. But there are also other rulings, consistent with the Thuringia ruling, that have been determined on the basis of an evaluation of the legality of party objectives.[26] Here again we can begin to detect the outlines of a tendency to downplay the sphere of legal norms (which demand an exact determination of the illegality of a party's political means) in favor of repudiating illegitimate social goals unacceptable to the administrative apparatus. In the process, it no longer makes much of a difference whether the administration reaches this result by presuming the legality or illegality of party action that is binding within its jurisdiction, or whether the judiciary announces that in the face of the illegality of the social goals, any evidence pointing to the legality of the political means used by the group is simply irrelevant.

V

Although the concept of the legitimate party, like the system of rule by emergency decree and administrative practices, still faces obstacles stemming from Germany's democratic and constitutional political structure, it nonetheless has managed to become relatively commonplace in the area of labor law. Theoretically, German labor law is distinguished from fascist labor law by its refusal to outfit bargaining parties with a legally based monopoly position. The system of labor contracts simply presupposes the existence of bargaining units having the will and the capacity to wage labor disputes, to conclude collective agreements, and to adhere to them. No one could have blamed the judiciary for taking special care before acknowledging the bargaining position of economically independent organizations whose reliability in the sphere of labor law was still untested, especially to the extent that the political character of such organizations raised serious questions about their interest in respecting labor contracts. Yet such doubts would have only been permitted to take on legal significance until the opposite was proven. When the Federal Labor Court refused to recognize the bargaining status of the *Allgemeine Arbeiterunion*[27] despite the fact that this organization not only had proven capable of settling labor disputes by means of collective bargaining agreements but clearly had respected such agreements over the course of many years, it was evidently relying on the increasingly widespread notion that the illegitimacy of a particular set of social goals can lead to a permanent denial of the right to make use of legal rights in a legal way. The concept of the legitimate works council is accompanied by the concept of the legitimate bargaining unit. Does the Works Council Law permit the election of an individual to the works council committee who is willing to exercise his authority within the framework of the Works Council Law but who belongs to an organization which in principle hopes to satisfy the needs of the working class by means of revolutionary class struggle?[28] According to the principles of the legal order that had been in existence, the only thing that matters is whether the individual's actions are in agreement with the law in question. As soon as the principle of legitimacy is taken as a basis, however, it is inevitable that the right to be a member of the works council committee is declared to be incompatible with membership in the Revolutionary Union Opposition (Revolutionäre Gewerkschaftsopposition).[29] But the idea of a legitimate bargaining unit or even of legitimate organizations forming the works council is not the judiciary's only invention. Its most dangerous creation is a concept of legitimacy that focuses on the nature of the aims of labor disputes; it threatens to hinder the working class's capacity for waging labor disputes. The following characteristic statement of the Federal Labor Court provides evidence enough for this trend:

> One of the consequences of concluding a bargaining agreement is the duty to abandon unjustified labor disturbances and to initiate hostile actions only when economic aims are pursued, or when there is a legitimate cause for such action. If such measures ensue without economic aims being pursued or a

justified cause being evident, this signifies, even if no contractual responsibilities are concerned, that a breach of the general duty to maintain peaceful relations, based in the collective bargaining agreement, has occurred.[30]

The freedom to engage in union activity is thereby vastly limited. The simple assertion of labor union claims to power—when no evident economic goal is at stake—is now impermissible. The labor court alone decides which goals are of an economic nature (that is to say, have a legitimate character) and which are political (that is, illegitimate)[31]—a typical example of how the administrative apparatus is both fencing in and submitting the labor unions, which understandably are trying to act in a unified fashion against their economic opponents, to a system of licensing.

VI

The prospects of every system of legality-based political rule depend on the possibility of incorporating the dialectic of historical change more smoothly than a system of rule based on an appeal to legitimacy can accomplish. The latter is only capable of surviving to the extent that it succeeds in attributing the appearance of eternal validity to the political and social conditions of a particular historical moment. It was the unheroic task of the German legal order of unstable coalition governments to undertake to balance social antagonisms at the level of the existing relations of power between social classes and groups without being able to get rid of the underlying sources of social tension. The independence of that part of the bureaucracy that remained intact grew to the extent that an increasingly trying set of conditions nationwide made it impossible to achieve autonomous compromises between key power groups by means of parliamentary laws. On the basis of its position as a neutral mediator, functioning as a trustee in a situation of rough balance between social constituencies, the bureaucracy became the decisive power in the political system; the closed character of its ranks and filial ties to the armed forces facilitated this development. The bureaucracy is the champion of a new system of legitimacy-based rule that is superseding the epoch of legality-based parliamentary democracy. This new system legitimizes itself by means of the concept of a legitimate government, it undermines the autonomy of its intransigent foes by means of the idea of a legitimate party, and, armed with the notion of a legitimate bargaining unit and legitimate labor dispute, it proceeds to dominate the sphere of labor law by bureaucratic means. Nonetheless, the social basis of this system is too weak to permit the bureaucracy to function as a truly independent mediating force, standing above and beyond feuding economic groups and capable of achieving genuine compromises between them and thereby preserving the presuppositions of the political unity of the German people.[32] Certainly, the bureaucracy "makes the formal spirit of the state or the true spiritlessness of the state a categorical imperative,"[33] and its neutrality and nonpartisan character are only an ideological veil for the fact that the bureaucracy takes itself to be the "final end goal of the state." But this static social ideal can only be realized by the bureaucracy if it gains support from social groups having an interest in stabilizing the process of capitalist development at a stage that may appear relatively auspicious to a retrospective observer. By repeatedly commenting that we need to go back to the more simple and frugal economic foundations of the prewar years, it is Chancellor Brüning who is giving expression to the aspirations of the bourgeoisie, petty bourgeoisie, and bureaucracy. Eternal value is attributed to something that has irreversibly vanished in the stream of social development. In opposition to such restorative aspirations, the progressive will of the democratic populace must seem to be a dangerous anachronism. The present emergency situation seems to provide the best opportunity for permanently squelching that will. Popitz—a prominent and so-typical representative for the entire bureaucracy—has made the liquidation of this anachronism the starting point for his consciously weighted proposals for revising financial relations among political units within the federal system.[34] Of course, those phenomena that for us perhaps seem to be explosive manifestations of rapid transformations undergone in the postwar period are attributed by Popitz to party corruption, abuse of power, irresponsibility, and the ills of partisan political deals; these ills are then unfavorably contrasted to the civic-mindedness and sense of duty allegedly characteristic of the prewar years. But is not a social order forced to appeal to a concept of legitimacy based on the borrowed luster of an idealized past, and incapable of achieving legitimacy by internal means, doomed to fail even before it has been fully realized?

(Translated by Anke Grosskopf and William E. Scheuerman)

NOTES

1. Editor's Note: Kirchheimer here is making use of the famous typology of *legitimacy* developed by Weber in *Economy and Society*, but the historical reference suggests that Kirchheimer is also relying on a second possible meaning of the term "legitimacy": he believes that he can draw parallels between authoritarian legal trends in Germany and the ideas and practices of one variety of nineteenth-century royalist political thought, *legitimism*. For helpful surveys of legitimist political thought see Charlotte Touzalin Muret, *French Royalist Doctrines Since the Revolution* [New York:

Columbia University Press, 1933]; John A. Hawgood, *Modern Constitutions Since 1787* (New York: D. Van Nostrand, 1939).

2. See Carl Schmitt, "Grundsätzliches zur heutigen Notverordnungspraxis," *Reichsverwaltungsblatt* 53 (1932): 161.

3. Raymond Carre de Malberg, *La Loi expression de la volonte generale* (Paris, 1931).

4. Editor's Note: The French Constitution of 1875 consisted of a set of concise rules overwhelmingly *organizational* in character. It limited itself to a set of *formal procedures* that described the manner in which governmental officials were to be chosen and the respective jurisdictions of distinct governmental bodies defined. As discussed in the Introduction, the Weimar Constitution outlined a similar set of organizational norms (in Part I), but a lengthy additional section included provisions for nearly seventy "fundamental rights and duties" that often possessed a rather indeterminate legal character. A few examples might provide some sense of the character of these clauses: Article 119 announced that marriage constituted "the foundation of family life" and should enjoy "special protection"; Article 133 demanded that all citizens have a duty to "perform special services for the state"; Article 151 entailed that "the organization of economic life must conform to the principles of justice to the end that all may be guaranteed a decent standard of living." Although Kirchheimer qualifies his criticisms in the subsequent "Remarks on Carl Schmitt's *Legality and Legitimacy*," here he refers to the potential dangers of a constitution including a panoply of amorphous, so-called material clauses. In Germany, they allegedly provide a constitutional starting point for undermining the principle of formal legality and the political authority of the democratically elected parliament.

5. Carl Schmitt, *Der Hüter der Verfassung* (Tübingen, 1931), p. 91.

Editor's Note: The reference here is to Schmitt's claim in *The Guardian of the Constitution* that intense political polarization in Weimar Germany had led to a situation where no universally acceptable concept of legality was any longer possible. In Schmitt's eyes, the concept of legality had become nothing but an instrument of political struggle; references to it constituted a "veil" (*Schleier*) for the power interests of particular political groupings. Political groups described all conceivable practices essential to achieving their aims legal, whereas their opponents were inevitably deemed illegal. A "pluralism of concepts of legality" thus results.

6. Editor's Note: Article 48 read as follows:

> If a state fails to carry out the duties imposed upon it by the national constitution or national laws, the President of the Republic may compel performance with the aid of armed force.
>
> If public safety or order are seriously disturbed or threatened within the German Reich, the President of the Reich may take the necessary measures to restore public safety and order; if necessary, with the aid of the armed forces. For this purpose he may temporarily suspend in whole or in part the fundamental rights enumerated in Article 114 (inviolability of the person), Article 115 (inviolability of the private resident), Article 117 (the inviolability of the mails), Article 118 (the right to free speech), Article 123 (the right to assembly), Article 124 (the right to form associations), Article 153 (the right to property).
>
> The President of the Reich must immediately communicate to the Reichstag all measures taken by virtue of Paragraph 1 or Paragraph 2 of this Article. On demand of the Reichstag these measures may be abrogated.

If there is a danger in delay, the state ministry may, for its own territory, take such temporary measures as are indicated in Paragraph 2. On demand by the President of the Reich or by the Reichstag such measures shall be abrogated.

Detailed regulations (of this Article) shall be prescribed by a national law.

A vast literature on Article 48 exists both in German and English. A helpful comparative analysis is provided by Clinton Rossiter, *Constitutional Dictatorship: Crisis Government in Modern Democracies* (Princeton: Princeton University Press, 1948); see also Hans Boldt, "Article 48 of the Weimar Constitution: Its Historical and Political Implications," in *German Democracy and the Triumph of Hitler,* ed. A. Nichols and E. Matthias (London: Allen & Unwin, 1971).

7. Compare the decisions of the state court in *Juristische Wochenschrift* 61, no. 7 (1932): 513.

Editor's Note: A contemporary commentator has made the same point: "The most curious thing of all is that these decrees were never annulled, and that several of them are in force to this day." Boldt, "Article 48 of the Weimar Constitution," p. 92.

8. Editor's Note: In other words: those rights that can be legally suspended in accordance with Article 48 of the Weimar Constitution.

9. Horst Grüneberg, "Das neue Staatsbild," *Die Tat* (January 1932): 822.

10. This was the view of Prussian Minister President Marx in the parliamentary debates that took place in the Prussian state legislature on March 27, 1925.

11. See the remarks of Stier-Somlos who, like many others, believes that this is possible without providing an adequate justification for this view: "Geschäftsministerium, laufende Geschäfte, ständiger Ausschuss und Notverordnungen nach preussischem Verfassungsrecht," *Archiv des öffentlichen Rechts* 9 (1925): 218.

12. Ernst Huber, "Die Stellung der Geschäftsregierung in den deutschen Ländern," *Deutsche Juristenzeitung* 37 (1932), beginning at column 194.

Editor's Note: This issue took on special significance in 1932 and 1933: the federal government's usurpation of regional authority proved crucial to the rise of the authoritarian state in Germany. A particularly egregious example of such a usurpation took place in the conflict between the Social Democratic Prussian state government and the right-wing Papen regime in the summer of 1932. Enthusiastically endorsed by authoritarian jurists such as Carl Schmitt, the Papen government managed to remove the freely elected Prussian Social Democrats. Despite the blatant unconstitutionality of this act, the German judiciary tolerated it.

13. The text of the law is available in F.-A. Aulard, *Histoire politique de la revolution francaise* (1921), p. 365f.

14. Otto Koellreutter, "Parteien und Verfassung im heutigen Deutschland," in *Festgabe für Richard Schmidt* (Leipzig, 1932), beginning on p. 107.

Editor's Note: The reference here is to Otto Koellreutter, an authoritarian jurist who became one of the most enthusiastic defenders of the Nazis. For a fine introduction to his ideas see Peter Caldwell, "National Socialism and Constitutional Law: Carl Schmitt, Otto Koellreutter, and the Debate Over the Nature of the Nazi State, 1933–1937," *Cardozo Law Review* 16 (1995).

15. Haentzschel, "Der Konfliktfall Reich-Thüringen in der Frage der Polizeikostenzuschüsse," *Archiv des öffentlichen Rechts* 20 (1931): 385.

16. Editor's Note: This is possibly a reference to Karl Renner's highly influential account of the transformation of capitalist private property in *The Institutions of Private Law and Their Social Functions* (London: Kegan & Paul, 1949).

17. Such a position is defended by the well-known political theorist Maurice Hauriou in *Precis de Droit constitutionnel* (Paris, 1929), p. 239.

18. See Carl Schmitt's comments in *Handbuch des Staatsrechts* (Tübingen, 1930), paragraph 101, point II.

19. On the relationship between revolutionary thought and the legal order see Georg Lukacs, "Legalität und Illegalität," in his *Geschichte und Klassenbewusstsein Studien uber marxistische Dialektik* (Berlin, 1923).

20. See the Decree of July 3, 1930, which has been printed in the *Justizministerialblatt* (Berlin, 1930), p. 220.

21. Editor's Note: The reference is to a set of decrees from January 29, 1932, that reversed the previous policy of preventing Nazis from belonging to the military.

22. See Glockner in *Die politische Betätigung der Beamten* (Bühl, 1930), an expert opinion issued on behalf of the teachers' organization in Baden.

23. Editor's Note: The KPO refers to the Kommunistische Partei Opposition, a group of "rightist" Communists who were driven from the (Stalinist) Deutsche Kommunistische Partei (KPD) in 1928 and thereafter set up their own organization.

24. Reprinted in Koellreutter, "Parteien und Verfassung im heutigen Deutschland," p. 122.

25. See the ruling of the Prussian Disciplinary Court for tenured bureaucrats who do not exercise judicial capacities, reprinted in the *Frankfurter Zeitung* on February 25, 1932.

26. See the decision of the Lübeck Disciplinary Court in Koellreutter, "Parteien und Verfassung im heutigen Deutschland," p. 128.

27. *Entscheidungen des Reicharbeitsgerichts* 6 (1931): 63.

Editor's Note: It is not quite clear which labor union Kirchheimer has in mind; in the legal decision cited here, the reference is to the *Freie* Arbeiter Union.

28. Editor's Note: Article 165 of the Weimar Constitution called upon workers and employees "to cooperate in common with employers, and on equal footing, in the regulation of salaries and working conditions, as well as in the entire field of the economic development of the forces of production." The Works Council Law of 1927, regulating councils for the purposing of advancing working class economic goals, was intended to help provide the rather ambitions aims outlined in Article 165 with substance.

29. See the resolution of the state labor court in Ulm, discussed by Ernst Fraenkel in *Justiz* 7, no. 4 (1931/32): 194.

Editor's Note: The Revolutionary Union Opposition (RGO) was a labor organization allied with the Communist Party.

30. See *Entscheidungen des Reichsarbeitsgerichts* 5 (1930): 252. A precise evaluation of these tendencies is provided by Otto Kahn-Freund, "Der Funktionswandel des Arbeitsrechts," *Archiv für Sozialwissenschaft* 67 (April 1932).

31. The contrast of "political vs. economic" is based in a set of pure value judgments about social behavior. Since a more detailed justification of these categories is usually not provided by the administrative bodies in question, it is difficult to de-

termine in general to what extent the courts are conscious of the contemporary significance of this problematic. See Carl Schmitt, *Der Begriff des Politischen* (München: 1932).

32. Compare Ernst Huber, *Das Deutsche Reich als Wirtschaftsstaat* (Tübingen: Mohr, 1931), p. 29.

33. Karl Marx, *Kritik der Hegelschen Staatsphilosophie*, in his *Der Historische Materialismus, Frühschriften I* (Leipzig, 1932), p. 78.

34. Johannes Popitz, *Der künftige Finanzausgleich zwischen Reich, Ländern und Gemeinden* (Berlin: Verlag von Otto Leibmann, 1932). See the comments by Rinner in *Die Gesellschaft* 9 (April 1932).

THREE

Remarks on Carl Schmitt's *Legality and Legitimacy*

Otto Kirchheimer[1]

Carl Schmitt's *Legality and Legitimacy* analyzes the core principles of the Weimar Constitution as well as the present and future status of German constitutional trends.[2] A substantial portion of Schmitt's arguments attempt to demonstrate that there is a contradiction between democracy's underlying justification and specific elements contained in the Weimar Constitution or arising from its application. Schmitt fails to discriminate sufficiently between providing a justification for a particular system of normative ideals and analyzing empirical political reality. He conflates two different tasks—an analysis of normative political ideals (*Sollensideen*) that focuses on their logical structure, and an examination of specifically political forms of human behavior (which can be intended by normative ideals) concerned with the question of whether a system of normative ideals can "function" properly when put into effect. Implicitly, Schmitt assumes that the internally contradictory character of a system of political ideas based on a definite system of normative ideals in itself constitutes evidence that the political system in question cannot "function" properly—signs of a strand of conceptual realism in his theory.[3] Since almost all of Schmitt's claims presuppose a certain justification for democracy, a discussion of this part of his theory seems necessary. Schmitt defines democracy as the fundamental principle of making decisions on the basis of simple majorities. He furthermore argues that democracy can only be justified within the context of a homogeneous society. Thus, he comments that "the method of will-formation by means of simple majority decisions only makes sense and can only be tolerated if a substantial homogeneity of the people can be presupposed."[4] But since it seems that homogeneity refers to an empirical condition and thus by itself cannot

Editor's Note: Originally appeared in *Archiv für Sozialwissenschaft und Sozialpolitik* 68 (1933).

constitute an ultimate justification, the postulate that democracy can only be realized in a homogeneous society seems to be the result of a somewhat more fundamental argument within Schmitt's theory. His *Constitutional Theory* explains in greater detail the significance of the need for homogeneity for democracy.[5] There, Schmitt grounds his view by referring to the principle of equality, which he claims constitutes the presupposition of every democratic system. But in opposition to Schmitt, we need to keep in mind that the principle of equality by itself does not suffice as a justification for democracy; it does not necessarily follow from the equal treatment of all members of society that the majority should decide.[6] Since Schmitt undertakes to do precisely this, majority rule inevitably seems senseless to him.[7] Instead, majority rule only becomes understandable if the demand for equality is integrated into a demand for the realization of freedom, defined here as an agreement between an unhindered process of will-formation among citizens with the will of the government; the demand for freedom then takes the form of trying to realize it for as many people as possible.[8]

The concept of liberty has many different meanings. In constitutional theory it has been used to describe two domains that historically have long appeared alongside one another. Nevertheless, these two domains differ. First, the concept of liberty can refer to the process by which norms are created, but, second, also to the relationship between the contents of particular norms and spheres of individual activity. So far, our comments here have been concerned with the former. In this first sense, liberty refers to political liberty (liberty *within* the state); in the second sense, liberty refers to individual liberty (liberty *from* the state). Individual liberty, which traditionally has been associated both with rights that guarantee the liberty of the individual as well as those rights that permit individuals to come together and form groups, possesses two key attributes. First, individual liberty guarantees that the process of political will-formation can take an unhindered form. This function can be described in terms of the *rights of citizenship*. Freedom of the press, freedom of opinion, and the rights of assembly and association belong under this rubric.[9] They constitute a necessary supplement to so-called *political rights,* such as voting rights and the right of equal access to all governmental posts. Political rights are naturally a component of liberty *within* the state and fundamental to the process of democratic will-formation.[10] At the same time, individual liberties are the precondition for a private sphere of freedom for the individual; here, we can speak of *private rights*. First and foremost, the right to property and religious freedom belong to this category, as well as other liberties, insofar as they do not serve political goals.[11] It is simply not the case that all three types of liberties—political rights, the rights of the citizen, and private rights—have always coexisted in history.[12] "Political liberty," in the narrow sense of fundamental participatory rights, even exists to some extent in nondemocratic states such as Italy.[13] Specific to democracy is the full realization of political rights alongside the full realization of the rights of the citizen: only this combination can guarantee an unhindered process of will-formation. In contrast, private liberties do not represent a necessary feature of democracy. The existence of private rights, and even to some extent the rights of citizenship, may even prove to be independent of the amount of political freedom realized at a particular historical juncture.[14] Schmitt's definition of liberty places special emphasis on the liberty of the individual; in addition, he distinguishes between the liberty of the isolated individual and the liberty of individuals interacting with other individuals. Since Schmitt conceives of liberty in terms of a sphere of individual action beyond the scope of the state and fails to consider whether individual freedom stands in some relationship to the process of democratic will-formation,[15] he is incapable of acknowledging the distinction between the rights of citizenship and private rights; in our definition, private liberty is merely described in reference to the intention underlying individual behavior, and it is therefore irrelevant whether this aim is pursued by an isolated individual or by individuals acting together. Schmitt defines political liberty according to its scope, but its significance only emerges [for Schmitt] in relation to the postulate of equality; liberty becomes a correlate of equality. Consequently, Schmitt obscures the dual character of the rather heterogeneous complex of ideas that make up the concept of liberty: it constitutes the foundation both of citizenship rights necessary for democracy and private rights. This all serves to suggest, as Hans Kelsen has shown,[16] that majority rule constitutes an institutional guarantee for the realization of a greater degree of freedom than other decision-making procedures. In accordance with Rousseau's *Social Contract,* we have to assume the inevitability of the emergence of special interests within every society. Admittedly, as the scope of such special interests decreases—and here we can only think in terms of quantitative shifts—so too does the sphere of heteronomy decrease. After all, under such conditions the probability of differences of opinion, and the concomitant chance of being outvoted by a majority, decline. Nonetheless, the total transcendence of all differences in opinion has to be seen as constituting a utopian idea because it would imply the destruction of individuality itself. If we start from the relatively uncontroversial claim that an acknowledgment of the virtue of a particular value necessitates that we try to realize it as fully as possible even if it turns out to conflict with competing values, and even if the real world is likely to present challenges to our undertaking, we can come to the following conclusion: even given some relatively high degree of heterogeneity within society, the mere acknowledgment of the principles of equality and freedom demands that we still strive to realize them as completely as can be achieved. It is not possible to show within the confines of this essay that a justification of democracy along these lines has been historically dominant or that precisely this view is the basis for the Weimar Constitution and its self-legitimization as the world's most liberal. In order to prove the accuracy of this interpretation, we merely need to refer to the often-cited speech of former Secretary for the Interior David—a rather moderate politician who was a contemporary of the Constitution's architects—as well as to the preamble of the Constitution itself, which speaks of the German people's quest to revitalize and secure a political system according to the principles of freedom and justice.[17]

The justification for democracy suggested here is only one of many possibilities. We can distinguish between two different basic types of justification. One grounds the democratic principle of political organization by recourse to the "formal" values of freedom and equality, independently of the objective content of concrete decisions that result from democratic decision-making procedures. Another justifies this organizational principle only because of the objective character and basic correctness of democratically derived decisions. The concepts of democracy developed by Rousseau—and, apparently, Kelsen as well—depend on both types of arguments.[18]

One reason why Schmitt rejects democracy is that he believes that "whoever possesses a majority position (namely, 51 percent of the votes) no longer commits injustice, but simply attributes to all of his actions the status of law and legality. Because of these implications, the concept of a functionalistic principle of legality devoid of any substance is pursued *ad absurdum*."[19] But there is a *quaternio terminorum* in the use of the term *injustice* here. Certainly, it is true that it is perfectly legal in a parliamentary democracy for a 51 percent majority to pass some set of material-legal norms as long as this is done in accordance with the existing constitutional system's underlying organizational norms. But that might change nothing from the perspective of some citizens, who might consider the legal norms in question unjust. This seems to be the type of situation that Schmitt has in mind in the passage just quoted: those who felt that a particular set of legal norms were unjust would have to belong to a minority. In a nondemocratic state, the same type of situation would arise when an indeterminate number of dissenting voices, but in this case potentially amounting to more than 49 percent of all subjects, considered as subjectively unjust a set of norms that are considered by the holders of power to be just.[20] In the case that the supreme power does not consider these norms unjust, there is only one way in which a difference between a democratic and nondemocratic state could result: only if the nondemocratic state institutionalized an authoritative decision-making body to which dissenters could appeal with a claim that injustice had been done to them. But even then the unavoidable problem of *quis custodiet ipse custodes* would remain as unresolved as beforehand. Even absolutism failed to institutionalize a constitutional device of this type.[21]

Incidentally, the establishment of such a device would not only transform existing democratic bodies into nothing but a set of intermediate powers for a "jurisdictional state" (*Jurisdiktionsstaat*), like that recently criticized by Schmitt, but it would similarly disfigure institutions of a new type of plebiscitary authoritarianism like that suggested by Schmitt.[22]

So far, we have only considered those possibilities for justifying democracy that focus on the direct acceptance of values obligatory for their own sake. But the relationship of democracy to a particular set of values can also be "instrumental" in an indirect fashion. At any given point in time, a democratic system may not directly realize a given set of values. Nonetheless, it may be believed that at some point in the future democracy will effect the realization of those values. This position can insist on either the maintenance or the abandonment of democracy once the values in question have been realized. In both cases, democracy is justified because it is a means to something else; for the first category of justifications mentioned above, democracy is a goal in itself. The political theory of Marxism is an example of this view of democracy, whereas National Socialism is an example of an instrumental view, seeking the abolition of democracy.

Yet Schmitt does not simply claim that democracy cannot be justified in a heterogeneous society. He also claims that democracy cannot function amidst heterogeneity because it does not allow all people to act in a universally legal manner.[23] But we can point to a whole series of phenomena that are difficult to square with this thesis. One cannot claim that France was homogeneous in the period between the Panama Dispute and the railway strike of 1910. The proletariat had yet to be integrated into the mainstream of French politics, and issues of "*politique et idéologie pure*" still played a pivotal role in political consciousness. The ideological legacy of the French Revolution has divided the French people since 1789. Now that these ideas have become hegemonic, they serve to integrate social groups into a stable society. Yet at the turn of the century, during a critical period in the history of the Third Republic, this ideological legacy still had real force. It had the capacity to polarize the French, yet the process of democratic will-formation was not disturbed.[24] In Great Britain, increasing heterogeneity is becoming ever more apparent: the consolidation of the Labour Party helped put a process into motion in which pronounced social divisions now take the form of divisions among political parties. The fact that there are situations where a concept of substantial national homogeneity is consciously employed as an instrument of political integration could just as easily be interpreted as a symptom of an overall weakening of the extent to which national homogeneity is self-evident. This process is all the more significant in the face of the fact that it was linked to the unprecedented "*hors de la nation*" declaration of a major British party—in short, to an attempt to limit the ideology of national homogeneity to a mere portion of the electorate. Significant national and social heterogeneity in Belgium has resulted in a transformation of political parties into typical integrative parties, but until now no serious threat to the functioning of democracy has been evident there.[25] The ongoing trend toward heterogeneity is the source of the fact that ideas of homogeneity important for contemporary political consciousness decreasingly correspond to political reality; homogeneity is thus largely founded on ideology in the sense given the term by Karl Mannheim.[26] A "false consciousness" of this type can be generated by a process in which the "superstructure" lags behind transformations of the social substructure. The contents of a particular form of consciousness may once have been "right" insofar as they corresponded to a particular set of real conditions, but they become "false" as soon as substantial changes in those conditions have taken place. For example, until recently a virtually unlimited faith in the virtues of a form of egotistical calculation, namely interest-based solidarity, functioned as a powerful integrative instrument in the United States. Its efficacy can be demonstrated simply by comparing the manner in which nationally heterogeneous groups have been assimilated in America to similar attempts at assimilation in Europe. But if it proves to be the case that the economic depression means that North American capitalism has entered a new stage in its history, it would seem that this quasireligious calculative worldview is going to be put to a difficult test as it comes up against a set of real conditions that conflict with it. Particularly in light of its pragmatic structure, it is questionable whether this worldview is going to prove able to survive the test at hand. With remarkable sociological consistency, the dream of a "new prosperity" is now being used as an instrument of social integration in the United States. Social coherence once was founded on the fact that the expectation of social mobility suggested itself to the individual. Now an ideologically denatured form of this reality is supposed to cement social bonds.[27] But a democratic ideology may not be "false" simply because it lags behind transformations of real social conditions. In addition, an ideology may be misleading because it interprets democratic reality in the light of a preconceived utopia that is incorrectly seen as being already realized in the existing democracy. This tendency is evident in the ideological development of broad segments of the European working classes, whose original allegiance to social democracy seems to have been transferred to existing political democracy. Parallel to the ongoing decline of subjective homogeneity, contemporary democracy is faced with the transformation of its very foundations, and thus a "foundational crisis" is taking place. It is impossible to deny that those moments when such transformations are necessary are precisely those when democracy often finds itself in a critical situation. But in the face of both the inadequate inductive basis for the argument and significant empirical evidence to the contrary, Schmitt's bleak assessment of the impossibility of democracy's situation in a heterogeneous society has not been sufficiently grounded. After all, new potential solutions to this problem are becoming evident: they take the form of an increasingly consistent "instrumental" view (*Mitteleinstellung*) to democracy. As long as constitutions had to represent the interests of relatively uniform social classes, little attention was paid to the significance of the instrumental relationship between distinct social classes and democracy. This remains true even though Charles Beard has recently claimed that the American Constitution originally rested on a coalition of "money, public securities, manufactures, and trade and shipping."[28] This instrumental conception currently manifests itself most clearly in the written norms of the constitution having a material-legal character, like those found in the Weimar Constitution (which is founded on the "social contract" of the Legien-Stinnes agreement)[29] and the recent Spanish Constitution.[30] It reflects the experience of parties that support a democratic constitution because they see it simply as that political apparatus best capable of achieving a necessary degree of political unity in a heterogeneous society. From the perspective of parties of this type, democracy's basic virtue lies in the fact that it provides a better chance for each of the respective parties to exercise power than a nondemocratic system can provide. The increasingly pervasive status of this instrumental view of democracy—compatible in style with so many other facets of the ongoing "disenchantment of the world"[31]—admittedly contributes to the instability of democracy to the extent that political shifts may suggest to key parties or power groups that democracy no longer functions as an adequate instrument for reaching their particular goals. This appears to be the case in Germany; its significance is arguably even greater for understanding recent developments in Germany than those factors described by Carl Schmitt.[32] It is clearly impossible to make generally valid statements about the relative frequencies of positive and negative instrumental views of democracy among various social groups. But recent experience does suggest that a positive instrumental view of democracy is capable of generating political stability (Germany between 1925 and 1929, Belgium, Czechoslovakia, Australia, perhaps even Spain).

So far our discussion of the functioning of democracy in a heterogeneous society has ignored questions concerning the strains put on modern constitutions by material-legal constitutional standards that go beyond the traditional set of organizational norms and guarantees of freedom.[33] But Schmitt not only claims that parliamentary democracy outfitted with a traditional set of basic rights is incapable of functioning properly, but that material-legal constitutional standards (regardless of whether they are exempt from amendment or possess special protection because they can only be amended by means of qualified majorities) constitute an additional source for the inevitable instability of contemporary democracy.[34] Before we can explicate this thesis, it is appropriate to categorize the relevant main types of material-legal standards found in the Weimar Constitution and of interest to Schmitt in his study.[35] The standards at hand include those demanding that the administration and judiciary immediately seek to achieve their concretization (in other words, norms of fixation [*Fixierungsnormen*], such as Article 143, paragraph 3, Articles 144 and 149),[36] as well as those that contain no such obligation. In the latter group, we find standards that constitute demands on the lawmaker to act in a specific manner but do not allow citizens to sue if they believe they have been left unfulfilled (programmatic norms, such as Articles 151, 161, and 162)[37] and those that merely authorize the legislator to act in a certain way (authorization norms, for example, Article 155, paragraph 2, Article 156, paragraphs 1 and 2, Article 165, paragraph 5).[38] It only makes sense to establish authorization norms when it seems at least questionable that their goals would have been admissible without the authorization; programmatic standards, however, make sense even when their admissibility was not questioned beforehand because they put "moral pressure" on the legislator. To the extent that fixation norms are realized by means of norm-based legal action undertaken by governmental authorities, they have real substance. When they fail to be fulfilled, programmatic and authorization standards lack such substance.

How does the existence of such norms affect the functioning of democracy in different settings? In situations characterized by a *relatively unchanging distribution of power*, norms of fixation play the following role: by removing certain objects from the immediate access of simple majorities they make it more difficult for those objects to become the target of everyday political struggles. They reduce tensions and hence tend to improve the functioning of democracy.[39] When they are chosen correctly, that is, they correspond to the specific political constellation, they anticipate political results that otherwise would first have to have been achieved by means of a political struggle. Such fixation norms thus seem to amount to introducing the principle of planning into the system of competitive democracy. At the same time, fixation norms deny simple majorities that stand in a relationship of enmity to those institutions protected by the norms a safety-valve for achieving their wishes. Such standards thus may result in a situation where dissatisfied mass movements fail to reach their goals because of the especially restrictive basis of the legal order and eventually opt for radical antidemocratic alternatives; this is a real possibility especially if a *variation in social power relations* has taken place. But there is still a noteworthy compensatory element that works against this possibility. Groups that are attached to the institutions protected by a particular fixation norm tend to have a positive relationship to democracy in general. A good example for both tendencies—that is, for a potential increase as well as decrease in democratic stability—is provided by the special constitutional protections enjoyed by the civil service. The constitutional guarantees provided to the civil service in

Article 129[40] (as well as by Article 41 of the new Spanish Constitution) limit the scope of political spoils. This reduces the intensity of struggles between parties because the opportunities for political patronage are diminished. At the same time, the parties' respect for the principle of legality is subject to a tough test if they believe that the realization of their political goals is tied to the rapid replacement of personnel in the state bureaucracy.

The same effect is evident in the sphere of programmatic and authorization norms as long as they are not realized in a situation characterized by *a constant distribution of power*. Here, the potential beneficiaries of these norms are brought into a positive relationship to the democratic system (Articles 156, 165, paragraph 2) because of the Constitution's endorsement of their ideal values as well as the political opportunities offered by the norms.[41] What consequences do such norms have for the operation of democracy when there is a *variable distribution of power* and a particular political majority attempts to realize the goals set out in an authorization norm? They would seem to contribute positively to the functioning of democracy to the extent that an increase in power of the group in question is permitted to take a legal form—in other words, to the extent that an expansion in the power status of a particular group is secured by legal means. In this fashion, both the Weimar Constitution and the new Spanish Constitution would allow the transition from an agricultural order dominated by big landed property to a more egalitarian one by means of a simple legislative act (Article 155 of the Weimar Constitution, Article 44 of the Spanish Constitution). To summarize: the material determinations of the second part of the Weimar Constitution are quite indeterminate as far as the question of the functioning of democracy is concerned. Whether an integrative or disintegrative function dominates is determined by their particular content and social milieu. All we can do here is limit ourselves to fleshing out their possible consequences.

Schmitt makes the further point that the introduction of material standards in the Constitution's second section alters the organizational core of parliamentary democracy in such a way that parliamentary sovereignty is abrogated in favor of a system based on the primacy of jurisdictional elements.[42] Schmitt is right to identify trends pointing in this direction, but—significantly—they emerge where the causes Schmitt identifies are not present. According to Schmitt, such changes in organizational structure occur especially where we find constitutions with "special material constitutional clauses that can only be changed by amending the constitution."[43] But the most significant example of a "jurisdictional state" is the United States. If we ignore the Eighteenth Amendment for a moment, the American Constitution clearly represents an example of one "limited to organizational and procedural rules and basic liberties."[44] It is the "due process clause" in the Fifth and Fourteenth Amendments of the American Constitution—both originally had a purely procedural character—that the Supreme Court (and the lower courts which follow its lead) has relied upon in order to outfit itself with impressive controls over both federal and state legislation.[45] One interpretation of this jurisdictional element in the American political system goes so far as to speak, not at all unjustly, of the "supremacy of the federal judiciary in matters involving persons and property."[46] As far as matters related to private property are concerned, the supremacy of the legislature in the United States has been effectively destroyed. Although the American courts do not "confront the state in the role of a guardian of a social and economic order that remains basically unchallenged," as Carl Schmitt claims,[47] but rather are conscious architects of a conservative "upper house" intent on defending propertied interests in opposition to legislatures elected on the basis of universal suffrage,[48] no threat to the functioning of the transformed American political system has resulted. None of the opponents of the Supreme Court's "usurpation" of power has even tried to make this type of claim. Whereas the contours of jurisdictional supremacy can be clearly identified in the American case, the German constitutional system has only taken relatively modest steps in this direction—despite the fact that Germany, in contrast to the United States, exhibits all the preconditions of this development emphasized by Schmitt. The only movement toward an expansive constitutional interpretation has occurred with regard to the politically irrelevant Articles 131 and 153 of the Constitution.[49] The interpretation of the constitutional guarantee of property does provide evidence of certain similarities to the jurisprudence of the American Supreme Court, but it remains fundamentally different because the concept of property at the base of German jurisprudence remains much narrower. Besides—and this is decisive for our discussion here—the protection of property does not belong among the familiar basic rights.[50] Nor have the courts made use of the possibility of relying on Article 109 as a starting point for establishing a system of jurisdictional supremacy.[51] In the face of the "administrative state"—which Schmitt rightly sees as characteristic of the system of emergency-based decree rule now found in Germany—possibilities for the expansion of jurisdictional power are gaining substantially in scope. There is now a real possibility that a new political system based on a mixture of specifically administrative and jurisdictional elements will be able to emerge. But that is a process that transcends the scope of this essay; Schmitt himself believes that such a process stands in opposition to positive constitutional norms for the most part only because of legal customs (*Gewohnheitsrecht*).[52] This is simply not the place to examine the entire constellation of issues that Schmitt discusses under the title "the exceptional legislator *ratione necessitatis*."[53]

As noted above, Schmitt's view of democracy leads him to posit the existence of a series of contradictions between democracy and the underlying justification of a number of central elements of the Constitution. By demonstrating that democracy can be justified within the context of a heterogeneous society, we at the same time have implicitly shown that there may be good reasons for a democracy to institutionalize special constitutional protections of a material-legal type. For heterogeneity implies the need for special protection. Schmitt argues that even if the heterogeneity of Weimar democracy constitutes a case where there may be a legitimate motive for special constitutional protections, and even if the need for them is quite substantial,[54] their establishment nevertheless generates a contradiction. This contradiction arises between the first section (with the exception of Article 76)[55] and its founding principle and the second section of the Weimar Constitution and its respective founding principle. The justification of the first part of the Constitution allegedly demands an unrestricted "functionalism"—in other words, a constitution that simply consists of organizational standards with the exception of guarantees of basic rights. Schmitt calls this type of democracy a parliamentary legislative state (*parlamentarische Gesetzgebungsstaat*) if it possesses the characteristics of a legislative state and its decisive manifestations can be found in norms established by Parliament.[56] At the same time, Schmitt claims that the basic justification of the Constitution's second section requires the abrogation of Article 76; it should either be fully exempt from amendment, or only the competent organs of the estate-based (*ständestaatlich*) state should be allowed to amend it.

> If we are logically consistent, recognizing the necessity of providing special protections for certain interests or groups from political majorities has to culminate in a situation where those interests or groups are placed completely beyond the range of functionalistic parliamentary and democratic decision-making procedures. It would be consistent to grant them a full exemption from amendments *itio in partes* or the acknowledgement of a right to exodus and secession.[57]

Thus, Article 76 contradicts the founding principle of the second as well as the first section of the Constitution.[58] Schmitt simply excludes the possibility that there could be a compromise between the imperatives of "functionalism" and the need for special constitutional protections. He explicitly repudiates the compromise found in the Weimar Constitution as unreasonable by characterizing it as an attempt to uphold "neutrality" between the principle of neutrality and the principle of nonneutrality. Yet the point is not that we simply need to identify a neutral position between these two alternatives. Instead, it is a question of distinguishing between impeded and unimpeded neutrality. Beyond this, Schmitt's conclusion that a decision to opt for neutrality here in fact implies a nonneutral decision appears to be wrong. Schmitt succumbs to a mistake made by Pascal: "*et ne point parier que Dieu est, c'est parier qu'il n'est pas.*" But Voltaire pointed out long ago that it is obviously incorrect to make this statement, for those who are filled with doubts and in search of enlightenment probably place their bets neither on behalf of God's existence nor against it. The decisive point is this: it is not clear why it should be acceptable for some objects to be fully exempted from the operations of the functionalism of the first part of the Weimar Constitution (which Schmitt believes necessarily has to be unrestricted), but why it then should be intolerable to impede the legislative regulation of such objects by political majorities as the Weimar Constitution has tried to do. In both cases, it is a question of compromises between the value of democratic forms and the value of definite objective values; the Weimar Constitution is characterized by an emphasis on the former. Its underlying support for democratic forms has merely been moderated in such a way that voting procedures have simply been altered for a specified set of objects. Undoubtedly, a ceiling to special protections would have to be established in such a way that if a constitution were to transgress it, the amount of democratic procedures remaining would be so minimal that one might just as well have established procedures justifying the possibility of abolishing democracy.[59] But no one can claim that the second section of the Weimar Constitution has reached such a limit. The justification of democracy that we have tried to sketch out here makes it possible to claim that in principle there is no contradiction between the existence of Article 76 and the core of the second section of the Weimar Constitution (that is, with the exception of the basic rights promulgated there). The facts of the case are different as far as the applicability of Article 76 to the Constitution's basic organizational norms is concerned. In his earlier *Constitutional Theory*, Schmitt relied upon a distinction between the Constitution and constitutional laws[60] to make the case that some constitutional norms are unalterable. He distinguishes these norms by determining whether they belong to the fundamental structural decisions of the Constitution. If we identify democracy's basis with an ultimate decision in favor of the principles of freedom and equality, and if we in principle accept Schmitt's distinction between the Constitution and constitutional laws, a very different assessment of the nature of the Constitution's unalterable core would nevertheless result. On the basis of the justification of democracy developed above, we can examine the question of exemption from amendment procedures from two competing perspectives. The first axiom could take the form of claiming that Article 76 should only be used to lead to variations in the system of constitutional standards that satisfy the following conditions: compromises between democratic forms and concrete values should still only be allowed to appear in the second part of the Constitution (which can be altered by constitutional annulments, supplements, and extensions); basic liberties need to be excepted from the sphere of such compromises.[61] Variations in the organizational part of the Constitution and in its closely related provisions for basic liberties are only permissible if they are necessary for achieving the greatest realizable degree of freedom and equality when structural changes in the political community require new organizational forms. If we view the problem from this perspective, it becomes clear that some constitutional standards or parts of them are always *sine qua non* and will therefore be basically unalterable. These include those that guarantee an identity between the wills of 51 percent of the citizens and the will of the government: in short, those that guarantee universal, equal, secret, and proportionally based elections, as well as a system of representation with a certain minimum of elected representatives and a maximum term of office. This is not to deny that changes in active and passive suffrage might be permitted under some circumstances when the political community has undergone structural transformations. For example, evidence for a change in the average time it takes for individuals to gain maturity might constitute justification for altering Article 22; the voting age stated there is apparently only supposed to give expression to a particular age at which individuals are thought to reach maturity. In contrast, an abrogation of the principle of "one person, one vote" or any "unjustified" increase in the minimum voting age would constitute an illegitimate impairment of political liberty. Constitutional standards that contribute to an unrestrained process of will-formation—in other words, the rights of citizenship—are inalienable.[62] But all "private" rights can be amended. The Hobbesian theorem that the abrogation of political freedom can be democratically justified contradicts the concept of political freedom that we have developed here: our justification emphasizes the importance of the existence of inalienable institutional opportunities for every citizen to reconcile state action with his will—in other words, to make sure that freedom and equality are the individual freedom and equality of all citizens. Thus, an abandonment of liberty along Hobbesian lines cannot be democratically justified.

Instead of this system of inalienable rights, there might be another way to solve the problem. According to an alternative interpretation, Article 76 could be relied upon so that a compromise between democratic forms and definite concrete objects could manifest itself in any section of the Constitution and, thus, even in its organizational core and in its guarantees of basic liberties. Some minimum of the principles of political freedom and equality would still have to be realized here, however; otherwise, not a "compromise" but a "rape" of democratic procedures would have taken place. From this standpoint, one could justify slightly lengthening the legislature's term of office.[63] But the legal establishment of a hereditary monarchy would not be permissible. And constitutional reforms, like those outlined by Schmitt in the final chapter of his study, would no longer prove up to the task of guaranteeing the necessary minimum of freedom and equality. If we had to make a choice between these two approaches toward the problem of constitutional amendment described here, the former seems to be in greater accordance with the basic idea of democracy. This solution insists that despite any compromise that democracy must make, the principle of *equal* participation by *everyone* is absolutely sacred. This suggests that the organizational core of the Constitution, along with provisions for basic rights that properly belong to that core, constitute—as Schmitt's position itself clearly points out—a "relativistic holy sanctuary." Its destruction would mean the death of democracy itself.[64]

Schmitt's remarks suggest that democracy cannot be justified merely on the basis of the idea of equality. In addition, an "equal chance" to become part of a political majority is essential to the "principle of justice underlying this [parliamentary-democratic] system of legality."[65]

First, we need to clarify the different meanings attributable to the idea of an "equal chance" in this context. In the process, we will examine the question of whether it is essential for developing a justification of democracy. Finally, we will comment on Schmitt's view of the relationship between the principle of an "equal chance" and the existence and effective functioning of a democratic system.

The term "equal chance," it seems, is chiefly used to describe two different basic states of affairs.

First, it can refer to the equal treatment of all persons, parties, and legislative proposals at certain stages in the generation of democratic laws. In the context of an election, first, an equal chance is guaranteed when every individual candidate or list of candidates—or proposed law in the case of a referendum—is admitted indiscriminately. The second application of this principle refers to the manner in which votes for representative bodies or a referendum are counted. In this context, realizing the principle of equal chance demands, on the one hand, that every vote is counted equally and, on the other hand, that parties gain representation in proportion to the number of votes gained by them; in short, there should be a proportional system of representation. Finally, the principle of equal chance directly concerns parliamentary proceedings. It requires that, on the one hand, the same type of majority is necessary for passing all types of laws, and that, on the other hand, there has to be an equal legal chance for every party to participate in a political majority. This condition is satisfied either when every form of coalition is illegal or when every form of coalition is permissible. Proposed reforms of parliamentary procedure that have the aim of only allowing parties to cooperate in toppling a government by a vote of no confidence when they share a unified set of reasons for doing so reduce the chances of any extremist party for belonging to a majority coalition—after all, these reforms only make sense when the opposition is divided. Reforms of this type improve the chances for neighboring, more moderate parties, insofar as they can opt for either side.

The principle of equal chance also has a second meaning. An equal chance to make up a political majority can be achieved only when the right of every party to gain this status is left undisturbed by legal standards. The relevant standards here are the material norms of the Weimar Constitution and so-called "political norms." The latter refer to every standard, regardless of how it has been made into law, that exercises an immediate influence on political organization and on the activity of the citizen within the process of public opinion formation. By means of an examination of Schmitt's analysis of this issue, we need to determine to what extent norms of this type disfigure the process in which both the governing party and the opposition are supposed to have an equal chance of gaining majority status. The governing party is likely to benefit whenever we find amorphous legal standards—and they exist in every legal system—that can be employed in a discretionary manner to restrain the activities of opposition parties. This is part of what Schmitt has in mind when he refers to the "political premium resulting from a legal possession of power." Schmitt believes that the following standards are among those which might function in this way: "public security and order, danger, emergency, necessary measures, constitutional subversion, vital interests."[66] Another source of a political advantage for the ruling party stems from the *absence* of *specific* norms, which we will describe in more detail. Constitutional clauses such as the rights of citizenship described above fall into this category, as do legal norms that make it difficult for ruling parties to benefit from "spoils." An example here is the attempt to regulate campaign funds by legal means.[67] Finally, an "unequal chance" between a governing party and the opposition can occur when ruling groups simply act in a manner that conflicts with the law. Because it benefits from the presumption of the legality of government actions, a *fait accompli* can be achieved that even judicial review may prove unable to undo.[68]

Now that we have tried to distinguish among the different meanings of the idea of equal chance, we need to examine the problems posed by the principle of "equal chance" for the justification of democracy that Schmitt suggested.

Schmitt believes that equal chance constitutes the "material principle of justice for a democracy." In the following section, we will try—to the extent that the idea of equal chance can be shown to be necessary for democracy—to explain this necessity as deriving "monistically" from the principles of freedom and equality.

It seems uncontroversial to claim that the view of democracy that we offered above requires the institutionalization of "one person, one vote" as well as the indiscriminate admission of all individual candidates and parties to elections. The same can be said for a proportional electoral system. For only this type of voting system offers both an institutional guarantee that a specific number of voters will match a corresponding number of representatives and that 51 percent of the representatives will be chosen by approximately 51 percent of the voters. This is essential for a parliament to function as a "plebiscitary intermediary."

As far as the second basic definition of the principle of equal chance is concerned, the "unhindered" structure of democratic opinion-formation, described above as an essential element of political liberty, means that opposition parties should be discriminated against by means of neither the discretionary use of indeterminate nor the determinate legal norms mentioned above. Furthermore, it is evident that a system that presupposes respect for the principle of legality cannot possibly justify illegal government action—that is, the third potential source of "unequal chances" between governing and opposition parties.

The normative justification of democracy formulated above hardly by itself necessitates material-legal norms—either within a constitution or outside it—to realize an equality of chances among political parties. By the same token, this does not preclude the possibility that such norms may be required by the postulate of "social" equality or "social" freedom. Historically, the coincidence of political *and* social forms of freedom and equality has often been of the greatest significance. Both liberalism and socialism demand both forms of freedom and equality.[69] This leads directly to the thesis that today freedom and equality can only be total: they have to be realized both in the political and social sphere, or we are not likely to achieve them at all.

Still, there is an immediate causal relationship between the principle of equal chance between political parties and the realization of freedom and equality within the political sphere: only the institutionalization of the ideal of an "equal chance" could mean that the "formally" unhindered process of public opinion-formation (that is, the impossibility of legal restraints on it) is "materially" unhindered as well. All currents of socialist thought have seized upon this state of affairs for polemical purposes, and it plays the key role in, for example, Lenin's *State and Revolution*.[70]

Schmitt thus considers the existence of an "equal chance" essential for the justification of democracy. Yet he also believes that this ideal is incompatible with the everyday operations of modern democracy. Democracy is thus confronted with a choice: it is either unrealized or unjustified. In what follows, we examine Schmitt's thesis by discussing its implications for the different types of democratic regimes described in his analysis.

What are the facts of the case in a parliamentary democracy where the sphere of basic freedom (*Freiheitsrecht*) is exempt from amendments? In this system, we see no meaningful limits to the possibility of realizing the principle of equal chance as initially defined above—with the exception that we would have to distinguish between some permissible and impermissible legal norms resulting from the existence of a sphere of freedom possessing special protective status.

As far as the existence of "political norms" that influence the relationship between the governing and opposition party is concerned, the possibility of an abuse of such standards undoubtedly exists in this type of political system. Yet a belief in the possibility of eliminating this danger altogether would truly have to be described as a "normativistic illusion." The same can be said—as Schmitt himself concedes[71]—for a certain amount of amorphousness within legal norms. But historically it has been typical of precisely this type of political system that it has tried to reduce legal indeterminacy as much as possible.

In regard to dangers resulting from the absence of certain *specific* norms, it needs to be said that it is *exactly* one of the special characteristics of this type of constitutional system—and this is what distinguishes it from other types of democracy—that it makes at least some such norms as unassailable as possible. The constitutional structure of this system includes provisions for what historically have been described as basic liberties and what we have categorized above in this article as the rights of citizenship. In this way, the right to property can function as an instrument that helps protect the possessions of oppositional organizations and thus secures its contributions to the process of public opinion-formation.

But the example of property shows exactly how the same right that in some ways helps to preserve the principle of "equal chance" between the government and the opposition can also serve altogether different, and even contrary, purposes. By means of the results of its effects on the economic structure, the right to property, as well as that to personal liberty, brings about an inequality of political chances among social groups. If the democratic socialist position—that its economic structure could bring about "equality of opportunity" while preserving the rights of citizenship—were justified (which we need not examine here), this would indicate that a type of democracy with a specifiable normative content exists, in which a maximal approximation of the ideal of "equal chance" in *every* sense of the term has been achieved. Schmitt is right to argue that parliamentary democracy cannot establish full "equal chances" for all parties, but he is wrong to claim that this failing results chiefly from parliamentary democracy's basic organizational structure. Instead, such failures can be traced back to the concrete content of specified private rights and certain other material-legal standards.

The second type of democratic system that we need to consider would be one outfitted with basic liberties and material-legal norms, like those examined above, that could be suspended by a qualified majority and whose particular contents still need to be specified. The same can be said about this system of government that was said about the previous one: with the exception of the rules concerning qualified majorities, the principle of "equal chance" in the sense of the first basic definition could be realized here.

However, this system would generate *greater* possibilities for *inequalities* between governing parties and the opposition than we were able to identify in the previous case. This stems from the fact that this system relies not only on amorphous norms like those just discussed but also on additional indeterminacies within the material-legal section of the Constitution. Article 137, paragraph 5 of the Constitution, for example, declares that religious bodies that are not public corporations can only gain this status "if, by their constitution and the number of their members, they give assurance of permanence." The indeterminacy of the words used here inevitably provides substantial room for governmental discretion; this is likely to produce some of the consequences described above. But material-legal determinations of this type might also function to assure *increased equality* between governing parties and the opposition insofar as they are not amorphous. Each clause of this type works to protect the core of a particular institution from intervention. Such protection becomes effective when the relevant institution stands in opposition to the governing parties, that is, when it is connected with an opposition party in some fashion. Inasmuch as ties between the relevant set of institutions and a particular party take on real significance for a party's electoral chances—and that is all that matters for us right now—these electoral chances become independent of whether the party in question belongs to the governing coalition or the opposition to the extent that the relevant institutions are clearly supported by a constitution. A tendency toward the equalization of electoral chances results as potential political norms are eliminated. This is valid, for example, in the case of the institutional basis for the labor unions provided by Articles 159 and 161 of the Constitution.

Norms of fixation contribute either to equalities or to inequalities between parties according to whether they are apportioned "unequally" or "equally" among parties and their respective institutional supports. Attributing constitutional status to labor's right to organize, for example, increases the independence of labor-based parties in relation to the government while altering their status in relation to other parties that (either directly or indirectly) may be "more" or "less" protected by a constitution.

So what can we ultimately say about Schmitt's claim that it is simply impossible to realize the principle of "equal chance" in a democracy?

During the course of the conceptual distinctions that we have made here, we saw that Schmitt's thesis primarily refers to the "equal chance between governing parties and opposition parties in the face of the existence of political norms." In the case of two possible causes of inequality between the ruling party and the opposition—namely, where we find amorphous legal standards and where governmental action conflicts with the law—we reached the conclusion that they could occur in a democracy, but only because, as Schmitt himself puts it, "no political system can do without" phenomena of this type.[72] Above and beyond that, democracy is capable of eliminating one of the main causes of such inequalities to the extent that it gives basic rights a legally binding character. Moreover, it is reasonable to believe that any additional illegal advantages potentially enjoyed by those in power could be disposed of by means of appropriate legislation.

If we compare *an oppositional group's chance* of attaining power in a nondemocratic state with the "*equal chance*" *of gaining 51 percent of the votes in a democracy*, democracy does greater justice to the principle at hand. True, the utopia of a *perfect* realization of the ideal of an "equal chance"—which, as Schmitt concedes, is impossible in any political context; the presumption of the legality of governmental action and the immediately enforceable nature of governmental decisions are essentially *differentia specifica* of public law—cannot be achieved. Yet democracy is the only political system that provides an institutional guarantee that even the most decisive transitions of power need not threaten the continuity of the legal order. In addition, democracy is best able to approximate the goal of an "equal chance" in the manner that we have tried to describe here.[73]

Schmitt claims that the justification for parliamentarism contradicts the underlying justification for direct democratic decision making outlined in Article 73, paragraph 3.[74]

> The dualism that exists between these two forms of legislation is a dualism between two distinct systems of justification—a system of parliamentary legality and a system of plebiscitary democratic legitimacy. The possible race between them is not simply a competitive struggle between two decision-making instances, but between two very different conceptions of what law is.[75]

This thesis presupposes a conception of parliament that does not see it as justified by the social and technical requirements of the division of labor. Instead, special emphasis is placed on the specific material character of the norms typically created by parliament.[76] On the basis of this view, Schmitt believes that there is a qualitative difference between parliamentary norms and unmediated expressions of the popular will as well as—once the superior character of parliamentary law is acknowledged[77]—an argument for disqualifying the people from engaging in direct democratic decision making. At the same time, Schmitt does not go so far as to suggest that there could be a political system resting purely on direct democracy and characterized by the absence of any representative elements whatsoever, since every state allegedly requires some representative features.[78] When applied to the Weimar Constitution, the following seems to follow from Schmitt's thesis for the relationship between direct democratic and parliamentary lawmaking: within the framework of the Weimar Constitution, Parliament has the authority to supersede law that the people have previously endorsed by a referendum. This is because parliamentary and direct decision-making procedures are both similar in function and incommensurable in status; of decisive importance is the fact that no norm explicitly prevents Parliament from revoking a popular referendum.[79] This shows that Schmitt's view of the contradictory relationship between parliamentary and direct democratic decision making ultimately depends on a particular justification for the existence of parliament. If we rely on the traditional conception of parliament as a "plebiscitary intermediary" (which Jacobi has most recently made use of)—in Schmitt's view, this interpretation necessitates making concessions to parliament's "degraded" form in contemporary society—it becomes possible to see parliamentary lawmaking and direct democracy as compatible within the same constitutional system. In addition, this view allows us to suggest an answer to the positive legal question that arose; representatives should not be allowed to act in opposition to the express will of the people because the representative must remain silent when the people speak.[80] Moreover, it is crucial that we apply this insight not simply, as Schmitt has done, to direct democracy—in other words, to the executive (there is no other representative instance there)—but to parliament as well.[81] Thus, it seems correct to argue that "because the institutions of direct democracy are an inevitable consequence of a *democratic state*, they should be superior to the institutional mechanisms of *indirect* parliamentary democracy" (as Schmitt puts it, although he fails to assume this for the Weimar Constitution). Schmitt—who interprets "the system of *parliamentary legality* as an intellectually and organizationally unique and independent complex that stands in no intrinsic relationship to democracy or the will of the people"—refuses to apply the deductions made above to the Weimar Constitution, reasoning that in Weimar, "alongside the exceptional plebiscitary decision-making complex, the overall organizational features of a parliamentary system are still present."[82] But this argument would only be correct if the Weimar Constitution really were a parliamentary legislative state in Schmitt's meaning of the term—in other words, if Weimar's architects had sought a system of parliamentary democracy in which the centrality of the *"législateur"* was justified by the Schmittian theory of parliamentarism. Only then could we conceive of parliament as altogether independent of any type of democratic foundation. As far as recent attempts to justify parliament are concerned, there are many signs that the type of classic argument developed by Schmitt in *The Crisis of Parliamentary Democracy* is on the decline; this corresponds to a more general retreat of certain early liberal positions in contemporary thought. Increasingly, parliament is justified as a "plebiscitary intermediary."[83] Parliament's decreasing significance constitutes the ideological background for this trend.[84] Still, this says nothing about parliament's potential role as an organ of democracy (*Transformationsorgan*). Charges directed everywhere against the chaos of "power blocs" in fact refer to a real set of problems: parliament is no longer a site for autonomous opinion-formation, but is simply an institution where preformed opinions are registered. This suggests that the institution at the heart of the problematic at hand may no longer be the technical apparatus of parliament but, instead, political parties that now function as unmediated organs of mass democratic politics. The general ideological trend has been captured by many interpretations of postwar constitutional government.[85] Indeed, in the case of the Weimar Constitution, its founders on several occasions explicitly endorsed an interpretation of Parliament that emphasizes its direct democratic functions. Jacobi has discussed this issue in great length in his discussion of the problem of prioritizing constitutional elements with special emphasis on Article 1, paragraph 2 of the federal constitution.[86]

Such a justification of Parliament would not require—but it also would not contradict—the demand that if a norm is to be given legally binding status by a parliament, more votes should be necessary for approving it than are necessary in direct democratic mechanisms. If this is the case, then another purported contradiction within the Constitution that Schmitt has identified, namely that concerning the participation requisite for the two allegedly competing systems of legislation,[87] can be resolved. Above and beyond that, the alleged factual basis does not appear to be proven. There are three conceivable cases at hand.

In order to *amend the Constitution*, Article 76 states that a simple majority of eligible voters (at least 51 percent) suffices in a referendum. In the case of constitutional amendments undertaken by Parliament, Article 76 demands a two-thirds majority. Moreover, at least two-thirds of the members of Parliament need to attend the vote. In opposition to Schmitt's claim that "in Parliament, a two-thirds majority is necessary to amend the Constitution, whereas direct democratic mechanisms only require a simple majority," it is important to note that under certain circumstances the number of votes in Parliament required to amend the Constitution could be less than is required in direct democratic decision making. First, this can happen whenever a proportion of representatives who are present sinks below a certain level; if the maximum legally acceptable number of parliamentary absences occurs, a mere 44 percent of the representatives are needed to amend the Constitution. This case presupposes 100 percent participation by those in attendance, and it does not include the possibility of a forfeiture of votes. Second, less than 51 percent of the eligible representatives suffices if 100 percent do attend but a certain number abstain or forfeit their votes.[88]

When parliamentary and direct-democratic devices lead to a conflict concerning a particular *legislative statute,* a majority of at least 50 percent of elected representatives is needed to pass a parliamentary resolution.[89] Passing the referendum in opposition to such a resolution requires the agreement of a majority of all votes cast; in addition, a majority of eligible voters has to have taken part in the direct democratic vote (Article 75).[90] So the minimal acceptable number of votes necessary for passing a parliamentary resolution is always less than the number needed in order to pass a referendum in opposition to the parliamentary law, as long as participation is less than 100 percent and some votes are lost (i.e., they were cast for a candidate who received no mandate). Schmitt argues against this point by claiming that it is not factually significant that a *majority* of voters needs to take part in passing a referendum, since *everyone* who participates in a successful direct democratic campaign, in accordance with Article 75, is likely to support the proposal in question in the first place.[91] Thus, there allegedly is no meaningful distinction between statutory and constitutional lawmaking when undertaken by direct democratic means. But one can counter this interpretation by pointing to the possibility—and reality—of the "terror" that can be unleashed against those who embrace a minority position in a referendum; this can lead them to change their material "no" (expressed most effectively by a simple refusal to participate in the referendum) into a formal "no." To the extent that the number of such "terrorized" is fewer than the number of "terrorists" and the absolute number of the "terrorists" includes more than 25 percent of eligible voters, this "no" may generate results diametrically opposed to the original purpose. If these preconditions are not met, "terror" is likely to be senseless, and surely harmless.[92]

Where there is no conflict between parliamentary and direct-democratic devices, 60,000[93] votes for Parliament are necessary to pass a legislative statute, whereas at least one vote is required through direct democratic means. If we ignore this factually insignificant difference for a moment, there does not seem to be any qualitative difference between the proportion of votes required for direct-democratic in relation to parliamentary mechanisms. Keeping the turnout rate of the vote undetermined within certain limits here corresponds to keeping those numbers undetermined in a referendum, since—in contrast to the second case—here the secrecy of the ballot is effectively preserved.

This alternative argument suggests that Schmitt's decisive distinction between legality and legitimacy can no longer be defended. Although Schmitt does not explicitly define these terms, it seems that "legality" refers for him to the underlying justification of parliamentary lawmaking—this justification is linked to the allegedly immanent character of parliamentary *lex*—whereas "legitimacy" refers to the justification of direct plebiscitary lawmaking. But Parliament's place in the German constitutional system no longer rests on the intrinsic *ratio* of parliamentary activity. Instead, it depends on the same attributes that provide a justification for direct democratic decision making. *They are therefore different organizational forms of the same type of legitimacy.* Beyond the question of suspending parts of the Constitution that we addressed above, there is no structural difference between the people acting by means of constitutionally ordained direct-democratic mechanisms and Parliament; both are expressions of the "*pouvoir constitué.*"

But this, of course, is no longer the case once we cease to interpret the Weimar Constitution (and other democratic constitutions having a similar structure) and instead focus on the imperatives of an ideal constitution and corresponding political system modeled in accordance with the values and justificatory universe of Carl Schmitt. Within Schmitt's intellectual world, legality and legitimacy certainly can diverge. In fact, legality can be fully dislodged by legitimacy. The need to eliminate parliamentary legality results for Schmitt merely from the demonstration that its underlying justification is no longer manifest in empirical reality. Monolithic plebiscitary legitimacy is supposed to take the place of parliament. But even if the highest organ of the state can be elected in a democratic manner, we could no longer use the term "democratic" to describe it. The point here is that according to common usage, democracy depends, if not on the existence of a central parliamentary body, then at least on the operation of a plurality of representatives. The reason for this is that the degree to which freedom and equality can be realized is inversely related to the degree to which representation is concentrated. The election of a member to parliament of my liking presupposes that I have voted alongside 59,999 other citizens who also supported him; participation in the presidential election presupposes that—taking into account that the number of candidates ultimately tends to be reduced (and assuming that all voters support candidates whom they genuinely endorse, and thus ignoring the possibility of mere protest candidates)—it is necessary for me to vote alongside a far larger number of fellow citizens. In contrast to parliamentary elections, presidential elections require a much more far-reaching form of unity between my will and the will of others. But as the scope of this unity grows, the average distance between the individual will and the will of the candidate correspondingly increases: in other words, my freedom is reduced because more compromise was necessary. The same trend toward a reduction of the amount of realizable political freedom—brought about by a hypertrophy of a unification of wills—is manifest in Schmitt's model of plebiscitary decision making, in which the people are permitted to say "yes" or "no" to questions posed to them by a governmental body.[94] But here the choice of alternatives is reduced even more: in the case of presidential elections, we *tend* to have two choices, whereas in a plebiscite we *inevitably* have *only* two choices. Even if one wants to try to justify a legally based reduction of popular political activity by means of anthropological arguments,[95] the consequences that we have just described for political freedom would result in any event. But might this concept of democracy justify a transition from the type of democracy represented by Weimar to a type along the lines just sketched out, in part because it would guarantee greater political stability? This question concerns the applicability of Schmitt's general theoretical claims to particular characteristics of constitutional development in contemporary Germany. His main thesis can be easily identified: like many other participants in contemporary political debate, Schmitt believes that the Weimar Constitution is collapsing. In his version of this argument, the source of this development is to be located in the internal contradictions of the Weimar Constitution. Here, we have tried to offer a critical examination of this position.

Schmitt's diagnostic thesis is followed by a prognostic one: a constitution reformed according to his plans could presumably provide for more political stability. Both parliamentary democracy and its caesaristic modification constitute constitutional systems that allow for legal regulations embodying—so long as they are in accordance with material-legal constitutional standards—many conceivable contents; thus, both are value-neutral to some extent. The legislative mechanisms of both constitutional systems are clearly distinct from traditional ones to the extent that they both attempt to integrate this great invention of modern democracy. But this says nothing about their factual stability, and it provides no answer to the question of whether historical development will prove capable of making good use of the relatively open-ended constitutional forms made available to it. In our view, the answer to this question—and this points to the limits of this study without trying to claim that we have by any means completely answered all the questions raised by it—depends chiefly on many different factors that determine the structure of political action today. The dependence of political behavior on so many interrelated factors leads to a situation where a variation in just one factor can lead to disproportionate disturbances in the political equilibrium. This makes it very difficult to come up with reliable prognoses, even if we ignore the antinomy underlying those prognoses whose character as *arcanum* becomes a precondition for their accuracy. Would we be able to make all the comments typically heard today about the stability and continuity of French democracy if the successor to Charles X had not favored the flag of lilies over a second restoration,[96] if Boulanger had not been the prototype of a "*dictateur manqué*,"[97] if intact, antidemocratic elements in the leadership of the French army during the Dreyfuss period had recognized the real significance of this legal case?[98] Might not we be talking today about Russian democracy's auspicious source of constancy in the relatively homogeneous peasant masses if the February regime had anticipated the battle phrases of the Bolsheviks? To pose these questions does not mean that we can provide an affirmative answer to them. It only means that if we are to provide an accurate assessment of the *possibilities for constitutional development* available, we need to take *every conceivable extraconstitutional factor into consideration*. It seems that only if constitutional theory tackles this task by working in close cooperation with all those disciplines concerned with social experience[99] will it gradually be able to convey general solutions to such problems.

(Translated by Anke Grosskopf and William E. Scheuerman)

NOTES

1. Editor's Note: With Nathan Leites.
2. Carl Schmitt, *Legalität und Legitimität* (Munich: Duncker & Humblot, 1932).
3. See Erich Voegelin, *Zeitschrift für Öffentliches Recht* 11 (1931): 108–109.
4. Schmitt, *Legalität und Legitimität*, p. 31.

Editor's Note: Schmitt long had argued that majority rule within genuinely heterogeneous societies inevitably resulted in political majorities "raping"—as Schmitt repeatedly phrased it—political minorities whose interests and ideals were distinct and even "alien" to those of majorities. Thus, majority rule only made sense as a decision-making procedure if substantial political homogeneity could be presupposed; only in a homogeneous setting could a majority decision genuinely claim to represent the democratic community's common good or "general interest."

5. Carl Schmitt, *Die Verfassungslehre* (Munich, 1928), pp. 169, 235.
6. Hans Kelsen, *Vom Wesen und Wert der Demokratie* (Tübingen, 1929), p. 9. (Here, Kirchheimer is relying on Hans Kelsen's interpretation of the principle of majority rule in order to criticize Schmitt. Whereas Schmitt grounds the principle of majority rule in a substantialist interpretation of the democratic principle of equality, Kelsen insists that majority rule is only defensible if democracy is understood as involving the quest to realize *both* equality *and* freedom. In Kelsen's interpretation, when a majority determines the nature of governmental action, more than half of the political community's wills can be said to shape governmental activity autonomously. Accordingly, majority rule allows a relatively impressive real-life approximation to the idea of a fully autonomous community. Kelsen, *Vom Wesen und Wert der Demokratie*, pp. 3–13, 53–68.)

7. Schmitt, *Die Verfassungslehre*, p. 278.
8. For a discussion of the view that both freedom and equality constitute the basic principles of democracy, see W. Starosolsky, *Das Majoritätsprinzip* (Vienna, 1916), beginning on p. 84. More recently see Dietrich Schindler, *Verfassungsrecht und soziale Struktur* (Zurich, 1932), p. 133; G. Salomon, *Verhandlungen des 5. deutschen Soziologentages* (Tübingen, 1926), pp. 106–109.

9. When one accepts the thesis that only a truly "humane" social order could provide maximal possibilities for political autonomy, then the scope of the rights of citizenship increases dramatically. See Luiz Jimenez de Azua, *Zeitschrift für ausländisches und öffentliches Recht* 3 (1932/1933): 3, 377.

10. For a discussion of their relationship to the concepts of "autonomy" and "individual responsibility," see Pribram, *Verhandlungen des 5. deutschen Soziologentages*, p. 100.

11. On the necessary organizational structure of this type of liberty in a democracy see Heinz Ziegler, *Die moderne Nation* (Tübingen, 1931), p. 237. Of course, Ziegler's thesis that democracy replaces individual freedom with collective freedom is only correct to a limited degree, for precisely the necessary organization of liberty guarantees a chance for the individual to break with a majority and then stand in opposition to it.

12. On the different concepts of liberty and the possibility that they may not coexist see James Bryce, *Modern Democracies* (London, 1921), vol. 1, beginning on p. 60. Harold Laski, *Liberty in the Modern State* (London, 1930) recognizes the different functions of liberties, but his pluralist theoretical background prevents him from formulating clear conceptual distinctions. See also his *A Grammar of Politics* (London, 1925), beginning on p. 146.

13. See Schmitt's categorization of rights in *Die Verfassungslehre*, pp. 168–169, and *Handbuch des deutschen Staatsrechts*, vol. 2 (Tübingen, 1932), p. 594; Franz L. Neumann, *Koalitionsfreiheit und Reichsverfassung* (Berlin, 1932), p. 16.

14. On the coexistence of absolutism and individual freedom: Ferdinand Tönnies, "Demokratie und Parlamentarismus," *Schmollers Jahrbuch* 51 (1927): 7.

Editor's Note: This is a peculiar—and somewhat disturbing—account of "private rights." How humane could a democratic society without guarantees of religious freedom possibly be?

15. Carl Schmitt, *Freiheitsrechte und institutionelle Garantien der Reichsverfassung* (Berlin, 1931), beginning on p. 27.

Editor's Note: Basic rights are essentially privatistic according to Schmitt: in his own words, "basic rights in the most authentic sense of the term include only [the classical] liberal rights of the individual person" (Schmitt, *Die Verfassungslehre*, p. 164). As Kirchheimer is arguing here, this leads Schmitt to obscure the relationship between democratic decision making and individual liberties. Even more immediately, it seems to imply that basic democratic rights—like the principle of "one person, one vote"—somehow partake less completely of the status of "rights" than, for example, the right to private property. This view also leads Schmitt to debunk the demand of many of his left-wing contemporaries for so-called "social rights," which clearly are distinct from classical liberal private rights. For Schmitt's account of basic rights see Schmitt, *Die Verfassungslehre*, pp. 157–182. For his peculiar distinction between "the liberty of the isolated individual" and the liberty of "individuals who act in unison with other individuals," see esp. pp. 165–166, 170.

16. Kelsen, *Wesen und Wert der Demokratie*, pp. 9–10.

17. This is in reference to David's speech from July 31, 1919. The preamble is referred to in many different attempts to interpret the Weimar Constitution. For examples of this see Hans Liermann, *Das deutsche Volk als Rechtsbegriff* (Berlin, 1927), beginning on p. 166; Rudolf Smend, *Verfassung und Vefassungsrecht* (Munich, 1928),

pp. 8–9. For an interpretation of the democratic significance of the ideals of freedom and equality here see Richard Thoma in *Handbuch des deutschen Staatsrechts*, ed. Gerhard Anschütz and Richard Thoma (Tübingen, 1930–1932), vol. 2, p. 190.
Editor's Note: David was a cosigner of the Weimar Constitution.
18. Smend, *Verfassung und Verfassungsrecht*, p. 114
19. Schmitt, *Legalität und Legitimität*, p. 33.
Editor's Note: Schmitt's argument here is a complex one. In a nutshell, he claims that the abandonment of the classical demand that legitimate parliamentary action should be required to take a *general* form effectively robs parliamentary decision making of one of its last remaining normative guarantees. Without the assurance of some degree of justice as provided by the classical liberal legal norm's general structure, and without any sensible reason for assuming that a particularly impressive degree of rationality inheres in contemporary parliamentary rule making, majority-based parliamentary rule making provides no protection against injustice—or even tyranny.
20. On the problems that result when governmental authorities see a particular set of legal norms as unjust see Gustav Radbruch, *Rechtsphilosophie* (Leipzig, 1932), p. 82. For a sociologically well-grounded analysis, but one that remains imprisoned within the problematic epistemology of value-relativism, see Thoma's comments in *Handbuch des deutschen Staatsrechts*, vol. 2, p. 142.
21. For the French case and the role of "lit de justice" as an uncontestable legal instrument in the absolutist period see Robert Holtzmann, *Französische Verfassungsgeschichte* (Munich, 1910), p. 350. English constitutional history does not seem to be familiar with the problem; see A. V. Dicey, *Introduction to the Study of the Law of the Constitution* (London, 1915), beginning on p. 224; Frederic William Maitland, *Constitutional History of England* (Cambridge, 1908), beginning on p. 266; Julius Hatschek, *Englische Verfassungsgeschichte* (Munich, 1913), beginning on p. 499. In the discussion of the dispute between Coke and the crown found in these accounts, emphasis is placed on the power of the crown in relation to judicial action (and not the power of the judge in relation to the crown) and on the question of administrative authority to issue arrest warrants.
22. Carl Schmitt, *Der Hüter der Verfassung* (Tübingen: Mohr, 1931), chapter I.
Editor's Note: A "jurisdictional state" is defined by Schmitt as a state in which

> a judge who decides a legal dispute, and not the legislature that issues norms, has the final say. . . . A typical expression of the jurisdictional state is a concrete case-oriented legal decision, in which "rightful" law, justice, and reason are made apparent without having been mediated beforehand by general legal norms. Thus, this type of political system does not exhaust itself in the normativism of mere [parliamentary] legality. (Schmitt, *Legalität und Legitimität*, p. 9)

23. Schmitt, *Legalität und Legitimität*, pp. 43, 90.
24. Incidentally, it is striking that the fascination with the problems of democracy, as exhibited by so many different types of political ideologies, obscures the fact that democracy—with the exception of the American case—is a relatively new phenomenon in historical terms. France has only had equal voting rights since 1852, Italy since 1911, Great Britain since 1918, and Belgium only since 1921. The accelerated psychical dynamics of contemporary history manifests itself in the fact that a

new set of institutions can seem antiquated even before they have had a chance to prove themselves. See Moritz Jaffe on political parties and democracy in *Archiv für Sozialwissenschaft* 65 (1931): 106–108.

25. On the concept of integrative parties see Sigmund Neumann, *Die deutschen Parteien* (Berlin, 1932). On the trend toward heterogeneity in Belgium see Bourquin in *Jahrbuch des öffentlichen Rechts* 18 (1930): 187. He speaks of a substitution of the "ministères homogènes" by the "minstères mixtes."

26. Karl Mannheim, *Ideologie und Utopie* (Berlin, 1929).

27. On the transformation of the spirit of the frontier into a system of conscious mass manipulation see Charlotte Lütkens, *Staat und Gesellschaft in Amerika* (Tübingen, 1929), beginning on p. 176.

28. Charles Beard, *An Economic Interpretation of the Constitution of the United States* (New York, 1923), p. 324.

29. Editor's Note: The Stinnes-Legien agreement of November 15, 1918, required employers to withdraw all support for "yellow dog" unions and helped establish the principles of collective bargaining within Weimar.

30. Recall Hugo Preuss's comments at the Constitutional Committee of the National Assembly: "A uniform orientation is not dominant here. Instead, what we see is the coming together of different orientations that otherwise would have distinct goals. Together, they may generate a constellation that allows these goals to be linked together."

31. Of course, for those who believe that democracy should be maintained even when a particular set of goals has been achieved, the instrumental character of their view of democracy is inevitably reduced. It is important to recognize that the problem of justifying democracy—as undertaken earlier in this essay—is an essential task for many who see democracy as a mere instrument.

32. See Albert Jovishoff, "Kapitalismus und Demokratie," *Zeitschrift für öffentliches Recht* 12 (1932), beginning on p. 625.

33. See Karl Löwenstein, *Erscheinungsformen der Verfassungsänderung* (Tübingen, 1931), p. 3.

34. Schmitt, *Legalität und Legitimität*, p. 47.

35. See Schmitt's typology in *Handbuch des deutschen Staatsrechts*, vol. 2, paragraph 101.

36. The term "norm of fixation" is used in a broader sense than Schmitt does: *Handbuch des deutschen Staatsrechts*, vol. 2, p. 604.

Editor's Note: Article 143, paragraph 3: "The teachers in public schools shall have the rights and duties of state officials"; Article 144 states that "the entire school system shall be under the supervision of the state; the latter may cause the municipalities to participate therein. The supervision of schools shall be carried on by technically trained officials"; Article 149 begins with the demand that "religious instruction shall be part of the regular school curriculum with the exception of non-sectarian (secular) schools."

37. Editor's Note: Article 151 requires that "the organization of economic life must conform to the principles of justice to the end that all may be guaranteed a decent standard of living"; Article 161 requires that "the Reich shall, with the controlling participation of the insured, establish a comprehensive scheme of insurance for

the conservation of health and of the capacity to work;" Article 162 reads, "The Reich shall endeavour to secure international regulation of the legal status of workers so that the entire working class of the world may enjoy a universal minimum of social rights."

38. Editor's Note: Article 155 postulates that "the distribution and use of landed property shall be controlled by the state in such a manner as to prevent abuse and to promote the object of assuring to every German a healthy habitation"; Article 156, paragraph 1: "The Reich may by law, without prejudging the right of compensation, and with due application of the provisions in force with regard to expropriation, transfer to public ownership private economic enterprises suitable for socialization"; and paragraph 2: "In case of pressing need, the Reich may, in the interests of collectivism, lawfully combine . . . economic enterprises and associations in order to secure cooperation in production"; Article 165, paragraph 5: "Powers of control and administration may be conferred upon workers' and economic councils within the spheres assigned them."

39. The elimination of such tensions can be interpreted as an attempt to uncover an underlying sphere of homogeneity within political consciousness (recall Hugo Preuss' comments cited above). But if one accepts the thesis that only homogeneity allows democracy to function, *this* type of homogeneity does not seem to suffice. Thus, Ernst Fraenkel's claim (*Die Gesellschaft*, no. 10 [1932]: 38) that the second part of the federal constitution is a *conditio sine qua non* as far as the particular function of interest here is concerned, is just as dubious as Schmitt's opposing thesis.

40. Editor's Note: Article 129: "Officials shall be appointed for life except as otherwise provided by law. . . . Duly acquired rights of officials shall be inviolable."

41. Editor's Note: Article 165, paragraph 2: "Workers and employees shall, for the purpose of looking after their economic and social interests, be given legal representation in factory works councils as well as in district works councils organized on the basis of economic sectors and in a works council for the entire Reich."

42. Schmitt, *Legalität und Legitimität*, pp. 57–58, 61.

Editor's Note: In other words: material-legal standards provide a starting point for attempts by the judiciary to gain substantial decision-making authority. Recall that Kirchheimer seemed to endorse this view in "Legality and Legitimacy." Here, he qualifies that argument.

43. Schmitt, *Legalität und Legitimität*, p. 60.

44. Schmitt, *Legalität und Legitimität*, p. 60.

45. John Commons, *Legal Foundations of Capitalism* (New York, 1924), p. 333. More recently, see the polemical account provided in Louis B. Boudin, *Government by Judiciary* (New York, 1932), chapters 33 and 34, and the German-language account in Heinrich Rommen, *Grundrechte, Gesetz und Richter in den USA* (Münster, 1931), p. 89.

46. Charles Beard, *American Government and Politics* (New York, 1931), p. 49. Also see the very cautious but ultimately positive assessment of this set of practices in Ernst Freund's informative "Constitutional Law," in *Encyclopedia of the Social Sciences*, vol. 4 (New York, 1930), p. 254.

Editor's Note: The discussion here concerns the *pre-New Deal* Supreme Court and its repeated assaults on legislative-based social reforms.

47. Schmitt, *Der Hüter der Verfassung*, p. 254.

48. Although there have been different evaluations of this trend, the basic facts of the case are uncontroversial: John Burgess in *Political Science Quarterly* 10 (1896): 420; Charles Warren, *Congress, the Constitution, and the Supreme Court* (Boston, 1925), pp. 176–177. For a critical analysis see Boudin, *Government by Judiciary*, chapter 2.

49. Editor's Note: Article 131: "If an official in the exercise of public authority vested in him is guilty of a breach of his official duty towards a third party, responsibility shall attach primarily to the state or to the public body for which the official serves"; Article 153: "Property shall be guaranteed by the constitution. Its nature and limits shall be prescribed by law."

50. Editor's Note: This is a peculiar comment, unless one reads Kirchheimer simply as pointing out that the Weimar Constitution's codification of property rights was no longer placed in that portion of the constitution (Article 109 to Article 118) outlining traditional *individual* liberal rights. Weimar's founders believed that private property should no longer enjoy the same status as the inviolability of the person (Article 114), or the freedom of speech (Article 118).

51. For a survey of this debate see Albert Hensel, *Die Reichsgerichtspraxis im deutschen Rechtsleben*, vol. 1 (Berlin, 1929). On the jurisprudence of Article 109, see Gerhard Leibholz's comments in *Archiv für öffentlichen Rechts* 9 (1930): 428. For a typical treatment of Article 109 by the upper courts see *Entscheidungen des Reichsgerichts in Zivilsachen* 136: 221.

Editor's Note: Article 109 assures the legal equality of all German citizens.

52. Schmitt, *Legalität und Legitimität*, beginning on p. 71. Rule by emergency decree in contemporary Germany is no longer merely a provisional facet of a basically democratic constitutional system. It now is reminiscent of the situation of a "suspended constitution" like that found in 1848 and 1849, see Johannes Heckel in *Archiv für öffentlichen Rechts* 22 (1932): 309.

53. Editor's Note: The reference here is to part 2, chapter 3 of Schmitt's *Legalität und Legitimität*, where he outlines an argument that openly calls for the destruction of traditional parliamentary democracy and its replacement with a dictatorial "administrative state."

54. Schmitt, *Legalität und Legitimität*, p. 43.

55. Editor's Note: Article 76:

> The constitution may be amended by legislative action. However, resolutions of the parliament for amendment of the constitution are valid only if two-thirds of the members are present and two-thirds of those present give their assent. Moreover, resolutions of the federal council (Reichsrat) require a two-thirds majority of all the votes cast. If by popular petition a constitutional amendment is to be submitted to a referendum, it must be approved by a majority of the qualified voters.
>
> If the parliament adopts a constitutional amendment over the veto of the federal council, the President shall not make this law valid if the federal council demands a referendum within two weeks.

56. Schmitt, *Legalität und Legitimität*, p. 7.

57. Schmitt, *Legalität und Legitimität*, p. 44.

58. Editor's Note: According to Schmitt, Article 76 contradicts the "functionalism" of formal parliamentary rule-making devices by demanding a qualified majority for amendments to the material-legal clauses of the Constitution's second section. In other words, Article 76 implicitly abandons a perfectly "value-free"

perspective. At the same time, the "value-laden" character of that second section demands that some of its objects stand altogether outside the scope of "functionalistic" decision making; thus, Article 76 *also* contradicts the Constitution's "substantial" second section.

59. When Hans Kelsen (in *Wesen und Wert der Demokratie,* p. 55) describes a qualified majority as a closer approximation to the idea of freedom than a simple majority, this is only possible because he has both private and political freedom in mind. For a discussion of why it is necessary to distinguish between these types of liberties, see the comments at the beginning of this essay.

60. Schmitt, *Die Verfassungslehre,* beginning on p. 26. Also, Carl Bilfinger in *Archiv des öffentlichen Rechts* 11 (1926): 118, and in his *Nationale Demokratie als Grundlage der Weimarer Verfassung* (Halle, 1929). For a survey of the literature see Thoma in *Handbuch des deutschen Staatsrechts,* vol. 2, p. 154, and Walter Jellinek, *Grenzen der Verfassungsgesetzgebung* (1931).

Editor's Note: As Franz Neumann notes below in "The Change in the Function of Law in Modern Society," Schmitt

> was of the opinion that amendments to the Constitution could not assail the "Constitution as a basic decision. Constitutional amendments might modify only certain aspects of the Constitution. The fundamental decisions regarding value preferences which the Constitution embodies, Schmitt thought, could not be modified even by the qualified parliamentary majority which had the power to amend the Constitution.

Neumann might have done a better job of describing the nature of the fundamental "decision" that Schmitt had in mind: it is truly "political," which for Schmitt means that it is an "existential," "pure decision not based on reason and discussion and not justifying itself, that is, an absolute decision created out of nothingness." Carl Schmitt, *Political Theology: Four Chapters on the Concept of Sovereignty* (Cambridge: MIT Press, 1985), p. 66.

61. The expressions used here are to be understood in the sense attributed to them in Löwenstein, *Erscheinungsformen der Verfassungsänderung,* beginning on p. 114.

62. From this perspective, the abolition of direct democratic decision-making procedures by means of a two-thirds majority is not permissible: Walter Jellinek in *Handbuch des deutschen Staatsrechts,* vol. 2, p. 185; Thoma's view is found in the same volume on p. 114, and Jacobi's in *Die Reichsgerichtspraxis im deutschen Rechtsleben,* pp. 257–258. Both Thoma and Jacobi believe that amendments can be made in these procedures, but that the possibility of amending them is subject to a referendum. This position ignores the fact that the people organized into a political system do not have the same rights as the people as "*pouvoir constituant.*"

63. In a similar vein, but by means of an argument that emphasizes the intent of the Constitution's architects, see Walter Jellinek in *Handbuch des deutschen Staatsrechts,* vol. 3, p. 185. See also Gmelin's comments in *Archiv für öffentlichen Rechts* 19 (1930), beginning on p. 270.

64. Although both of them refer to Schmitt's *Legalität und Legitimität,* neither Thoma nor Jellinek develop a principled argument for why some organizational norms and basic rights cannot be altered. Thoma's comments on the principles of freedom and justice in *Die Grundrechte und Grundpflichten der Reichsverfassung* (Berlin, 1929), vol. 1, p. 47, only refer to the question of impermissible individual measures,

even though there is explicit reference to "bills of attainder." He does not seem to acknowledge that some parts of the Constitution are unalterable because of reasons of principle. This becomes clear in *Handbuch des deutschen Staatsrechts,* vol. 2, p. 154. On the questions of amending the Constitution, see also Gerhard Anschütz, *Kommentar zur Reichsverfassung* (Berlin, 1932), beginning on p. 385. There, he expresses opposition to the "new" teaching [that is, the idea that there must be some core to the Weimar Constitution that cannot be altered by means of Article 76—ed.] about this issue because he believes that it implies the existence of an obligatory referendum about the constitution itself. This argument is unacceptable: this would be a referendum of the *"pouvoir constitué,"* but a power reserved to the *"pouvoir constituant"* is at stake here. This whole set of problems serves to encourage the elaboration of a set of general constitutional structures. Such "inherent limitations on the legislation" do not, however, have the same political relevance as the formula of "due process of law" for a concrete economic system. See Ernst Freund, "Constitutional Law," *Encyclopedia of the Social Sciences* (New York, 1930), p. 251.

65. Schmitt, *Legalität und Legitimität,* p. 36.

Editor's Note: For Schmitt, parliamentary democratic decision making seems at the very least to presuppose a commitment to the minimal normative ideal that every party should have a chance to make up a political majority; otherwise, there is no reason why any particular political constituency should opt to respect the mechanisms of majority rule in the first place. Schmitt then proceeds to argue that even this rather minimal condition is continually violated in contemporary democracy. Governing majorities take advantage of a "political premium" deriving from their possession of state authority: 1) they interpret amorphous legal concepts ("public order," "emergency," etc.) in a manner that suits their own political aims and harms their opponents [*Ermessenshandhabung*]; 2) they enjoy the benefits of the presumption of the legality of their actions [*Legalitätsvermutung*]; 3) in situations where their acts may be of a questionable legal character, they enjoy the advantage of control over the administration. This allows them to execute their decisions even before there is a chance for the opposition to appeal to a court [*sofortige Vollziehbarkeit*] [Schmitt, *Legalität und Legitimität,* pp. 35–40]. As we will see, Kirchheimer and Leites also critically scrutinize this claim. But it is important that Schmitt's intention here is clear: he wants to demonstrate that even the most minimalistic interpretation of democratic decision making is a failure—and thus that democracy cannot possibly live up to those standards that it claims to be in accordance with.

66. Schmitt, *Legalität und Legitimität,* p. 35.

67. On possibilities for legal regulations of the financing of elections see Edward Sait, *American Parties and Elections* (New York, 1927).

Editor's Note: This claim is inadequately explicated. But Kirchheimer seems to be suggesting that the *lack* of some constitutional norms or legal rules—such as a constitutional clause assuring free speech or rules regulating campaign financing—can also undermine "equal chances" for different parties.

68. Schmitt, *Legalität und Legitimität,* p. 36.

Editor's Note: Schmitt's original argument here is described in note 64 above. Kirchheimer and Leites seem to alter his original position somewhat in their account of the nature of a "political premium resulting from the legal possession of political power."

69. R. H. Tawney, *Equality* (London, 1929), p. 125.

70. Editor's Note: For a critical discussion of Lenin's *State and Revolution*, see Otto Kirchheimer, "Marxism, Dictatorship, and the Organization of the Proletariat," in *Politics, Law, & Social Change: Selected Essays of Otto Kirchheimer*, ed. Frederic S. Burin and Kurt Shell (New York: Columbia University Press, 1969).

71. Schmitt, *Legalität und Legitimität*, p. 35.

72. Schmitt, *Legalität und Legitimität*, p. 35. See also Lester Ward's comments in *Reine Soziologie* (Innsbruck, 1907), vol. 1, p. 305. Roffenstein (in *Schmollers Jahrbuch* 45 [1921]: 109) summarizes Ward's view: "Every gain in power provides an additional advantage in the struggle to gain more power."

73.

> The contemporary law-based democratic state depends first and foremost on free and equal political competition, and a legally guaranteed equal chance for every group to advance its ideas and interests by political means. This legally equal opportunity can in fact seem dubious because of inequalities in education and property; this can happen to such an extent that a proletarian dictatorship may seem to fulfill this egalitarian ideal more effectively than the contemporary law-based state. But the impressive degree to which this political ideal still corresponds to social reality can be seen in postwar Italy in the emergence of the Catholic Popular Party with its extremely radical social demands.

Hermann Heller, *Europa und der Fascismus* (Berlin, 1931), p. 100. There clearly are parallel examples in contemporary Germany.

74. Editor's Note: Article 73 outlines procedures for a referendum:

> A law passed by parliament shall, before it becomes valid, be subject to a referendum if the President of the Reich, within a month, decides.
>
> A law, whose validity has been deferred on the request of one-third of the members of parliament, shall be subject to a referendum upon the request of one-twentieth of the qualified voters.
>
> A referendum shall also take place, if one-tenth of the qualified voters petition for the submission of a proposed law. Such petition must be based on a fully elaborated bill. The bill shall be submitted to the parliament by the ministry accompanied by an expression of its views. The referendum shall not take place if the bill petitioned for is accepted by the Reichstag without amendment.
>
> Only the President may order a referendum concerning the budget, tax laws, and salary-related regulations.
>
> Detailed regulations in respect to the referendum and initiative shall be prescribed by a federal law.

75. Schmitt, *Legalität und Legitimität*, p. 69; see also p. 66.

Editor's Note: Schmitt believes that the Weimar Constitution's direct-democratic elements conflict with its traditional liberal-parliamentary features. This stems from the fact that Weimar's founders (allegedly) sought a parliament in accordance with traditional liberal conceptions of parliamentary government. In other words, they emphasized the classical ideals of rationalistic liberal parliamentarism—for example, the aspiration to guide political affairs by general norms stemming from a process of free-wheeling rational discourse. According to Schmitt, plebiscites are guided by an altogether distinct logic: whereas Parliament is based on *ratio*, referenda necessarily are guided by an irrational, emotional expression of *voluntas*. According to Schmitt, this contradiction manifests itself in a series of inane decision-making devices within the Weimar Constitution; Kirchheimer addresses some of these arguments below. Schmitt, *Legalität und Legitimität*, pp. 62–69.

76. On the problem of justifying Parliament see Gerhard Leibholz, *Wesen der Repräsentation* (Berlin, 1929), especially p. 71.

77. Qualities that help justify the special status of the legislature in Schmitt's eyes include "reason" and "moderation." Schmitt, *Legalität und Legitimität*, p. 68; see also pp. 13, 15.

Editor's Note: For Schmitt's discussion of parliamentarism see *The Crisis of Parliamentary Democracy* (Cambridge, MIT Press, 1985). For his discussion there of the special character of parliamentary law, see esp. pp. 44–48.

78. Leibholz, *Wesen der Repräsentation*, p. 170, footnote 3.

79. Schmitt, *Legalität und Legitimität*, pp. 63, 69.

80. This only applies if nothing crucial occurred between that juncture when the referendum took place and that moment when Parliament passed a law. If something relevant for the law in question has taken place in the meantime, then the representative function of Parliament demands of it that it reconsider the legislative proposal in question in the spirit of the referendum that had been approved by the people. A parliamentary law that contradicted a referendum could come into existence if it substantiated a shift in public opinion that had resulted because of changes in the political situation. See Jellinek in *Handbuch des deutschen Staatsrechts*, vol. 2, pp. 181–182. Unfortunately, his example is not well chosen. It is not evident why alterations in the use of the death penalty abroad should have an immediate effect on the political perspective of the majority of the German people.

81. Schmitt, *Legalität und Legitimität*, p. 64.

Editor's Note: Recall the special place accorded the executive in the provisions of Article 76—reprinted above—for a referendum.

82. Schmitt, *Legalität und Legitimität*, p. 63.

83. The liberal-democratic oriented literature describes this process in terms of the "distrust to parliament." This expression is meant to capture the loss of parliament's autonomy, but it says nothing about parliament's technical functions. As far as the role of parliament in democracy is concerned, this "distrust" is an eminently democratic virtue: Harold Laski, *A Grammar of Politics* (New Haven, 1925), p. 321; Agnes Headlam Morley, *The New Democratic Constitutions of Europe* (Oxford, 1926), p. 32.

84. See the extensive analysis provided by Karl Löwenstein in his "Soziologie der parlamentarischen Repräsentation nach der grossen Reform," *Archiv für Sozialwissenschaft* 51 (1924). Also see *Annalen des Deutschen Reichs 1923–1925*, p. 4:

> Since the emergence of mass democracy, the cabinet is only formally subordinate to the lower house. The ruling power is in the hands of the electorate. The lower house is no longer the master of the state, but rather a mere transmission belt and instrument of control for the electorate.

The possibility of replacing parliament in a democratic state is discussed in Graham Wallas, *The Great Society* [reprint: Lincoln, Neb., 1967]; Ferdinand Tönnies, "Parlamentarismus und Demokratie," *Schmollers Jahrbuch* 51 (1927). Despite his criticisms of it, James Bryce acknowledges the technical necessity of parliament in *Modern Democracies* (New York, 1924), vol. 2, p. 377.

85. This transition from a substantial justification of Parliament to one that emphasizes its sociotechnical functions is described by Ziegler, *Die moderne Nation,* beginning on p. 285. But he does so without acknowledging the significance of this development for the attempt to provide a justification for contemporary parliament.

86. See Jacobi, *Reichsgerichtspraxis im deutschen Rechtsleben,* pp. 244–245; Thoma in *Handbuch des deutschen Staatsrechts,* vol. 2, p. 114.

87. Schmitt, *Legalität und Legitimität,* p. 67.

Editor's Note: One consequence for Schmitt of the Weimar Constitution's attempt to synthesize traditional liberal parliamentarism with new forms of plebiscitary decision making is that contradictions emerge concerning the number of votes needed to pass laws by means of these two distinct legislative "systems." See note 74.

88. Focusing attention on the problem of parliamentary absenteeism is justified because parliamentarians may fail to show up to vote for political reasons.

89. When this type of conflict arises need not be discussed here. See Schmitt, *Legalität und Legitimität,* pp. 67, 69.

90. Editor's Note: Article 75 reads that "a resolution of the parliament shall not be annulled unless a majority of the qualified voters participate in the election."

91. Schmitt, *Legalität und Legitimität,* p. 67.

Editor's Note: Schmitt writes there that

> in parliament, amendments to the constitution require a two-thirds majority instead of a simple majority; in the case of a referendum, no one dares to demand a qualified majority of the present, unmediated people; this would constitute an all too obvious contradiction of the basic democratic ideal of majority rule. So Article 76 requires a simple majority of qualified voters in order to amend the constitution by means of a referendum. In contrast, Article 75 requires the participation of a majority of qualified voters in a referendum if it is to result in the annulment of a parliamentary resolution. . . . Today, things have reached such a state that only those who plan to vote "yes" in a referendum take part in it. If they constitute a majority of qualified voters, a referendum will be passed which at the same time always necessarily satisfies the conditions outlined in Article 76 for constitutional amendments by means of a referendum. In practical terms, any distinction between statutory and constitutional lawmaking thereby vanishes.

92. On the question of "terror" in the context of direct democratic decision making see Karl Tannert, *Die Fehlgestalt des Volksentscheids* (Breslau, 1929).

93. Editor's Note: That is, the approximate number of votes needed to elect a member to the parliament at the time Kirchheimer and Leites authored this essay.

94. Schmitt, *Legalität und Legitimität,* beginning on p. 93.

95. As far as the possibility of an identical system of norms having a diversity of possible theoretical justifications is concerned, it is striking that the view that the people have preeminence *within* the constitutional system (as Jacobi's theory argues), and the view that they have preeminence *outside* of it (Schmitt's view), can be linked to contrary assessments of the basic character of the people. Jacobi, *Die Reichsgerichtspraxis im deutschen Rechtsleben,* p. 243, p. 247, note 30.

96. See Georges Bernanos, *La grande peur des bien-pensants* (Paris, 1931), p. 104.

97. See Charles Seignobos, *Histoire de la France contemporaine* (Paris, 1921), p. 139.

98. Seignobos, *Histoire de la France contemporaine,* beginning on p. 202.

99. See John Dewey, *The Public and Its Problems* (New York, 1927), p. 171.

PART II

Law and Politics in the Authoritarian State

FOUR

The Change in the Function of Law in Modern Society[1]

Franz L. Neumann

Fascist and social-reformist critics conceive of the liberal state as a "negative" state, and Ferdinand Lassalle's characterization of the liberal state as a "nightwatchman state" is a generally accepted formulation in these circles. The fact that liberalism too regards its nonexistence as the highest virtue of the state is so evident that no proof is needed. According to this ideology, the state must function imperceivably and must really be negative. One would, however, fall a victim to a historical fallacy if one were to identify "negativeness" with "weakness." The liberal state has always been as strong as the political and social situation and the interests of society demanded. It has conducted warfare and crushed strikes; with the help of strong navies it has protected its investments, with the help of strong armies it has defended and extended its boundaries, with the help of the police it has restored "peace and order." It has been a strong state precisely in those spheres in which it had to be strong and in which it wanted to be strong. This state, in which laws but not men were to rule (the Anglo-American formula)—that is, the *Rechtsstaat* (the German formula)—has rested upon force and law, upon sovereignty and freedom. Society required sovereignty in order to destroy local and particularist forces, to push the church out of temporal affairs, to establish a unified administration and judiciary, to protect boundaries and to conduct war, and to finance the execution of all these tasks. Political liberty has been necessary to modern society for the safeguarding of its economic freedom. Both elements are indispensable. There is no modern theory of law and state which does not accept both force and law

---

Originally appeared in German in *Zeitschrift für Sozialforschung* 6, no. 3 (1937). Reprinted here from *Selected Readings, Second Year Course in the Study of Contemporary Society* (Social Science II), 8th ed. (Chicago: University of Chicago, 1939).

even if the emphasis accorded to each of these components has varied in accordance with the historical situation. Even when it is asserted that sovereignty must be the function of the competitive process, force, unregulated by law, is still demanded independently of the competitive process.

Juridical terminology expresses this actual contradiction in the two concepts of objective law and subjective rights (in German, both meanings can be covered by the term *Recht*). "Objective law" means law created by the sovereign or, at any rate, law attributable to the sovereign power; subjective rights are the claims of an individual legal person. The one negates the autonomy of the individual; the other presupposes and affirms it. Various theories have attempted to reconcile the contradiction expressed by these two terms. Sometimes the subjective rights are simply declared to be mere reflections of the objective law—a proposition which completely denies the autonomy of the individual. (This German theory, which was developed and flourished at the end of the nineteenth century, has been adopted by Italian fascism.) Sometimes the difference between objective law and subjective rights is denied altogether. Subjective rights appear as nothing but objective law itself insofar as the latter, by force of the claim to obedience which it establishes, addresses itself to a concrete person (obligation) or is directed against such a concrete person (legal claim). Other theories again reduce objective law to patterns of behavior on the part of those subject to the law.

I

The work of the classic liberal Locke does not contain the term "sovereignty," but the idea is there. Locke, like all liberal theorists of the state, conceived of man as being good in the state of nature. He thought of the state of nature as a paradise that is supposed to persist even after the formation of the state. It is true, according to Locke, that laws will prevail (he called them "standing laws") whose material content cannot be altered even by democratic procedures. But even Locke approves of extralegal force. He does not, however, call it *sovereignty* (ever since the frank discussions of Hobbes and the absolutism of the Stuarts the word has had an unpleasant connotation in England) but *prerogative*. By prerogative he referred to the power to act, at discretion, beyond or even against the law. Man, after all, sometimes is evil, and Locke recognized that the positive laws of the state are but imperfect copies of the laws of nature. Whenever these evil tendencies find expression there must be a power to lead man back to his state of natural goodness. The prerogative, the force unregulated by law, is most developed in the "federative power," which Locke puts beside the legislative and the executive. He acknowledged it as a third independent power. The prerogative operates in the conduct of foreign affairs which cannot be based on abstract general norms but necessarily must "be left in great part to the prudence of those who have this power committed to them, to be managed . . . for the advantage of the commonwealth."[2]

This fundamental duality is perhaps even more clearly expressed by absolutists like Hobbes and Spinoza. Although law for Hobbes is pure *voluntas*, identical with all the sovereign's measures, and notwithstanding the fact that outside the state there can be no law, he restricts his monistic theory by basing the state (and hence law) on a natural law which is not only *voluntas* but also *ratio* because it is oriented toward the preservation and defense of human life. In case of a conflict between the measures of the sovereign and the *ratio* of the law of nature, he concedes clear priority to the law of nature. "Contracts, which prohibit the defense of one's own body, are null and void." No one is obliged to confess to a crime, no one to commit suicide or to kill a fellow man. Universal military service is against natural law. Lacking his usual lucidity, he writes that the Law of Nature obliges always in conscience (*in foro interno*) but not always *in foro externo*.[3] The point where the obligation of obedience ceases and the right of disobedience (which is only granted in individual cases) commences again is ambiguously defined.

> If the sovereign command a man, though justly condemned, to kill, wound, or maim himself; or not to resist those that assault him; or to abstain from the use of food, air, medicine, or any other thing without which he cannot live; yet hath that man the liberty to disobey.[4]

Here again Hobbes's ambivalent attitude is obvious. In accord with requirements of this epoch the emphasis is put on sovereignty, legally unchecked force, and on the demand for a strong state that is independent of the warring groups. But liberty is also stressed, however weakly.

The conflict in question is even more evident in the case of Spinoza, who really developed two theories: a theory of the state and a theory of law, between which there exists a dialectical relationship. In Spinoza's theory of the state, state absolutism is at least as unlimited as in Hobbes. The rights of the individual are lacking even though freedom is postulated as the ultimate aim of the state. Even in matters of religion the subject is entirely subordinated to the measures of the sovereign, which are called laws. "It is obedience which makes the subject." Only thought is free. In Spinoza's *Tractatus politicus* even the last traces of the rights reserved to the individual have been eliminated, probably owing to the impression that the murder of his friend DeWitt left on him. "If we understand by law the law of civil society . . . then we cannot say that the state is bound by law or can infringe on it." The laws of civil society are entirely dependent on the state and in order to protect its own freedom the state should act only out of consideration for itself and should "regard nothing as good or evil except what according to its own judgment is good or evil for itself."[5] Beside this absolutist theory of the state, however, there stands his theory of law, which really represents a correction of his theory of the state.

> The natural right of the totality of nature and consequently of every individual extends just as far as its power. Accordingly, whatever a person does in following the laws of his own nature, he does in accordance with the highest natural law and the justice of his action is proportionate to his power.[6]

Under normal circumstances the state has supreme power, and hence it has the highest right. Should, however, an individual or a group acquire power, then they will be right to a corresponding extent. Spinoza's theory, therefore, is not a system in which the relationship of state and society is rigidly determined. The line of demarcation is flexible. If a social group possesses enough power, it may acquire for itself as much liberty as its power allows in the face of the power of the state. It may ultimately succeed to the direction of the state and transform its power into law and justice. The absolutism of the state is based on considerations identical with those operative in the case of Hobbes. But the freedom of individuals is guaranteed by power that becomes legal and just and that they are to apply in order to conduct commerce, to exchange goods, and to cooperate in a society that is based on division of labor. The theory, according to which might is right, serves primarily to control the masses which Spinoza hated, but at the same time it combated monarchy. Spinoza's theory is the theory of an opposition that feels its strength and that hopes soon to transform its social power into political power.

II

The antithesis of sovereignty and law corresponds to two different concepts of law: a political and a rational concept. In a political sense every measure of the sovereign power, regardless of its material content, constitutes law. Declaration of war and conclusion of peace, tax laws, and the code of civil law, the policeman's command and that of the bailiff, the decision of the judge and the legal norm upon which the decision is based—in fact, all utterances of the sovereign, because they are utterances of the sovereign, are law. This concept of law is exclusively genetically defined. Law is *voluntas* and nothing else. Insofar as a legal theory accepts this political concept of law, it may be called a "decisionist" theory. However, there is also the rational concept of law, which is based not on the source of law but on its material content. Not every measure of the sovereign, and not only measures of the sovereign, are law. Law is here a norm that is intelligible and contains an ethical postulate which is frequently that of equality. Law, then, is *ratio* and not necessarily *voluntas* at the same time. This rational law need not, but can, emanate from the sovereign. For this theory of law, especially in the form of the theory of natural law, asserts that material laws may exist without reference to the will of the sovereign. It defends the validity of a system of norms even when the positive law of the state ignores its postulates. Today there two concepts of law are strictly separated.

There is no such separation in the Thomist system of natural law. There *voluntas* and *ratio* are still one. Not every measure of the authority is law. Only those measures are law that also correspond to the requirements of the law of nature. Law is the basis, the standard, the *regula artis*, by means of which a just decision is to be obtained. Against a law that contradicts the principles of *lex naturalis*, passive resistance is not only justified but it becomes rather a duty, because even God cannot dispense with the *lex naturalis*. In the Thomist system, the law of nature is sufficiently concretized and, in part, institutionalized: Thomism derives from it a number of concrete demands on the legislator. At the same time the recognition of the right of, at least, passive resistance makes possible the realization of the law of nature in the face of a conflicting law of the state.

The separation of the two concepts of law is undertaken by the Nominalists and in the conciliar theory. Since then law has been viewed as the conscious creation of civil society. The detachment of the political concept of law from nonsecular natural law was consummated in the course of the struggles between church and state and of the internal conflicts within the church and the temporal order. The Nominalists, who represented specifically bourgeois interests, opposed the papal demand for the subordination of the temporal power. During these conflicts natural law underwent a series of metamorphoses, serving at one time a revolutionary function and at another a conservative one, at still another a critical function, and then an apologetic one. Whenever a political group attacks the powerfully entrenched positions of another group, it will use revolutionary natural law as an implement and will derive from natural law even the right to tyrannicide. Whenever such a group has succeeded, it will abjure all its former ideals, suppress the revolutionary implications of natural law, and transform it into a conservative ideology. Marsilius of Padua, owing to his antagonism toward the ecclesiastical claim for temporal sovereignty, was forced to restrict the rule of the temporal sovereign by recognizing a type of natural law that supported demands for freedom. The legislator, the *pars principans*, is not without restrictions, but is placed under the domination of universal norms of natural law, which are, to a high degree, concretized and institutionalized. At the same time, however, Marsilius, in order to receive sufficient popular support, was forced to postulate democratic rights of participation in which he conceives of the people not as the totality of all free and equal citizens but only as the *pars valentior*. The conciliar theorists, Gerson and Nicolas of Cusa, were driven to the acceptance of the same postulates in consequence of their conflict with the claims of the pope for ecclesiastical sovereignty.

Gerson reduced the will of the church to the individual wills of the members of the ecclesiastical aristocrats who were assembled at the council. Nicolas of Cusa went even further and made the ecclesiastical power subject to the general norms of natural law while denying the validity of papal measures which contradicted these universal laws.

Beginning with the fourteenth century, the identity of political and rational law ceases to be insisted on. The political law is regarded only as the measure of the sovereign. Natural law, as expressed in universally, generally valid norms, stands in opposition to the political law and plays a restrictive role with reference to it; natural law points in a definite direction and contains social demands which usually refer to the preservation of private property and to political liberties. Furthermore, it contains the demand for equality before the law. This type of natural law, as in the case of the Monarchomachs, is always put forward by an attacking group. Bodin, who produced the first modern system of legal and political theory, accepts sovereignty as an absolute and permanent power as unequivocally as he accepts rational law which restricts that absolute power.

III

In the age of liberalism, natural law declines to the same degree as democracy and the social-contract theory find acceptance. The generality of the positive law acquires a position of central importance in the legal system. Only a norm, which has a general character, is regarded as law. It is sometimes asserted that the difference between the general law and the individual measure is only a relative one, because each command of the superior to the subordinate has some degree of generality with respect to the act to be executed since the executor always possesses a certain amount of initiative, however, small. Those legal theorists who accept as legitimate only those concepts that lend themselves to a logically unambiguous formulation, and who will reject every decision as subjective and therefore arbitrary, will also reject the distinction between general norms and particular measures. We conceive of a legal norm as a hypothetical judgment of the state regarding the future conduct of its subjects, and the statute is the principal form in which this legal norm appears.

Three elements are relevant in the characterization of the law: the law must be general in its formulation, its generality must be specific, and it must not be retroactive. Rousseau formulated the claim for the generality of formulation as follows:

> When I say that the object of law is always general, I mean that the law considers subjects *en masse* and actions in the abstract, and never a particular person or action. Thus the law may indeed decree that there shall be privileges,

but cannot confer them on anybody by name. . . . In a word, no function which has a particular object belongs to the legislative power.[7]

This first requirement is insufficient, however, for

right receives only by becoming law not only the *form* of its generality but also its true determinateness. Therefore in considering the nature of lawmaking, one should not dwell only upon the first formal aspect of a law, namely that it declares something as the universally valid rule of behavior. Rather it is more important and essential to consider the contents of a law and to recognize that these contents partake of a specific, defined generality.[8]

But what is the substantive content of this generality? In order to deduce this concrete definition, we distinguish between specific laws and "legal principles" or legal standards of conduct (*Generalklauseln*, as they are called in German jurisprudence). Propositions like the following, that contracts that violate public policy or are unreasonable or immoral (Section 138 of the German Civil Code, BGB) are null and void, or that he who damages someone in a way that violates good morals is responsible for indemnities (Section 826), or that he "who commits an act which has been declared punishable under the law or which is deserving of punishment because it is in conflict with healthy popular sentiment" shall be punished (Section 2 of the Criminal Code for the German Reich as formulated by the Law of June 28, 1935), are not specific laws with true generality. They embody rather a spurious generality. Because in present-day society there can be no unanimity on whether a given action, in a concrete case, is immoral or unreasonable, or whether a certain punishment corresponds to or runs counter to "healthy popular sentiment," they have no specific content. A legal system which derives its legal propositions primarily from these so-called general principles (*Generalklauseln*) or from "legal standards of conduct" is nothing but a mask under which individual measures are hidden. On the other hand, rules like the following, that the legal existence (rights and responsibilities) of a person begins with his birth (Section 1 of the German BGB), or that the transfer of landed property is effected by agreement of the parties concerned and registration in the registry of landed property (Section 873 of the German BGB), are real legal norms because all the essential facts to which the norm refers are clearly defined and because there is no reference to moral standards that are neither generally binding nor accepted as binding. If the fundamental principles or the essential parts of a legal system are placed under the rule of such *Generalklauseln*, then one can no longer speak of the rule of a general law.

The formal structure of a general law—and herein lies the third element of generality—contains also a minimum of substantive content. The general law which is defined in such a manner guarantees to the judge a minimum of independence because it does not subordinate him to the individual measures of the sovereign. Likewise a general law contains the demand for the inadmissibility of retroactivity. A law which provides for retroactivity contains particular commands inasmuch as the facts to which the law refers already exist.

The facts that are regulated by general laws are to be found either in spheres of free choice or in institutions which guide and control behavior. Liberty, in the legal sense, has an exclusively negative meaning. It is merely "absence of external compulsion" (Hobbes). This

> negative freedom or this freedom as conceived by the intellect is onesided; but this onesidedness always contains in itself an important determination. It is therefore not to be discarded. The shortcoming of the intellect is, however, that it elevates a onesided determination into an exclusive and dominant one.[9]

It is necessary, however, to do more than indicate the existence of a sphere of freedom from the state. It is important in this connection to point out a distinction, however superficial, between the various kinds of legal freedom. We distinguish in general four separate legal freedoms:

1. Personal freedom, which comprises the rights of the isolated individual, such as the provision that a person can be arrested only on the basis of laws and by means of legal procedures; and domiciliary and postal inviolability.
2. Political freedom, which is political because it obtains its significance only on the basis of an organized social life within the framework of the state. It includes, for example, freedom of association and assembly, freedom of the press, and the right to the secret ballot. These rights are liberal as well as democratic. They are liberal in so far as they guarantee freedom to the individual in certain spheres of life and democratic insofar as they are means to the democratic determination of state policy.
3. A third category is constituted by economic freedom, that is, freedom in trade and industry.
4. In the period of democracy the political rights of liberty find expression also in the social sphere by the recognition of a right of association on the part of employees.

This fourfold classification does not claim exhaustiveness either logically or historically. These freedoms ordinarily are not constitutionally guaranteed as unrestricted rights. Such guaranties would be absurd. They are guaranteed exclusively within "the framework of the law." Interference with these rights is therefore permitted only on the basis of legal provisions. It is the most important and perhaps the decisive demand of liberalism that interference with the rights reserved to the individual is not permitted on the basis of individual but only on the basis of general laws.

In addition to defining areas of freedom, general laws also regulate human institutions. By institution we mean an enduring, dominational or cooperative association for the continuance of social life. (These relationships can be formed either between different properties or between different people or between persons and properties.) This definition is purely descriptive and has nothing to do with pluralistic theories of the state or with Thomism or the National Socialist philosophies of law, both of which have attached central significance to "institution." This concept includes all sorts of associations, the foundation, the factory, the business enterprise, the cartel, and the institution of marriage. Above all, it comprises the most important institution of all historical societies—private property in the means of production. Private property as such is a subjective and an absolute right which lends to the proprietor legal defenses against anyone who interferes with possession or enjoyment of the property. In addition, however, private property in the means of production is also an institution. It is destined to be enduring; its functions in the maintenance and continuance of social life; it assigns to man a place in a dominational structure.

There are definite and definable relations between institutions and the various liberties. A certain liberty may be a principal freedom and for the guaranty of its operation it may require a complex of auxiliary liberties and auxiliary institutions. An institution likewise may also require auxiliary liberties. Private property as the central institution of modern society in the age of competitive capitalism requires the decisive auxiliary liberties of freedom of contract and freedom of enterprise. The owner of capital must have the liberty to establish or discontinue a business enterprise; he must have the right of concluding all sorts of contracts, since he can operate only if these particular rights are recognized. These economic liberties are not protected for their own sake, but only because in a particular phase of economic evolution their protection is necessary for the functioning of the principal institution. The contract—that is, the legal form in which man exercises his liberty—is, in the period of free competition, a constituent element of modern society. The contract terminates the isolation of the individual proprietors and constitutes a means of communication between them. It is therefore as indispensable as property itself. To bring about "that I may own property not only by means of a thing and my own subjective will, but also by means of another will, and thereby in a common will—this constitutes the sphere of contract."[10]

Liberalism regards as the rule of law exclusively the rule of statute law, and not that of customary or natural law. Actually, natural law disappeared in England under the rule of Henry VII. It was during this period that both the supremacy of parliamentary laws and the duty of the judge to obey these laws became undeniable. Hence, already in the sixteenth century the prevailing formula of the rule of law meant only the rule of laws passed by

Parliament. During the Puritan revolution, of course, there emerged strong natural-law tendencies, which were used not only by the Republicans in their struggle against monarchism but were also employed by the Royalists in defense of their own position. Since that time the rule of natural law has never been asserted either in juridical literature, jurisprudence, or judicial practice. Even Blackstone (1723–1780), who in the first volume of his *Commentaries,* copied the natural-law system of Burlamaqui and who acknowledged the rule of an eternal and immutable natural law, was compelled to admit (when discussing the sovereignty of Parliament) that Parliament can do whatever it desires and that he knew of no way of realizing the rule of the natural law that he postulated.

In Germany natural law experienced a different fate. At first it changed its character; finally, it disappeared altogether. Natural law can provide a theory of liberty. In this form it represents the critical theory of a bourgeois opposition at war with absolutism, or it appears as an apologetic doctrine legitimating not a liberal system but the sovereignty of the state. In England there was no reason for the further retention of either of these kinds of natural law—for neither the liberal type, since the bourgeoisie had acceded to political power in the seventeenth century, nor the absolutist type, because since Henry VIII the unity of the state had been unquestioned (even during the Puritan revolution). In Germany, however, neither of these events had yet occurred. The most pressing task was the establishment of a unified state in order to provide an important precondition for industrial and commercial expansion. Pufendorf's system of natural law, which exerted extraordinary influence upon the jurists of the seventeenth and eighteenth centuries, served the purpose of justifying, by means of natural law, the power of the state. Human nature, according to his theory, is dominated by two impulses—the impulse of sociability and the impulse of self-preservation. Since there is no natural harmony among these instincts, harmony must be achieved by compulsion. Natural law, however, because it has no sanction at its disposal, is unable to accomplish this task. The execution of the law of nature is entirely dependent on the *foro divino et conscientiae.* This, however, is insufficient. Sanctions, therefore, are applied by the state, which has been founded by contract and which must be an absolutist one. The law of the state is the command of the sovereign; it is pure *voluntas.* The right of resistance which Pufendorf includes in his system is only of secondary significance. In Christian Thomasius's system, natural law offers only a body of counsel from which certain moral obligations follow. However, as law and morality are distinctly separated and as the supreme criterion of law is its compulsory character, Thomasius's system of natural law likewise serves to make compulsion on the part of the state legitimate. However different Christian Wolff's point of departure is, however determinedly he stresses the validity of a *Lex aeterna,* he too arrives at the conclusion that only the state is able to assure a well-ordered social life. The only difference from the rationalistic theories of Pufendorf and Thomasius lies in the fact that Wolff assigned to the state the additional tasks of promoting welfare and culture. His system was as adequate to the governments that Frederick II of Prussia and Joseph II of Austria had set up, as the systems of Pufendorf and Thomasius were expressive of the state that the Elector Frederick William I had established.

If Kant's legal theory is examined apart from his ethics, it is found that natural law has completely disappeared from it. The state is viewed as an organization that is to guarantee that individuals can be free without interfering with the freedom of their fellow men. But the decision is delivered not by the autonomous individual but by the absolute state, which is the logical postulate derived from the state of nature under which, in turn, the existence of provisional private property and of the rule of *pacta sunt servanda* are already asserted as a dogma. According to Kant, the freedom of the legal subject is guaranteed solely by the requirement that the state must rule only on the basis of general laws. But this postulate is asserted with rigorous consistency. Kant even rejects the softening of the strict legal system, as it is codified by (statutory) general laws, through the law of equity. For "equity is a dumb goddess who cannot claim a hearing of right. Hence it follows that a Court of Equity for the decision of disputed matters of Right would involve a contradiction."[11] From the time of Kant until the end of the nineteenth century the demand for the generality of law forms the center of German legal theory. By demanding that the domination of the state be based on general laws, Kant adopted the theories of Montesquieu and Rousseau.

The demand that the state must rule only by means of general laws is perhaps most clearly voiced in Montesquieu's *Esprit des Lois*. Montesquieu, by way of Malebranche, was influenced by Descartes. The universe, according to Descartes, is governed by general mechanical laws which even God is unable to alter because individual measures are alien to him, and because God withdraws from the universe and becomes *immense, spirituel et infini*. According to Montesquieu, the laws of the state are general and inaccessible to the measures of the sovereign in the same way. The French Revolution was most profoundly affected by the doctrines of Rousseau and Montesquieu. Mirabeau, the chairman of the committee for the drafting of the Rights of Man, proposed, on August 17, 1789, the following provision: "Being the expression of the general will [*volonté générale*], the law must be general with respect to its object." Hence, one article of the Declaration of the Rights of Man and Citizen contains a provision that the law is the expression of the general will (*volonté générale*). This was restated in Article 6 of the Declaration of 1793 and in Article 6 of the Constitution of the Année III. During the Revolution, in the Constitution of 1791 and the Jacobinist Constitution of 1793, a distinction was made between laws (*lois*) and decrees (*décrets*). The

Girondist Constitution of 1793, which was under the decisive influence of Condorcet, emphasized sharply in Section 2 of Article 4: "The distinctive characteristics of laws are their generality and their unlimited duration," and it distinguishes laws from measures (*mésures*) for an emergency case.

The German doctrine is deeply indebted to the French doctrine but, toward the end of the nineteenth century, it diverged widely from it. Robert von Mohl, Lorenz von Stein, and Klueber viewed the demand for the generality of the law as the central problem of political theory. Yet under the pervasive influence of Paul Laband this doctrine became enfeebled and was replaced by the distinction between formal law and material law. Every utterance of the will of the state is considered as formal law, whereas only those utterances which contain a legal norm, that is, which produce subjective rights and duties, are considered as material laws. The budgetary law, in this sense, is not a material law since it only enables the state to make expenditures within the framework of the budget. This dualistic theory was generally accepted by German jurisprudence.

Notwithstanding the fact that the theory of the supremacy of Parliament was victorious in England, there too the general character of law was not neglected. Blackstone even asserted that an individual law is "a declaration rather than a law."[12] Even Austin, the most extreme representative of Hobbes's concept of political law, asserted that one could speak of a law only if it has a general character. But in the only case in which an English court dealt with the question of whether individual measures have the character of law, this question was answered in the affirmative. This decision is of the greatest interest because the judges discussed the reasons why in this particular case an individual measure must be a law. The decision deals with the validity of a measure of a colonial high commissioner, by which a native was deprived of his freedom. The question was how far such an individual measure could suspend liberties that had been guaranteed by the Habeas Corpus Act. Lord Justice Farwell deduced the legality of the measure as follows:

> The truth is that in countries inhabited by natives who outnumber the whites, such laws [Habeas Corpus], although bulwarks of freedom in the United Kingdom, might very probably become the death sentence of the whites if they were applied there [i.e., in the colonies].

Lord Justice Kennedy added that legislation that is oriented toward a single person is a privilege, and "generally, so I hope and believe, such legislation recommends itself to a British legislator just as little as it appealed to the legislators of ancient Rome."[13] This case clearly stresses the double-edged character of the general law in a society characterized by decisive conflicts of interests.

The postulation of the generality of law is accompanied by the repudiation of the retroactivity of law.

Retroaction is the most evil assault which the law can commit. It means the tearing up of the social contract, and the destruction of the conditions on the basis of which society enjoys the right to demand the individual's obedience, because it deprives him of the guarantees of which society assured him and which were the compensation for the sacrifice which his obedience entailed. Retroaction deprives the law of its real legal character. A retroactive law is no law at all.

This is the way in which Benjamin Constant characterized the retroaction of laws.[14] This notion, too, is directly derived from Rousseau's theory. It was adopted by the *Declaration of the Rights of Man and Citizen*, by the Constitution of 1793 and by the Constitution of the Année III, although today there exists neither in England nor in France any obstacle against the enactment of retroactive laws. In Republican Germany, however, the Weimar Constitution assigned the status of a constitutional guaranty to the prohibition of retroactive criminal laws.

Such a theory of the formal structure of law leads automatically to a specific theory of the relation between the judge and the law. If the law and nothing but the law rules, then the judge has no other tasks than cognitive ones. Judges, as Montesquieu had remarked, are only "the mouthpieces of the law and inanimate things." Owing to this alleged insignificance, the acts of the judge are *en quelque façon nul*.[15] This phonographic theory of the judicature is, of course, closely bound up with the theory of the separation of powers, that is, with the assertion that creation of law and legislation are identical, and that, apart from the process of legislation, law can be created neither by society, by judges nor by administrative officials. Cazalès expressed this notion most clearly when he said, "In any political society there are merely two powers, one that creates law and another one that sees to its execution. The power of the judges . . . exists only in the plain and simple application of the law."[16] Similar ideas, however, were already to be found in the *Federalist*, in Hobbes, and in Hale's *History of the Common Law*.

The legal system of liberalism, therefore, was regarded as a closed system without gaps. All the judge had to do was to apply it. The juridical thinking of this epoch was called positivism or normativism, and the interpretation of the laws by the judge was called the dogmatic interpretation (in Germany) or exegetical interpretation (in France). Bentham, too, in order to achieve complete intelligibility and clarity in the legal system, recommended the codification of English law, for

> a code formed upon these principles would not require schools for its explanation, would not require casuists to unravel its subtleties. It would speak a language familiar to everybody: each one might consult it at his need. . . . No decision of any judge, much less the opinion of any individual, should be allowed to be cited as law until such decision or opinion have been embodied by the legislator in the code. . . . If any commentary should be written on this

code, with a view of pointing out what is the sense thereof, all men should be required to pay no regard to such comment, neither should it be allowed to be cited in any court of justice in any manner whatsoever. . . . If any judge should in the course of his practice see occasion to remark any thing in it that appears to him erroneous in point of matter . . . let him certify such observation to the legislature with the reasons of his opinion and the correction he would propose.[17]

It is of great importance that, above all, the French Revolution was not content with the merely doctrinal form of the proposition that judges may not create law but attempted to institutionalize it. This development started with the famous formulation of Robespierre:

The statement that law is created by the courts . . . must be expelled from our language. In a State which has a constitution and a legislature, the jurisprudence of the law courts consists only in the law.[18]

The decrees of August 16 and 24, 1790, consequently, prohibit the interpretation of laws on the part of the judge and request him to appeal, in all doubtful cases, to the legislature. The functions of the so-called Référé Législatif were fulfilled later by the Tribunal de Cassation and, subsequently, by the Cour de Cassation, which institutions were constituted not as courts but as a part of the legislative. Later, owing to the influence of Portalis, this impracticable doctrinaire attitude was given up, and in the Code Civil freedom of interpretation on the part of the judge was re-established. According to Portalis, the judge is supposed to fill any legal gaps in accordance with "the natural light of legal sense and common sense." But this idea was not incorporated into French legal theory; on the contrary, especially after 1830, the exegetical school was victorious. The year 1830 really is the turningpoint in French legal theory. Henceforth laws are interpreted in a dogmatic manner, the legal system is regarded as a closed one, the "phonograph" theory is rigorously applied, and the law-creating function of the judge is denied. Henceforth there is no recourse to considerations of justice or appropriateness.

Similar developments took place in Germany. On April 14, 1780, Frederick II of Prussia prohibited the interpretation of laws. Article 4 of the Introduction of the *Allgemeines Landrecht* prohibited interpretations which conflicted with the literal sense of the words of grammatical contexts in which the laws were framed. Feuerbach is probably the author of the Bavarian order of October 19, 1813, which prohibited the writing, by officials and private scholars, of commentaries on the Bavarian code of criminal law of 1813. On this point Feuerbach's adversary, Savigny, took the same view. Savigny and the historical school of law regarded only law, the folk-spirit, and customary laws as genuine sources of law. Savigny likewise viewed the legal system as closed, unified, and complete, the judge having only to apply the truth, not to create it. During the whole of the nineteenth century the German theory of the application of law was dogmatic.

The theory of the separation of powers, upon which this theory of legal application depends, does not imply, however, that the three divided powers are of equal value. Since Locke it has always asserted the preeminence of the legislative power. Hence, during the whole of the nineteenth century, and in Germany until 1919, the right of the judiciary to examine laws that have been properly enacted was denied. German constitutional theory was split in this respect, the liberals favoring judicial review, the conservatives rejecting it. Yet although the majority at the fourth annual meeting of German jurists in 1863 declared itself in favor of judicial review, the number of its proponents declined rapidly under the rule of Bismarck. In practice such a right was consistently rejected and only the examination of laws with reference to the compatibility of state law and federal law was permitted.

What are the social causes and consequences of the theory of the rule of law, of the denial of natural law, and of the absolute subordination of the judge to the law? In England, in Germany, and in France the belief in the rule of law expressed both the strength and the weakness of the bourgeoisie. The proposition of the supremacy of statutory law implied the additional proposition that social change may be carried out only by legislation. The priority of legislation is maintained because the middle classes, at least in England and France, participated to a significant degree in the legislative process. Laws, however, always involve interferences with liberty or property. If such interferences can only be undertaken on the basis of laws, and if the bourgeoisie is, to a decisive degree, represented in Parliament, then this doctrine implies that the social class which is the object of intervention will itself determine the content of those interferences and will, of course, see to it that its own interests are taken into account. If Parliament is the chief agent of social change, then the rule of the laws of Parliament will also operate as an instrument to prevent, or at least to retard, social progress. This doctrine, therefore, veils the unwillingness of the ruling classes to give way to social reforms, for the slowness of the parliamentary machinery transforms the sole means of legal change into a means for the preservation of the status quo. Finally, the doctrine has an ideological function, namely, that of disguising the real holders of power in the state. The invocation of the law as the sole sovereign and the dictum that sovereignty is "a government of laws and not of men" make it superfluous to mention that, in reality, men do rule, even when they rule within the framework of the law. Hence, the supremacy of the laws of Parliament forms the center of the constitutional doctrine only as long as the middle classes are able to wield decisive influence in Parliament. As soon as this influence wanes, there appear new natural law doctrines that are designed to reduce the predominance of a Parliament in which representatives of the working classes also exert influence. At the same time, the doctrine of the supremacy of Parliament hides the weakness of the middle classes. The dictum that social changes can be attained only through laws enacted by parliament, and that administrative agencies and judges may only apply law but not create it, is an illusion that also serves to deny the law-creating capacity of extraparliamentary forces. This doctrine clearly reveals the ambivalent position of modern man—the emphatic assertion of the autonomy of man is accompanied by the equally passionate insistence on the rule of the state.

The rule of law is, moreover, necessary as a precondition of capitalist competition. The need for calculability and dependability in the legal system and in administration was one of the motives for restricting the power of the patrimonial princes and of feudalism, leading ultimately to the establishment of Parliament, with the help of which the bourgeoisie controlled the administration and budget while participating in the modification of the legal system. Free competition requires the generality of law because it is the highest form of formal rationality. It requires also the absolute subordination of the judge to the law and therewith the separation of powers. Free competition depends upon the existence of a large number of competitors of approximately equal strength who compete in a free market. Freedom of the commodity market, freedom of the labor market, free selection within the entrepreneurial class, freedom of contract, and, above all, calculability of the decisions of the judiciary are the essential characteristics of the liberal competitive system which, through continuous, rationalistic, and capitalistic enterprise, produces a steady flow of profits. It is the primary task of the state to create such a legal order as will secure the fulfilment of contracts. A high degree of certainty of the expectation that contracts will be executed is an indispensable part of the enterprise. However, this calculability and predictability, if the competitors are approximately equal in strength, can be attained only by general laws. These general laws must be so definite in their abstractness that as little as possible is left to the discretion of the judge. In such a society the judge, therefore, is forbidden to have recourse to *Generalklauseln*. The state, if it intervenes in the individual's disposition of his liberty or property, must render its interventions calculable in advance. It may not interfere in a retroactive manner, for that would negate all existing expectations. It may not intervene extralegally because such an intervention would be unpredictable. It may not intervene by individual measures because such an intervention would violate the principle of the equality of competitors. The judge, moreover, must be independent and litigations must be decided without regard for the desires of the government. Hence there must be a separation of powers which, quite apart from its political significance, is of the greatest importance for the organization of the competitive system since it provides for a division of competences and fixes the limits among the various activities of the state, guaranteeing thereby the rationality of law and its application. This scheme solves the apparent contradiction in the liberal attitude toward legislation. This contradiction, which Roscoe Pound detected in the attitude of the American Puritans, consists, on the one hand, in the negative attitude toward every kind of legislation and, on the other hand, in the firm belief in legislation associated with the rejection of customary law and the law of equity. This is the attitude not only of Puritanism but of liberalism as a whole. The latter postulated the superiority of parliamentary legislation in order to prevent legislation or, as far as that is impossible, to make this legislation serviceable to the interest of the bourgeoisie. In principle, liberalism always disliked state intervention.

The theory of the rule of general laws has, of course, never been fully realized in any stage of the development of competitive capitalism. Liberal society is not a rational one, and its economy is not planfully organized. Harmony and equilibrium are not, at any given moment, automatically restored. Measures of the sovereign and "general principles" are, at all stages, indispensable. The contract becomes the instrument for dislodging free competition, terminating therewith the rule of the contract and of the general law on which the contract in the economic sphere is based. According to the legal theory of liberalism (and there it is in opposition to Adam Smith), freedom of contract implies the right of the entrepreneur to form organizations, cartels, corporations, syndicates, employers' associations, and finally the monopolistic trust which dominates the market. Since the legal theory of liberalism discarded the social postulates of Adam Smith's classical liberal theory—namely, his objection to *unrestricted* competition,[19] his demand that the competitors be equal, his fight against monopolies, his declaration for the unification of the capital-providing and the managerial functions in the same individual (that is, in the property-owner), and, accordingly his fight against the joint stock company—it arrived unanimously at the conclusion that freedom of contract meant nothing but the freedom to conclude freely any kind of contract if there were no express legal prohibitions, even such contracts as would mean the end of free competition. The transformation of the concept of the freedom of contract from a social concept, implying the exchange of equal values among equally strong competitors, into a formal, juridical concept contributed to the development of the system of monopolistic capitalism, in which contract and general laws were to play a strictly secondary role.

IV

Yet general laws and the principle of the separation of powers have still another function. This function is ethical in character and is most clearly expressed in Rousseau's philosophy of law. The generality of laws and the independence of the judge guarantee a minimum of personal and political liberty. The general law establishes personal equality, and it forms the basis of all interferences with liberty and property. Therefore the character of the law that alone permits such interference is of fundamental significance. Only when such interferences are controlled by general laws is liberty guaranteed, since in this manner the principle of equality is preserved. Voltaire's statement that freedom means dependence on nothing save law[20] refers only to general laws. If the sovereign is permitted to decree individual measures, to arrest this man or that one, to confiscate this or that piece of property, then the independence of the judge is extinguished. The judge who has to execute such individual measures becomes a mere policeman. Real independence presupposes the rule of the state through general laws. Generality of the laws and independence of the judge, as well as the doctrine of the separation of powers, have therefore purposes that transcend the requirements of free competition. The basic phenomenon underlying the generality of law—namely, the legal equality of all men—has never been disputed by liberalism. Equality before the law is, to be sure, "formal," that is, negative. But Hegel, who clearly perceived the purely formal-negative nature of liberty, already warned of the consequences of discarding it.

All three functions of the generality of laws—obscuring the domination of the bourgeoisie, rendering the economic system calculable, and guaranteeing a minimum of liberty and equality—are of decisive importance and not just the second of these functions, as the proponents of the totalitarian state claim. If one views—as, for example, Carl Schmitt does—the generality of laws as a means designed to satisfy the requirements of free competition, then the conclusion is obvious that with the termination of free competition and its replacement by organized state capitalism, the general law, the independence of judges, and the separation of powers will also disappear and that the true law then consists either in the Führer's command or the general principle (*Generalklauseln*).

V

The juridical forms that were created by the competitive society of the nineteenth century were different in Germany and England. The specifically German phenomenon is the *Rechtsstaat*; the specifically English phenomenon is the supremacy of Parliament combined with the rule of law.

The idea of the *Rechtsstaat* is perfected in Kant's system. There it appears as the creation of the German Bürgertum—an economically ascending but politically stagnant class. This class was content with the legal protection of its economic liberty and was resigned to its exclusion from a share in political power. The essence of this concept of the *Rechtsstaat* consists in the distinction of the legal form from the political structure of the state. This isolated legal form, independent from the political structure, was to constitute the guaranty of freedom and security. This was the fundamental difference between German and English theory. In the former the *Rechtsstaat* did not develop into a specifically juridical form of democracy, as was the case in England. It rather assumed a neutral attitude toward the form of the state. This indifferent attitude is most clearly expressed in the writings of Friedrich Julius Stahl.

> The state should become a *Rechtsstaat*. This is the solution of our problems and the motivating force of our age.... The state should define and secure the modes and limits of its own activities as well as the citizens' sphere of freedom in strict accordance with law. It should not realize the ethical idea directly (i.e., in a coercive manner) beyond the limits of legality—which means it should, in this sphere, not attempt to do more than the most indispensable "fencing in." The concept of the *Rechtsstaat* does not mean that the state merely manages the legal order without administrative aims nor that it merely protects the rights of the individual. It does not refer to the goal or content of the state's activity at all but only to the mode and character of their realization.[21]

Stahl's definition was accepted even at times explicitly by the liberal theorists of the *Rechtsstaat*: Gneist,[22] Robert von Mohl,[23] Otto Baehr,[24] and Welcker.[25] This conception of the *Rechtsstaat*, which Stahl elaborated in passionate criticism of de Maistre and Bonald, culminates in the denial that the monarch is the Lord's representative on earth and concludes with the assertion that the monarch may rule not against the law but only together with the representatives of the people and only by means of the bureaucracy. Stahl's definition reveals two things distinctly: 1. the state also has administrative tasks which are not controlled; 2. the legal form, on the other hand—that is, the rule by law—is independent of the form of the state.

In English constitutional theory both factors—sovereignty of Parliament and the rule of law—receive equal emphasis. This was already visible in Blackstone. The English middle classes, in contrast to the German, safeguarded their economic freedom not materially, that is, by establishing barriers against the legislation of Parliament, but genetically, that is, through participation in the making of laws. The English theory is, however, not really indifferent toward the structure of the concept of law (cf. Dicey's famous *Introduction to the Study of the Law of the Constitution*).[26] The German theory of law had little interest in the genesis of laws and concerned itself with the interpretation of positive laws regardless of their origin. The English middle classes took an essentially political interest in the genesis of laws. The German theory is liberalist-constitutional; the English theory is democratic-constitutional. The English bourgeoisie expressed its preference through the medium of Parliament; the German bourgeoisie found the laws of constitutional monarchy in existence and systematized and interpreted them in order to secure a minimum of economic liberty in the face of a more or less absolute state. In the English theory, therefore, there is no serious discussion about the formal structure of laws, whereas, German theory is replete with investigations into the nature of law.[27] The German theory, in the views of its foremost representative, Paul Laband, whose ideas also became those of the dominant circle of legal theorists, clearly manifests the political weakness of the German bourgeoisie.

After 1848 the independence of the judge was no longer contested. He applied the laws literally. Discretion, which is most visible in "general principles" (*Generalklauseln*), plays no role. In the first thirty volumes of decisions of the Supreme Court, "general principles" are hardly ever mentioned.[28] The police article of the *Allgemeine Landrecht,* the most important "general principle" of administrative law, likewise had fallen into oblivion. As late as 1912 the Second Congress of German judges adopted the following resolution:

> (1) The power of the judge is subordinated to the law. The judge, therefore, is never allowed to deviate from the law. (2) Ambiguity of the content of a law does not entitle the judge to decide according to his own discretion; doubts are to be dissolved by interpretation of the law with regard to its meaning and purpose, and, wherever possible, by analogy. (3) If a law is subject to divergent interpretations, the judge has to give preference to that interpretation which corresponds best to legal understanding and to current social needs.[29]

This attitude of the judges toward the law during the period of William II is understandable. The state, then, knew how to retain its influence over the judge despite the latter's independence. The social position of the judge was definitely fixed. He began his career as a reserve officer and thus learned the significance of obedience and discipline. Chief justiceships and court presidencies were almost exclusively filled by former state attorneys, who, in contrast to the judges, had previously been public officials controlled by orders from above. Having become court presidents, they still knew how to fulfil the wishes of ministers, even when these were not distinctly expressed. Finally, the Prussian judge, especially if compared with his English colleague, was a poorly paid official. He had to wait for years before he was finally appointed, so that only members of the moderately well-off middle classes could afford to enter the profession. The judge of this period exhibited all the characteristics of the class of his origin: resentment against the manual worker (especially when he was organized and well paid), reverence toward throne and pulpit, and, at the same time, complete indifference toward financial capitalism and monopoly capitalism. The judges represented the alliance between crown, army, bureaucracy, landlords, and bourgeoisie. Their interests and those which sprang from the constellation of the above strata were identical, and since the laws corresponded to these interests, there was no reason to apply them in any but a literal manner. Neither was there any room for any kind of natural law. The German bourgeoisie was satisfied with its relations with the state. Judges and jurists no longer had to appeal to a natural-law system in order to fight a system of positive law which was hostile to them. Hence, both natural law and philosophy of law disappeared. Positivism was victorious not only as regards the application of law (in that respect it was progressive) but also as far as the theory of law was concerned, which amounted to doing away with all legal theory and uncritical acceptance of supine relativism. The complete repudiation of natural law during the second half of the nineteenth and the beginning of the twentieth centuries was most definitely voiced by Windscheid: "Yes, we do not mind saying it: The law which we have and which we create is not the law. In our eyes there is no absolute law. The dream of natural law has been dissipated."[30] This striving for legal security was sharply expressed by Karl Bergbohm when he remarked that whoever thinks of a law "which is independent of human creation" has been "corrupted" by the idea of natural law.[31]

Even though it represented the coalition of the ruling classes, the *Rechtsstaat* was not, however, a despotism. The generality of the law and the independence of the judge contained both elements transcending the functions of obscuring the actual distribution of power and the maintenance of calculability. The separation of powers was, it is true, not only an organizational division of powers; it was, at the same time, a distribution of political power among the various groups of that coalition. Yet this class rule was calculable, predictable, and, hence, not arbitrary. Furthermore, owing partly to the fusion of the Prussian-conservative proponents of the police state with large-scale industrialists and partly to the concessions that the state had to make to the proletariat which was increasing in strength, the poor and the workers benefited to a large extent from the rationality of law. This was all the more true after the development of a system of law permitting poor persons to sue without cost, which after 1918 experienced an extraordinary expansion and made the legal system of the Weimar period the most rationalized system in the world. It was rational not only in the sense of creating calculability but also in an eminently social sense, insofar as the advantages of rational law also benefited the working classes and the poor. This evolution represents a contrast to England, where even today a rationality which favors the status quo is guaranteed by the totally inadequate development of the poor law and by the fact that owing to the extraordinarily high costs of legal proceedings and the concentration of the administration of justice in the High Court of Justice the broader strata of the population are practically without legal protection. The legal system of the period under discussion thus centers around the following elements: personal, political, and economic liberties that imply the priority of these liberties vis-à-vis the state. The structure of the system may be summarized as follows:

1. The formal structure of the legal system. These liberties were guaranteed by formal, rational law, that is, by general laws and by their strict application by independent judges, by the rejection of legislation by the judiciary, and by the opposition to "general principles" (*Generalklauseln*).
2. The material structure of the legal system. This legal system was oriented, economically, toward free competition. It found expression in the auxiliary guarantees of private property and in the freedom of contract and enterprise.
3. The social structure of the legal system. Socially it was oriented toward a situation in which the working class did not constitute a serious threat.
4. The political structure of the legal system. Politically it was oriented toward a system in which the separation and distribution of political power prevailed: in Germany, toward a situation in which the bourgeoisie did not play a politically decisive role; in England, on the other hand, toward one in which the bourgeoisie determined the content of the law and in which the power of Parliament was distributed among crown, aristocracy, and bourgeoisie.

VI

During the period of monopoly capitalism, which in Germany began with the Weimar Republic, legal theory and legal practice have undergone a decisive change. To facilitate an understanding of these legal changes, it is more useful to consider the political structure of the Weimar democracy than to describe economic developments which have moreover been extensively treated elsewhere. The decisive political characteristic of the German republic was the significance of the workers' movement after 1918. The middle classes were no longer able to ignore the existence of class conflicts as the earlier liberals had done. They had rather to acknowledge this conflict and to try somehow to construct a constitution in light of it. Here, too, the contract was the technical means used since it alone makes possible the necessary political compromise. The contention that civil society originated the social contract implies the insight that contractual relations represent a deeply important component in the functioning of society. Modern society does, indeed, exist in large measure through contractual relations, and not only in the economic sphere. Powerful social groups unite, make their interests appear as the only legitimate ones, and thereby sacrifice those of the population at large. The formation of the German Republic laid bare the true function of the social contract. The Republic began with the following contracts: the most important one was the contract between Ebert, on the one hand, and Hindenburg and Groener, on the other hand (its conditions have been outlined by Groener as one of the witnesses of the "stab in the back" trials at Munich). This contract provided, on the positive side, for the reestablishment of "peace and order," and, on the negative one, for the fight against bolshevism.[32] The so-called Stinnes-Legien Agreement of November 15, 1918, was to effect the same result in the social sphere; employers promised not to tolerate "yellow" labor unions and to recognize only independent unions, to cooperate with them, and to fix working conditions by means of wage contracts. Actually this agreement not only meant the end of bolshevism but it also meant the end of the possibility of any kind of socialism and provided the basis of the system under which Germany lived from 1918 to 1930. On March 4, 1919, the Social Democratic Party of Berlin and the Reich government agreed on the introduction of factory councils and the legalization of their position in the Constitution. It was made clear that such factory councils would have nothing to do with the revolutionary workers' and soldiers' councils or Soviets. By the agreement of January 26, 1919, between the Reich and the federal states, the federal set-up of the Reich was preserved. The fifth and final contract (which really included all the preceding ones) between the three Weimar parties—the Center, the Social Democratic, and the Democratic parties—provided for the preservation of the old bureaucracy and judiciary, rejected the Soviet system, stabilized the political power of the church, sanctioned civil liberties, even though they were somewhat restricted by new social fundamental rights, and introduced parliamentary democracy.

The Weimar system has been called "collectivist democracy" because, ostensibly, the formation of political decisions was to be achieved not only through the summation of the wills of individual voters but also through the agency of autonomous, social organizations. The state was to remain neutral vis-à-vis these free organizations. To the extent that this occurred, the Weimar state fulfilled the program of political pluralism.[33] The sovereignty of the state was no longer to be exercised by an independent bureaucracy, by the police and the army, but was supposed to rest in the hands of the entire populace which, for this purpose, would organize itself in voluntary associations. This pluralistic system did not ignore the class struggle but attempted rather to transform it into a form of interclass cooperation. Hence, the Weimar democracy rested to a decisive extent on the idea of parity—a parity between social groups, between Reich and states, and between the various churches. Although this phenomenon occurred in its purest form in Germany, parallel tendencies existed in England and France.

A contractual system can exist only as long as the parties exist, as long as they desire to maintain the contracts, or if, in the event that they do not wish or are unable to fulfil them, there is a coercive agency which can enforce their execution. In Germany, however, the Democratic party disappeared almost completely. New parties—above all, the National Socialist Party—were founded which, by 1931, surpassed the old parties in numerical strength. The developing crisis made it impossible for the capitalistic partners to the contracts to fulfil their contractual obligations, especially those bearing on the maintenance of the social institutions. A neutral coercive power naturally did not exist, the idea of the neutral state being only a fiction. As already mentioned, in the sphere of public law as well as in that of private law, the contract necessarily produces power. In other words, the system of contracts, in the political sphere too, contains within itself the elements of its own destruction. The proponents of pluralism who seek to realize the "people's state" by reducing the part played by the independent bureaucracy, by the army and the police, and by handling the affairs of the state through agreements of voluntary associations, increase in reality the power of bureaucracy, reduce the political and social significance of the voluntary associations, and thus strengthen the tendencies which lead to the authoritarian state. In Germany, by 1931, the system of wage bargaining had almost ceased to function. While compulsory arbitration by the state was, according to the original intention, to come into play in the relations between employers and employees only when, in exceptional cases, the parties were unable to agree, state intervention actually became the normal case and voluntary agreements were reached only in order to avoid compulsory intervention. Moreover, structural changes in the organization of production and distribution—for example, the rationalization and mechanization of industry—had powerful consequences for the working class. The balance of power shifted and the decisive position of the old unions of highly skilled workers passed, on the one hand, to the foremen and other supervisory workers, and, on the other hand, to the large mass of unskilled and semi-skilled workers, who were more difficult to organize. This development, of course, impaired the power of the labor unions very considerably. They were further weakened by the economic crisis and by the strength of their monopolistic adversaries. Strike statistics demonstrate how little will to fight they retained. The equilibrium of the classes had found its constitutional expression in the second part of the Reich Constitution, which bore the title "Fundamental Rights and Fundamental Duties of the German Citizenry." There the old classical and the new social rights are juxtaposed in an unrelated manner, so that it was justifiable to say that the Weimar Constitution was a decisionless constitution.[34] Structural-economic changes in conjunction with the increasing impotence of Parliament added tremendously to the strength of the bureaucracy. The increment in strength was especially great in the case of the ministerial bureaucracy.

These changes in the economic and political structure were accompanied by profound changes in legal theory and legal practice.[35] It has been stated already above that, under the influence of Laband, German legal theory had discarded the concept of the generality of laws and had set up instead a division into formal and material laws. Suddenly, however, the postulate of the generality of laws was revived, particularly in the writings of Carl Schmitt and his school. Schmitt asserted that the term "law," as far as it had been used in the Weimar Constitution, referred merely to general laws, and that the Reichstag, therefore, could only create general laws. The legislative power of the Reichstag consequently was restricted by its inability to decree individual measures. In order to prove his thesis he referred to the historical developments mentioned above, and to Article 109 of the Weimar Constitution, which states that all Germans are equal before the law. The theory that the state may rule only through general laws applies to a specific economic system, namely, one of free competition. But it was exactly with respect to the economic sphere that Schmitt's theory indicated the postulate of the rule of general laws. The political meaning of this renaissance is not difficult to perceive. Schmitt himself developed this thesis at first for the purpose of showing that the laws providing for the expropriation of the German princes had been unconstitutional because they violated the principle of equality before the law and the postulate of the generality of laws. Yet Schmitt's theory presupposes that the principle of legal equality relates not only to the administration and the judiciary but also to the legislative power, that is, in Schmitt's opinion the principle did not mean only what it had meant formerly, namely, that promulgated laws must be dutifully applied by state officials regardless of differences in the status of citizens, without hatred, and without prejudice. For Schmitt it also meant that the principle binds the legislative power itself and prevents it from creating laws in which equal situations were differently treated. It is of course true than Haenel, the liberal constitutional jurist and politician, once supported this thesis in his arguments against Bismarck's laws expropriating the Polish minority. But his thesis had been universally rejected. Now this old idea was revived in order to add new checks to the sovereignty of Parliament in addition to those which were already provided by constitutional clauses concerning changes in the Constitution. Heinrich Triepel was the first to try to prove that the principle of equality would prohibit, in the case of the federal decree concerning gold balances, depriving stockholders of the value of their shares. Soon an enormous literature arose in order to prove that this principle of legal equality, at bottom, represented the basic fundamental right and that the Parliament was as much bound by it as were the administration and the judiciary.

But even if the principle of equality before the law is also supposed to be binding for the legislative, it does not at all follow that such equality is attainable *only* through general laws. The assertion that equality can be realized only by general norms is a reiteration of Rousseau's demand which, in his case, is reasonable and intelligible because he was discussing general law with reference to a society in which there was to be only small property or common property. Private property, which is sacred and inviolable, according to Rousseau, is property only to the extent that it remains an individual and particular right.

> If it is regarded as common to all citizens, it is subject to the general will [*volonté générale*] and may be infringed on or denied by this will. Thus the sovereign has no right to touch the property of one or several citizens. But he may legitimately seize the property of all.[36]

On the other hand, Rousseau also postulates the rule of general laws for situations in which property is socialized, as he has described it in his projected Corsican Constitution.

> Far from desiring that the state be poor, I prefer on the contrary, that it should possess everything and that individuals share in the common wealth only in proportion to their services.[37]

Thus Rousseau believed that the *volonté générale* could be expressed in general laws only in societies with equally distributed small property holding or with socialized property. The rule of law really obtains in Rousseau's system, and there is no room for force since in the social system which Rousseau postulated the state has no functions.

> Since individual property ownership is so slight and dependent, the government has little need for force and controls the citizenry with gestures of the finger, so to speak.[38]

In a monopolistically organized system the general law cannot be supreme. If the state is confronted only by a monopoly, it is pointless to regulate this monopoly by a general law. In such a case the individual measure is the only appropriate expression of the sovereign power. Such an individual measure neither violates the principle of equality before the law nor runs counter to the general idea of the law, as the legislator is confronted only with an individual situation. Thus in the economic sphere the general law presupposes economic equality within the capitalist class. German legislation between 1919 and 1932 did indeed create special measures with regard to individual monopolistic enterprises; the emergency decree of the president of the Reich of July 13, 1931, prohibited the application of the regulations concerning insolvency to the insolvent Darmstaedter Bank, and therewith ordered a special regulation for one powerful monopoly because only this one vital bank was in danger. The postulate that the state should rule only by general laws becomes absurd in the economic sphere if the legislator is dealing not with equally strong competitors but with monopolies which reverse the principle of the free market. The renaissance, under the Weimar democracy, of the notion of the generality of laws and its indiscriminate application to personal, political, and economic liberties, was thus used as a device to restrict the power of the Parliament which no longer represented exclusively the interests of the big landowners, of the capitalists, of the army, and of the bureaucracy. Now the general law, within the economic sphere, was used in order to preserve the existing property system and to protect it against intervention where such was regarded as incompatible with interests of the above-named groups.

Before 1914 the discussion concerning the formal structure of laws was exclusively theoretical, because, as has been stated, the examination of laws on the part of the judge (judicial review) was not permitted. Now these theoretical discussions became political questions of great practical importance because the German supreme court suddenly accepted the principle of judicial review. In its decision of April 28, 1921,[39] the supreme court asserted that it had always upheld its right of examining whether laws were constitutional—an assertion which, as the technical literature stated almost unanimously, was a sheer falsehood. At any rate, the recognition of judicial review represented a redistribution of power between state and society. The greater the power of the state, the more readily will the judge submit to its authority. The weaker the state, the more he will try to realize his private class interests. The recognition of judicial review operated favorably to the existing social order. This is unmistakably shown by an analysis of all those decisions which affirmed the court's power of review.[40] All these decisions dealt with the question of whether a particular law violated Article 153 of the Weimar Constitution, which guaranteed the security of private property. The supreme court likewise accepted the theory that the principle of legal equality bound the Parliament, so that "arbitrary" laws were to be considered as being unconstitutional. Thus, in both theory and practice Articles 109 and 153 of the Weimar Constitution served to prevent interference with the existing property system.

This recourse to the ideas of legal equality and generality is really a disguised revival of natural law that is now fulfilling counterrevolutionary functions. The older system of positivism would, in the period after 1918, have imperiled the position of monopolies because the positive legal order no longer corresponded with the interests of the monopolies. Hence the existence of a system of natural law was now openly discussed. Carl Schmitt, by adopting the American theory of the "inherent limitations upon the amending power," tried to distinguish between amending and violating modifications of the Constitution. He was of the opinion that amendments to the Constitution could not assail the "Constitution as a basic decision." Constitutional amendments might modify only certain aspects of the Constitution. The fundamental decisions regarding value preferences that the Constitution embodies, Schmitt thought, could not be modified even by the qualified parliamentary majority which had the power to amend the Constitution. The members of the supreme court were moved by a similar thought when, during a meeting in 1924, they commented upon the revaluation decree (which was the first emergency taxation decree). They decided:

> This notion of good faith [*Treu und Glauben*] stands beyond individual laws and beyond individual positive-legal provisions. No legal order which deserves this title of honor can exist without this principle. Hence, the legislator, by his power, cannot obstruct a result which is imperatively demanded by good faith [*Treu und Glauben*]. It would be a grave offense against the prestige of the government and the sense of justice if someone who based his claim on a new law would be dismissed by a law court because his appeal to the law violated the principle of good faith.[41]

The judges of the supreme court likewise announced that a contractor of a mortgage who would base his claim on the above-mentioned emergency taxation decree would lose his case because his defense against the mortgagee would have to be considered as violating the principle of good faith. James Goldschmidt, professor of criminal and civil procedure at the University of Berlin, supported the judges of the supreme court, and in order to prove the correctness of their decision he invoked the old principles of natural law and the right of resistance of the people against the unlawful exercise of power by the state.[42] Hermann Isay even went farther and conceded to the judge the right of examining each law as to its compatibility with the popular sense of justice. A vast body of literature was written on the subject, and a new kind of natural law seemed to be in the process of establishment.

However, a kind of secret natural law had been continuously applied throughout this period. The period from 1918 to 1932 was characterized by the almost universal acceptance of the doctrine of the "free law" school, by the destruction of the rationality and the calculability of law, by the restriction of the system of contracts, by the triumph of the idea of command over that of the contract, and by the prevalence of "general principles" over genuine legal norms. The "general principles" transformed the whole legal system. By their dependence on an extralegal order of values they negate formal rationality, give an immense amount of discretionary power to the judge, and eliminate the line of division between judiciary and administration so that administrative decisions—for example, political decisions—take on the form of decisions of the ordinary civil courts. Before the war of

1914–18 the "free law" school had conducted an energetic but hopeless battle against legal positivism.[43] According to this school, law is not exclusively contained in statutes and the legal system is not closed and free of gaps. The filling of these gaps, then, must be accomplished through legal norms, for the decision of the judge must be a legal one. And the norms must have a general character because the administration of law must follow the principle of legal equality. These norms are to be created by the judge, who has therefore not only the task of applying law but also that of creating it. This free-law theory of legal sources is usually connected with a new policy in the application of law. This postulate is most clearly stated in the famous pamphlet of Hermann Kantorowicz[44] and in the numerous publications of Ernst Fuchs. It demands that the freedom that must be conceded to the judge with regard to legal provisions must be as vast as possible so that the free discretionary power of the judge may be elevated to the rank of the basic principle of the application of law. These two aspects of the "free law" school, the theoretical and the political, must be strictly distinguished. To the extent that the "free law" school demands a new theory of the application of law, it demands the substitution of formal-rational law by "general principles." Kantorowicz, the founder of this school in Germany, in his later writings focused his attention more on the theoretical problems of the school. His disciples, however, who were less qualified in theoretical matters, dealt rather with its policy for the application of law and insisted, as in the case of Ernst Fuchs, that the German civil code contained only one good passage, namely, where it ceases its abstract treatment of cases and erects a signpost with the inscription "Entrance to the free sea of legal needs." This passage is Section 242, and for Fuchs it is the Archimedian point permitting the old legal system to be transformed. It was this practical aspect of the doctrine of free law which became dominant.

Before 1918 the "free law" school demanded discretionary power for the judge in order to infuse progressive ideas into a reactionary legal system. But already in 1911 Max Weber warned,

> [i]t is moreover not at all certain that the classes which today enjoy only negative privileges, particularly the working class, can expect the gains from an informal administration of law that the jurists assume will flow from it.[45]

In order to point out the function of "general principles" it is necessary to examine the fields of law where "general principles" are invoked and the functions they fulfil there. To begin, it may be stated that "general principles" are always invoked when the state is confronted by powerful private groups. Whenever parties which do not have the same rights engage in the exchange of goods and where one powerful party faces other less powerful private parties or the state, rational law ceases to obtain and "general principles" are resorted to. The decision of the judge then takes the form of a political or of an administrative order by which antagonistic interests are adjusted. This political order employs, however, the form of a court decision. It is interesting to investigate the utilization of "general principles" in the field of labor law which regulates the legal relations between employees and employers. The power of private groups is most clearly perceivable in the field of labor relations. According to German law, the legal admissibility of labor conflict was determined by the standard that is provided for in Section 826, BGB. This law provides that he who causes damage to someone else in a way that violates "good morals" is liable to the payment of indemnities. What violates "good morals" can never be decided in a universally binding way. The supreme court for many decades had employed the formula that those actions are contrary to "good morals" which contradict the sense of equity and justice of the whole people. This, of course, is a purely tautological definition which adds nothing to what the law has already expressed. A binding standard as to the legality of a strike is not attainable on this basis. An employer, at bottom, sees every strike as a disturbance of the sacred order, whereas an employee will regard no strike as a violation of "good morals." Every "concrete" formulation which the Reichsgericht has enunciated on this question is nothing but a reiteration of the tautological definition. Or, to discuss another difficult problem of labor law: if a worker accepts a lower wage than the contracted one, has he renounced the difference between the contracted wage rate and the wage actually paid? The supreme court always decided this question on the basis of Section 242, BGB, which provides that the debtor has to fulfil his obligation with regard to good faith (*Treu und Glauben*). The federal labor court consequently refused to decide unambiguously either way. It preferred to decide each case on the basis of the concrete situation, to take into account all details that might have been relevant—above all, the question of whether the worker, when he accepted the lower wage rate, had been subjected to "economic pressure." Another central question of labor law was the question whether a worker who is willing to work loses his claim for pay when the employer cannot put him to use for some such reason as technical disruptions, fluctuations in the market, or such social disturbances as a strike in his own or in another's factory. This question is, as such, clearly dealt with by Section 615, BGB, which provides that the worker in such cases may claim his wages, the legislators having intended to fasten the risks on the entrepreneur. Both supreme court and federal labor court declined, however, to apply the unambiguous norm of Section 615, basing their decision solely upon Section 242, BGB. In this case, too, the specific individual circumstances are to be taken into account in each case. Following this decision, the federal labor court developed a number of principles that were of extraordinary juridical and political significance. It declared the Factory Council Law had created a "working and factory community" between worker and entrepreneur and that, consequently, the worker is to share in the fate of the enterprise. If the enterprise is shaken in its foundations by some disturbance, the worker has to bear the whole or part of the risk. There is another principle that was developed on this occasion and which is of far-reaching importance. If a plant is slowed down or shut by a strike in another plant or by a strike of certain workers in the same plant, the claim for payment of wages on the part of workers who are prepared and willing to work is to be denied because of the bond of solidarity among all workers: the responsibility for any strike, therefore, must be attributed to every individual worker who is not working because of it. These are only a few examples from the very important field of labor law.

The rediscovery of "general principles" serves to destroy a system of positive law that had incorporated many important social reforms; it destroys the rationality of law. The structural changes within the economic system led to important changes in the functions of "general principles." Having formerly been stepchildren of law, they now become its darlings. Section 1 of the law against unfair competition prohibits the use of unfair methods of competition by merchants. This prohibition has definite and specific functions in a competitive economy. By prohibiting certain forms of advertising, the announcement of irregular clearance sales, etc., it secures equal opportunities for the competitors in a free market; this "general principle" is, therefore, an important element in a competitive economy. This is, however, modified in the instant at which a competitive economy is replaced by a monopolistic economy. This general principle ceases at this moment to be an instrument for the preservation of equal opportunities in a free market and becomes a means for establishing monopolistic control over the market. This functional change has an important bearing on the price-fixing of trade-marked articles. If the state sanctions the price-fixing among manufacturers of trade-marked commodities, and, moreover, threatens wholesalers and retailers who do not adhere to these price schedules with punishment, then the private price-fixing of the monopoly assumes a public character. Hence, the application of the "general principle" becomes a sovereign act of the state, which orders the consumers, who are dependent on the monopoly, to recognize and to put up with the price rules of the private monopolies.

The foregoing examples are intended to illustrate the proposition that "general principles" occupy a central role when competition gives way to monopoly. "General principles" support the power-position of the monopolies. However, this thesis must be qualified in one direction. From 1919 to 1931 "general principles" in labor law served to effect a compromise between enterprisers and workers. A precise analysis of all its decisions shows that during this period the federal labor court used "general principles" to effect a compromise between the antagonistic interests of capital and labor.

At that time the constitutional idea of parity among the various groups in German society still had the character of political reality. From 1931 onward, when the political influence of labor parties and labor unions was waning, the idea of parity became nothing but pure ideology, and "general principles" again became a means for giving sanction to the interests of capital.

The conclusion is justified, therefore, that in a monopolistic economy "general principles" operate in the interest of the monopolists. The irrational norm is calculable enough for the monopolist since his position is so powerful that he is able to manage without the formal rationality of the law. He can manage not only without rational law; frequently the latter operates even as an impediment to the full development or, if desirable for him, to a restriction of production facilities. For rational law, as has been pointed out, has not only the function of rendering the process of economic exchange calculable, but it serves at the same time to protect the weaker partner. The monopolist can do without the assistance of law courts. His power is a sufficient substitute for the judicial action of the state. Even when utilizing the form of the contract, his economic power enables him to impose upon consumers and workers all those rules that he deems indispensable and that the other parties are forced to accept if they want to continue to exist. The contracts of the monopolists burden the consumer with all imaginable risks, while the consumer himself has to fulfil all the obligations required by the law. The monopolist can force him to comply without appealing to the courts. Moreover, the monopolist tries to abolish the supplementary guaranties of private property in the means of production—namely, freedom of contract and enterprise—and to have the formal rationality of the law completely terminated. Freedom of contract comprehends the right of the outsider to remain out of a cartel, the right of a cartel member to retire from the cartel under certain contractual conditions, and, finally, the right of the employee to form unions. Freedom of enterprise permits any capitalist to establish competitive enterprises and to compete with the monopolies. Hence in the eyes of the monopolist these supplementary guaranties lose their value. They are consequently restricted or even completely abolished. The direct commands of the sovereign state, the administrative acts that directly protect the interests of the monopolist and restrict or abolish the old guaranties, now assume the function of a new auxiliary institution. The apparatus of the authoritarian state realizes the juridical demands of the monopolists.

VII

The significance of "general principles" becomes even clearer in the authoritarian state because all restraints are abolished which parliamentary

THE CHANGE IN THE FUNCTION OF LAW   133

democracy, even when functioning badly, had erected against the unlimited execution of the requirements of monopolies. The function of "general principles" is even extended. Thanks to their ambiguity, they served, in the period of transition, to bring pre-National Socialist positive law into harmony with the demands of the dominant group, and formally with the commands of the leader [Führer], to the extent that it had been in contradiction with these. Despite certain differences of opinion, National Socialism postulates that the judge is absolutely bound by the law. But the "general principles" enable decisions to be made in accordance with the dominant political opinions even where positive law contradicts them. For, in applying "general principles" the judge must not have to resort to his free discretion, since "the principles of National Socialism are the direct and exclusive authorities in the application and use of the 'general principles' by the judge, the lawyer, and the jurist."[46] Thus, the "general principle" is a means for realizing the political command of the leader against a contradictory positive law. Furthermore, National Socialist literature is entirely unanimous in holding that the law is nothing but the command of the leader for it is only due to the will of the leader that "prerevolutionary" law is valid. "All the political power of the German people is embodied in the leader. . . . All law emanates from him." The "leader of the ethnic group" is characterized by his attachment to the law of life of the ethnic community which he expresses by laws, decrees, and so on. It is this direct "administration" of law which appears "as a singular monstrosity to all those whose mode of thinking is still under the influence of the nineteenth century. To them 'law' can only be what is provided for by statutes, and they call law only that which Parliament as a so-called 'popular representation,' according to orderly proceedings, has decided on as law. Above all, it is inconceivable to them that even the highest judicial authority of the 'ethnic community' is embodied in the leader. They established their bourgeois *Rechtsstaat* under the auspices of the separation of powers and regarded the 'independence of the judge' in the face of the state as one of the most essential guarantees of their individualistic freedom. Yet history has definitely decided in favor of us Germans and against those disintegrating liberalistic principles. Today we know that the leader protects the law and that he, in a case of emergency, will immediately act in an executive capacity. The destiny of the whole community rests on his shoulders."[47] Numerous nongeneral laws having the character of privileges have been decreed. The principle that laws may not have retroactive force has been discarded. Even the fundamental principle of the *Rechtsstaat*, the principle of equality before the law, has ceased to be a rule of the National Socialist theory of law which, claiming to derive its theory from Hegel, seeks to base itself upon the "concrete personality"[48] and forgets that Hegel, although recognizing the purely negative nature of the principle of formal equality, was not in favor of discarding it. The independence of the judge has also been changed. Even if one disregards all extralegal interferences with the judicature, the repudiation of the general character of law reduces the status of the judge to that of a policeman. If law and the leader's will are identical and if the leader can have political foes killed without legal trial and this action is then celebrated as the highest realization of law,[49] then one can no longer speak of law in a specific sense. Law in this case is nothing but a technical instrument for the execution of certain political objectives; it is nothing but the command of the ruler. The legal theory of the authoritarian state is accordingly decisionism, and law is nothing but an *arcanum dominationis,* that is, a means serving the stabilization of power.

This, however, is not the juristic ideology of the authoritarian state. This is rather represented by "institutionalism" or, as Carl Schmitt calls it, the "theory of concrete orders and communities."[50] Institutionalism is distinguished from decisionism as well as from normativist positivism. We have already characterized the main tenets of legal positivism as including the proposition that law can be found only in statutes, that the legal system is free of logical contradictions and is consequently a completely coherent system of general norms, and that the judge has only to apply this system of norms so that, in spite of the fact that the application is effected by human beings, the norm prevails in all its purity. The principal concepts of this theory are (a) the legal person, which comprises as well the physical as the juridical person; (b) the subjective private rights, which express personal freedom based upon objective law (and the highest form of which is the right of private property); and (c) the contract, to which all human relations must be reduced, including the state and the club, marriage and sales agreement, church and labor union. According to the positivist theory, the state, too, was a legal person. The bearer of sovereignty was not social groups but the *Staatsperson* itself which acted through agencies. The individual possessed subjective public rights vis-à-vis the state.

The legal person is the economic mask of the property relationship. As a mask it covers the true face and obscures the fact that private property is not only a subjective right but is, at the same time, the basis of "master-slave relationships." The contract, being the auxiliary guaranty of private property, is a contract between free and equal legal persons. But this freedom and equality exists only in the legal sphere. The legal equality of the contractual partners hides their economic inequality. The labor contract in particular is a contract between the legally equal worker and entrepreneur. Its form does not reveal the fact that in actuality the entrepreneur is more powerful than the worker. The *Staatsperson* alone is supposed to be the bearer of sovereignty, and the positivist theory of the state refuses, therefore, to speak of the sovereignty of an agency or an organ. This theory obscures the domination of some men over other men.

Institutionalism proclaims itself as a progressive and "debunking" theory because it attacks the concept of the person and replaces it by the concept of the institution which does not hide differentiations as the liberal concept of the legal person does. Thus the two concepts of the *Staatsperson* and of sovereignty are eliminated.[51] The state becomes an institution like a parallelogram of forces; it becomes a community that rests organically upon communities of a lower order. The concept of sovereignty becomes superfluous because the power that is exercised by this state has ceased to be an external power. It is rather the power of the organized community itself. This power is supposed, moreover, to be subsumed under eternal natural law or under the "eternal law of life of the ethnic group."

Even more rigorous are the changes that the theory of property undergoes. For positivism the plant is the technical unit in which the owner produces and the enterprise is the economic unit through which he executes his business policy. Institutionalism transforms the plant into a "social work and factory community" in which the worker is not only an instrument of the entrepreneur but also "a living member of the working community of entrepreneurs and workers." The law regarding organization of national labor of January 20, 1934, legalized the foregoing definition of the federal labor court, the consequence being that the contractual relationship between worker and employer is replaced by the obligation of faithfulness which is derived from this community.

> Not the materialistic Roman *locatio conductio operarum* [sale of service] but the German legal form of a faith-contract [*Treue-vertrag*] determines the relation between employer and employee. It is not the reciprocal obligations of exchange but common work, work in the community and a common task and aim, which are decisive.[52]

This formulation, which does not consider the labor contract as a contract but as an organizational relationship or as a personal legal bond, was first put forth by Gierke,[53] who asserted that the labor contract is nothing but the continuance of the Germanic "faith-contract" (*Treue-vertrag*) between lord and vassal. Hugo Sinzheimer transposed this theory into the German labor law. The business enterprise, then, becomes a social organism, and the corporation is transformed from a union of legal persons with property into an institution. Property, briefly speaking, ceases to be the subjective right of a legal person and becomes an "institution," that is, a reified, objectified, and deindividualized social relationship. The contract is not only pushed aside in practice, as we have seen, but it also ceases to play a role in legal ideology. Rights and duties are no longer connected with the will of legally equal persons but rather with objective facts. What is decisive, now, is the status that man possesses in society.

The chief representative of institutionalism, Georges Renard,[54] summarized the institutionalist demands and opposed them to juridical positivism, which he calls Jacobinism. The core of institutionalism is the elimination of the legal person from the legal system, the separation of the institution from the legal person, and the absolutization of the institution. The concept of the legal person is supplanted by the "concrete legal status of the member of the ethnic community"[55] since the retention of the old liberal concepts would destroy the "ethnic community."[56] According to Renard, the institution is an organism or a legal structure that serves the commonweal. It is not a simple relationship; it is "existential." It is a unit, "a whole" in which the single individuals are integrated. "The institutional relationship is an internalization, a *consortium, invicem membra*." Thus the enterprise is divorced from the entrepreneur, the corporation from chairman and board. With the subjective public right, the person and sovereignty of the state disappear.[57]

How is this development to be explained? The legal principles of positivism certainly had a veiling function. The concept of the legal person doubtless is a social mask. But this mask only disguises; it does not eliminate its bearer, which can still be sensed behind the mask. In the period of competition it was not necessary that the proprietor should disappear since, as an individual, he did not exercise much economic and social power; for it was not the single individual but the totality of those individuals, that is, the system which exercised power over man. Under monopolistic capitalism, however, this power is concentrated in the hands of a few. If the mask were removed, the true situation would be revealed. In a monopolistic economy the power that is exercised by a few can be easily perceived. Institutionalism, as the legal theory of monopolism, eliminates this mask from the theory of law, but it also eliminates its bearer, the proprietor himself. One does not speak any more of proprietors but of plants and entrepreneurs. One discards the concept of the "person of the state [*Staatsperson*]." This concept, in the positivist theory of the state, disguised the fact that, in reality, a social group exercised the power that was attributed to the "person of the state." However, if political power is as strongly concentrated as is the case in the authoritarian state, then it is desirable that the concepts of the "person of the state" and of sovereignty be abolished and replaced by the concept of the community led by the leader. Henceforth the state is called a "formation" or "configuration" (*Gestalt*) and is called "the political configuration of the German people."[58] To the extent that commands, and not contractual agreements, become decisive, the legal theory of positivism disintegrates and is supplanted by institutionalism:

> If, during the last centuries, it was necessary for the continuation of economic life that promises were kept without continuous intervention of power, in the

meantime this necessity has become less important due to the progressive accumulation of capital. The ruling class has ceased to consist of numerous persons who conclude contracts, now it is composed of large powerful groups controlled by a few persons, which compete with one another in the world market. They have transformed vast areas in Europe into gigantic labor camps characterized by a rigid discipline. The more competition in the world market turns into a sheer struggle for power, the more rigidly organized will these labor camps become both internally and externally. The economic basis of the significance of promises becomes less important from day to day, because, to an increasing extent, economic life is characterized not by the contract but by command and obedience.[59]

Entirely disparate political theories have made use of institutionalism, including reformist theory, especially that of the trade unions, as well as the theory of the authoritarian state. This fact is indicative of the confusion that at present is characteristic of legal thought. It is indeed true that the theory of institutionalism seems to be more correct empirically than the theory of juridical positivism. That the plant, the enterprise, the corporation, and the monopoly are declared to be social institutions expresses the fact that property is no longer the private affair of the individual but has become a social institution in a specific sense. Institutions are, of course, more tangible than norms. Hence in Germany, France, and England this theory was adopted by progressive labor-unionism or collectivism. But actually this realism is only apparent because the institution is divorced from the context of power relationships without which it is unintelligible. Institutionalism tears institutions from their social context. Just because the concept of the institution has such a vague character, which can be expressed in such high-sounding sentences, just because it was divorced from social reality, institutionalism in Germany became the theory of social reform on the part of the trade unions. Particularly the theories of labor law of the various trade unions were based upon institutionalistic concepts. In England, especially under the influence of Gierke's theory of the association (*Genossenschaft*), conservatism as well as Fabianism employed the institutionalist concepts in order to reform the relationship between state and society. In France institutionalism is substantially neo-Thomistic and has been extraordinarily strengthened by the papal encyclical "*Quadragesimo anno*."

The legal theory of National Socialist Germany avoids the word "institutionalism" and, "in order to distinguish itself from neo-Thomism," prefers to call itself "the juristic-theory of order" or "the theory of community." It is supposed to be "configurational or structural thinking." National Socialism experiences this "configuration of things" in the activities of the monopolies. The close kinship between institutionalism and monopolistic capitalism was implicitly admitted by Carl Schmitt when he characterized Gottl-Ottlilienfeld's "theory of structures" as the truly appropriate German economic theory. Gottl-Ottlilienfeld, a leading German economist, eliminates the economically active individual entirely from his economic theory and replaces him by social structures which are either "elementary" or "instrumental" structures.

Hence, juridical positivism is eliminated from the legal theory of the authoritarian state; yet it is not replaced only by institutionalism. The decisionist elements are preserved and are enormously strengthened: first, by the elimination of the rational concept of law, and second, by the exclusive rule of the *political* concept of law. The reason is that the institutionalist theory is never able to answer the question of which institutions, in a given situation, are "elementary" and which are merely "instrumental structures"; neither is it able to state which acts of intervention and which type of regulation of institutions are "appropriate to the situation." Nor is it able to decide of itself what the "concrete status of the group-member" is to be. This decision must be made by the apparatus of the authoritarian state which utilizes the command of the leader as a technical means.

If the general law is the fundamental form of law and if law is not only *voluntas* but also *ratio,* then one must state that the law of the authoritarian state has no legal character. Law as a phenomenon distinct from the political command of the sovereign is possible only if it manifests itself as general law. In a society that cannot dispense with power as a principle, complete generality of law is impossible. The limited, formal, and negative generality of law under liberalism not only makes possible capitalistic calculability but also guarantees a minimum of liberty, since formal liberty has two aspects and makes available at least legal chances to the weak. For this reason there develops a conflict between the law and the liberties based thereon, on the one side, and the requirements of a monopolistic economy, on the other side. Under monopolistic capitalism, private property in the means of production as the characteristic institution of the entire bourgeois epoch is preserved, but general law and contract disappear and are replaced by individual measures on the part of the sovereign.

NOTES

1. This article is an abbreviated translation of "Der Funktionswandel des Gesetzes im Recht der bürgerlichen Gesellschaft," *Zeitschrift für Sozialforschung,* 1937, pp. 542–596. The translation and editing have been done by Klaus Knorr and Edward A. Shils. The article no longer fully represents the views that I hold, as will become apparent by comparison with the subsequent article "The Concept of Political Freedom."

Editor's Note: Neumann added this comment in 1953.

2. John Locke, *Second Treatise of Civil Government* (Oxford, 1948), chap. 12, sec. 147.

3. Thomas Hobbes, *Leviathan*. In *The English Works of Thomas Hobbes of Malmesbury*, ed. William Molesworth (London, 1839–1845), chap. 15, p. 145.
4. Hobbes, *Leviathan*, p. 204.
5. Benedictus de Spinoza, *Tractatus politicus* (Hilversumi, 1928), chap. 4, par. 5.
6. Spinoza, *Tractatus politicus*, chap 2, sec. 4.
7. J. J. Rousseau, *The Social Contract, and Discourses*, trans. G. D. H. Cole (New York, 1913), pp. 35 ff.
8. G. W. F. Hegel, *Philosophy of Right*, trans. T. M. Knox (Oxford, 1942), sec. 211.
9. Hegel, *Philosophy of Right*, sec. 5, suppl.
10. Hegel, *Philosophy of Right*, sec. 71.
11. Immanuel Kant, *The Philosophy of Law*, trans. W. Hastie (Edinburgh, 1887), p. 51.
12. William Blackstone, *Commentaries of the Laws of England* (New York, 1851), vol. 1, p. 44.
13. Rex v Crewe; ex parte Sekgome (1910), 2 K.B. 576.
14. Benjamin Constant, *Le Moniteur Universel*, June 1, 1928, p. 755.
15. Montesquieu, *L'Esprit de lois* (Paris, 1868), pp. xi, 6.
16. Cazalès, in *Archives parlementaires* (Paris, 1862–1919), ser. 1, vol. 11, p. 892.
17. Jeremy Bentham, *Works*, vol. 3: *General View of a Complete Code of Laws*, ed. John Bowring (Edinburgh, 1843), pp. 209–210.
18. Maximilien Robespierre, in *Archives parlementaires* (Paris, 1862–1919), ser. 1, vol. 20, p. 516.
19. "One individual must never prefer himself so much even to any other individual as to hurt or injure that other in order to benefit himself though the benefit of the one should be much greater than the hurt or injury of the other." Adam Smith, *The Theory of Moral Sentiments* (Boston, 1817), vol. 1, pt. 3, chap. 3, p. 564. Further: "In the race for wealth and honors and preferment, each may run as hard as he can and strain every nerve and muscle in order to outstrip all his competitors, but if he should jostle or throw down any of them, the indulgence of the spectator is entirely at an end" (vol. 1, pt. 2, sec. 2, chap. 2).
20. "*La liberté consiste à ne dépendre que des lois.*"
21. F. J. Stahl, *Rechts- und Staatslehre*, 3d ed. (n.d.), vol. 2, pp. 137–146.
22. Rudolph Gneist, *Der Rechtsstaat*, 2d ed. (1872), p. 333.
23. Robert von Mohl, *Geschichte der Literatur der Staatswissenschaften* (Erlangen, 1855), vol. 1, pp. 296 seq.
24. Otto Baehr, *Der Rechtsstaat, eine publicistische Skizze* (Cassel, 1864), pp. 1–2.
25. Karl Welcker, "Staatsverfassung," in *Das Staats-lexikon*, ed. Karl von Rotteck and Karl Welcker (Hammerich, 1834–1843), vol. 15.
26. A. V. Dicey, *Introduction to the Study of the Law of the Constitution* (London, 1915).
27. On the German theory, the best discussion is in Raymond Carré de Malberg, *Contribution à la théorie générale de l'Etat* (Paris, 1920), vol. 1.
28. See J. W. Hedemann, *Die Flucht in die Generalklauseln* (Tubingen, 1933).
29. Quoted in E. Forsthoff, "Zur Rechtsfindungslehre im 19 Jahrhundert," *Zeitschrift für die Gesamte Staatswissenschaft* 96 (1935): 63.
30. Bernhard Windscheid, *Recht und Rechtswissenschaft* (1854), p. 23.
31. Karl Bergbohm, *Jurisprudenz und Rechtsphilosophie* (Leipzig, 1892), p. 131.

32. *Der Dolchstossprozess in München* (Munich, 1925), p. 224.

33. H. J. Laski, "The Pluralistic State," in his *Foundations of Sovereignty and Other Essays* (London, 1931), p. 232 seq.

34. O. Kirchheimer, *Weimar und was Dann?* (Berlin, 1930). [Published as "Weimar—and What Then?" in *Politics, Law and Social Change: Selected Essays of Otto Kirchheimer,* ed. Frederic S. Burin and Kurt Shell (New York: Columbia University Press, 1969).]

35. This is based upon an analysis of the following: Hedemann, *Die Flucht in die Generalklauseln*; H. Heller, in *Veroeffentlichungen der Vereinigung der Deutschen Staatsrechtslehrer,* no. 4 (1928); H. Isay, *Rechtsnorm und Entscheidung* (Berlin, 1929); C. Schmitt, *Verfassungslehre* (München, 1928); H. Triepel, *Goldbilanzenverordnung und Vorzungsaktien* (1924); F. Dessauer, *Recht, Richtertum und Ministerialbuerokratie* (Munich, 1928); O. Kirchheimer, *Grenzen der Enteignung* (Berlin, 1930).

36. J. J. Rousseau, *Emile* (London, 1911), bk. 5.

37. J. J. Rousseau, *The Political Writings of Jean Jacques Rousseau,* ed. C. E. Vaughan (Cambridge, 1915), vol. 2, p. 337.

38. Rousseau, *The Political Writings of Jean Jacques Rousseau,* vol. 2, p. 355.

39. Official collection, vol. 102, p. 161.

40. Vol. 102, p. 161; vol. 111, p. 320; vol. 103, p. 200; vol. 107, p. 370; vol. 109, p. 310; vol. 111, p. 329; Kirchheimer, *Grenzen der Enteignung* (Berlin, 1932); vol. 111, p. 329.
Editor's Note: These seem to refer to the published proceedings of the German Supreme Court.

41. *Juristiche Wochenschrift* (1924): 90.

42. *Juristiche Wochenschrift* (1924): 245.

43. Eugen Ehrlich, *Freie Rechtsfindung und freie Rechtswissenschaft* (Leipzig, 1903), and *Grundlegung der Soziologie des Rechtes* (Munich, 1913).

44. Hermann Kantorowicz, *Der Kampt um die Rechtswissenschaft* (Heidelberg, 1906).

45. Max Weber, *Wirtschaft und Gesellschaft* (Tubingen, 1922), vol. 2, p. 511.

46. Carl Schmitt, *Fünf Leitsätze für die Rechtspraxis* (Berlin, 1933).

47. Hans Frank, in *Zeitschrift der Akademie des deutschen Rechts* 4 (Jahrgang, 1936): 290.

48. Karl Larenz, *Rechtsperson und subjektives Recht* (Berlin, 1935), p. 9.

49. Carl Schmitt, "Der Führer schützt das Recht," in *Deutsche Juristen-Zeitung* (1934): 945.

50. Carl Schmitt, *Über die drei Arten des Rechtswissenschaftlichen Denkens* (Hamburg, 1934).

51. Reinhard Höhn, *Die Wandlung im staatsrechtlichen Denken* (Hamburg, 1934); Leon Duguit, *Droit constitutionnel* (Paris, 1907).

52. R. Dietz, *Gesetz zur Ordnung der nationalen Arbeit,* 4th ed. (Munich, 1936).

53. Otto von Gierke, "Die Wurzeln des Dienstvertrages," in *Festschrift für Heinrich Brunner* (Berlin, 1914), pp. 37 ff.

54. Georges Renard, *L'Institution, fondement d'une rénovation de l'ordre social* (Paris, 1931).

55. Larenz, *Rechtsperson und subjecktives Recht,* p. 225.

56. E. R. Huber, "Die Rechtsstellung der Volksgenossen," *Zeitschrift für die gesamte Staatswissenschaft* 96 (1935): 448.

57. Reinhard Höhn, *Staat und Rechtsgemeinschaft*; Thomas Maunz, "Das Ende des subjectiven öffentlichen Rechts," *Zeitschrift für die gesamte Staatswissenschaft* 95 (1934): 656 and 96 (1935): 71.

58. E. R. Huber, "Die deutsche Staatswissenschaft," *Zeitschrift für die gesamte Staatswissenschaft* 95 (1934): 28.

59. Max Horkheimer, "Bemerkungen zur philosophischen Anthropologie," *Zeitschrift für Sozialforschung* 4 (1935): 14.

FIVE

State Structure and Law in the Third Reich

Otto Kirchheimer

THE RULE OF LAW AND JUDICIAL INDEPENDENCE

To what extent traditional views of the rule of law are reconcilable with the essence of National Socialism remained a controversial issue in German legal thought and practice for a considerable period of time. But after the authoritative comments by Minister of the Reich, Dr. Frick, Reich Law *Führer* and Minister of State, Dr. Frank, the Secretary of State for the Chancellory of the Reich, Dr. Lammers, and Secretary in the Reich Ministry of Justice, Dr. Freisler, all practical reservations against conceiving the National Socialist state as embodying the ideals of the rule of law dissipated. Theoretical clarity concerning how we are to understand the National Socialist version of the rule of law, the so-called "German *Rechtsstaat* of Adolf Hitler," can be gained in particular from the writings of a member of the state council, Professor Carl Schmitt. A penetrating examination of the history of the nineteenth century seems to have taught Schmitt that the rule of law was merely a clever construction of the ruthless and unscrupulous individualism of the liberal epoch. To demonstrate that the rule of law functioned merely as a pretence for security and calculability, he relies on old Rothschild's remark to the effect that whoever wants to sleep peacefully needs to buy Prussian government bonds. The predictability of law, as Max Weber demonstrated, provided the basis for the functioning of a developed commercial capitalist social order. All acquired social positions were protected by a legal referent, the development and potential riskiness of which was calculable to all parties in advance. This hollow law-based state [*Gesetzesstaat*], which acknowledged the existence of reciprocal obligations between citizens

---

Editor's Note: Originally appeared as a brochure, published under the pseudonym of Dr. Hermann Seitz, that was smuggled into Nazi Germany in 1935.

and the state, now has been superseded by the National Socialist version of the rule of law. The technical concept of the rule of law henceforth takes on an altered significance. The rule of law of old Rothschild was identical with a form of society organized according to the principles of competitive capitalism. It was the function of the state to place an elaborate and minutely composed legal order at the disposal of individuals in pursuit of their rights. Society was proud that the legal order and the coercive apparatus resulting from it was, at least theoretically, at the disposal of every citizen in a nondiscriminatory fashion.[1]

The transition from competitive to monopoly capitalism meant that the need for such legal forms tended to vanish. Large capitalist firms—large banks as well as monopoly concerns—long ago ceased to depend on court proceedings in order to conduct their affairs with members of other social groups. Because they could announce a ban on lending or could simply rely on the fact that they employed an army of hirelings, they came to dominate the government. Governments fulfilled the particular needs of these firms by means of statutes and emergency decrees. A number of developments rendered the traditional court system virtually meaningless: the economic crisis made it questionable whether legally binding claims would be fulfilled, the government tended to hinder legal foreclosures even of relatively sizable agricultural properties, and the responsibility of paying off foreign debts ultimately no longer depended on the legal validity of a judicial decision but rather on decisions made by administrative bodies concerned with the operations of the foreign exchange market.

Even those activities that traditionally belonged to other areas of the law now take a different form. First, the economic crisis generated a purely quantitative increase in the activities of the criminal courts and thus dramatically reduced the significance of traditional legal protections. The criminal courts then took over a new set of activities: the elimination of all political opponents, undertaken in conjunction with the realignment of all judicial activity with the political ideals of National Socialism. In this way, the face of the criminal justice system was decisively changed.

Even before the seizure of power by the National Socialists, unemployment and the attack on the labor union apparatus had already limited the scope of labor court activity. The process of replacing marxist-oriented workers with followers of National Socialism occurred uninhibited by the labor courts. The demise of collective labor law litigation—the regression of labor law to a system befitting the regulation of personal service (*persönliches Dienstrecht*)—has totally eliminated law from an area of social life into which it had first made its way during the Weimar period.

After National Socialism tried anew to stabilize the hegemony of monopoly capital and big landed property, the National Socialists proceeded to furnish the new situation with an appropriate timely ideology. Traditional views of law underwent a fundamental revision. The restriction of law to an ethical minimum was abandoned, and the identity of law and morality has been elevated to a guiding principle of the new order. In practical terms this meant the following: now that the affairs of the state's dominant social strata are regulated by means of the Führer's statute or by means of direct agreements between the bureaucracy and monopoly capital, the National Socialists want to provide the middle and poorer social strata with the illusion that for them as well there is an escape from the monotonous misery of their everyday existence; there is a right to satisfy their individual needs that is found outside the text of the law. The National Socialists are trying to trace the growing impoverishment of ever-broader social strata in part back to the failure of formal law to permit the recognition of the masses' legitimate demands on the entire nation. Law—in particular, much-maligned Roman law—hence gets blamed for conditions caused by unemployment, economic decline, and monopoly capital.[2]

Auxiliary legal means (*juristische Hilfsmittel*) were supposed to enable the generous use of vague legal standards (*Generalklauseln*), in accordance with the principle of "good faith" (*Treu und Glauben*). A vehicle for a newly awakened natural law, vague legal standards did in fact offer the possibility of stripping the whole law of its normative and obligatory character without requiring the alteration of a single positive legal statute.[3] Embodied in a novel version of the doctrine of judicial independence, a new dynamism has seized control of German legal thought and practice. After being purged of those elements hostile to National Socialism, the irremovability of the judiciary was freshly secured. But this type of judicial independence, as many have correctly noted, is no longer comparable to the type of independence previously possessed by the judiciary. Independence formerly meant the freedom of judging on the basis of statutes while at least trying to maintain neutrality in relation to distinct social and political groups. The new form of judicial independence is characterized by the fact that law at any juncture can be changed by the Führer and retroactively canceled at any point in time, without any legal formalities having to be respected. Furthermore, as shown above, law is only valid provided its "conformity with the National Socialist worldview." "In the National Socialist way of thinking, a certain instinctive political sense is a presupposition even of judicial independence. It implies independence in one's attachment to the main principles of the folk-based state of the Führer."[4]

Whereas the rule of law once represented a quest for objectification by means of legal guaranties and the formulation of clear standards, an opposing ideal is now transformed into the quintessence of Adolf Hitler's German rule of law. Guarantees of justice are no longer located in the statute, but in the extent to which the individual decision accords with National Socialist thinking.

What consequences does this have for specific areas of the law?

MATERIAL AND PROCEDURAL CRIMINAL LAW WITH REGARD TO THE QUESTIONS RAISED AT THE ELEVENTH INTERNATIONAL PENAL AND PRISON CONGRESS[5]

Domination by National Socialist modes of thought was achieved much more swiftly and radically in the realm of criminal law than in other legal fields. Even before the complete reworking of criminal law could be engineered, National Socialism attended to the elimination of the final remnants of "folk-destructive liberalism" from the penal law. It also made sure that the most important National Socialist lines of thought were put into practice. An "outmoded concept of legal security with its emphasis of bourgeois calculability, which in no way corresponds to the type of human being now created by National Socialism," was dropped from the administration of criminal law.[6] National Socialist criminal law is organized according to two basic ideas: the protection of the German folk's "present roaring, intoxicating life and its future," and the tearing down of all barriers that might hinder the court's attempt to achieve material justice.[7]

In particular, the criminal trial has undergone comprehensive reforms. These reforms aim to ensure that the concerns of the individual and individual protections are forced to recede behind the interests of the government and of "material truth" [*materielle Wahrheit*]. But this poses a serious dilemma both for criminal law and the procedures of the criminal trial. What is material truth in the context of criminal law? In his widely heeded *Politische Strafrechtswissenschaft,* one of the most well-known contemporary German criminal law experts argues for the "necessary alignment of the institutions of criminal law with the principle of political consistency." Yet we need to ask whether methods "based on the principle of political consistency"—that is to say, methods corresponding to the interests of the political and social elite—can still serve the quest for material truth. It has become quite customary to interpret procedural guarantees of the criminal law that are now being liquidated purely from the standpoint of the individual. But that is clearly inadequate. For criminal trial procedures—the guarantee of having a defense, or a hearing of the evidence, for example—are primarily supposed to provide a complete picture of the facts and thus knowledge of the material truth.

Perfect justice is no abstract ideal in the legal world of National Socialism. Instead, National Socialism identifies perfect justice with its interpretation of the vital life interests of the German folk, thus rapidly descending from the heights of an abstract ideal to the subordination of the coercive tools of criminal law to the political goals of National Socialism. "We know that the essence and purpose of the criminal law cannot be recognized independently and in isolation. Rather, they have to be seen as emanating from the highest political principle forming the state in question."[8]

The first result of the subjection of justice to politics is the expansion of the sphere of penal law. The protective functions of criminal law are being sacrificed to a drive toward greatly expanding its sphere of application. This is taking place even though countless new individual regulations have created some new criminal offences and have made the punishment for existing offences more severe during the past two years. The explicit introduction of analogous legal reasoning[9] is not only likely to have practically unforeseeable consequences, but it undermines the very foundations of judicial procedure. The new wording of paragraph 2 of the criminal code— "Punishment is to be inflicted on anyone who commits an act which has been declared punishable under the law or who deserves to be punished according to the fundamental principles of a criminal statute and healthy popular sentiment"—at first seems to suggest that only analogous reasoning in reference to a legal statute [*Gesetzanalogie*], but not in reference to the spirit of the legal system as a whole [*Rechtsanalogie*], is intended by the alteration of the criminal code. An act can be punished when it conflicts with the basic idea of an existing statute but cannot be subsumed under a precisely formulated definition of the criminal offence. First of all, the practical necessity of a determination of this type—which, by the way, is unknown in other central and western European countries—is questionable. In an authoritarian state where the Führer can issue any laws he deems appropriate at any time, any demonstrable lacuna in the law can be immediately filled. In addition, the express wording, which explicitly refers to the "healthy popular sentiment," does not seem to eliminate reliance on analogous reasoning in reference to the legal system as a whole. This second type of analogous reasoning does not simply consist of applying a legal statute to a situation that seems equivalent to that referred to in a statute; instead, it leads to legal deductions that generate entirely new criminal offences based merely on National Socialist ideology. It constitutes an authentic example of judicial legislation, and its introduction into any political system anywhere would signify that the judiciary had become a political authority. If tomorrow German judges decide to punish racially mixed marriages on the basis of the new criminal code, even though existing laws only have illegalized them for civil servants and members of the armed forces, they are acting as legislators and not as judges. Their independence—which until now was seen as resulting from the fact that they were strictly bound to the letter of the law—is thereby destroyed. The judiciary is required to take into account National Socialist ideology not only as it has been imprinted into the structure of the legal statute. Even more significantly, courts are supposed to comply with everyday political currents, "healthy popular sentiment," as they have been interpreted by politicians of the ruling party. Of course, in the totalitarian state "healthy popular sentiment" is simply what the Führer takes it to be.

National Socialism waited until June 1935 before explicitly legislating the abolition of the principle of *nulla poena sine lege*.[10] But it tossed another equally important and universally respected legal guarantee of individual freedom overboard as soon as it gained power: the prohibition of retroactive laws. It is revealing that the Eleventh International Congress of Criminologists will only be concerned with the issue of retroactive laws to the extent that a *liberalization* of criminal punishment is in question.[11] From the perspective of a forum of international jurists, the mere possibility of making criminal punishment more *harsh* by means of retroactive criminal penalties is simply inconceivable. Merely to discuss it would mean robbing all of European criminal law of its most basic foundations. It would mean applying an inherently unjust standard to lawbreakers, a standard that, at the time an act was committed, not even the highest court or most powerful judicial authority would have considered justified.

National Socialism, however, has been infringing on precisely this universally accepted legal ideal since March of 1933. Only on the basis of a punishment that was retroactively made more severe was it possible to condemn van der Lubbe to death and then execute him.[12] Only with the help of such murderous legal constructions—the very possibility of which the International Criminologists' Congress refused to discuss—was it possible to execute political opponents; jurists of the Third Reich someday will have to answer for these deaths. Even if we forget for a moment that many have been condemned to death and hanged even though *fact-based* findings simply could not be made, we still must deal juristically with a situation where laws from 1933 to 1935 were applied to acts that took place between 1930 and 1932. An act that would have been treated as a disturbance of the peace before Hitler's seizure of power or, if the necessary set of causal relationships could be proven, as an assault having fatal results, at the very most would have been punished with a prison sentence. Now, the very same act is punished with death. At times the courts are punishing "offences" that are alleged to have taken place years before Hitler's seizure of power. The mere fact that the prosecution's proceedings against many who are now condemned to death were originally abandoned proves that the instruments of a regularly functioning judiciary were not able to prove anything against them. Just to mention a few examples, this is how

> Twenty-one-year-old Paul Foelz and nineteen-year-old Ewald Szody were condemned to death on July 24, 1933, for an incident that took place on May 12, 1932;
> Ernst Sander was condemned to death in Hamburg on December 23, 1933, because he allegedly killed a policeman on December 3, 1930;
> Twenty-year-old Joseph Reitinger was executed on November 21, 1934, because he allegedly shot a member of the SA on June 4, 1932;

A member of the Reichsbanner, Karl Jänicke, was hanged on July 5, 1935, because SA members claimed under oath that he shot a member of the SA in a clash with them on March 28, 1931;

Johannes Becker from Kassel was hanged on December 7, 1935, because he allegedly shot a policeman on June 12, 1931.

The tendency to focus less and less on visible features of the offence than on the *will* of the perpetrator is noticeable both in the revised edition of the criminal code and in several special laws establishing new political offences. The partial justification for this is that it corresponds to the special nature of the Aryan conception of law that the will, and not the act, is at the core of investigation; moreover, reference has been made to the fact that a writer of a related Aryan people titled one of his works *Crime and Punishment* and not *Act and Punishment*.[13] But here as elsewhere, arguments based on a vague concept of race simply function to veil the true state of affairs. The bourgeois legal system is anachronistic not because it is the product of Roman legal traditions and Jewish intellectual influence, but rather because it is the expression of a capitalist social system that has reached its final stages. Similarly, we should hesitate before interpreting the unchecked growth of subjectivistic theories of criminal law as a renaissance of Aryan customs and mores. Instead, this trend constitutes a desperate defensive measure by a universally threatened social order that fancies it can gain security by making maximal use of the criminal law.

The introduction of the volitional concept of penal law (*Willensstrafrecht*), emphasizing the criminal will rather than a concrete act, simultaneously serves to isolate individual will and to deny the roots of criminal behavior in social conditions. It used to be a general maxim of the criminal law that the extent to which a person's capacities and resources allowed him a real chance of respecting the statute should be taken into consideration; now the social situation of the accused is ignored completely. The principle of "you can, because you shall"[14] is established. In the process, the criminal law is clearly founded on the interests of the dominant class, instead of an understanding of the actual opportunities that are provided to individuals by the existing social order. As a result, the penal law's remedial functions are eliminated from the very outset. If the rules of the penal law serve nothing but the preservation of a system of domination in which conformity to civilized norms is only possible in exceptional cases, then the criminal law's remedial aims have been rendered null and void. In that case, the penal law is nothing but a form of pure repression directed against social, religious, and political foes. So, the first question discussed in Section II of the International Criminologists' Congress is answered with a resounding "no" in Hitler's Germany.[15] The argument made in an authoritative article in the

Völkischen Beobachter from December 2, 1934, refers to the combative character of National Socialist criminal law: criminal law should not simply react to illegal actions, but should additionally ensure that all hostile political groupings are eliminated by a permanent series of purges. This is an open admission that the volitional concept of criminal law is based on political revenge and thus transcends any penal concerns.

Even if we disregard such general objections against the recasting of penal law into a political weapon of the ruling political group, a number of serious reservations of a purely juristic nature regarding the application of the volitional concept of criminal law still remain. Its concrete meaning becomes most apparent in the manner in which the legal definition of an *attempt* (*Versuchsbegriff*)[16] has taken on inflationary characteristics and has been robbed of any basis in an objective determination of the facts of the particular case. Claiming that the best defense of the political order lies in fighting against attempted crimes[17] may sound impressive. But in reality it leads, as an author as enthusiastic about National Socialism as Oetker has noted, "to plague comrades who act in accordance with the law with doubts about whether or not their doings can be justifed or whether they are already violating penal prohibitions against placing others in jeopardy (*Gefährdungsverbot*); excessive regulations in this area are handicapping initiative and the motivation to act."[18]

It is important to note that initial applications of the basic principles of the volitional concept of criminal law have greatly damaged the international reputation of German legal practice. The fact that political opponents of the regime in Germany are sentenced to death merely on the basis of so-called intellectual authorship—where even the most minimal evidence of their actual participation in a criminal act is lacking—has not met with much understanding abroad.[19] Special damage is done to the reputation of the German judiciary when foreign civil servants have to deal with such theories. The Swiss Bundesrat, for example, was recently presented with a formal petition to extradite a former member of the German Parliament, the communist Heinz Neumann, who was accused of having committed murder. The act of murder—more precisely, the incitement to murder—was seen as demonstrated by the fact that Neumann had once allegedly talked about two police officers and asked whether "that pig is still alive?" Since the policemen to whom Neumann was referring were soon thereafter shot by unknown assailants, Neumann was accused of incitement to their murder, even though no argument was made that he had any connection to the murderers. Of course, the Swiss Bundesrat was forced to reject this rather mysterious application of the volitional concept of crime; it did not even bother to ask the upper federal court to take a position on the extradition request. In the face of such developments, it is no surprise that a prominent legal expert from Poland—a nation with such friendly ties to our own—feels forced to come to the following less-than-flattering assessment of the international reputation of German jurisprudence: "The period of contemporary lawmaking is undoubtedly diminishing the international interest in the reforms of the German criminal law."[20]

Apart from the sphere of politically oriented legal persecution, it is especially striking that reforms of the material criminal law since the so-called national revolution have not been characterized by the creation of new definitions of criminal offences. The alteration of legal clauses (as in the case of the reference to "breach of trust" in paragraph 266) has generated nothing objectively new in character. Such changes have merely provided pre-existing court practices with a legal sanction. On the contrary, the National Socialists have exercised great restraint in many important areas of the law such as, for example, in the corporate finance laws. The underlying intent there surely has most likely been to avoid placing excessive restraints on business initiative. Yet the recent Lahusen case,[21] which continues to unfold under the new regime (unfortunately employing very old window-dressing tactics), has proven that especially in this area of the law drastic reforms are needed.

While profoundly changing its spirit, the totalitarian state has generated an unprecedented boom in the legal persecution of political opponents. A law issued on May 26, 1933, broke with an old tradition by abolishing the punishment of political offences with a period of imprisonment (*Festungshaft*). According to Under-Secretary of State Roland Freisler, political disturbances must be seen as constituting particularly dishonorable crimes. For Freisler, the reason for this is that the state is "nothing but the expression of the *folk*, from which it originates and whose basic customs and morals the state is in agreement."[22]

It is difficult to consider it a moral victory for National Socialism that it has hammered into people's heads the idea that those with different political views are "subhuman." As far as the idea of a moral order under attack by political opponents is concerned, however, criminal law would do better to leave it to history to decide which political party or group can be rightfully identified with the moral order of the people. Although the discriminatory treatment of political prisoners unfortunately suggests that Freisler's view of the morally subhuman character of the political opposition is increasingly dominant, not everyone has accepted his view. For example, Zimmerl argues that since "heroic types"—one thinks of George Dimitrov or Ernst Thälmann—also make up the ranks of the political opposition, not all political opponents can be classified as "cowardly subhumans." According to Zimmerl, such individuals cannot rightfully be ranked alongside common criminals.[23]

The dominant interpretation of a politically motivated crime defines it according to whether the offence has been committed by followers of the ruling party or by its opponents. Whereas even the most minimal offence committed by the political opposition will be pursued and severely punished, followers of the ruling party generally go unpunished. Even when courts find them guilty, political allies of the regime are likely to gain a quick pardon or amnesty. The wording of the Criminal Immunity Law from August 7, 1934, was consciously formulated so that criminal offences committed by members of the ruling party, including the looting and physical abuse of defenseless prisoners, fall under the law as long as such acts occur "in the excessive zealousness of the struggle on behalf of the National Socialist movement." The possibility of gaining amnesty, however, is unavailable to the regime's political opponents. Amnesty is inapplicable to the most important political offences, treason and high treason, but it is also inapplicable to other offences "if the inspiration for the act reveals a vicious spirit." The National Socialist judicial system simply presumes that all expressions of political opposition fall under this category.

The scope of political offences has been expanded beyond all limits. Any activity of a political, social, or religious nature that is not expressly condoned by the government can be punished with a severe prison sentence or the death penalty. Judicial decision makers give themselves the widest possible freedom in the interpretation of criminal regulations that already are formulated rather broadly. This is how it was possible to punish participants of a recent Catholic youth meeting on the basis of government decrees issued against revolutionary communist acts that threaten the state (issued on February 28, 1933): the justification provided was that activities of the Catholic youth group might lead to such unrest that a revival of communist terrorism could thereby be promoted.

Another rather idiosyncratic feature of this type of legislation makes it possible to punish undesirable expressions of opinion even when their truthfulness can be demonstrated. The pertinent legal texts (the March 21, 1933, Decree for the Repulsion of Malicious Attacks Against the Government of National Renewal, as well as paragraph 90 of the Criminal Code, which deals with treason by inflammatory slander), refer to "slanderous claims that distort the truth." But the special courts (Sondergerichte)[24] fail to provide the accused with a chance of proving his assertions in his own behalf. Rather than undertaking a nonpartisan examination of the evidence of the case, the regime's view is automatically assumed to be truthful, and everything else is dismissed as slanderous claims that distort the truth. For the regime, even worse than the injustice done to the accused is that this approach permits no criticism of state authorities. Instead of channeling dissatisfaction by legalizing the most harmless forms of expression, the regime forces all discontent into the uncontrollable sphere of illegality. The criminal persecution of the political opposition in contemporary Germany hence is not subject to severe criticism simply from a liberal or humanitarian viewpoint; even from the perspective of Germany's ruling elite, its usefulness is limited. Legal procedures of this type are purely repressive, and they fail to perform any positive maintenance functions. It is well known that the success of a purely repressive system is very questionable in the long run.

Because they aim to secure the rights of the criminally accused, traditional criminal procedures are accused of embodying liberal ideals alien to the spirit of the German folk and state. The attempt has been made to obliterate all such "humanistic confusions" and to alter criminal regulations inspired by them. The formal law of evidence has been mostly done away with, the accused's possibilities for legal appeal have been limited substantially, and the prohibition on *reformatio in peius*[25] has been wiped out. Is the administration of justice improved by these changes? Is the investigation of material truth, which even the National Socialists take to be the central task of the penal law, served well by these trends? Experience has shown that courts and public prosecutors have no greater inherent skills than do any other bureaucratically organized institutions. But since the task of making decisions about the rights and welfare of their fellow human beings is both much more difficult and demanding of so much more responsibility than are the activities of most other bureaucratic instances, judicial authority traditionally has been outfitted with greater safeguards—most significantly, rights that are guaranteed to anyone whose fate is being determined by the courts. An American lawyer recently published statistics comparing the frequency of acquittal among the criminally accused who freely chose their own lawyers and among those given a public defender. He found that when the accused pick their own lawyers, the number acquitted is 40 percent higher than when the accused are forced to rely on a public defender. German criminal statistics do not permit us to determine with certainty whether the situation in Germany is identical. But anyone with practical experience in these matters will confirm that the results would be no different if a similar study were undertaken in Germany. Only the possibility of an effective legal defense, laws that demand the examination of all relevant evidence, and liberal possibilities for legal appeal make it possible to ascertain material truth in the courtroom. But to the extent that the judicial process becomes bureaucratized and nothing more than another instrument of administrative authority, and as the criminally accused is reduced to an object controlled by administrative power, the chances of ascertaining the material truth are substantially diminished.

When the delegates at the International Criminologists' Congress grapple with the second question of Section I of their meeting—"What measures are to be recommended in order to shorten the so-called monster trials?"[26]—they will have to take all the points mentioned in my argument into consideration. The abridgment of legal procedures can result in nothing but the curtailment of the rights of the criminally accused and the defense. In addition, it means increased power for the judicial bureaucracy to the point where it is outfitted with full discretionary authority. Regardless of how we attempt to define the concept of the "monster trial," it will always include trials that gain substantial public attention and that could for various reasons become unpleasant for ruling groups. The development of German criminal law described here should at least help show non-German jurists what measures are to be avoided if the judiciary in their respective countries is to be kept from regressing to arbitrariness and barbarism.

The destruction of all protections for the criminally accused does not exhaust the changes endured by German criminal procedure in recent years. In addition, court structure has been altered so that opportunities for popular participation in criminal proceedings have been extinguished. Representatives appointed by the ruling party replace jurors and lay assessors. This eliminates any influence on the criminal judiciary by the population at large; the judiciary becomes nothing but an apparatus of the party. In addition, every form of public control is eliminated. To the extent that the proceedings fail to offer possibilities for embarrassing dominant political, social, and military groups, they are allowed to maintain their public character. But there no longer is any independent court reporting. Instead, the judicial bureaucracy, with the help of the court's public relations department, makes the materials available to the court reporter, which he alone is allowed to publish.

Such conditions surely make it extremely difficult to ascertain material truth in the criminal process. But a set of additional conditions makes it virtually impossible to do so where *political* cases are concerned. First of all, the prosecuting authority in such cases is not the ordinary state prosecution operating in accordance with traditional bureaucratic imperatives; now it is the central state prosecution belonging to the Ministry of Justice, which receives its orders for every individual case directly from the government. Moreover, the police in such cases are no longer ordinary policemen, but members of the secret state police (Gestapo). The government is undoubtedly finding their services to be of exceptional value: they are permitted to use any methods they deem necessary to get the results sought by their supervisors. Whether they submit evidence, acquired by means of oftentimes suspect methods, to the state prosecutor and thereby initiate a trial or whether they simply stick the prisoner in a concentration camp without a conviction is left up to the discretion of the Gestapo. It is thus perfectly legitimate to conclude that political justice in Germany is primarily administered by policemen who punish the accused by means of discretionary powers and with methods unheard of in legislation elsewhere. Only if it happens to be opportune for them do they even bother to complete their investigations and hand the case over to a people's court (Volksgericht)[27] or a special court for an additional hearing. Even then, court proceedings take place on the basis of evidence gathered by the police by means of its rather impressive powers.

As for the people's court itself, it is an ad hoc appointed commission composed of administrative functionaries from the civil service, military and NSDAP and judges who have proven their trustworthiness to the regime. It autocratically decides how much evidence should be examined. Its decisions cannot be contested. Even the right to a lawyer of one's own choosing—the last remaining, though in itself inadequate, protection for the accused against a partisan instrumentalization of the penal law—has been made into a farce. In Hitler's state, the lawyer generally has the responsibility of representing the interests of his client only as long as they remain compatible with the welfare of the National Socialist regime. If the lawyer takes a step beyond these limits, he can count not only on being subjected to disciplinary action,[28] but also on a prison sentence having an indeterminate period of time. (An example of this is provided by the imprisonment of the Berlin lawyer Rötter, who could be accused of nothing except having announced that he was willing to defend the leader of the Communist Party, Ernst Thälmann, in court.) The law regulating the procedures of the people's court reveal in the clearest possible form this trend toward undermining any possibility of truly defending the interests of the accused. A defense attorney who not only has to ask for the court's permission to be allowed to take over a case, but then can be stripped of that right at any stage in the proceedings and without any reason having to be supplied, is robbed of any real autonomy and is hardly in a position to provide real help to his client. Hence, the people's court cannot be described as a court at all. The nature of its composition, its dependence on the preparatory work of the secret police, and the restraints it places on the counsel for the defense prove that the people's court is interested simply in eliminating political opponents, and hardly in an unbiased investigation of the facts of any particular case. The people's court is nothing but a politically motivated administrative body that has been outfitted with unlimited discretionary power over the fate of all German citizens.

Not only did the depression result in an increase in the prison population, it simultaneously led to substantial declines in the living standard of the imprisoned: the daily ration for the provisions of a prisoner in a Berlin prison amounts to 30 to 32 pfennig today in comparison to 50 to 60 pfennig in 1932. It is inconceivable that so many authors believe that this dramatic deterioration of the prisoners' living conditions is not simply a regrettable consequence of present economic conditions and that they celebrate it as a much-improved penal instrument that ought to be permanently employed.

Equally unfathomable is the apparently sadistic drive motivating State Secretary Freisler's quest for more severe methods of imprisonment. In his most recent book he makes a number of suggestions along these lines that have to sadden anyone genuinely concerned with the reputation of German law.[29] He justifies every attempt to make criminal punishment more unpleasant by referring to the imperatives of general prevention, to the need to deter the general population from crime. The pain suffered by the individual, resulting from a system of treatment that consciously abandons any educational aspects and is likely only to strength asocial tendencies and the desire to commit further crimes, is supposed to deter the remainder of the population from committing criminal offences. The fact that German prisons are crowded to an unheard-of degree demonstrates that the aim of Freisler's proposals has yet to be achieved. In Prussia the number of prisoners was 56,928 in 1933, compared to 37,982 who were imprisoned in 1932—in short, a 50 percent increase. State Prosecutor Schäfer's remarks in a speech given in Königsberg suggest that the number of prisoners has doubled since 1930, and his calculations do not even include the 49,000 individuals presently detained in concentration camps.

Just as unconvincing are those arguments that try to justify the ever more extensive use of the death penalty. Freisler believes that the death penalty's usefulness has been demonstrated by the fact that terrorism directed against the National Socialist regime has subsided since its introduction. This is misleading: he knows quite well that antifascists have disavowed murder as a political instrument as a matter of principle. Neither at the time of their proclamation nor today—as Freisler's own comments concede—has there been an adequate justification for the antiterror decrees. It should be impossible to understand even from the viewpoint of Friesler why the death penalty should be used against someone like Rudolf Claus, who simply chose to remain an active member in the proletarian self-help organization Rote Hilfe.

PUBLIC AND ADMINISTRATIVE LAW IN THE THIRD REICH

> Adolf Hitler resolutely marches forward with the task of leading the entire folk into the national community. Correspondingly, the folk is no longer the sum of all subjects; this would contradict the *Führerprinzip*. Instead, the people consists of the followers of the Führer on the way to the realization of the national community.

Certain difficulties have arisen from this undeniably more metaphysical than real view of the position of the Führer because it is hard to make juristic distinctions among his various announcements. In addition, the significance of the Führer's proclamations for the legal order often remains unspecified. Even today, the status of the so-called law that declared the actions of June 30, 1934, legitimate because they were committed during a national emergency is still unclear. It was necessary to refer to the metajuristic concept of the Führer in order to make the fusion of administrative execution, judicial decision making, and post facto justification in the form of an individual law—issued by the same authorities who made and then executed this judicial "judgment"—comprehensible.[30] Such difficulties are also evident in the debate about whether everyday political remarks made by the Führer can be distinguished from his legal statutes. In academic and bureaucratic circles, it is common to refuse to attribute a quasilegal binding character to each and every one of the Führer's statements because of "the confusion that would result in public life." Others would at least like to let remarks of the Führer supersede preexisting law. Evident in this dispute is a conflict between the conservative traditions of the state bureaucracy and the National Socialist Party's interest in political agitation. Parliament, where battles between distinct social and political interests were once played out, still meets, but only to receive the Führer's proclamations one to three times a year. (By the way, what do its 600 National Socialist members—who take home four or five times the income of the average "folk comrade"—really get paid for?) The Führer is all-powerful and sovereign; nonetheless, within the person of the Führer, different influences and tendencies intersect.

In the real world of the German Reich, the Führer is chiefly the leader of a civil war–based party that was able to seize control of the state apparatus by astutely exploiting the political crisis. The seizure of the state machinery is expressed in terms of public law by the installation of the leader of this party as the formally unlimited ruler of the German Reich. In addition, special privileges have been granted Hitler's "civil war army." With the help of the Law for the Restoration of the Civil Service,[31] leaders of this "army" were granted official posts in the state apparatus. The attempt was made to give the first 100,000 members of the party lower-level posts in the civil service that were vacant after marxist workers and employees had been chased away from their positions. An additional provision was allotted to "fighters for the National Socialist National Renewal" who suffered injuries in the battle against the banished marxists.[32] In order to offset excessive financial demands on government funds that might result from this initiative, the system of veteran's compensation was altered at the same time so that war-based injuries to members of oppositional political parties no longer guaranteed a right to compensation. Regulations of compensation for civil law claims (*Gesetz über den Ausgleich bürgerlich-rechtliche Ansprüche*) served to secure civil war booty in the form of houses, real estate, and newspaper businesses. The law confirms that "National Socialism does not even think of allowing the outcome of the events of January 30, 1933, to be taken away from it by means of a civil law dispute, or even by means of a judgment by default (*Versäumnisurteil*)."[33] In order to stifle any attempt to compete with the ruling party from the start, the organization of new parties has been illegalized. In order to suffocate any signs of opposition within the National Socialist Party itself, governmental legislation has established a system of internal party disciplinary courts. In addition, the strictest possible centralization of the entire organization of the party has been achieved. Only recently were the NSDAP's internal subdivisions and welfare organizations denied autonomy in the use of their financial resources. Their employment of these funds is now dependent upon the approval of the party's national treasurer.

But the legal presuppositions of the political hegemony of the NSDAP still fail to tell us anything about the social groups that exercise a predominant influence in governmental operations. Party Führer Hitler can only protect his party comrades' newly acquired sinecures and loot by joining ranks, as Führer of the political community as a whole, with Germany's dominant social groups. Alongside his rank as leader of the party, Hitler thereby becomes representative of the most powerful social interests. As long as they are willing to acknowledge the dominance of the party and of its leader, Hitler guarantees the unassailability of their economic resources. The army seems to be taking on an ever more significant role within this system of reciprocal guarantees and obligations. Juristically, this expresses itself in the fact that it is no longer possible for civilian authorities to intervene in the internal affairs of the army. Virtually as a reward for the army's positive attitude toward Hitler's ascent to governmental power, the old internal military courts were reestablished within the very first days of the Third Reich. As a way of averting party intervention in the army, the new military laws explicitly state that anyone who joins the army is required to suspend his membership in the NSDAP and in any related organizations for the duration of his stay in the military. If to all this the fact is added that in the Third Reich there no longer are elected parliamentarians in a position to scrutinize the military budget, it should be obvious why the outlines of a powerful, independent military apparatus—even more impressive than pre-1918 Imperial Germany's—are beginning to take shape.

In addition, Hitler is bound to support those social classes that promoted the rise to power of his party by many different forms of support; these groups still represent the most powerful social bloc in Germany. Hitler secures the inviolability of two guarantees of the interests of industrial and finance capital: the exclusive control over the means of production and the domination of wage labor. Admittedly, National Socialist writings maintain that the concept of property constitutes nothing more than an administrative function in National Socialism.[34] It is correct that in contemporary Germany the acquisition and maintenance of economic power no longer rests simply on the exercise of a formal-legal title to property. To a great extent, economic status now depends on government economic regulation and social policy. But in itself the fact that intervention takes place in the sphere of property is not crucial; rather, what is decisive is *how* this intervention influences the social power and the living standard of different social classes. When existing price controls no longer allow a salesman to establish a certain price by referring to the prospective costs of production, then the state undoubtedly is taking control of his working capital. When a worker is prohibited from joining a union in order to improve wage conditions, the state is effectively limiting the worker's use of his means of production, his labor power, while providing economic advantages to the worker's economic opponent, the entrepreneur, by means of the very same set of actions (controlling wages). When inheritance laws make it impossible for the farmer to take a mortgage and thus keep him from gaining credit on his real estate, then the state is similarly limiting his right to use his property as he sees fit. But has the National Socialist state infringed upon the basic structure of German heavy industry? On the contrary, has not the National Socialist state provided new instruments of power to heavy industry by means of legally sanctioned compulsory cartels? Has National Socialism changed anything fundamental about the system of industrial and agricultural feudalism? Has not the pursuit of the axiom of "a strong economy in a strong state" generated benefits for the rich and massive sacrifices from the unpropertied? (One only needs to think of how the new inheritance laws worked to the benefit of the wealthy, or how the government has abandoned legal proceedings against all so-called national elements who refused to pay their taxes as a way of accelerating the demise of the Weimar Republic.)

The establishment of the totalitarian state has also brought about the death of genuine municipal and local self-government. Municipal self-rule was totally abolished by means of the German municipal code of January 30, 1935, and mayors and mayoral deputies were reduced to government functionaries. Guaranteeing local party organizations certain, albeit rather limited, possibilities for political participation did not change this situation. Municipal councils are purely decorative. The relevant legislation unintentionally concedes this by explicitly requiring the councils to express an opinion on matters of public interest if it varies from prevalent views. But if they were capable of giving authentic expression to popular aspirations and possessed real opportunities for influencing the administration, the municipal councils would not need to be legally obligated by such truisms. The elimination of any real possibility of influencing local affairs goes hand in hand with the curtailment of the municipality's jurisdiction. Making the mayorship an honorary, unpaid position in municipalities having less than 10,000 members at first glance may appear as the height of fiscal good sense. In practical terms, however, it serves to exclude members of the lower classes even within the dominant party from seeking the mayorship. This means that the post is handed off to wealthy interests cognizant of the fact that even an honorary mayorship ultimately can pay off quite nicely. Similarly characteristic is a regulation found in a Prussian law from July 17, 1933, which since has become part of the municipal code: the state forbids municipalities from engaging in any activity that might be seen as constituting competition with the private economy. Whereas fierce battles have erupted in other political systems—such as the United States and France—about the possibility of putting large utilities into public hands, National Socialism prefers to follow the example of fascist Italy and burden the population by leaving utilities in the hands of private capital.

To what extent possibilities are available for legal appeal against administrative acts in the Third Reich remains unclear. The widely accepted view that "there are neither individual rights nor rights of subgroups of the community against the Führer, since that would totally contradict the concrete legal nature of the Führer"[35] is quite apt since, in fact, no legal protection against the secret police is possible. Possibilities for legal appeal that might provide guarantees for the most important legal goods, freedom and life, are totally missing.[36]

There is another object that is not subject to review by civil and administrative courts owing to its dynamic character: the activities of lower administrative bodies—in particular, the actions of some factions of the National Socialist Party against the non-Aryan population. Their concerns are known to be regulated according to various legal acts of the Führer. Nonetheless, National Socialist legislation in the area of race has come nowhere close to realizing all the points sketched out in the party program.[37] A court thus was able to rule that in the future mixed marriage would not be prohibited because, in its view, courts lack the authority to attribute validity to National Socialist ideals beyond the scope of those areas to which National Socialist legislation has limited itself.[38] It is well known that not all of the lower courts have fully accepted this ruling. Quite recently, the registrar of marriages in Wetzlar refused to permit a mixed marriage and was subsequently supported in this decision by a ruling of the regional state court. Similarly, the permissible scope of Jewish small business has not been subjected to any special legal regulations. But that does not keep certain elements within the National Socialist movement from demolishing Jewish businesses and forcing their closing. It is yet to happen that public authorities in such cases have ordered the reopening of the business in question or the payment of financial compensation to affected businessmen. On the contrary, administrative authorities work from the presupposition that disturbances to the peace do not stem from those who plunder and attack Jewish businesses but from the Jewish businessmen who dare to file complaints about acts of violence committed against them. Especially in the case of the "Jewish Question," the development of so much of the German legal system remains in a state of flux. Indeed, the dynamic nature of National Socialism conflicts with any attempt to establish a set of determinate legal guarantees. At least to the extent that the emotional rather than the social interests of the lower classes are at stake, the regime does by no means disdain attempts to base legal principles on the immediate imperatives of political agitation or distraction.

NATIONAL SOCIALIST LABOR LAW

As noted above, the basic traits of National Socialist labor law are determined by the fact that the Führer is trying to gain the absolutely crucial support of the industrialists. In order to achieve it, he guarantees their monopoly over the means of production and permits them to determine labor relations as they see fit. This, the National Socialist solution to the problem of labor organization is clearly distinct from that pursued in other countries. In England, France, and Belgium—all states having a highly developed, privately owned, capitalist industrial system—labor relations are determined by the conflict between two organized social groups: employees and employers. Work conditions and salary depend on the strength and the degree of organization found in these two groups. State intervention only occurs when and to the extent that the two groups prove unable to reach a collective agreement. But the National Socialist seizure of power put an end to the open struggle between capital and labor. The National Socialists replaced the marxist unions with the German Labor Front, whose tasks are more psychological than social in nature. The Labor Front has been outfitted largely with the special task of reeducating marxist "infected" workers with the "ideals" of National Socialism; rulings of higher courts refer to this task in order to make it unambiguously clear that the German Labor Front is not responsible for fulfilling the legal obligations of the marxist unions that it replaced.[39] Although the German Labor Front has taken full possession of all the properties of the marxist-oriented unions, the former employees of the dissolved organizations, who have lost any material claims that they had against the marxist unions, are now supposed to be consoled by the "ideal" nature of the mission of the Labor Front.

Whereas the Labor Front's activities are limited to the pursuit of a set of ideological goods, the Law for the Organization of National Labor procures the widest possible authority for the so-called factory leader (*Betriebsführer*) in all social matters.[40] It must have been a mere lucky coincidence that led the ministerial bureaucracy to entrust the formulation of this law to a former corporate lawyer, Dr. Werner Mansfeld. Even during "marxist" times, Mansfeld had worked to make sure that entrepreneurs possessed unlimited authority within their factories. Intimately knowledgeable of the true needs of the factory leader, Mansfeld realized the basic ideas of economic Führerdom in the law; the system of collective agreements has been destroyed, and the center of all social norms has been shifted to the factory. There, the factory leader, armed with a sense of responsibility, regulates the relations of his "followers" (*Gefolgschaft*) (that is, his employees) in the best interests of the "factory community" (*Betriebsgemeinschaft*). At least the state continues to exercise a number of supervisory and participatory functions through the government-appointed trustee (*Treuhänder*). The much-maligned system of politically determined wages has not been fully abolished, and the trustee can participate in the determination of wages by the factory leader; hence, he can participate in accordance with economic and political necessities. But the trustee's right to intervene in the core activities of the factory leader remains limited. It would be a mistake to assume that the trustee has the power to expropriate an entrepreneur who acts in a socially irresponsible fashion. Nor does the trustee possess the authority to dissolve cartels that he deems socially counterproductive. Granting such authority to the trustee would conflict with the basic principles of a capitalist economy, which National Socialism acknowledges and protects like every other noncommunist state.

In the sphere of labor-capital relations, National Socialism thus has generated nothing but the unprecedented domination of the employees by their factory leader. To ward off growing discontent within the working class that has resulted from this situation, the National Socialists have introduced one of their boldest juristic innovations—the *social courts of honor* (*soziale Ehrensgerichte*). True, these courts fail to challenge the entrepreneur's monopoly over the means of production. But they are supposed to force him— at least as far as nonmaterial issues are concerned—to treat employees with the respect deserving of fellow "German ethnic comrades." In exchange, the worker is supposed to learn to treat the entrepreneur without bias and as deserving of his confidence despite differences in social status. In other words, to protect the existing social order more effectively, the psychological atmosphere within the factory should be improved. Like the German Labor Front, the social courts of honor do not serve the material interests of the working class. These are faithfully entrusted to the entrepreneur. Instead, the social courts of honor serve the "preservation of economic peace and undisturbed community work."[41]

The number of proceedings that have taken place so far—sixty-one in

1934, fifty-six of which were directed against the factory leader—does not measure up to the significance attributed the new social courts of honor in the legal literature and in political propaganda. Clearly, employees cannot gain much by undertaking legal proceedings against the factory leader in the social courts of honor. After all, the courts offer no basis whatsoever for material complaints—despite their profound significance to the workers. Even if the factory leader loses his position because of a blatant failure to fulfill collective responsibilities based on the idea of the factory community, his employees do not take possession of the factory. Consistent with the general aim of preserving capitalist property, the social courts of honor in such cases merely are allowed to institutionalize a division between the overall management of a factory and its immediate direction in the hands of a factory leader. The only controversial aspect here is whether the trustee should have the authority to name the new factory leader[42] or whether the owner should have the power to choose his own replacement as factory leader.[43] The formal alternation of the factory leader means virtually nothing for the employees. In order to avoid troubles with the authorities, even the factory leader often gladly hands over his post to a person who possesses good ties to the state bureaucracy; this practice is especially common among non-Aryan firms. As a series of decisions by the social labor courts demonstrates, the factory leader is freed of any real obligations as soon as he carefully selects a factory supervisor knowledgeable of the relevant legal regulations.[44] Thus, even the attempt to realize the mere psychological goals of the Law for the Organization of National Labor is failing. Given the fact that personal responsibility no longer plays a decisive economic role in developed capitalism, this is unsurprising.

It was widely believed that intensified community spirit within the factory, as well as outfitting the entrepreneur with additional responsibilities, would result in better guarantees of job security for the "working folk comrade" than had been provided by previous formal legal regulations with their marxist-oriented works councils. But even this soon proved deceptive. National Socialism itself was forced to acknowledge this in the wording of the Law Against Unfair Dismissals of January 30, 1934: to a greater degree than had been expected, entrepreneurs are failing to fulfill their responsibilities and are refusing to rescind unfair dismissals. Even though the continuation of employment would have been a reasonable demand in individual cases, they preferred paying compensation, thereby trying to buy themselves free from obligations appropriate to the true spirit of the factory community.[45] Consistent with capitalist modes of economic thinking, National Socialist legislators did not conclude from the entrepreneurs' inadequate community spirit that it would be appropriate to demand that those unfairly dismissed should be rehired on a compulsory basis. Instead, they merely increased the maximum compensation amount to be paid from four to six months' wages. In addition, the entrepreneur possesses unlimited power to fire not only any of his employees but also any of the members of the Employee's Advisory Council (Vertrauensrat), whose members he chooses. More feudal than capitalist in its basic structure, the conceptual paraphernalia of German labor law makes it extremely difficult to act successfully against unfair firings. Expressions of political opposition naturally lead to immediate dismissals. In other words, any criticism of economic or social policy can be interpreted as a disturbance of community spirit and as constituting sufficient reason for immediate dismissal.

Neither its legal structure nor the manner in which the owner chooses its members allows the Employees' Advisory Council to become an effective organ for representing worker interests. This has culminated in a situation where the material position of the contemporary German worker is decidedly less advantageous than that of his predecessor in the Weimar Republic. Since the shift in social power has been so disadvantageous to the working class, it may very well endanger National Socialism's enthusiastic attempt to destroy "class spirit." In response to this danger, an attempt has recently been made in Leipzig by the State Labor Ministry, State Economic Ministry, and German Labor Front to try to improve the structure of the National Socialist labor policy. Mansfeld has described the resulting agreement from March 26, 1935, as the perfection of German social policy.[46] The agreement represents a partial and rather inconsistent step back toward a system of collective economic self-administration involving worker participation. In reality, the agreement shows that even today the Third Reich lacks a coherent set of social policies. Instead, it is inevitably following the party of the economically dominant; only in response to occasional crises does it even make a pretence of trying to fill its (unfulfillable and inevitably unfulfilled) promises to the weaker social party, the working class.

First, the Leipzig agreement aims to eliminate tensions among the two state bureaucracies, the German Labor Front, and entrepreneurs by trying to amalgamate them. Furthermore, it hopes to funnel growing worker dissatisfaction with the employer-dominated employees' advisory councils by establishing a system of sector-specific work councils based on a system of parity-based representation. Yet a fusion of the Labor Front with the state economic bureaucracies by no means signifies a shift in the relations of power between capital and labor. This fusion fails to give the Labor Front social functions that alone could transform it into a genuine representative of employee interests; more likely, it might lead to a situation where the ideological and educational functions of the Labor Front will be exercised by economic bureaucracies dominated by the entrepreneurial views. Committees based on a parity-based system of representation, where a consensus between distinct social groups is supposed to be worked out, have been fearfully prevented from gaining genuine decision-making authority. In particular, they have been denied the possibility of intervention in the affairs of individual factories. It makes sense that even parity-based committees of this type could not succeed in heightening the "feeling of spiritual participation" among employees. Every feature of the Leipzig agreement proves nothing more than that, even in the third year of the "Renewal of the Nation," the reorganization of labor relations in National Socialism still faces serious difficulties. It proves something else as well: to ward off an open revolt against National Socialist labor organization by those groups most directly affected by it, particular features of its formal structure repeatedly need to be altered.

HEREDITARY ESTATE LAWS[47]

One of the most striking legal innovations of the Third Reich, the Hereditary Estate Act, aims to "preserve the source of German blood, the farming community, by securing the continued existence of old German inheritance customs." In three different respects, this law signifies a radical break with previous laws. First, it prevents non-Aryans—defined in the broadest possible sense of the term—from acquiring even average-sized agricultural properties. The second decisive legal change consists of making it illegal to mortgage a hereditary farm or to put it up for sale. Only in exceptional circumstances, and then only with the approval of a court, can this rule be disregarded. But this also means, as the legislature was well aware, that the hereditary farmer is prevented from gaining credit on his real estate. Instead, he is advised to seek personal credit.[48] Since failure to repay a personal loan legally cannot result in a foreclosure of the farm, the farmer has no practical way of gaining access to personal credit. The third substantial legal change concerns the right of inheritance. The law eliminates the possibility of dividing farm properties, and it stipulates that a single descendant, generally the eldest son, should inherit the entire farm. Other descendants have a legal claim only to basic living provisions of produce and other assets (which are usually nonexistent) and only as long as such provisions cannot be converted into cash. Since farmers who do not fall under the clauses of the Hereditary Estate Act can gain credit on their real estate and divide their property into lots, they and their heirs are eager to escape its blessings, which prevent them from gaining credit and inheritance. Distinguishing between those who fall under the new law and those who do not is extremely complicated and often paradoxical. If a farmer with little landed property is so diligent that he is able to cover all of his family's expenses with the proceeds from his farm, he still cannot attain the legal status of a hereditary farmer since it is impossible to ascertain whether a somewhat less hardworking heir would be able to support his family in a similar manner.[49] When, as is common in southern Germany, some type of business related to agricultural production is operated in conjunction with the farm, the agricultural unit in question becomes incorporated as a hereditary estate; that means that there are still possibilities for the farmer to gain credit on his real estate. In contrast, the hereditary farmer who simply engages in farming, and thus lacks the regular access to cash revenue possessed by his peer, is deprived of any chance of gaining such credit. The new regulations inevitably lead to a proletarianization of those offspring denied an inheritance, regardless of whether they receive financial compensation for leaving the farm. If they decide to stay, they are nothing more than servants—the only difference being that they cannot be dismissed from their positions. Understandably, many victims of this process are not content with their proletarian fate. Thus, they try to bring attention to aspects of the hereditary farmer's conduct that might justify a court decision to strip him of his special legal status. Although legal requests to disband the hereditary farmer's special status thus far primarily have come from creditors rather than members of his own family, this merely stems from the novelty of the law. In other words, it stems from the fact that the decision about who is to fall under the new law's provisions has yet to be made everywhere, as well as the fact that the overall number of relevant cases has remained relatively limited. We can already begin, however, to identify trends that suggest that the very aim of the law—the preservation of stable families—is likely to be undermined by it. The struggle to gain land and property, whether undertaken by a creditor who is trying to foreclose on a farm, an impatient son, or a brother threatened by the spectre of proletarianization, is now being waged with moral arguments rather than simple juristic means. Although the short period in which the Hereditary Estate Act has been in effect prevents us from reaching any final conclusions about its consequences, the social disadvantages resulting from it certainly seem to outweigh its advantages. It fails to resolve the question of small farms; the attempt to distinguish between hereditary farmers and other types of farmers creates artificial separations within otherwise homogeneous sections of the population; the credit problems of the average farmer are rendered irresolvable; all the farmer's offspring but one are driven into the ranks of the proletariat. Through this, and through new legal instruments that allow family members to discredit the hereditary farmer and then grant his special privileges to another sibling, familial harmony is destroyed.

CONCLUSION

Although changes in administrative, labor, and agricultural law might create the impression that they intend to provide economic relief for those who have suffered from the economic crisis, such changes have in fact only resulted in a reshuffling of positions within the social structure: individual members of the economic and bureaucratic elite have profited at the expense of the public as a whole. It is evident that the measures undertaken by Hitler's regime against the economic crisis are a failure. That should be no surprise to those who understand that National Socialism's political roots are utterly reactionary and that the social mission of National Socialism is to represent the interests of a minuscule upper class.

Changes in the criminal law are functioning primarily to produce a system of total state repression unforeseen in the annals of modern civilization. Fewer years of imprisonment were passed in the eleven years of Bismarck's antisocialist laws than during one month of National Socialism. Fifty political convicts have been executed within two-and-a-half years of Hitler's regime; more than ten people are still sitting on death row. As these lines are being written, a new practice of the criminal "justice" system is getting tested: all political opponents are being systematically condemned to death. This is how the people's court justified the death sentence for the former communist parliamentarian Kaiser on August 4: with the comment that "he was active on behalf of communist ideas dangerous to the state and folk." This is how they similarly sentenced the leader of Rote Hilfe, Rudolf Claus, to death a few days earlier. The same thing can happen at any moment to any functionary in the antifascist movement, or leader of the union movement or Catholic Church. A new and unthinkable radicalization of judicial terror has occurred. The spectre of the death sentence haunts Germans of every social class. Judges and lawyers, who are increasingly hesitant to participate in the operation of this apparatus, no longer can close their eyes to the fact that a political system dependent on this type of criminal law ultimately cannot endure.

The task of future jurists will be to put an end to the National Socialist campaign of annihilation in all elements of the legal order. In the process, the groundwork for the legal system of a socialist Germany can be prepared.

(Translated by Anke Grosskopf and William E. Scheuerman)

NOTES

1. Editor's Note: Carl Schmitt long had argued that the rule of law constituted an essentially bourgeois ideal. In accordance with middle-class liberalism's basic hostility to the imperatives of a political universe characterized by the need for dramatic "decisions" incapable of being rationally justified, the rule of law functioned as an "antipolitical" instrument for restraining authoritative political action and forms of state power; its spirit corresponded to a typically middle-class preference for deliberation and "chatter." The emphasis of the rule of law-ideal on the virtues of regu-

lating political action by means of cogent general legal statutes allegedly represented an attempt to subdue politics to a set of inappropriate "normativistic" criteria.

At a first glance, this position seems similar to marxist-inspired analyses of the rule of law like that developed by the Frankfurt School scholars; it certainly parallels important features of orthodox marxist views of the rule of law. But the following passages from Kirchheimer's 1935 essay already point to two significant differences. First, Neumann and Kirchheimer believe that "the transition from competitive to monopoly capitalism" tends to undermine the "bourgeois" character of the rule of law-ideal. In the simplest terms: the rule of law becomes economically dysfunctional in organized (or "monopoly") capitalism. Second, the rule of law always contained an "ethical minimum." That is, it serves a set of essential protective functions. The benefits of this "ethical minimum" chiefly accrued to privileged social strata, but others have also been able to benefit from it at least during some historical periods.

2. Editor's Note: In order to discredit liberal legal forms, Nazi jurists—including Carl Schmitt—typically traced their roots back to Roman and Jewish sources purportedly alien to the spirit of "Germanic" law.

3. Editor's Note: Kirchheimer is making a point here about Nazi legal practice during the regime's early years that more recent scholars have also made: as Stanley L. Paulson recently commented,

> [r]ather than waiting for the introduction of new statutory law, judges and other officials in Nazi Germany simply departed from the language of existing law whenever and wherever that was called for . . . [T]ime-honored guarantees of the rule of law or *Rechtsstaat* were eliminated in one fell swoop—not legislatively, but rather in the judicial practice of the new regime.

Stanley L. Paulson, "Lon L. Fuller, Gustav Radbruch, and the 'Positivist' Theses," *Law and Philosophy* 13 (1994): 313–359.

4. Fauser, "Das Gesetz im Führerstaat," *Archiv für öffentlichen Recht* 26 (1935): 149. The author refers to the Beuthen decision as an example of the ills of the pre-National Socialist legal order. In that decision "an instinctive political sense" of National Socialist ideology was clearly missing because "several German folk comrades were condemned to death on account of a Pole."

Editor's Note: In August of 1932, a Polish Communist was brutally murdered in Upper Silesia by a group of Nazis. Despite the fact that the Nazi leadership openly sympathized with the murderers, the regional court in Beuthen sentenced five Nazis to death. The ruling was followed by Nazi-organized riots in which Jewish businesses and the offices of republican newspapers were plundered.

5. Editor's Note: The 1935 Berlin International Criminologists' Congress focused its discussion on the following questions:

Section I.
1. What powers must the judge in a criminal court possess in the execution of penalties?
2. What measures can be recommended to shorten the so-called "monster trials"?
3. Should the attenuation of penal legislation influence judgments which are already enforceable? What influence may a change in the legislation regarding the execution of penalties be allowed to have on the penalties which were definitely imposed before this change or the execution of which had already commenced?

Section II.
1. Are the methods applied in the execution of penalties with a view to educating and reforming criminals calculated to bring about the effects aimed at, and are these tendencies generally advisable?
2. What influence does industrial and agricultural unemployment have on the work of the prisoner in time of crisis, and by what means can the harmful consequences which it causes be avoided or reduced? In fixing the standard of life of the prisoner, must account be taken of the standard of life of the population in general?
3. How must the execution of penalties restrictive of liberty differ from the execution of measures of security involving deprivation of liberty?

Section III.
1. In what cases and according to what rules should sterilization be applied in the modern penal system, whether by castration or by vasectomy or salpingectomy?
2. Is it desirable to introduce into the penal legislation provisions authorizing the judge to prohibit persons condemned for offences connected with their profession from carrying on that profession?
3. Is it desirable to establish homes for discharged prisoners?

Section IV.
1. Should juvenile courts be given the power to decide on the measures to be taken with regard not only to erring children and youths but also to children and youths in moral danger?
2. How would it be possible, in the organization of the detention of minors pending trial, to reconcile the requirements of procedure with the interest of the moral protection of the minor against the dangers of detention?
3. What is the best way to organize moral and material assistance for children and youths when they leave schools or other institutions in which they have been placed by order of the court and by whom and in what manner should such assistance be granted?

Reprinted from *Actes du Congrès Pénal at pénitentiare International de Berlin, Août 1935* (Bern, 1936), pp. 78–94.

6. See the very important remarks on this in Heinrich Henkel, *Strafrichter und Gesetz im neuen Staat* (Hamburg, 1934).

7. Rudolf Freisler, *Gedanken zur Strafrechterneuerung im nationalsozialistischen Strafrecht* (Berlin, 1933), p. 9.

8. Friedrich Schaffstein, *Politische Strafrechtswissenschaft* (Hamburg, 1934), p. 28.

9. Editor's Note: *Black's Law Dictionary* defines legal analogy in the following manner: "In cases on the same subject, lawyers have recourse to cases on a different subject-matter, but governed by the same general principle." *Black's Law Dictionary* (St. Paul, Minn., 1979).

10. Editor's Note: This refers to the idea that "there can be no punishment without law."

11. Editor's Note: The reference here is to Section I, Question 3:

Should the attenuation of penal legislation influence judgments which are already enforceable?

What influence may a change in the legislation regarding the execution of penalties be allowed to have on the penalties which were definitely imposed before this change or the execution of which had already commenced?

12. Editor's Note: Under a set of mysterious circumstances, van der Lubbe allegedly set the Reichstag on fire on February 27, 1933. His actual role in the fire was never clarified. The fire played a crucial role in securing Hitler's rise to power.

13. Ebert, *Deutsche Justiz* 96 (1934): 480–485; see also Rudolf Freisler's comments in *Zeitschrift der Akademie für deutsches Recht* 1 (1934): 82.

14. Editor's Note: The German expression here is *"Du kannst, denn du sollst."* In other words, since something is legally decreed, it must be possible, even if there is no real possibility for a particular, concrete individual to do so.

15. Editor's Note: The question reads: "Are the methods applied in the execution of penalties with a view to educating and reforming criminals calculated to bring about the effects aimed at, and are these tendencies generally advisable?"

16. Editor's Note: In contemporary American criminal law, "attempt" is defined by *Black's Law Dictionary* as "an effort or endeavour to accomplish a crime, amounting to more than mere prevention or planning for it, which, if not prevented, would have resulted in the full consummation of the act attempted, but which, in fact, does not bring to pass the party's ultimate design."

17. Freisler, in *Zeitschrift der Akademie für deutsches Recht* 1 (1934): 82.

18. See Oetker's comments in *Nationalsozialistisches Handbuch für Recht und Gesetzgebung*, ed. Hans Frank (Munich, 1935), p. 1346.

19. Just to mention a further example: the French newspaper *Le Temps* published a report on May 27, 1935, about the case of Rudolf Claus, who was a functionary in the Rote Hilfe. After summarizing the reasons given by the Nazi people's court for the penalty, the article closes with the comment: "So what are the crimes that the condemned is accused of? Nothing very precise was made public about this."

Editor's Note: Rote Hilfe was a Communist Party charity organization.

20. Stanislaus Rappoport, who is a member of the Polish Supreme Court and a professor at the University of Warsaw: "Le Futur Code Pénal du Troisieme Reich," *Revue internationale de droit pénal* 39, no. 3 (1934).

21. Editor's Note: I have been unable to gather any further details about the case referred to here.

22. Rudolf Freisler in *Grundzüge eines allgemeinen deutschen Strafrechts. Denkschrift des Zentralausschusses der Strafrechtsabteilung der Akademie für deutsches Recht* (Berlin, 1935), p. 103.

23. Zimmerl in *Deutsche Juristenzeitung* 39 (1934): 442.

Editor's Note: Dimitrov was a famous Bulgarian Communist and analyst of fascism; Thälmann was leader of the German Communist Party.

24. Editor's Note: For an accessible discussion of the Nazi *Sondergerichte* see Ingo Müller, *Hitler's Justice: The Courts of the Third Reich* (Cambridge: Harvard University Press, 1991), pp. 129–137.

25. Editor's Note: This refers to the principle that legal bodies are not permitted to alter a court ruling in a manner that works to the detriment of the condemned.

26. Editor's Note: The accompanying explanation for the question at the Congress reads:

> It has been found on various occasions that ordinary provisions governing criminal procedure and in particular the provisions regarding the furnishing of evidence . . . are only suitable for trials of more or less normal length while, in the case of very big trials,

they lead to an excessive and unreasonable extension of the substance of the trial. The question therefore arises whether, in such cases, it could be left to the court to decide on the extent to which evidence should be furnished.

27. Editor's Note: The "people's court" was outfitted with the special task of persecuting political opponents. A contemporary German jurist describes it as "first and foremost an instrument of political terror . . . with the goal of exterminating political opponents." Günter Gribbohm, "Das Volksgerichtshof," in *Juristische Schulung* (1969), p. 109. See also Ingo Müller, *Hitler's Justice: The Courts of the Third Reich*, pp. 140–152.

28. See von der Goltz, *Deutsche Juristenzeitung* 39 (1934): 182.

29. Freisler, *Grundzüge eines allgemeinen deutschen Strafrechts*, p. 100.

30. Editor's Note: On June 30, 1934, SA Leader Röhm was murdered by the Nazi leadership. Kirchheimer very well may be referring here to the rather peculiar legal justification of the Nazi leadership's act that Carl Schmitt provided in an infamous 1934 article, "Der Führer schützt das Recht" ("The *Führer* Keeps Watch Over the Law"), reprinted in Carl Schmitt, *Positionen und Begriffe im Kampf mit Weimar-Genf-Versailles, 1923–1939* (Hamburg, 1940).

31. Editor's Note: Issued on April 7, 1933, this decree made it illegal for Jews and "Marxists" (in other words: Social Democrats and Communists) to maintain positions within the civil service.

32. See *Reichsarbeitsblatt* from March 5, 1934.

33. These were the words used by the lawyer and District Führer Dr. Römer in the *Westfälische Zeitung*.

34. F. Wieacker in *Deutsche Juristenzeitung* 40 (1935): 1449.

35. Theodor Maunz, *Neue Grundlagen des Verwaltungsrechts* (Hamburg, 1934).

36. Editor's Note: The original here contains a number of typographical errors that render it very difficult to translate.

37. Editor's Note: The reader should keep in mind that the essay appears to have been authored in the summer or autumn of 1935. Obviously, this situation soon changed dramatically.

38. *Reichsgesetz* 134, p. 1.

39. *Juristische Wochenschrift* 64 (1935): s. 1338.

40. Editor's Note: The basis of Nazi labor law was the *Gesetz zur Ordnung der nationalen Arbeit* from January 20, 1934. It gave the proprietor the status of the workplace or factory "*Führer*" (leader); employees were now "*Gefolgschaft*" (followers), and both leaders and followers were given the duty of cooperating "in the best interests of the folk and state." The democratically elected Weimar labor councils (*Betriebsräte*) were replaced by a system of Employees' Advisory Councils (*Vertrauensräte*), which was given the responsibility of "deepening the spirit of trust within the factory." In order to become a member of this council, a worker's candidacy for it had to be approved by both the Factory Leader and the factory "cell" representative for the National Socialist Party. For a detailed account of Nazi labor law see Franz L. Neumann, *Behemoth: The Structure and Practice of National Socialism* (New York, Harper & Row, 1944), pp. 419–427. Also see Taylor Cole, "National Socialism and the German Labor Courts," *Journal of Politics* 3 (1941): 169–197; Nathan Albert Pelcovitz, "The Social Courts of Honor of Nazi Germany," *Political Science Quarterly* 53 (1938): 350–371.

41. Von der Goltz in *Juristische Wochenschrift* 64 (1935): 1281.

42. This is the view of Ernst Huber, who primarily seems to have its propagandistic benefits in mind, see *Deutsche Juristenzeitung* 39 (1935): 207.

43. This view, which is more consistent with the functioning of capitalism, is endorsed by analysts such as Werner Mansfeld and Pohl.

44. See the decisions reprinted in *Juristische Wochenschrift* 64 (1935): 1302.

45. *Reichsarbeitsbatt* (1934), 1, 274.

46. *Juristische Wochenschrift* 64 (1935): 1284.

47. Editor's Note: The *Erbhofrecht* analyzed here was made law on September 29, 1933. According to it,

> the peasant (only if racially a pure Aryan, of course) was tied to the land. Upon his death, it passes to one heir, undivided and unencumbered. The order of succession is fixed: the son, his offspring, the father, brothers or daughters and their offspring, sisters. To be a hereditary peasant one must be *bauernfähig*, that is, capable of managing the farm.

Neumann, *Behemoth*, p. 394.

48. See the discussion of this issue in *Nationalsozialistisches Handbuch für Recht und Gesetzgebung*, ed. Hans Frank (Munich, 1935), p. 1064.

49. See the decision of the Hereditary Estate Court in Karlsruhe, printed in *Juristische Wochenschrift* 64 (1935): 2014.

SIX

Criminal Law in National Socialist Germany

Otto Kirchheimer

The first period after the downfall of the Weimar Republic was marked by the rise of authoritarian ideology. An authoritarian criminal theory, mingled with elements of the old classical school, dominated the academic field. In the criminal courts the transition was immediately reflected by the imposition of harsher punishments and by a weakening of the status of the defendant.

In this early period, the genuine national socialist contribution is to be found in the theory of the volitional character of penal law (*Willensstrafrecht*). This theory, the ideological offspring of Dr. Freisler, Undersecretary of Justice, completely shifted the emphasis from the objective characteristics of the criminal act to its subjective elements. It asserted that the state is justified in demanding greater self-control from the individual and also in considering criminal intent as the main object of the offensive action of the authorities. The content and even the style of these ideas were copied from Nietzsche, who characterized penal law as war measures used to rid oneself of the enemy.[1]

The most important practical consequence of this more or less deliberately vague theory was a disappearance of the distinctions usually separating criminal attempt and the consummated criminal act.[2] Neither doctrine, however, made much headway. When German theorists discovered that Germany is not an authoritarian state but a racial community, authoritarian criminal theory lost its theoretical foundation.[3] The doctrine of the volitional character of the penal law, although never officially discarded and still considered as a clue to national socialist law,[4] ran into a maze of contradictions and theoretical difficulties. At first it seemed to foreshadow the

Editor's Note: Originally appeared in *Studies in Philosophy and Social Science* 8, no. 3 (1940).

conversion of punishment of consummated acts into prohibitions against the commission of acts which would merely endanger the community. In effect, the new legislation of 1933, relating primarily to treason and the protection of the people and the government, has made punishable a large number of mere preparatory acts which, although not having done any actual damage, might, had they been consummated, have endangered the community.[5] The theory, although justifying the punishment of such preparatory undertakings in the case of high treason and related subjects, nevertheless fought with all available arguments against the unlimited extension of the penal sanctions.[6] The measures of security—one of the cornerstones of the national socialist penal legislation—introduced in 1933 are intended to protect society from future misdeeds and therefore aim also at wholly or partially irresponsible persons.[7] These measures, too, defy classification under a system of volitional penal law. Moreover, the doctrine would not apply to the whole field of negligence.

The so-called *Kieler Schule* (Phenomenological School) gained some theoretical following and its doctrine superseded, at least to a limited extent, the volitional penal law doctrine. With the beginning of the present war its influence could even be noticed in the formulation of governmental decrees and court decisions, which were seeking a concept to minimize the legal requirements for punishableness. In its theoretical foundation, this doctrine shares Carl Schmitt's attack on general conceptions, on normativism and positivism, and stresses, instead, the concrete order of life. Intuition and essence are introduced as the true method of discovering the criminal agent. His innate character can never be educed by mere logical deduction from the statutory requisites. "A person who takes away a movable object not belonging to him does not necessarily classify himself as a burglar. Only the very nature of his personality can make him such."[8] Vehement controversies rose around this doctrine. Its chief adversaries tried to prove that a penal code retaining rational and teleological elements was more in line with the aspirations and needs of National Socialism than was the *Kieler Schule*.[9]

For practical purposes it was sufficient to abandon the *nulla poena sine lege* rule[10] and to substitute the postulate of material justice (legitimacy) for mere formal deduction from the law (legality). These devices and, more effectively, the constant stream of new and sometimes retroactive statutes and decrees, coupled with the increasing subordination of the judiciary to the orders of the central authorities, worked to fashion the new fabric of national socialist penal law. The postulate, always recurrent in the national socialist literature of penal law, that mere formal wrongdoing must be superseded by the motive of material justice, leads to the demand that the eternal tension between morality and law, dominant in the liberal philosophy of law, must disappear.[11] The social order of the racial community postulates the identity of law and morality. With this identification the given order is theoretically accepted as unquestionable and just. On the practical side, however, German literature no longer holds that acts formally forbidden by statute but performed in the higher interest of the country are not punishable per se. As in any other established order, there is still the contradiction between legal and legitimate. If there is an urgent need to suspend the validity of criminal sanctions—and many such cases are found in the Germany of today—the reference to a legitimacy beyond the law does not seem to be sufficient. In 1934, in the case of Röhm and his followers, a special law was promulgated, retroactively covering murder in these cases with a cloak of legality.[12] With regard to the recurrent criminal acts of overzealous Party followers, amnesty laws with *nolle prosequi*[13] clauses intervene, thus maintaining the fiction of a coherent legal order. The main importance of the attempted unification of the moral and legal order lies, therefore, in the symptomatic desire to broaden the scope of the penal law, and to extend its activities to new fields. We abstain from remarking on mere changes of phraseology which, in order to justify more severe punishment, try to find a foundation for secondary social rules in the new mores of the country. Under the pre-Hitler penal code, a person who abused a position of special trust was punished for breach of trust; the new prescription retained the old definition but added to its scope the violation of the duty to take care of other people's financial interests. Corruption was to be attacked through this comprehensive definition.[14] The mass of published decisions contains no hint of an intensified drive against corruption, but what quite naturally happened was that heavy pressure was brought to bear upon contract partners by initiating criminal prosecutions. The Reichsgericht was compelled to side against such attempts at enlarging the content of the penal law by explaining that mere violation of contractual relationships does not come under the modified prescription, and that the duty to protect other people's financial interests must be the essential content and not a circumstantial element of the contract in order to enjoy the protection of the modified Section 266.[15]

More far-reaching than this attempt to raise the standard of business ethics was the extension of the category of crimes committed by omission.[16] This extension was carried through by new legal rules as well as by judicial interpretation. Section 330c of the Penal Code makes it a legal duty for all people to render assistance in cases of accident or common danger, and the neglect to do so may be punished by imprisonment for two years. But still more important is the way in which judicial interpretation has extended the legal necessity of action. Every conceivable statute, whether in the realm of civil or of criminal law, may create such duties. An attorney who does not prevent his client from lying to the court when under oath may be punished

CRIMINAL LAW IN NATIONAL SOCIALIST GERMANY   175

for participation in perjury, as Section 138 of the modified Code of Civil Procedure requires the parties to give complete and true accounts.[17] The wife of a hereditary farmer has the duty of extinguishing fires on the property because the hereditary farm law and the legislation in the field of agricultural production aim at raising production.[18] The Reichsgericht's interpretation creates special duties for people living in a family or in a domestic community. Here the Reichsgericht decides that the moral duty of Christian charity becomes a legal duty, the neglect of which results in punishment.[19] There have been many objections to this method of converting moral into legal duties whenever the court likes to inflict punishment.[20] The previously mentioned Kieler school has therefore tried to replace the moral-legal duty argument by increased emphasis on the nature of the criminal. Motives, general disposition, criminal antecedents, and personal character here largely replace objective characteristics, making the uncertain boundaries between legal and illegal still more indeterminate.[21]

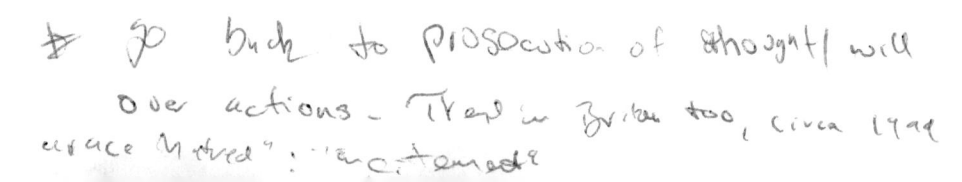

The "sound feelings of the people" occupy a special position among the attempts to enlarge the scope of criminal law. In some instances—as in the previously mentioned Section 330c, and in the analogy prescription Section 2—they were explicitly inserted in the statutes. But in addition to that, they play an important part in the general reasoning of the courts. It may be doubtful, though, in particular instances, what the "sound feelings" of the people amount to. It is interesting to know that in such cases the individual judge is not supposed to act as an independent source of the "people's feelings." He is directed to find the authoritative expression of the "people's feelings" in two sources: first, in the pronouncements of the nation's leaders, and second, in the homogeneity of conceptions developed by the similarity of educational and professional standards among members of the judiciary. That is to say, the people's feelings are crystallized by the authentic interpretation first, of the executive, and second, of the judicial bureaucracy.[22] Most important of all, because of its wide field of application, is the mention of the "people's sound feelings" in the analogy prescription. The application of Section 2 is allowed only when two conditions coincide: first, that the fundamental idea underlying the statute can be applied to the case in question, and second, that "the people's sound feelings" require such application. If the fundamental idea of a statute is conceived as something fixed once and for all at the time of the statute's perfection, Section 2 serves only as a permissive clause for closing gaps unintentionally left open by the legislator. But it would not be permissible to extend this application to new facts which the legislator could not foresee.[23] In Germany, criminal law theory embraces all shades of opinion. Representatives of a very conservative application[24] are found side by side with advocates of an opinion which allows for changes in the fundamental idea,[25] and both are outdone by a number of extremists who start by emphasizing the "people's sound feelings." Of course, in the phraseology of the statutes, "sound popular feeling" only takes second place after the mention of the fundamental idea of the statute. But for these extremists the analogy has little meaning as they acknowledge the legal prescriptions only as signposts for the judge, to guide him in his creative endeavor to form the conception of material wrong doing.[26] The numerous opinions delivered by the Reichsgericht on this question show a remarkable restraint in the use of Section 2 in contrast to the practice of the lower courts.[27] It would be futile to pin down the Reichsgericht to a well-defined doctrine, but it constantly refused to lend support to the more extremist views, and even recently it declared that no dispensation of the judge from obeying the statute follows from Section 2.[28] The following are among the most important decisions: the application of Section 2 in order to punish false accusations of unknown persons is denied, since the legislator intentionally refrains from punishing such accusations.[29] Merely immoral acts cannot be punished as incest because the legislator has deliberately demarcated the realm of punishable acts.[30] The cases in which the abuse of the dependency relationship is punishable are also explicitly limited and no extension into new fields may take place.[31] Neither did the interesting attempt to extend rape into the field of matrimonial relations find favor.[32] Manslaughter cannot be interpreted as murder simply because the accessory circumstances were especially atrocious.[33] A wide domain was more or less completely closed to the application of Section 2 when the Reichsgericht argued that the analogous application of prescriptions given by the national socialist legislator must be examined with the utmost care in order to make sure that the lawmaking authorities did not intend to erect a barrier against extension by analogy.[34] Of the less frequent cases where the Reichsgericht approved of the application of Section 2, we mention only two significant ones. The first case is concerned with the receiving of stolen goods. If a person, instead of receiving stolen goods, did receive the gains obtained by selling or exchanging them, he will nevertheless be punished. In this case, of course, the Reichsgericht admitted a change of the fundamental idea on which this prescription rests. The original prescription was directed against the hiding of stolen property, whereas in the new interpretation the idea of attacking participation in, and profiting through, crime prevails.[35] Embezzlement by employees of the party and related organizations is dealt with as embezzlement by public officials.[36] But it is interesting to know that so far the Reichsgericht utilizes only old tactics from the postwar revolutionary period (1918–1919) when it convicted revolutionary organs of "malfeasance in office," as if they were public officials. Throughout the decisions of the Reichsgericht there is an evident tendency to maintain rationality in the realm of criminal law. This rationality requires that the statute is preserved as a main focus for the decisions of the individual cases. On the other hand it pays for its attempt to maintain a certain coherence in the legal system by complete submission when cherished ideas of the new regime are at stake. Thus, for instance, its decisions regarding race defilement fall in line with the interpretations of the most ardent adherents of the official dogma and try to extend the range of this legislation as far as possible.[37]

It is especially interesting to note the willingness of the Reichsgericht to extend legislation on race defilement to include foreigners who have contravened this German legislation on foreign soil.[38] It is just a preliminary stage of the realization of the ambitious plan to extend the limits of criminal jurisdiction over foreigners in foreign countries. This plan aims at extending the jurisdiction beyond the traditional limits of high treason, felony, and so on to embrace the punishment of all violations of German interests.[39] This principle remained a mere postulate, without much actual importance, as long as Germany's rule was restricted to her own territory. But at the point at which she began successfully to invade other countries, the retroactive extension of part of the German criminal legislation, as done by decree of May 20, 1940, to foreigners acting in foreign countries, served the double purpose of giving a cloak of legality to persecutions of foreign political enemies who fell in German hands and then frightening into submission the population of still unconquered territory by indicating the legal consequences involved in any move against Germany—a kind of legal counterpart to the *Blitzkrieg* movies shown to the upper classes in the countries about to be invaded.[40]

But it is questionable how far the influence of the Reichsgericht extends. The changes in appeal practice, no longer allowing many cases to come up to the Reichsgericht for review, limit the sphere of influence of the highest court. Where the influence of the Reichsgericht has diminished, the administration has stepped in with its much more effective weapons for coercing judges to fulfill its wishes not only as regards the general ideas but also as regards decisions in concrete cases. Whenever the government so desires, it can compel the judiciary to mete out sentences according to its wishes by means of retroactive statutes. This method was used in two types of cases. First, in the "cause célèbre" of van der Lubbe (Reichstag fire) the retroactivity served to obtain a desired sentence in an individual case. Second, retroactive statutes were later issued as, for instance, the statute against kidnapping and the statute against car holdups with the help of traps, as well as in the more recent war legislation. Here the retroactive death penalty was introduced in order to achieve an immediate deterrent effect. The executive influence on the administration of criminal justice has been further increased by the gradual abandonment, since 1937, of judicial self-government. The assignment of tasks within the court is no longer carried out by the president of the court in connection with the presidents of the various sections and the highest ranking associate judge, as independent organs of the court, but by the president of the court alone as representative of, and on orders from, the ministry of justice. The assignment may be changed during the year not only for specific reasons, for example, illness, but also in the interests of the administration of justice.[41] This development, which tends to lower the judiciary to the status of a mere administrative agency, finds its logical conclusion in new regulations issued at the beginning of the war. These regulations grant the ministry of justice the right to change and unify jurisdictions and to abolish the immovability of judges, by ordering them to accept all assignments within the jurisdiction of the ministry of justice.[42] The dismissal and the compulsory retirement of judges, at first only planned as a transitional measure for the stabilization of the regime, have become a permanent device. The judges are subjected to Section 71 of the civil service statute, which provides for the compulsory retirement or dismissal of officials if they do not give sufficient guarantees of adherence to the National Socialist regime. The removal may, however, not be ordered by reason of the material contents of a judicial decision. But the boundaries are difficult to draw and a decision not punishable in itself may nevertheless reveal just that personal unreliability on which the removal may be based.[43] The changed status of the judge is quite naturally reflected in the official ideology which, instead of formal independence, emphasizes the judge's incorporation in the racial community.[44] The central administration also increasingly influences the decision of individual cases through the medium of the public prosecutor's office. Legally speaking the courts are at liberty to deviate from the punishment asked for by the public prosecutor, but in practice they are strongly discouraged from doing so.[45] The effect is evident. The rate of acquittals fell from 15.06 percent in 1932 to 10 percent in 1938. Duration and severity of sentences have increased,[46] even if the share of fines in all punishments has not varied very much. From 56.6 percent in 1932 it went down slightly to 54.5 percent in 1938, an interesting sign that even the penal law of the racial community cannot dispense with such capitalist institutions as fines. There is also, so to speak, a certain type of public opinion which exerts heavy pressure on the courts from below. This public pressure is allowed to express itself in the more extremist organs of the National Socialist Party, which sometimes disagree violently with the judiciary and publicly express their opinion in their newspapers.[47]

There is another feature to which little attention has been paid and which seems, however, very seriously to have influenced the administration of criminal justice in Germany: that is the disappearance of a unified system of criminal law behind innumerable special competences (departmentalization). The ever increasing number of administrative agencies with independent penal power of their own has enormously diminished the scope of action of the regular criminal courts.[48] This curtailment of the judiciary's activity is a phenomenon of deep social significance. Special administrative units like the S.S., the National Socialist Party, the labor service, and the army have their members partially or totally exempted from the competence of the ordinary criminal courts. Under the special disciplinary rules of such organizations, the legal demarcation between permissible and illicit behavior may be fundamentally the same as in the ordinary law courts. But the primary object of such organizations is the unconditional maintenance of a strictly hierarchic order, and this colors and varies the application of the penal law. The reestablishment of special military courts, abolished under the Weimar Constitution, was one of the first fruits that Hitler's victory brought to the army. Since then, the organization of the military courts has been carried out with great thoroughness. From a purely legal point of view the compulsory labor service has only a rather restricted disciplinary power over its members.[49] But in practice two-thirds of all punishable acts committed by members of this service are handled by the labor service organs themselves.[50] The same applies to more exclusive organizations like the S.S. The exercise of this disciplinary power makes it impossible for rival bureaucracies like the judiciary, and, to a certian extent, the public, to get too many glimpses of the conditions prevailing in such services, which are thus more or less hermetically sealed against outside influences. But at the same time the peculiar mixture of special disciplinary and regular penal power, which prevails even if nominally special penal courts are set up in the particular administrative branch, appreciably increases the administrative pressure on the members of the service.

The facts that the demarcation lines between special disciplinary and general penal power[51] are insignificant and that both these powers are combined in one bureaucracy result in a guarantee of the complete subservience of the individual and an immense advantage for the service. The separation of functions between the entrepreneur and the coercive machinery of the state is one of the main guarantees of liberty in a state of affairs where few people control their own means of production. This separation has often been threatened and rarely completely achieved. Now, however, it is completely eliminated under this combination of disciplinary and penal power in the same administrative service.

Whereas the exemptions of the members of the labor service or of soldiers are personal and more or less complete exemptions, German practice also knows a considerable number of exemptions that are only attached to specific functions, while in other respects the competence of the ordinary criminal courts is upheld. We do not need to go into the treatment of political offenders by the *Volksgerichtshof*, which is one of these special agencies for a selected category of criminal cases. The importance of this agency, by the way, is diminished by the very fact that the Gestapo (Political Secret Police) are not obliged to abide by its decisions, but may keep in custody people acquitted by this court. The commercial part of the administrative penal law is only concerned with the professional activities of merchants, factory owners, their deputies, and the affairs of taxpayers in general. The term "exemption" is, strictly speaking, incorrect, as the German legal system provides for a dualist procedure. The administration is at liberty to carry the case to the courts or to impose fines of varying amounts on its own authority. The German theorists try hard to find a demarcation line between ordinary criminal law and commercial-administrative criminal law. They refer to the degree of immorality involved or call upon the difference between proven and presumed culpability for the different procedures.[52] In reality the completely discretionary power of the administrative agency as to whether it decides to initiate a criminal prosecution or prefers to deal with the offender by administrative methods defies theoretical classification. Criminal prosecution carries with it loss of social and economic position through imprisonment, publicity, and criminal records. The administrative procedure means a change in the basis of calculation, perhaps an alteration in the distribution of the social product between different participants in the process of production or distribution, perhaps only between entrepreneur and administration. This applies equally to tax evasion and to infringement of price, marketing, or production regulations. In many aspects such administrative procedure can be compared with the antitrust prosecution by the U.S. Attorney General whose last report expressly states: "The defendants are usually not members of what is ordinarily called the criminal classes."[53] But whereas the U.S. courts decide as sovereign bodies when to further and when to bar the industrial policies of the administration, the use of the administrative penal law in Germany represents an effective weapon of the administration's economic policy. It is applied, not to ascertain what the law of the land is in the question under dispute, but in order to coerce the merchant or industrialist to fall in line with the administrative regulations. In some cases private combinations, such as marketing organizations, were invested with disciplinary and penal power, and the official industrial associations (*Wirtschafts-Gruppen* and *Kammern*), which had similar powers, were mostly dominated by the most powerful affiliated corporations.[54] On the other hand, the choice of the administrative penal procedure in the field of taxation, marketing, or price fixing represents a noticeable advantage to the commercial and industrial classes in their typical clashes with the public order. Its consequences are of a financial nature and do not prejudice the social status of the persons involved. For a long time the administration has even acknowledged that these penalties form a part of the ordinary business expenses to be deducted when establishing the net income of corporations for tax purposes.[55] Behind these advantages, which the administrative penal procedure grants to the business classes, there is always, of course, an evident danger that the administration may use the weapon of criminal prosecution against a recalcitrant or otherwise unpopular member of the business classes.

Administrative penal procedure does not necessarily imply that the offender fares badly in the individual case, as its foremost task is not one of punishing but of enforcing the obedience of the individual to the administrative policy with its rapidly changing needs. These administrative needs have also been responsible for a completely changed treatment of petty criminality (minor offenders in ordinary criminal cases). The increasing maze of regulations, economic hardships, and fundamental processes of economic dislocation, with their inevitable consequence of loosening moral standards, have created an urgent problem of what to do with the enormous army of minor offenders. The theory that had elevated the criminal as such to the rank of the archenemy who has to be exterminated hastened to show that the essential nature of those petty offenders raises a totally different problem.[56] The administration coped with the problem in its own way. It institutionalized an expedient that democratic governments use only very hesitantly. In 1933, 1934, 1936, 1938, and at the beginning of the war in 1939, amnesties were issued for: a) minor offenses of all types, punishable with prison terms of one to six months, b) minor offenses of political enemies, covering sentences up to six months, and c) almost all types of offenses and sentences of overzealous political adherents. The amnesty laws applied to judged as well as to pending cases.[57] The magnitude of these amnesties may be seen from the figures shown in the table on the following page, although they are very incomplete.

The German solution to the problem of petty criminality by generous and regularly recurring amnesties is open to grave doubts. When, by sheer good fortune or by adroit manipulation, it is possible, even if discovered, to avoid punishment, the enforcement of the penal law assumes the character of a gamble. A purely technical consideration must also be added because of its specific weight. Whether the offender is classed as a first offender or as a recidivist merely depends upon the chance of whether, at the time of the amnesty, the proceedings had already advanced as far as the judgment stage and whether his records have therefore been transferred to the criminal files, or whether he is lucky enough to get away with the *nolle prosequi* and therefore keeps his criminal record "virgin," as the French like to say.[58] Let us agree, for a moment, that the lawyer is a mere administrative classifier. Even a purely classificatory practice will suffer in the long run if the administrative technique is completely reversed during the year, while the

Numbers of convicted for crimes and misdemeanors[1]			Amnestied	Nolle prosequi	Strafbefehle[2] asked for by prosecutor concerning trespasses and misdemeanors (in thousands)
1928	588,492				831
1932	566,042		139,899	64,839	695
1933[4]	491,638	Amn. Dec. 30, 1932, results for Prussia only (55% of Reich)	up to 6 mos.[3] polit. up to 5 years	51,933	643
1934	383,885	Amn. Aug. 2, 1934, Prussia only (55% of Reich)	up to 3 mos.[3] polit. 6 mos.	193,350 120,244 44,174 50,334	563
1935	429,335			6,305	648
1936	383,315	Amn. Apr. 23, 1936, Reich as a whole	1 month[3] overzealous adh.	240,340 254,674 1,592 1,940	525
1937	438,493				530
1938	335,666	Amn. Apr. 30, 1938, Reich as a whole, old territory	1 month[3] pol. 6 mos. pol. 1 month	437,000 238,000 6,428 12,163[5] 22,826	406

[1]) All figures are taken from the official statistics given in *Deutsche Justiz.*
[2]) *Strafbefehle* = written order of the court issued without hearing on request of the prosecutor and imposing prison terms up to 3 months (6 months since September 1939) and fines.
[3]) Persons with more than 3 months antecedents not allowed to benefit from amnesty.
[4]) Figures for 1933 amnesty not available.
[5]) Austrians included.

Amnesties and *nolle prosequi* refer to fines too.

aims to be achieved remain unchanged. And the most subtle differentiation will hardly be able to show why a larceny committed on April 23 is something different from one committed on April 24.

The war, as we have already had the opportunity to mention, brought a mass of new legislation. This legislation was doubtlessly influenced by special considerations of war policy, but it also contains matured concepts of National Socialist criminal policy.

Insofar as substantive law is concerned, the principal aim is to guarantee the security of the country in wartime by an extremely harsh policy of punishment. The chief weapon is the unsparing use of capital punishment. As early as August 17, 1939, a decree made the death penalty mandatory for any attempt at treason.[59] At the beginning of the war, the scope of application of the death penalty was also extended to crimes committed during the carrying out of anti-aircraft defense measures and also generally to all those who profit from the state of war in order to commit crimes. Whereas in these cases the death penalty is optional along with hard labor, it is mandatory for crimes involving danger to the public.[60] A more recent decree applies the mandatory death penalty to anyone committing rape, highway or bank holdup, or other crimes of violence involving the use of firearms or swords or daggers or other equally dangerous implements. The same decree makes the punishment provided for consummated acts mandatory for anyone only attempting or participating in a crime.[61]

The decree of October 4, 1939, concerning dangerous juvenile delinquents, also merits special attention.[62] Up to the war there was some tendency to spare juveniles the harshness of National Socialist criminal policy. The new decree, however, apparently a consequence of increasing juvenile delinquency, marks a break with the previous policy. It exempts juveniles between sixteen and eighteen from the jurisdiction of the juvenile court when the culprit, in view of his mental and moral development, could justifiably be regarded as a person over eighteen, and when the offense exhibits a particularly degraded criminal character or if the protection of the community requires such a punishment.[63]

The new evaluation of these criminal offenses shifts the emphasis from the personal motives, the direction of the criminal's will, to the special external circumstances under which the offense was committed.[64] The deterrent purpose prevails above all other considerations. Where the statutory formulation still gives equal weight to the evaluation of the offender's personality and to the protective needs of the community, the official interpretation makes it abundantly clear that the latter aim has absolute predominance. In this relationship, the doctrines that lay special stress on the type of the criminal gain official recognition. The war parasite, the precociously dangerous criminal youth, and the brutal criminal, as they appear in the war decrees, are criminal types for which the pictorial impression (*Bildtechnik*) prevails over precise legal definition (*Merkmalstechnik*). In decisions deriving from these decrees, this method has led to the use of antecedents for establishing the guilt in the crime in question, and guilt becomes guilt not in relation to the particular offense, but in relation to the whole career and the earlier ways of life of the criminal.[65] This method of considering antecedents not only in order to decide the punishment but also to judge the guilt in the offense before the judge helps in practice to establish the predominance of a rather crude form of social protection as the main content of the criminal law.[66]

In the field of criminal procedure before the war, opinions arose, even in the National Socialist camp, resenting the fact that no mutual trust could be established between the defense attorney and the court. Nor had the problem of providing an adequate defense for the overwhelming majority of indigent defendants found a solution.[67] The deterioration in the position of the defense attorney was, after all, very largely an unavoidable result of the transition from the liberal to the National Socialist system. Instead of improving the position of the defense attorney, the war increasingly shifted the main task from the judge to the public prosecutor, the member of the "militant" corps of the administration of justice. The war decrees have given the public prosecutor an almost completely free hand to choose before which judge he would like to bring a case. Competence in criminal matters is no longer regulated according to the nature of the offense, but depends on the sentence that the public prosecutor is prepared to ask for. Thus he has complete power to decide whether he intends to bring the defendant before the "one judge tribunal," which may prescribe hard labor up to two years and imprisonment up to five years and against the decisions of which there is no appeal, or before one of two kinds of "three men courts," which may prescribe any kind of sentence, including the death penalty. If he chooses to bring the defendant before the ordinary "three men court" (Strafkammer), an appeal to the Reichsgericht is possible. Incidentally, we should note here that the abolition of the principle of the inadmissibility of *reformatio in peius* now allows a conviction to be reversed to the detriment of a defendant, even if the decision has been appealed only by him. But if the prosecutor prefers to bring the case before the "special tribunal" (Sondergericht)—usually composed of the very same three judges who ordinarily sit as Strafkammer—no appeal is allowed.

The participation of laymen in criminal proceedings has been completely abolished as a measure of war economy, but even now it is still possible that the judges might not conform quickly enough to the policy of extreme deterrence initiated by the government. There were some instances where the "three men court," constituted as a "special tribunal," and issuing a decision that was legally unappealable, did not react quickly enough to the wishes of the government. To remedy the situation and to secure a jurisprudence in absolute conformity with the wishes of the political leadership, a special division was set up inside the Reichsgericht.[68] Before this division, the chief public prosecutor of the Reich (*Oberreichsanwalt*), as representative of, and on order from, the Führer, may directly bring—omitting the lower courts—certain cases which seem to him of special importance. Moreover, even cases which have been finally decided may be brought by him to a new trial before this division within a period of a year after the final decision of the lower court had been rendered. The decree provides for this new procedure in case there are grave objections to the accuracy or the justice of the judgment. But let us not misunderstand the position: when the chief public prosecutor demands a new trial, he at the same time stipulates the sentence which the division is expected to give.[69] Not without justification, the position of this special division has been compared to that of the princes in the seventeenth and eighteenth centuries, who had the sovereign right of confirming or modifying decisions of criminal courts, and, therefore, the possibility of increasing or decreasing the punishment. A slight difference, however, should not be overlooked. Frederick II of Prussia, whose memory the new German regime sometimes takes pleasure in invoking, exercised this jealously guarded right of "confirmation" in order to foster the humanization of the criminal law and not, as the present regime does, solely for the purpose of converting the criminal law into a system of deterrence and brutality.[70]

The situation of the German judiciary in dealing with criminal cases may be summed up as follows: like any other administrator of importance, the judge has the right and the duty to decide the particular case before him according to the existing laws of the land. Just as the administrator may receive, from his superior, a circular prescribing certain desired changes in administrative methods, so the judge may be presented with a retroactive decree ordering him immediately to change criminal practice. The difference between the administrator and the judge is the following: in particularly important cases the administrator usually receives orders from his superior, prescribing how to proceed and to decide. But a judge is legally bound only to decide according to the existing laws—subject, however, insofar as his person is concerned, to compulsory transfer or removal, and subject, insofar as the judgment is concerned, to the order of the Führer to the special division of the Reichsgericht to change the decision in the way indicated by the chief public prosecutor of the Reich. Of the many changes that the administration of criminal law has undergone in Germany since 1933, the most far-reaching one is its conversion into an administrative technique. New prescriptions are made and remade; the emphasis may shift from personality factors to the social situation; harsh punishment in one field and for one set of persons may be counterbalanced by wholesale exemptions for other violations and other groups of persons. And at the same time there is a continual process of leveling down the judiciary from the status of an independent organ of the state to that of an administrative bureaucracy. As early as the beginning of February 1933, the freedom of action of the judiciary became increasingly restricted through the replacement of the general law of parliament by the Führer's uncontrolled and incessant decree legislation, often applying to specific cases.[71] The wartime decrees, by making it possible to control individual criminal decisions, mark the last stage in the transformation of the judge from an independent agent of society into a technical organ of the administration.

One of the most serious consequences arose from the accompanying process of departmentalization. We have seen how the increased efficiency of state and industrial machinery was paid for not only by the loss of the benefits of abstract citizenship but also by the complete subordination of man in his productive relationships to the disciplinary and penal machinery built up by the special services and by private combinations invested with the garments of public authority. It is at this point that the inroads of the

National Socialist state machinery on the daily life of the average citizen appear to be most striking and that the exclusive predominance of strict power relationships will most likely create frictions.

The fight between normativism and the concrete conception of life did not affect developments in the field of criminal administration until a very late stage, when this conception could, by its very loftiness, be conveniently used to bridge theoretical difficulties in the recent campaign for ruthless extermination. The attempt of the legislator and of the judiciary to use the criminal law to raise the moral standards of the community, appears, when measured by the results achieved, as a premature excursion by fascism into a field reserved for a better form of society. In effect, it is difficult to see how the goal of improving public morality could be obtained by a state that not only operates at such a low level of satisfaction of needs but that also rests on a supervision and direction of all spheres of life by an oppressive political organization.

NOTES

1. Heinze, *Verbrechen und Strafe bei Nietzsche* (Berlin, 1939).
2. Rudolf Freisler in *Grundzüge eines Allgemeinen Deutschen Strafrechts. Denkschrift des Zentralausschusses der Strafrechtsabteilung der Akademie für deutsches Recht* (Berlin, 1934), pp. 13–14; see also the same author in the second edition of *Das kommende deutsche Strafrecht. Allgemeiner Teil* (Berlin, 1935), p. 26. The National Socialist ideology of penal law and the proposed changes in the penal code, as well as the changes already introduced, are dealt with in more detail, though without much regard for the actual administration of criminal justice, by Henri Donnedieu de Vabres in *La Crise Moderne Du Droit Penal, La Politique des Etats Autoritaires* (Paris, 1938).
3. See, for example, Georg Dahm, *Nationalsozialistisches und Faschistisches Strafrecht* (Berlin, 1935), beginning on p. 6, who speaks of the gulf separating the German people's community from the Italian ideology of state and nation. This is especially interesting because of the fact that the same author was one of the initiators of the authoritarian school two years before in Dahm and Friedrich Schaffstein, *Liberales oder Autoritäares Strafrecht* (Hamburg, 1933).
4. Graf Gleispach, "Willenstrafrecht," in *Handwörterbuch der Kriminologie* (Berlin, 1936), vol. 2, pp. 1967–1979.
5. See the decree of February 28, 1933, *Reichsgestezblatt* (henceforth: *RGBL*), (1933), 1, 83, paragraph 90 a–d and paragraph 92 a–f of the Penal Code.
6. Oetker (in *Grundzüge eines Allgemeinen Deutschen Strafrechts*, p. 48), among others, used the argument that such a policy would tend to weaken the reliance of the members of the community on their own ability to avert possible dangers.
7. *Strafgestzbuch*, paragraph 43 a–n. In Karl Larenz, ed., *Grundfragen der neuen Rechtswissenschaft* (1935).
8. Georg Dahm, *Verbrechen und Tatbestand* (1936), p. 46.
9. The whole controversy is surveyed by E. Wolf, "Der Methodenstrait in

der Strafrechtswissenschaft und seine Überwindung," *Deutsche Rechtswissenschaft* 4 (1939), beginning on p. 168.

10. Editor's Note: This refers to the idea that "where there is no law there can be no transgression."

11. See the second edition of the *National-Sozialistische Leitsätze für das deutsche Strafrecht*, ed. H. Frank (Berlin, 1935); *Das kommende deutsche Strafrecht*, pp. 17, 45.

12. See *Reichsgestz über Maßnahmen der Staatsnotwehr,* July 3, 1934, *RGBL* (1934), 1, p. 529.

13. Editor's Note: This refers to the plaintiff's choice not to proceed with his or her legal action, or with some part of it concerning certain defendants.

14. Dahm, in the special section of *Das kommende deutsche Strafrecht*, p. 339; Kohlrausch in the 34th edition of the *Strafgesetzbuch* (1938), paragraph 266, note 1.

15. Compare the *Reichsgericht* (henceforth: *RG.S*) decisions in criminal cases (*RG.S*, vol. 71, p. 90), and the decision of the same court quoted in the *Zeitschrift der Akademie für deutsches Recht* (henceforth: *ZA*) (1940): 15, with commentary by Nagler.

16. Editor's Note: For a discussion of this issue see Otto Kirchheimer, "Criminal Omissions," *Harvard Law Review* 54, no. 4 (February 1942): 615–642.

17. *RG.S*, vol. 70, p. 82.

18. *RG.S*, vol. 71, p. 193.

19. *RG.S*, vol. 69, p. 321; vol. 72, p. 373.

20. Helmuth Mayer, *Das Strafrecht des deutschen Volkes* (Stuttgart, 1936), p. 178.

21. On the whole problem there is an abundant though partially confused literature. See Drost, "Der Aufbau der Unterlassungsdelikte," *Gerichtssaal* 109 (1937): 1–63; Georg Dahm, "Bermerkungen zum Unterlassungsproblem," *Zeitschrift für die gesamte Strafwissenschaft* 59 (1939): 133–183.

22. Peters, "Das gesude Volksempfinden," *Deutsches Strafrecht* 3 (1937): 337–350.

23. The view that the underlying idea of the statute could itself undergo changes was warmly recommended to the 1937 Congress of the International Association of Penal Law in Paris by Professor Donnedieu de Vabres, although he would never have admitted that this extensive interpretation contemplated the abandonment of the *nulla poena sine lege* rule. See the report by Pierre Bouzat in *Revue Internationale de Droit Penal* (1937), beginning on p. 33.

24. Kohlrausch, *Strafgesetzbuch*, commentary on paragraph 2.

25. E. Mezger, "Der Grundgedanke des Strafgesetzes," *Deutsche Rechtswissenschaft* 4 (1939): 259–266.

26. Boldt, "Bericht über Stand und Aufgaben des Strafrechts," *Deutsche Rechtswissenschaft* 2 (1937), beginning on p. 47, who, however, is not very consistent; see his later and much more moderate programmatic formulation of principles in *Gerichtssaal* 112 (1938), beginning on p. 93.

27. See J. Hall, "Nulla poena sine lege," *Yale Law Journal* 40 (1937): 175.

28. *RG.S*, vol. 72, p. 93; The Reichsgericht in *ZA* (1940): 67.

29. *RG.S*, vol. 70, p. 367.

30. *RG.S*, vol. 71, p. 196; vol. 71, p. 306; The Reichsgericht in *ZA* (1940): 180.

31. *RG.S*, vol. 71, p. 94.

32. *RG.S*, vol. 71, p. 109.
33. The Reichsgericht in *Juristische Wochenschrift* (henceforth: *JW*) (1937): 1328.
34. *RG.S*, vol. 70, p. 218.
35. *RG.S*, vol. 72, p. 146.
36. *RG.S*, vol. 71, p. 390. The decisions on paragraph 2 are collected and systematized by Hans Bepler in *JW* (1938): 1553–1570, and in *JW* (1939): 257–266.
37. *RG.S*, vol. 72, p. 91, vol. 72, p. 149; vol. 72, p. 245.
38. The Reichsgericht in *Juristische Wochenschrift* (1940): 790. In this case one of the parties was a "non-Aryan" Czech, and the other was an "Aryan" German girl. The "crime" was committed in the sovereign republic of Czechoslovakia, before Munich, and the act was not punishable under Czech law.
39. Reimer in *Das kommende deutsche Strafrecht*, pp. 223–224; Maurach, "Treupflicht- und Schutzgedande," *Deutsches Strafrecht* 5 (1938): 1–15.
40. Incidentally, the retroactivity here, as in the Röhm case, also serves the German yearning for legal correctness. This longing for a wholly worthless legality is a strange sign in a legal order which, officially at least, rests on "material justice."
41. *RGBL* (1937), 1, p. 1286. E. Kern, "Die Selbstverwaltung der Gerichte," in *ZA* (1939): 47–50.
42. *RGBL* (1939): 1, p. 1658.
43. See Brandt, *Das deutsche Beamtengesetz* (1937), note 2 to paragraph 71.
44. Jaeger, *Der Richter* (1939), p. 69.
45. In a recent address given by Undersecretary of Justice Roland Freisler before the presidents of the special courts, he draws their attention to the fact that the public does not understand unimportant differences between the punishments asked for by the public prosecutor and the sentence given by the court. Freisler, "Die Arbeit der Sondergerichte in der Kriegszeit," *Deutsche Justiz* (1939): 1753.
46. George Rusche and Otto Kirchheimer, *Punishment and Social Structure* (New York, 1939), p. 186, table 23.
47. See the discussion between the Schwarze Korps and the Ministry of Justice, parts of which are reprinted, especially the arguments of the judicial bureaucracy, in *Deutsche Justiz* (1939): 58–59, 175–178.
48. Georg Dahm, "Wissenschaft und Praxis," *JW* (1939): 829.
49. Dienstrafordnung of January 8, 1935, *RGBL* (1935), 1, p. 5.
50. Bruasse, "Zur Frage einer Strafgerichtsbarkeit für den Reichsarbeitsdient," *ZA* (1938): 228.
51. See, for example, Hoder, "Erweiterte Disziplinarstrafgewalt im Krieg," *Zeitschrift für Wehrrecht* 4 (1940): 433–443.
52. Part of the field is now regulated by the decrees on punishments and procedures in regard to contravention against price regulations, *RGBL* (1939), 1, p. 999. As regards the literature, see Rauch, "Werdendes Wirtschaftsrecht," *Zeitschrift für die gesamte Strafrechtswissenschaft* 58 (1938): 75–98 and by the same, "Umgestaltung des Preisstrafrechts," *Zeitschrift für die gesamte Strafrechtswissenschaft* 59 (1939): 360–370. K. Siegert, "Zum allgemeinen Teil des Wirtschaftsrechts," *JW* (1938): 2516–2521.
53. *Annual Report of the Attorney General of the United States 1939*, p. 37.
54. See Drost, "Der Krieg und die Organisation der gewerblichen Wirtschaft," *ZA* (1940): 25–26.

55. The extent to which this administrative criminal procedure lacks any relationship with penal law may be seen in an example which at the same time shows the ascendancy of the administrative over judicial bodies. Up to the beginning of 1939 the revenue collectors, under the explicit rule of the highest judicial body in the field of taxation, the Reichsfinanzhof, maintained the practice of admitting the deduction of administrative penal fines from gross income when establishing the net corporation income. (See the decision of the Reichsfinanzhof of August 17, 1938, in *Reichssteuerblatt* [1939], p. 229.) It was reasoned that these fines represented a typical case of normal business risk. As these fines sometimes attain considerable amounts—in one case the amount was over one million marks—the finance ministry ordered the revenue collectors to stop the practice (order of January 4, 1939, p. 257). The Reichsfinanzhof, legally a completely independent judicial body, hastened to fall in line with the order given to the revenue collectors, thus completely reversing the decision that it gave nine months before (decision of March 8, 1939, in *Reichssteuerblatt* [1939], p. 507). It now argues that the administrative penal procedure also intends to punish guilt but with the difference that for reasons of mere convenience the guilt is often presumed and need not be proved. Its main argument for the abandonment of its earlier line are the changing aims and significance of the administrative penal procedure which leads to a change in the people's conceptions of such procedures. As it is very unlikely that the people have a definite conception of such intricate problems as the legal nature of administrative fines, we can safely assume that the order of the finance ministry is the real explanation of the miraculous change in the people's opinion.

56. Mayer, *Das Strafrecht des deutschen Volkes,* beginning on p. 84.

57. We have not taken into account the numerous special amnesty laws for the members of particular administrative services or for the inhabitants of special (mostly newly incorporated) regions.

Whereas the convictions for crimes and misdemeanors and the amnesties and *nolle prosequi* relate to numbers of persons, the *Strafbefehle* relate to numbers of cases. This difference is partly balanced by the fact that about 40 percent of the penal mandates are Bavarian cases (see *Deutsche Juristenzeitung* [1936]: 46). But in Bavaria the prevailing practice is to handle, through judicial *Strafbefehle,* all kinds of violations of police regulations (for example, traffic violations) elsewhere dealt with by the police and never appearing in any criminal record. It must also be noted that the "number of convicted" covers crimes and misdemeanors, the amnesties and *nolle prosequi* crimes of political adherents, less important misdemeanors, and probably also some major trespasses, whereas the *Strefbefehle* include only trespasses and minor misdemeanors. In spite of all this overlapping, which prevents accurate comparison, one result stands out very clearly: in the years 1932, 1935, and 1937, when the amnesties could have had no practical influence on the movement of criminality, the figures for convictions and for *Strafbefehle* are in general appreciably higher than in preceding or subsequent years, when the influence of the amnesty laws could be traced. We may notice, by the way, a secondary consequence of the amnesty policy with its numerous *nolle prosequi,* as well as of the transition from ordinary to administrative procedure: criminality figures based on convictions by ordinary criminal courts become meaningless. (Von Weber, "Die deutsche Kriminalstatistik, 1934," *Zeitschrift für die gesamte Strafrechtswissenschaft* 58 [1938]: 598–624, admits the deceptive nature of the German criminality figures. As regards the 1939 amnesty, the administration has ordered that, insofar as *nolle prosequi* are concerned, no material for statistical use should be collected. See *Deutsche Justiz* [1939]: 1432. This order makes it impossible to follow the application of the 1939 amnesty.) We cannot, therefore, obtain a statistically accurate picture of the development of that part of criminality usually handled by the repressive agencies of the government.

58. This state of affairs has led to proposals to introduce a file of pending criminal procedures: Seidel, *Deutsches Strafrecht* 6 (1939): 23.

59. *RGBL* (1939), 1, beginning on p. 1455. We do not comment on the aggravations of punishment for military and related offences.

60. *RGBL* (1939), 1, beginning on p. 1679.

61. *RGBL* (1939), 1, p. 2378.

62. *RGBL* (1939), 1, p. 2000.

63. Although the number of unemployed youths between 14 and 18 fell almost to zero between 1933 and 1937, the rise in the number of criminal youths in many towns was much higher proportionally than would have been justified by the 34 percent increase in the age classes between these years. In Hamburg, for example, their number rose from 658 to 1068, in Erfurt from 111 to 230, in Halle from 150 to 230. The figures are taken from reports on crime among youth in *Zeitschrift für die gesamte Strafwissenschaft* 54 (1934): 667, and 59 (1939): 187. The most obvious rise is in the field of morality; the percentage of moral offenses in the whole of youth criminality rose from 4.6 percent to 10 percent between 1934 and 1937 in the townships.

64. "The picture of the personality of the offender cannot be separated from the state of war": Roland Freisler in "Gedanken zum rechten Strafmaß," *Deutsches Strafrecht* 6 (1939): 329–342.

65. See the decision of the Stuttgart Sondergericht, in *JW* (1940): 442.

66. *RG.S*, vol. 71, p. 179, anticipates this trend when it explains that a state of diminished responsibility by no means excludes the application of the death penalty.

67. K. Siegert, "Die Lage des Strafverfahrens," *Deutsche Rechtswissenschaft*, vol. 2 (1937), pp. 47–57.

68. Decree of September 16, 1939, *RGBL* (1939): 1841.

69. Tegtmeyer, "Der ausserordentliche Einspruch," *JW* (1939): 2060. The decision of the special division, quoted in *ZA* (1940): 48, shows that the judges understood the orders given to them when they changed a sentence of hard labor into a death sentence.

70. E. Schmidt, "Staat und Recht," in *Theorie und Praxis Friedrichs des Grossen* (1936), beginning on p. 30. A later decree of February 21, 1940 (*BGBL* [1940], 1, p. 405), generalized the option of the chief public prosecutor of the Reich to take exceptions to final decisions during a period of a year following the decision. The decree allows him to challenge criminal sentences before the ordinary divisions of the Reichsgericht if he finds fault in the application of the new law. Conservative lawyers were eager to interpret this as a new nullification procedure in substitution of the extraordinary exception before the special division (K. Klee, "Die Verordnung über die Zuständigkeit der Strafgerichte," *ZA* [1940]: 90), but it was immedi-

ately authoritatively confirmed that the extraordinary exception did not yield to the new rules (Roland Freisler, "Die neue Methode der Strafgerichtszuständigkeitsbestimmung," *Deutsche Justiz* [1940]: 281). It seems, therefore, that in order to obtain the desired results in questions of practical importance, a new trial before the special division will be asked for, whereas in questions of more legal than practical significance, the unification of the criminal practice will be obtained by means of the nullification procedure before the ordinary divisions of the Reichsgericht.

71. Franz L. Neumann, "The Change in the Function of Law in Modern Society," reprinted above.

PART III

Toward a Critical Democratic Theory

SEVEN

The Concept of Political Freedom[1]

Franz L. Neumann

It is a fairly widespread academic doctrine that political theory is concerned with determining the limits of the citizen's obedience to the state's coercive powers. In this formula coercion appears legitimate, and the sole function of political theory is to erect a fence around such political power. The analysis of political power—its origin, manifestations, and techniques—belongs to another discipline, sociology. In both disciplines political power seems to be accepted as an ontological datum, a natural fact, and the role of political theory is to see to it that political power behaves with relative decency.

Insofar as political theory is concerned with the legitimacy of political power, it has, according to prevailing opinion, a mere ideological function. Political theory is conceived as a rationalization of existing power relationships. A theory's validity is thus determined by a pragmatic-utilitarian appraisal in terms of the assistance it gives in defending or conquering an existing power position, with its propagandistic-manipulative success the criterion of its truth.

This position expresses, often unwittingly, the political alienation of contemporary man: the fact that man considers political power a force alien to him, a force which he cannot control and with which he cannot identify himself, and which at best can be made barely compatible with his existence. The extraordinary decline in prestige of the political philosophies of Plato and Rousseau—theorists who attempted to solve the problem of man's political alienation—seems to confirm this view.

There is, of course, no doubt for any realistically minded person that politics is a struggle for power—a struggle between persons, groups, and states. The assertion that in politics Right fights Might, Idea combats Power—with

Editor's Note: Originally appeared in *Columbia Law Review* 53, no. 7 (1953).

the frequent addition that, after all, Right and Idea will ultimately be victorious—may be edifying and comforting to many but seems impossible of proof. In fact, whenever Right has had to contend with Power, Right has been defeated. Were we to stop at this formula, we ought to abandon political theory altogether (save as a technique of manipulation) and accept what one commonly understands by Machiavellianism: that nothing really changes in politics, that the "outs" always fight the "ins" for profit, prestige, and security. The wise observer will add that you cannot expect anything else, human nature being as it is—basically selfish and evil.

In a period of conflicts, of uncertainty, hatred, and resentment, this view—like pessimistic theories in general—seems especially attractive. St. Augustine's theory of man (as commonly interpreted), Machiavelli's view of politics, Metternich's conception of foreign relations—all are unquestionably fashionable today and if contrasted with a shallow misinterpretation of enlightenment philosophy they are certainly more realistic. Modern sociology and political science do not weary of stressing the view that politics consists in nothing but the manipulation of large masses by small elites, particularly through clever use of symbols: in order to beat an enemy, one must merely be cleverer. A theory then becomes an ideological statement which, if repeated often enough, will by its own weight change the political situation and produce victory.

But the ordinary man is repelled by these conceptions. Distinguishing the promotion of an idea from the sale of soap he refuses to accept the view that the legitimation of political power is a matter of individual preference. As a political man he deeply feels that his preference must be part of a more universally valid value system, a system of natural law or justice or national interest or even humanity.

Politics is indeed a struggle for power, but in this struggle persons, groups, and states may represent more than their egoistic interests. Some may really defend national interests or those of humanity, while their opponents may merely rationalize their egoistic-particular demands. The thought structure of the former would be termed an idea; the latter, an ideology—an *arcanum dominationis* designed to hide and rationalize concerns that are actually egoistic.

This formula, of course, answers no questions. How does one determine whether an interest is more than a particular one? The answer is difficult, more difficult today than perhaps at any other period of history, precisely because our thinking is so heavily permeated by propaganda that it sometimes seems hopeless to attempt to pierce the layers of symbols, statements, and ideologies and thus to come to the core of truth.[2]

Yet this is precisely the task of political theory. It is in this enterprise that political theory parts company with the sociology of knowledge. Sociology is concerned with description of the factual; political theory is concerned with the truth. The truth of political theory is political freedom.[3] From this follows one basic postulate: since no political system can realize political freedom fully, political theory must by necessity be critical. It cannot justify and legitimize a concrete political system; it must be critical of it. A conformist political theory is no theory.

Thus the concept of political freedom needs clarification. The present discussion has primarily a didactic function: to dissect the concept of political freedom into its three constituent elements—the juridical, the cognitive, and the volitional—with the hope that they may be reintegrated into an overall theory of political freedom.

THE CONCEPT OF JURIDICAL LIBERTY

Freedom is first and foremost the absence of restraints. There is little doubt that this view underlies the liberal theory of freedom, that it is the key concept of what one understands by constitutionalism, that it is basic to the understanding of what, particularly in the Anglo-American tradition, one understands by juridical liberty.[4] This is the formula of Hobbes (although he formulated it as a natural science theory), and of Locke, Montesquieu,[5] and Kant. Thus understood, freedom may be defined as negative or "juristic" freedom. In referring to this concept as negative we do not mean bad or objectionable, but rather that it is in the Hegelian sense[6] one-sided and therefore inadequate. The negative element may not be thrown out—to do so leads to the acceptance of totalitarianism—but it cannot, of itself, adequately explain the notion of political freedom. Translated into politics, the negative aspect of freedom necessarily has led to the formula of citizen versus state.

The real meaning of this formula needs clarification.

Its basic presupposition is philosophic individualism—the view that man is a reality quite independent of the political system within which he lives.[7] The positing of man against political power implies, in varying degrees, an acceptance of man's political alienation. Political power, embodied in the state, will always be alien to man; he cannot and should not fully identify himself with it. The state must not completely swallow up the individual; the individual cannot be understood merely as a political animal.[8] A political theory based upon an individualistic philosophy must necessarily operate with the negative-juridical concept of freedom, freedom as absence of restraint.

The idea that there are individual rights that political power may restrain and restrict but never annihilate is concretized in the civil rights catalogs of the various constitutions. Indeed, for practical purposes, juridical freedom largely coincides with these charters. An analysis of civil rights provisions thus seems equivalent to an analysis of the concept of juridical freedom.

Legally, civil liberties establish a presumption in favor of the rights of the individual and against the coercive power of the state. They are no more than presumptions because there is not, and obviously cannot be, a political system that recognizes the individual's sphere of freedom absolutely and unconditionally. Thus the state may intervene with the individual's liberty—but first it must prove that it may do so. This proof can be adduced solely by reference to "law," and it must, as a rule, be submitted to specific organs of the state: courts or administrative tribunals. There are thus three statements inherent in this analysis of civil rights:

> The burden of proof for intervention rests always with the state.
> The only means of proof is reference to a law.
> The method by which a decision is to be reached is regulated by law.

Clearly the political significance of this formula depends upon the meaning of the term "law." Abstractly, there are three possible definitions:

1. Law may mean a set of rules of behavior asserted to be objectively valid within any political system (as is the case in the Thomastic view).
2. Law may mean the sum total of individual rights allegedly existing prior to the political system and not being, in their essence, affected by it (the Lockean position).
3. Law may mean the positive law of the state, valid if enacted in accordance with a written or unwritten constitution.

The first two meanings of the term "law" can be dispensed with in our analysis. In the reality of political life, natural rights (in either meaning) have validity only if they are institutionalized, only if there is an authorized agency capable of enforcing them against opposing provisions of positive law. Thus medieval natural law norms were valid if the Church or the vassals were successful in asserting what they considered natural rights against imperial or royal legislation. The right of resistance was then indeed the institutionalization of "natural law."[9] With the emergence of the state, with its institutional monopolization of the means of coercion, "natural law" and "inalienable natural rights" have a political meaning only if they are recognized by organs of the state—and to this extent they become positive law. This is precisely the case with civil rights when they are incorporated into a written constitution or are recognized, as in the English system, in constitutional and legal practice.[10] The philosophic theories concerning civil rights may have shaped their enactment and may still be necessary for interpreting them in ambiguous situations, but they do not determine their legal validity.

Thus the "law" by which the state proves its right to interfere with individual rights can only be positive law.

Yet, the meaning of the term "positive law" is in itself a problem. Genetically, the validity of positive law is determined solely by the fact that it is enacted in accordance with certain written or unwritten procedural rules. Thus the Hobbes-Austin-Kelsen definition is correct, translating the concept of sovereignty into legal terms. Law is simply *voluntas,* or will.

But historically there has been a second definition, concerned with the formal structure of positive law, one which emphasizes its generality. Were law merely *voluntas,* the concept of a "rule of law" would have no ascertainable meaning for the protection of individual rights, for sovereignty, and law would then be synonymous. Actually there exists a steady tradition, stemming from Plato[11] and Aristotle,[12] holding that no matter what the law's substance, its form must be general (or universal, as it is sometimes termed). Even when natural law has been rejected, insistence upon the law's formal structure survives as a minimal requirement of reason for restraint of power. The generality of the law may thus be called secularized natural law.[13]

The generality of law means logically a hypothetical judgment by the state on the future behavior of legal subjects, its basic manifestations being the legislative statute or the *ratio decidendi* of the common law.

Two determinants are contained in this definition: first, law must be a rule that does not mention particular cases or individual persons but which is issued in advance to apply to all cases and all persons in the abstract, and second, it must be specific, as specific as possible in view of its general formulation.[14] This view of the nature of law determined legal and political thought from the seventeenth century on. It was common to Hooker and Locke and was most accurately formulated by Rousseau, in whose political philosophy this notion of law is virtually the sole institutionalized limit upon the community's sovereignty. This is how he defines the law:

> When I say that the object of the law is always general, I mean that the law considers the subjects in their totality and their actions in the abstract, but never a man as a single person and never an individual act. Therefore, the law may well provide that there shall be privileges, but it must never grant them to a named person . . . in a word: each statement referring to an individual object does not belong to the legislative power.[15]

France and England adopted this position. Even Austin, protagonist of the volitional theory of law, says: "Now where the law obliges generally to acts and forbearances of a class, a command is a law or rule."[16] Almost every theorist asserts that this ought to be the theory of law,[17] even where one has to admit that positive constitutional law permits the enactment of individual measures.[18]

From the simple proposition that there exists a presumption in favor of the individual's freedom there follows every element of the liberal legal system: the permissibility of every act not expressly forbidden by law, the closed and self-consistent nature of the legal system, the inadmissibility of retroactive legislation, the separation of the judicial from the legislative function. These concepts were—and seem still to be—accepted by the civilized world without question, with their logical connection with the doctrine of the law's generality well perceived.

If there is a presumption for the individual's right, it logically follows that only behavior that is expressly forbidden by law is punishable. This statement is universally recognized as being the foundation of legal liberty. Hence follows the inadmissibility of bills of attainder, which deny that a presumption exists for right against power and which permit power to enact individual measures directed against specifically named persons. By this token the bill of attainder is a legislative and judicial act in one.[19] The doctrines *nullum crimen sine lege* and *nulla poena sine lege* are latinistic formulations of the basic principle[20] against retroactivity.[21] Its inadmissibility follows logically from the structure of the general law as a hypothetical judgment about future behavior—a rule, therefore, for an indefinite number of concrete cases. A retroactive law covers, hidden behind the language of a general law, countable concrete cases, and is thus in reality a mechanical addition of individual measures.[22] The famous nazi *Lex van der Lubbe* of March 29, 1933, retroactively introducing the death penalty for arson, was enacted for the sole purpose of dealing with the alleged arsonist of the Reichstag.

Moreover, the generality of the law implies the doctrine of a separate judiciary. If the law is to be abstract, if it is to regulate an unknown number of future cases, then its application to concrete cases cannot be in the hands of those who make the general rule. Thus judicial or administrative functions are legally subordinated (no matter what may be the sociological theory of the judicial function) in such a way that the judge or administrator performs the routine function of subsuming a concrete case under a general law.

The liberal legal tradition rests, therefore, upon a very simple statement: individual rights may be interfered with by the state only if the state can prove its claim by reference to a general law that regulates an indeterminate number of future cases; this excludes retroactive legislation and demands a separation of legislative from judicial functions. The underlying assumption of the liberal legal system is the logical consistency of the law. The legal system is deemed to be closed so that new law can be created only by legislation; the judge or administrator must answer each case by reference to existing law.[23]

I have little doubt that this formula expresses, so far as any formula can, the creed of liberal legal thought. Yet there remains the question of what this theoretical system actually guarantees. I have distinguished three functions of the generality of law: a moral, an economic, and a political function.[24]

The moral (or ethical) function consists in the inherent elements of equality and security which it presupposes. A minimum of equality is guaranteed, for if the lawmaker must deal with persons and situations in the abstract he thereby treats persons and situations as equals and is precluded from discriminating against any one specific person. By the same token a minimum of security exists in the relation between the individual and the state. The individual knows in advance that an act, once performed, cannot be made punishable by a later law and that he alone cannot be made to suffer, unless others for similar reasons are also made to suffer. This is the ethical content of the prohibition against bills of attainder—a prohibition by which the Anglo-American countries have, on the whole, scrupulously abided. Even Great Britain, where the sovereignty of Parliament theoretically permits the enactment of attainder bills, has never since the seventeenth century resorted to them save in colonies against natives.[25]

Thus it seems correct to say that an ethical minimum is inherent in this formal structure. This basic idea is well expressed in Cicero's statement, "The magistrates who administer the law, the jurors who interpret it—all of us in short—obey the law to the end that we may be free,"[26] and still more precisely in Voltaire's dictum, "*La liberté consiste à ne dépendre que des lois.*"[27] Both have in mind the general law. If the sovereign may enact measures interfering with an individual's rights, the role of judge becomes transformed into that of a policeman or bailiff. The generality of the law is thus the precondition of judicial independence, which, in turn, makes possible the realization of that minimum of liberty and equality that inheres in the formal structure of the law.

The formal structure of the law is, moreover, equally decisive in the operation of the social system of a competitive-contractual society. The need for calculability and reliability of the legal and administrative system was one of the reasons for the limitation of the power of the patrimonial monarchy and of feudalism. This limitation culminated in the establishment of the legislative power of Parliaments by means of which the middle classes controlled the administrative and fiscal apparatus and exercised a condominium with the crown in changes of the legal system. A competitive society requires general laws as the highest form of purposive rationality, for such a society is composed of a large number of entrepreneurs of about equal economic power.[28] Freedom of the commodity market, freedom of the labor market, free entrance into the entrepreneurial class, freedom of contract, and rationality of the judicial responses in disputed issues—these are the essential characteristics of an economic system that requires and desires the production for profit, and ever renewed profit, in a continuous, rational, capitalistic enterprise.[29] The primary task of the state is the creation of a legal order that will secure the fulfillment of contractual obligations; the expectation that contractual obligations will be performed must be made calculable. This calculability can be attained only if the laws are general in structure—provided that an approximate equality in power of the competitors[30] exists so that each has identical interests. The relation between state and entrepreneur, particularly in regard to fiscal obligations and interferences with property rights, must also be as calculable as possible. The sovereign may neither levy taxes nor restrain the exercise of entrepreneurial activity without a general law, since an individual measure necessarily prefers one to another and thus violates the principle of entrepreneurial equality. For these reasons the legislator must remain the sole source of law. Thus seen, the alleged contradiction in the attitude of liberalism toward legislation vanishes. Roscoe Pound[31] maintained that the Puritans' view of legislation contained an inherent contradiction: on the one hand, hostility to legislation; on the other, firm belief in it and rejection of customary law and equity. But this is precisely the attitude of the whole liberal period, which, for obvious reasons, desires as little governmental intervention as possible—since intervention, by definition, interferes with private rights—but if intervention at all, then in the form of the legislative statute with clear, precise, unambiguous general terms.

The political function of the general law is manifested in the Anglo-American slogan "a government of laws and not of men"[32] and in the Prussian-German notion of the *Rechtsstaat* (state based upon law). Both formulations contain, obviously, an ideological element. The law cannot rule. Only men can exercise power over other men. To say that laws rule and not men may consequently signify that the fact is to be hidden that men rule over other men. While this is correct, the ideological content of the phrase "the rule of law" differs sharply according to the political structure of the nation that coins it. The English rule of law and the German *Rechtsstaat*[33] doctrines have really nothing in common. To the Germans, the *Rechtsstaat* merely denotes the legal form through which every state, no matter what its political structure, is to express its will.

> The state is to be a Rechtsstaat; that is the watchword, and expresses what is in reality the trend of modern developments. It shall exactly define and inviolably secure the direction and the limits of its operation, as well as the sphere of freedom of its citizens by means of law. Thus it shall realize directly nothing but that which belongs to the sphere of law. This is the conception of the Rechtsstaat, and not that the state shall only apply the legal order without administrative aims, or even only secure the right of the individuals. It signifies above all not the aims of the state, but merely the method of their realization.[34]

This is the formula of Friedrich Julius Stahl, founder of the theory of the Prussian monarchy. The last sentence is the decisive one; it has been fully accepted by the German liberal theorists. It means, of course, that neither the origin nor the goals of the law are relevant, but that the form of a general law gives to every state its legal (*Rechtsstaat*) character. That a conservative monarchist coined this theory is, of course, understandable; that the liberals adopted it merely expresses the collapse of German political liberalism in 1812, in 1848, and during the constitutional conflict with Bismarck in 1862. German liberalism remained content to defend its rights against the monarchy, particularly its property rights, but was no longer concerned with the conquest of political power. Indeed, as this formula indicates, it had traded political freedom for economic advance and security.[35]

In contrast, the English doctrine of the rule of law comprises two different propositions: that Parliament is sovereign, thus possessing the monopoly of lawmaking (the democratic legitimation of political power), and that the legislation enacted will comply with the requirements of a liberal legal system as defined above. Dicey recognizes the logical incompatibility of the two statements but believes that "this appearance is delusive; the sovereignty of Parliament, as contrasted with other forms of sovereign power, favors the supremacy of the law, whilst the predominance of rigid legality throughout our institutions evokes the exercise, and thus increases the authority of, parliamentary sovereignty."[36] The fact is that Dicey was, and probably still is, correct. The reason for this does not lie in a kind of preestablished harmony between power and right in the United Kingdom but probably in the self-restraint of Parliament, which in turn is the result of a functioning party system and a balanced and stable social structure.

The United States system lies between the two marginal cases of the *Rechtsstaat* and the English rule of law, the two elements often being, as now, in a rather precarious balance.

To sum up: the general character of the law and the presumptions in favor of the right of the individual and against the state play three roles in modern society: a moral, in that they guarantee a minimum of freedom, equality, and security; an economic, in that they make possible a competitive-contractual society; a political, in that in varying degrees they hide the locus of power. I should stress here that the moral function transcends both the economic and political contexts within which it operates. This is the legal value, the sole legal value, inherent in a legal system so structured. All other values realized in a legal system are introduced from outside, namely by power.

It is clear, I think, that our political, social, and economic life does not consist solely of rational—that is, calculable—relationships. Power cannot be dissolved in legal relationships. The dream of the liberal period was precisely that it could. From the end of the eighteenth century to the first half of the nineteenth this view of rational society assumed, one may say, utopian characteristics. All relevant relationships were deemed to be legal; the law was to be general in character; the judge was merely "the mouthpiece of the law," applying it through a logical process of subsumption.[37] Legal positivism is not only, as is commonly taught, the acceptance of political power as it is, but also the attempt to transform political and social power relationships into legal ones.

But this, of course, does not work. It never did and never could. If our social, economic, and political life were merely a system of rational, calculable relationships, the rule of law would of course cover everything. While power can at times be restrained, it cannot be dissolved. The nonrational element, power, and the rational element, law, are often in conflict.

The conflict may be resolved in two ways: the general law may, in its very formulation, contain an escape clause permitting purely discretionary decisions that are not the product of the subsumption of a concrete case under an abstract rule, or, if power so desires, the general law may be suspended altogether.

I shall consider only the first case. Every legal system employs legal standards of conduct—statements permitting the agencies of the state to act in a purely discretionary fashion while outwardly complying with the liberal tradition of a general law. These legal standards of conduct may be explicit (that is, written into codes or statutes) or implicit (that is, may be interpreted by courts into statutes). One may perhaps say that power enters rational private law through equity and rational constitutional law through prerogative (or some similar term).

I shall first take examples from private law, in order to show that the principle prevails even in the most rational section of the legal system.

Liberal legal theory was once violently opposed to equity (in the Aristotelian meaning, as a corrective to rigid general laws). Whether one reads Selden's *Table Talk*,[38] or Blackstone's *Commentaries*,[39] or Kant's *Legal Philosophy*,[40] to mention but a few, equity is denounced as incompatible with the calculability which is the primary requirement of liberal law. England, the home of modern European equity, was at once her gravedigger. According to Maitland, equity had become since 1875 merely "that body of rules which is administered only by those Courts which are known as Courts of Equity."[41] And in Lord Eldon's judgment, "The doctrines of this court ought to be as well settled and made as uniform almost as those of the common law, laying down fixed principles, but taking care that they are applied according to the circumstances of each case."[42] Similar statements by other English judges show basic agreement on the necessity of transforming equity into a rigid system of law in order to secure the calculability which economic transactions require.

But the rejection of equity is germane only to a competitive economic system. Equity considerations increase with the increase in concentrations of economic power and in interventionist activities of the state.

We may generally say that equitable rules are and must be applied where one has to deal with power positions.[43] When an interest approaches monopolistic control, its private power becomes quasilegislative and therefore public. Since each such interest affects public welfare in a unique way, the state can regulate it only through some form of individual measure. This is introduced into the liberal legal system through the equity approach. The English conspiracy doctrine as applied to restraints of trade, the American concept of "reasonableness" as applied to economic combinations, the German doctrine of "good morals" as applied to industrial disputes—are all clear evidence of this. The whole of the German law regarding the legality of strikes and lockouts is contained in the Civil Code provision that an act which inflicts damage upon another and violates good morals is a tort. Our whole antitrust law is really nothing but the statement that an unreasonable combination is illegal. Yet how can one rationally define such standards? They can be illustrated and described but never defined. Nor, without risking extreme rigidity, could we seek to do otherwise. The general law therefore operates best when it regulates the behavior of a vast number of competitors of about equal strength. If it has to deal with power concentrations it will be replaced by clandestine individual measures.

Similar methods are employed in the field of public law, appearing in three sets of problems:

1. No political system will fully uphold the legal value of calculability and legal security if it deems its own security endangered by it. Power will thus strive to set aside the juristic notion of freedom.
2. The fundamental presupposition of liberal legal theory is that the right of one will coincide with the right of others and that in case of conflicting rights the state will fulfill its arbiter function through the application of precisely defined general laws. But quite often the colliding interests seem to be of equal weight and the conflict can then be solved only by a discretionary decision.
3. No political system is satisfied with simply maintaining acquired rights. The juristic concept of freedom—as we have developed it—is naturally conservative.[44] But no system, even the most conservative one (in the literal meaning of the term) can merely preserve; even to preserve it must change. The values that determine the character of the changes are obviously not derived from the legal system. They come from outside, but for propagandistic reasons they are presented as legal demands, often allegedly derived from natural law.

To answer the first two of these problems it becomes necessary to define more accurately the amount of freedom that civil rights actually guarantee. To this end the traditional civil liberties must be classified, for it would be dangerous to speak of only one right: individual freedom. While all civil rights ultimately go back to this basic philosophical conception, historical development has led to a distinction among various types of rights with different functions and different sanctions.

Civil rights, as restraints upon power, are necessary as a means of preserving freedom. This formulation implies two statements: civil rights are indispensable for the realization of freedom, but civil rights do not exhaust freedom—they are but one of its elements. Freedom is more than the defense of rights against power; it involves as well the possibility of developing man's potentialities to the fullest. Only because we do not trust any power, however well meaning, to decide what is good or bad for us, do we insist on a realm of freedom from coercion. This is the fundamental and inalienable (the so-called negative or juristic) aspect of our freedom.

But what, concretely, is it that is inalienable? We may distinguish three types of traditional rights: personal, societal, and political.

Rights may be called personal if their validity is bound solely to man as an isolated individual.[45] The security of the person, of houses, papers and effects,[46] the right to a fair trial,[47] the prohibition of unreasonable searches and seizures[48] do not depend upon man's association with other men. Their protection is not dependent (or should not be) upon changes in the socioeconomic system, such as the change from competitive to organized capitalism, nor upon political expediency. What precisely constitutes a fair trial may be open to interpretation,[49] but reasons of state can never justify inroads into these principles. The criminal law provisions of our constitution are absolute personal rights; and probably no country has as many detailed constitutional provisions concerning these personal rights.[50]

Societal civil rights can be exercised only in relation to other members of society. They are, in a proper sense, rights of communication. Freedom of religion (as distinguished from religious conscience), freedom of speech, of assembly, and of property are such rights. One limitation is inherent in them: the exercise of these rights must not deprive others of theirs; in the language of Kant the rights of one must coexist with the rights of others. It is through such general laws as those of libel, slander, and trespass that this coordination is perfected.

There is a demonstrable relationship between personal and societal rights. While the personal rights are, so to speak, an end in themselves, they are also ancillary to the societal rights. Without security of the person there can be no free communication, since a person subject to arbitrary arrest and without the prospect of a fair trial will be reluctant to engage in free communication. But the additional ancillary character of the personal rights must not lead to the view that they are subject to the inherent limitations of the societal rights.

This seems simple, but the two problems raised above—the conflict of political power with juristic freedom and the conflict of two interests—create difficulties that, if conceived solely as legal problems, seem really insurmountable. The second problem is best illustrated by the Supreme Court decision in Kovacs v. Cooper,[51] in which the court upheld a local ordinance forbidding the use of sound trucks emitting "loud and raucous" noises.

But it is the first problem which is the really important one. Feiner v. New York[52] is a typical case, appearing in precisely the same form in every nation: the citizen exercises his right to free speech, the audience protests, disorder ensues, the police are called in, and they arrest the speaker for breach of the peace or for disorderly conduct and thus restore order. A study of the decisions of administrative or criminal courts in Germany and France will, as a rule, show that these courts, like our Supreme Court, uphold the discretionary power of the police to take such measures as they think fit to prevent disorder. In Germany, resistance by the speaker to such police action would be punishable as "resistance to the state power," while here the Supreme Court upheld the conviction for breach of the peace. Thus free speech is everywhere qualified by the proviso[53] that the agent of political power may determine at his discretion whether he will protect free speech or side with the power of the mob against it.

Some constitutional lawyers and political scientists detect a decisive difference between the United States and continental Europe in the different constitutional formulae: the First Amendment with its statement "Congress shall make no law . . . abridging the freedom," as against the typical continental formula, the right of free opinion is guaranteed within the framework of the laws.

There is indeed a difference, and there seems little doubt that the American pattern is preferable. Under our constitutional provision freedom of the press has developed remarkably better than under the numerous continental European press laws. But the decisive difference must be attributed less to different formulae than to more sensitive attitudes toward civil liberties, particularly on the part of the courts.

Beyond any shadow of a doubt the *calculable* relation between the rights of the individual and the power of the state is everywhere governed by an escape clause. In continental Europe it is the so-called reservation of the law; in the United States it is the "clear and present danger" formula.[54]

The clear and present danger test demonstrates the impossibility of clarifying the precise meaning of legal standards of conduct. David Riesman[55] goes so far as to assert that the Schenck decision does not permit the court to weigh the value of free speech against that of any governmental policy. This is probably an extreme interpretation but it does seem, in considering the range of decisions from Near v. Minnesota,[56] Board of Education v. Barnette,[57] Thomas v. Collins[58] to the Dennis case,[59] that the test has been watered down from "clear and present" to "clear and probable" danger, allowing the noncalculable element of political power to assert itself against the calculable limitation upon that power. Thus power, or "necessity," or "reason of state" cannot be effectively eliminated or restrained by constitutional law.[60]

Furthermore, not only do the objectively necessary or alleged requirements of political power interfere with the rule of general laws, they may even occasion the total suspension of civil liberties. The state of siege, martial law, emergency powers—these merely indicate that reasons of state may actually annihilate civil liberties altogether. Common to these institutions in most countries is the fact that the discretionary power of those who declare an emergency cannot be challenged. It is they who determine whether an emergency exists and what measures are deemed necessary to cope with it.

Civil rights (personal and societal) are to be distinguished from political rights, though they are closely related. Continental theory frequently distinguishes "human" and "civil" rights—the former, it is asserted, are inherent in the nature of man as a free and equal being, enjoyed by citizens, denizens, and visitors: the latter are derived solely from the political structure of the state.

This is correct if the term "political structure" is properly defined. If it simply says that a citizen has as many political rights as those wielding political power are willing to grant, it is meaningless. What is really meant is that the nature and extent of political rights are determined by the nature of the political system—that is, by what the political system claims to be.

Thus if a political system claims to be a democracy, specific rights must be implemented. On the whole, there is agreement on the minimal basic rights: equal franchise and equal access to all public offices, and equality of treatment in regard to occupations, professions, and callings.

The rights of the *status activus* (as these political rights are sometimes called) presuppose, as I have mentioned, the personal and societal rights. There can be no formation of the national will on the basis of equal suffrage without freedom of the person and without free communication. By definition, therefore, any abrogation of personal or societal rights necessarily involves an intervention with political rights—though not vice versa.

So far, quite traditional problems have been discussed—although it is hoped that they have been discussed in a more systematic setting than usual. The problems are traditional because they revolve around the old formula of citizen versus state, which is primarily thought of in a context of criminal law. In this setting civil rights can be, or at least could be, more or less effectively protected. But in modern society three new problems arise that are difficult or perhaps impossible to fit into this theoretical model: the effect upon civil rights of far-reaching changes in the socioeconomic structure; the application of social sanctions against dissenters; and the attempt to legitimize positive demands upon the state by means of "civil rights."

These questions indicate that the juristic notion of freedom covers only one element of freedom and cannot include all of political freedom. The confrontation of citizen versus state is inadequate for several reasons.

If political freedom were mere legal freedom, it would be difficult to justify democracy as that political system which maximizes freedom. A constitutional monarchy would do as well, and indeed there are continental historians and political scientists who take precisely this position and even assert its superiority over democracy. This view we believe to be untenable— but this compels us to define political freedom more concretely.

Furthermore, juristic freedom is static and conservative, while society changes. The problem was well stated by Justice Jackson:

> [T]he task of translating the majestic generalities of the Bill of Rights, conceived as part of the pattern of liberal government in the eighteenth century, into concrete restraints on officials dealing with the problems of the twentieth century, is one to disturb self-confidence. These principles grew in soil which also produced a philosophy that the individual was the center of society, that his liberty was attainable through mere absence of governmental restraints, and that government should be contented with few controls and only the mildest supervision over man's affairs. We must transplant these rights to a soil in which the laissez faire concept or principle of non-interference has withered at least as to economic affairs, and social advancements are increasingly sought through closer integration of society and strengthened governmental controls.[61]

Justice Jackson's view, moreover, leads to these doubts: the formula liberty versus government seems to comprehend two statements, that individual liberty increases with the decrease of governmental power (and vice versa), and that liberty has but one enemy, government. Neither of these implications can be accepted. It is historically impossible to maintain that governmental interventionism of itself decreases the scope and effectiveness of the citizen's freedom. A mere superficial acquaintance with history is quite enough to show that there is no logical connection between the two factors. A less interventionist Imperial Germany protected freedom far less effectively than a far more interventionist Weimar Republic. England during the less total World War I was not as sensitive to civil rights as during the more total World War II. In the United States, the Supreme Court decisions extending the scope of civil rights protection began in 1931. The historical links between interventionism and civil rights are but little investigated by the historians and political scientists. The theoretical falsity of the statement that liberty decreases with the increase of governmental intervention is obvious since the term "intervention" neither indicates its purposes nor the interests against which intervention is directed. The connection between the two situations is a political-historical one, requiring analysis of each concrete situation, for it is undeniable that a minimum of intervention—the maintenance of "law and order"—is always indispensable to the preservation of individual rights, so that the very existence of the state is a precondition for their exercise.

This, in turn, is closely tied up with the second implication of the formula liberty versus government, namely, that the state is the sole enemy of liberty. That this is fallacious reasoning should be obvious from the fact that private social power can be even more dangerous to liberty than public power. The intervention of the state with respect to private power positions may be vital to secure liberty.

Thus the juristic notion of liberty is inadequate in the following respects:

1. The protection of liberty through general laws does not take into account the content of the laws. The general law may be repressive in content. A state may brutalize its penal system and, for instance, threaten the death penalty for all petty crimes. Nothing in the theory of juristic liberty could possibly prevent this. Even Rousseau, the fanatic believer in the generality of the law, was compelled to admit[62] that the law may create privileges although it must not grant them to individual persons. Thus we cannot but repeat that the juristic notion of liberty can guarantee only a minimum of liberty. That minimum may mean much or very little, depending on factors nonlegal in character.
2. Even within the scope of the juristic concept of liberty, escape clauses like the clear and present danger formula permit political power to prevail over individual rights. Thus Justice Frankfurter's statement in the Dennis case that "civil liberties draw at best only limited strength from legal guarantees"[63] adequately formulates our position.

In short, the juristic notion of liberty, based upon the philosophic formula that freedom is the absence of restraint, opposes freedom to necessity, the two allegedly belonging to two different realms. There is no need here to resume the age-old debate on the correlation between freedom and necessity, but it seems necessary to restate the stages in the development of what we call the cognitive concept of liberty in order to show its political relevance.

THE COGNITIVE ELEMENT IN FREEDOM

The first step is to be found in Greek natural philosophy culminating in the philosophy of Epicurus. To him, as to Lucretius, the "terror then and darkness of mind must be dispelled not by the rays of the sun and glittering shafts of day, but by the aspect and the law of nature."[64] Their problem was to free men from the terror inspired by the superstitious belief that natural phenomena are due to the arbitrary intervention of the Gods—

THE CONCEPT OF POLITICAL FREEDOM

precisely the religious superstition that Plato[65] desired to maintain and even strengthen in order to keep the masses in hand. In opposition to this view Epicurus taught that external nature was governed by necessity, that is, by immutable natural laws. Understanding of this necessity makes man free, liberates him from the fear that the phenomena of external nature instill into the ignorant. "A man cannot dispel his fear about the most important matters if he does not know what is the nature of the universe but suspects the truth of some mythical story. So that without natural science it is not possible to attain our pleasures unalloyed";[66] and still more precisely, "necessity is an evil, but there is no necessity to live under the control of necessity."[67] Ever since Epicurus the development of natural science has occupied a decisive place in the growth of man's freedom; not only does the understanding of external nature free man from fear, but, as again indicated by Epicurus, it permits the utilization of natural processes for the betterment of man's material life. This powerful Epicurean tradition has continued to our day in the philosophy of Hobbes, Spinoza, the French enlightenment, and English utilitarianism.[68]

The second decisive step is the development of Spinoza's psychology,[69] with its application of the Epicurean principle to the understanding of man's mind: a man who lives according to the dictates of reason alone is a free man.[70] To be able to live according to reason man must understand his mind; he must classify his passions, understand them, and thereby subdue them. Only a slavish nature is ruled by passions. Freedom, to Spinoza, is thus insight into necessity.

It is in this scientific tradition that Freud stands. His understanding of the instinct of aggression and self-destruction[71] and his analysis of the need for identification as the emotional tie of one person with another[72] contain suggestions that have so far hardly been utilized in political theory. The fundamental proposition that Freud shares with Kierkegaard[73] is that our existence is shot through with anxiety. Both distinguish anxiety ("dread" in the English translation) from fear; the latter refers to "something definite," while anxiety is a state of existence produced by innocence and thus ignorance. Anxiety, the operation of the aggressive instinct, and the need for identification of the isolated human being are the psychological processes that permit the total annihilation of freedom in totalitarianism.

Yet it is possible that neither the understanding of external nature nor the knowledge of the operation of the mind will enable us to come to grips with necessity. There is no necessary correlation between freedom and an advanced state of knowledge of external and internal nature. The societal arrangements may, indeed, be such that natural science and psychology may become handmaidens of oppression. What one calls the "moral lag" expresses this possible developmental dichotomy.

A third step is necessary: the understanding of the historical process. If we are to believe historians of history it is Giambattista Vico[74] who first attempted a scientific analysis of the structure of political freedom in the frame of an historical analysis. The subject of his theory of history is universal, not national, history. The historical process is no longer considered a theological but a social one. History is the work of man[75] within a cultural setting, the setting, the totality of material culture. History is the conflict between man, nature, and culture. Since Vico, the conception of history as universal history, and of the historical process as an intelligible development, have become primary concerns in the analysis of the notion of freedom. Similar ideas, but more mechanistic ones, have been developed by Montesquieu,[76] whose concepts of political structure are related to historical processes. Montesquieu was the first to develop the notion[77] that the actor in the historical process may by his acts produce consequences that he intended to avoid. It is he who insisted on the interdependence of all social phenomena, rejecting attempts to isolate specific features of a social structure and attribute specific consequences to them.

From Vico and Montesquieu the road goes to Hegel and Marx. Both accepted the Epicurean-Spinozist formula that freedom is insight into necessity: one who understands what happens, and why it happens, is thereby free.[78]

The cognitive formula, however, is wrong if it is conceived as obedience to an abstract and fatalistic law of history. The historical process includes man's aspiration to secure more effective control of his environment, so that historical insight is critical and programmatic. The real function of the cognitive element is to expose the possibilities for realizing the human potentialities latent in different social situations. On the one hand it prevents us from repeating empty time-honored formulae. What is progressive today and conducive to freedom may be false tomorrow and a hindrance to freedom. On the other hand it curbs utopian radicalism. Since what man can achieve is bound to the stage of social development, the realization of freedom is not at the disposal of man's free will.

The fate of two key concepts of political theory, sovereignty and property, will demonstrate the significance of the cognitive element of freedom.

Today it is fashionable to defame the concept of sovereignty. Hobbes, in particular, has never been popular in Anglo-American countries, and Bodin, the creator of the word "sovereignty," has been interpreted to be a mild liberal. Some hold sovereignty responsible for all the ills of our present age. Nationalism, imperialism, even totalitarianism are deemed to be direct descendants of sovereignty, with Marsilius of Padua, Bodin, Calvin, Luther, Hobbes, and, of course, Hegel, the criminals. We do not want to raise the problem of how far a theory—even the most brilliant one—can be held responsible for political developments, but will assume here that this is possible. It is clear that this view follows directly from the equation of freedom with juristic freedom, that is, absence of restraint. Sovereignty of the state means, obviously, that the monopoly of coercion rests with an institution separate from society, yet connected with it, called the state. The progressive historical function of sovereignty has never been doubted, even if there is dispute as to the limits of the state's coercive powers. In a period of feudal rule, of exploitation of peasants and cities by feudal lords, of competing jurisdictions of monarch, vassals, guilds, and corporations, of secular and temporal powers, there arose one central power: the monarchy. It destroyed the autonomies, created (or attempted to create) one administration, one legal system, and transformed privileges into an equality of duties, if not of rights. How could our modern commercial and industrial society have arisen without this sovereignty which created large economic areas and integrated them legally and administratively? It was precisely middle class political theorists—Bodin, Spinoza, Pufendorf, Hobbes—who insisted on the powers of the monarch against the privileges and autonomies of estates, corporations, guilds, and churches. One may well interpret the French revolution of 1789 not as a reaction to the monarch's misuse of his absolute powers, but rather to his failure to use them. The theories of the Marquis d'Argenson, of the Abbé Dubos, of the Physiocrats, and particularly of Rousseau are indeed attempts to reconstitute the unity and efficiency of the central power in the state, be it monarchical or democratic, so that the freedom of the nation can be effectively realized.

The rise of the liberal theories (such as Locke's) is understandable and has meaning only if the monopoly of the state's coercive powers is no longer challenged, so that restraints upon sovereignty will no longer lead to its disintegration. I have elsewhere stated the problem of modern political theory in these terms:

> The problem of political philosophy, and its dilemma, is the reconciliation of freedom and coercion. With the emergence of a money economy we encounter the modern state as the institution which claims the monopoly of coercive power in order to provide a secure basis upon which trade and commerce may flourish and the citizens may enjoy the benefit of their labor. But by creating this institution, by acknowledging its sovereign power, the citizen created an instrument that could and frequently did deprive him of protection and of the boon of his work. Consequently, while justifying the sovereign power of the state, he sought at the same time to justify limits upon the coercive power. The history of modern political thought since Machiavelli is the history of this attempt to justify right *and* might, law *and* power. There is no political theory which does not do both things.[79]

In international relations, the concept of state sovereignty fulfilled similar functions.[80] By attributing sovereignty to the state, formal equality is attributed to all states and a rational principle is thus introduced into an anarchic state system. As a polemical notion, state sovereignty in international politics rejects the sovereign claims of races and classes over citizens of other states, thus limiting the state's power to people residing in a specific territory. The notion of state sovereignty is thus basically antimperialist. The equalizing and limiting functions of this doctrine appear most strikingly when contrasted with the National Socialists' racial imperialism (which rejected state sovereignty for racial supremacy) and with the doctrine of the sovereignty of the international proletariat, represented by the Third International.

Thus sovereignty in the modern period, though it formally appeared as the negation of the juristic concept of freedom, was in reality its very presupposition.[81]

Quite identical problems arise in connection with the property concept—a concept fundamental in every political theory. There is an almost universal agreement in political theory on the supreme significance of private property. But why is private property often raised to the rank of a natural right? Why should it be treated with such reverence, even in the work of the early Marx?[82] *[handwritten: Economic + Philosophic Manuscripts + Holy Family]*

It seems clear that it is conceived, throughout the history of social and political thought, as an instrument for the realization of the good (or at least the tenable) life. This is clearly Aristotle's position,[83] which is carried on in the whole medieval tradition.[84] It is equally the position of the more modern political thinkers—of Bodin, Spinoza, Hobbes, Kant, and Hegel—whether they believe property to be a natural right or a grant by positive law. The instrumentalist character of property is probably the strongest link among these varied political theories. The connection of property and liberty is, of course, most candidly stated in Locke's theory, where liberty appears as inherent in the overall concept of property. But property is defined as labor-property, and possessory theories of property are thus rejected, the legitimation of property resting in the transformation of external nature, particularly land, by the creative activity of man. It is precisely the labor theory of property that demonstrates its instrumentalist role and it is here a matter of indifference that Locke drew no consequences from his own theory, which he merely intended as a legitimation of capitalist property. But the recognition of the instrumentalist nature of property in regard to liberty makes it obviously necessary to redefine the social function of property in each historical stage, and thus to distinguish clearly between various types of property and of property owners.[85] If property is to serve freedom, and if freedom pertains to man only, then corporate property, while it may or may not be necessary socially, cannot claim to be a civil right of the same rank as freedom and religion and communications. Similarly, the substrata of the property right—land, consumption goods, production goods—may require different treatment.

Most of the Continental civil rights catalogs thus make a clear distinction between property and other civil rights, the protection of the latter being far more stringent than that of the former.[86] One very simple consideration will make clear the instrumentalist role of property: all constitutions permit the condemnation of private property with adequate compensation. Yet no civilized constitution could possibly permit the state to do away with a person's life or liberty for public purposes even with more than adequate compensation. The value of political freedom is absolute; that of property is merely relative to it. Thus the tasks of a political theory concerned with man's freedom are to analyze whether property fulfills its function as an efficient instrument of freedom and to discover what institutional changes are necessary to maximize its effectiveness.[87]

To sum up: Insight into the operation of external nature permits man to master nature. Our enlarged knowledge of man's psyche permits us to understand the psychological processes activating the anxiety that deprives him of freedom and tends to make him a slave to authoritarian and totalitarian leaders. Our understanding of the historical situation permits us to adjust our institutional framework to the increased knowledge of nature and of man.

THE VOLITIONAL ELEMENT IN FREEDOM

The above formula indicates, however, that neither the juristic nor the cognitive element of freedom is really exhaustive. Law limits political power; knowledge shows us the way to freedom; but man can actually attain freedom only through his own efforts. Neither God nor history grants freedom to him. In this insight rests the theoretical formulation of democracy as that political system that permits the maximization of political freedom. The volitional or activist element is as indispensable to the constitution of political freedom as are the juristic and cognitive elements. We have said before that if political and juristic freedom are equated no case can be made for democracy as that political system where, supposedly, political freedom is best preserved and that the constitutional monarchy might then be as good an institution—if not better.

Despite Aristotle's dislike of democracy, some kind of active participation in politics is to him the precondition for citizenship. This minimum he defines as a share in "the deliberative and judicial functions."[88] The freedom created by the *Polis*[89] can thus be attained solely through active participation in its politics—even if, for reasons of expediency, Plato and Aristotle deny full participation to the masses. In our terms, some kind of identification through action is necessary to prevent the total political alienation of the citizen.

This assumes, of course, a value judgment, namely the undesirability of political alienation. This is by no means shared in the history of political thought. The Epicurean school (Epicurus, Lucretius, Hobbes and many others) took the opposite point of view: the undesirability of political participation, thereby frankly admitting that political power, whatever its origin and form, is and will always remain a force hostile or alien to man, who should find his satisfaction not in a political system—which provides merely the outer frame of order—but rather outside it. Political Epicureanism may indeed be a necessary attitude in periods where two evil principles compete, and a third principle has no prospect of asserting itself.[90] The *homo politicus* may indeed then withdraw and cultivate his garden or his mind. As a rule, however, Epicurean attitudes will probably be expressions of either cowardice or indifference, playing directly into the hands of those bent on appropriating political power for their own ends. Whether or not one believes political power is alien to man, it determines his life to an ever increasing extent; thus the need for participation in its formation is imperative even for those who prefer the cultivation of individual contemplation.[91]

To stress merely the volitional aspect of freedom creates as dangerous a situation as does exclusive concentration on the juristic or the cognitive aspect. To define political freedom simply as individual will implies the negation of the obligations that we have toward our fellow man: one cannot assert one's will at the expense of another, nor attain one's own perfection by destroying another's. The protection of minorities and of dissenting opinions is ruled out if the activist element alone is deemed the equivalent of freedom. The juristic notion, therefore, cannot be dispensed with.

If we stress the supremacy of political action regardless of the historical situation within which the will must be realized, we arrive at a utopian putschism—the view that man can, in each historical stage, or rather regardless of the historical stage, realize his full freedom through his action. Bakunin, very strongly influenced by Fichte's philosophy,[92] espoused revolutionary action for its own sake, while Mussolini preached the virtue of a "heroic life" in contrast to the sordidness of bourgeois security.

Yet the element of political action by the individual is as indispensable as are the other two. Man can realize his political freedom only through his own action, by determining the aim and methods of political power. A monarch or a dictator may give him freedom—but he can as easily take it away. History may present magnificent opportunities for freedom, but they may be missed if one does not act or fails to act adequately.

Thus the democratic political system is the only one which institutionalizes the activist element of political freedom; it institutionalizes man's opportunity to realize his freedom and overcome the alienation of political power. All three elements of the notion of political freedom are given a chance in the democratic system. The rule of law (expressed in civil rights) prevents the destruction of minorities and the oppression of dissenting opinion; the mechanism of change (inherent in the democratic system) allows the political system to keep pace with the historical process; the need for self-reliance of the citizen gives the best insurance against his domination by anxiety. Political action obviously involves the possibility of a choice between approximately equal alternatives. Only with such alternatives can the choice—and hence the action—be free. It is this which, in turn, constitutes the connecting link between the volitional and juristic aspects of freedom. The citizen can choose between alternatives only if he can choose freely; that is, only if his personal and societal rights are protected.

The stability of the democratic system thus depends upon these three elements: the effective operation of the rule of law, the flexibility of its political machinery to cope with new problems, and the education of its citizens.

THE PRESENT CRISIS IN POLITICAL FREEDOM

All three elements of political freedom are equally important and therefore none can be dispensed with. All three are in danger.

That none of them exists in totalitarian societies needs no comment here. In totalitarian states the individual-state relationship is reversed. There is no longer a presumption in favor of right and against coercion; rather there is a discretionary authorization of the agencies of the state to act as they see fit. Increased knowledge of man and nature is not used for the betterment of man's fate; rather, it assists in the manipulation of oppression. The active participation of the citizen in the formation of the national will is a sham. The basic elements of the structure of totalitarianism are so well known that nothing need be added here. Far more difficult, however, is the analysis of our system of democracy.

In the present period our attention is focused on the juristic element of freedom—on the operation of the rule of law, particularly as it relates to personal freedom.

We have drawn attention to the fact that in the modern period the traditional sanctions of the criminal law are supplemented by socioeconomic ones which may undermine the traditional guarantees. The problem appears in the so-called Loyalty Program and the Taft-Hartley Act.[93]

In the Loyalty Program[94] two problems naturally arise: the dismissal of civil servants suspected of disloyalty, and the refusal to appoint suspects. There can be no doubt, of course, that a government has the right, indeed the duty, to dismiss disloyal employees. The major problem is how far the rights of the employee are to be protected, that is, how loyalty is to be defined and what procedures are to be adopted. Since no criminal charge is involved, it may be correct to say that the protective clauses in the Sixth Amendment do not apply; the dismissed employee does not, therefore, enjoy the guarantee of a fair trial, so that "without a trial by jury, without evidence, and without even being allowed to confront [his] accusers or to know their identity, a citizen of the United States" may be "found disloyal to the government of the United States."[95] This may well be law; one can argue that no "civil right" is involved and that the discretion of the executive agencies cannot be questioned. It may also be legally true that nobody has a right to a specific government position and that, therefore, executive discretion in the exercise of the government's hiring power cannot be challenged. Yet one of the political principles upon which democracy rests is that of equal access to all public offices. No doubt this principle permits the government to exclude disloyal persons from employment. But there remains the problem of protecting the rights of applicants against arbitrary action.

Similarly, it may also be legally accurate—as the Supreme Court maintains[96]—that trade unions that are private associations should have no access to the National Labor Relations Board if their officers fail to file the noncommunist affidavit required by the Labor-Management Relations Act of 1947.[97]

Yet our analysis of the relation between the three types of civil rights—personal, societal, and political—attempted to show that even the justified denial of societal and political rights need not and should not lead to a restraint upon personal rights, which are not (or should not be) bound to changes in the economic, social, or political structure. The requirement of a fair trial is the indispensable minimum of civil liberties.

That minimum is now increasingly denied by socioeconomic sanctions which are probably not unconstitutional. From this it seems to follow that the juristic conception of liberty can no longer adequately perform its function. A few years ago one could indeed regard as adequate the classical interpretation of the personal rights as protecting the physical integrity of the individual from arbitrary action by the state. This is no longer possible today. Governmental sanctions against economic status are now of infinitely greater importance. The size of government employment has grown tremendously, and if we add the private industries working for the government—where similar rules seem to apply—we must conclude that in many cases the application of economic sanctions means a sentence of economic death inflicted without a hearing.

Perhaps worse than the possibility of an economic death penalty are the psychological-social consequences of governmental action. Social ostracism may well be the result of firing—or refusing to hire—a person because of suspected disloyalty. In a period of growing political conformism the stigma attached to these governmental actions may transform the citizen and his family into outlaws, proscribed by his neighbors, shunned even by his friends.

It seems clear, therefore, that the traditional notion of juristic freedom can no longer cope with the new phenomena. Juristic freedom, indispensable though it is, guarantees merely a minimum. And this minimum, once covering a broad aspect of our freedom, although perhaps for a relatively small stratum of the people, is steadily shrinking.

Similar difficulties exist in the operation of such societal civil rights as the right of communication. The Supreme Court's decision in Kovacs v. Cooper,[98] the loudspeaker truck case, illustrates the problem. Justice Black, in his dissenting opinion, considered the loudspeaker van as the communication medium of the little man, permitting him to compete with highly organized and concentrated media of communication. But even assuming that Justice Black's view had prevailed and the local ordinance had been voided, the free and equal use of societal rights would still not have been possible. The economic imbalance cannot thus be restored. The problem appears in various forms and has given rise to the formulation of a new type of civil right, the so-called "social rights" designed by various means—such as intervention of the state in behalf of the economically weak, as in various types of social security legislation, or recognition of mass organizations by the state, as in labor legislation—to restore a balance of social forces jeopardized either by the concentration of power on the one side or by awakening of political and social consciousness on the other. It is extremely doubtful whether it is wise to designate as civil rights positive demands upon the state—whether for social security, trade union recognition, or even planning. These and similar demands upon the state have their legitimation in their social utility, which must be concretely demonstrated. Personal, societal, and political rights, by contrast, constitute the very essence of a democratic political system and need no demonstration as to their social usefulness. But the psychological attraction of natural right doctrines, with their presentation of specific interests as natural ones, is such that the category "social rights" will probably soon find general acceptance. Whatever language we choose, however, the fact is that the exercise of civil (and political) rights requires a fair degree of equality in the control of and access to the media of communication.

These problems may not appear so depressing if one considers political power not as an alien power (as expressed in the formula citizen versus state) but as one's own—that is, if the volitional or activist element of freedom is recognized as being of equal importance with the two others. This may be expressed in the formula: no freedom without political activity. Yet it is clear—and this is the eternal contribution of individualist political thought—that no matter what the form of government, political power will always be to some degree alienated. The theories of Plato and Rousseau are thus utopias. Postulating complete identity between the citizen and the political system, they fail to take into account the fact that the conditions under which such identification can be achieved have never been realized in history. The two alternatives—the wisdom of Plato's philosopher-king, and the complete social and moral homogeneity of the Rousseauist society—are but dreams, though they be potent ones. The most exalted ruler is subject to passions; every society is charged with antagonisms. Even the most democratic system needs safeguards against the abuse of power. Yet in its tendency to minimize the alienation of political power democracy makes possible a fair balance between the interests of the individual and the *raison d'état*.

But there is equally no doubt that today the citizen's alienation from democratic political power is increasing—in Europe at tremendous speed, more slowly, but still discernibly, in the United States. Psychologically, this fact is usually designated as apathy. The term is useful if one does not forget that three states of mind may thus be designated: the literal meaning, the "I-don't-care" attitude; the Epicurean approach, which holds that political life is not the area in which man can or should attempt to realize his potentialities; and the total rejection of the political system without a chance of effectively articulating an alternative. In varying degrees all three types of apathy play into the hands of demagogues, and all may lead to caesarism.

The last type, the most dangerous, is the result of the malfunctioning of the democratic state. Its symptoms and causes have often been analyzed: the growing complexity of government, the growth of bureaucracies in public and private life, the concentration of private social power, the hardening of political parties into machines that, because of the high cost of politics, tend to exclude newcomers from the political market.

These difficulties are enhanced by many of the remedies proposed. There is the assertion that democracy is "mass-participation in politics" and that the structure of a system of political representation makes a sham of participation. Some propose "occupational representation," a corporate system as a substitute for political democracy. But it need not be demonstrated here that corporate representation theories are mere fig leaves for dictatorships.

Others, more modest, want to transform "political" democracy into true "economic" democracy, or at least to introduce "democratic principles" into the organization of the economy and the executive power. They overlook the fact that the theory of democracy is valid only for the organization of the state and its territorial subdivisions, never for any specific function. There is but one democracy, political democracy,[99] where alone the principles of equality can operate. Plans for "economic democracy" or the German trade union demand for "co-determination" in the economy may be useful, but they cannot be legitimized as democratic.

Still others, frightened by the growth of government bureaucracies, desire to democratize the administration. This is clearly desirable if to "democratize" means—as in post-1918 Germany—to eliminate undemocratic and antidemocratic elements from the bureaucracies. If it means, however, to reform the executive branch of the government by destroying the hierarchic principle or by letting "interest groups" participate in the making of administrative decisions, then such reforms not only have nothing to do with democracy but may even create new threats to it. The democratic principles of equality cannot operate in a bureaucratic structure, where the weight of a clerk must necessarily be less than that of an executive, and where responsibility has meaning only as that of an inferior to a superior. Demands for equality in bureaucracies and for responsibility downward within the bureaucratic structures tend to destroy an orderly administration.

Still more fateful is the second alternative: the participation of interested groups in the making of administrative decisions—what the Germans call functional, as against territorial, self-government. Labor administration is thus defined as democratic if the interested employer and labor groups have a voice in the decision-making process, so that the state, represented by a civil servant, appears as a kind of honest broker between opposing interest groups. This is a fairly widespread pattern of administration in Europe—but a dangerous one.[100] The danger to democracy of these and similar devices lies in the following.

The agreement of opposing interest groups on specific problems does not by the mere fact of their compromise necessarily coincide with the national interest. If such agreements are reached in fields where the government has no jurisdiction, this is, indeed, the best method of decision making, for in such a case the government expresses by its hands-off policy the view that national interests are not necessarily involved. If the government has assumed jurisdiction, however, its reliance on agreement between interest groups and its withdrawal into the role of broker between the interests may amount to a dictate of these interests over the nation. In this recognition lies the great contribution of Rousseau: the *volonté générale* (the national interest) is not necessarily the result of a mechanical addition of particular wills. Indeed, such an addition may, if raised to a political status, pervert the general interest of the community. If, therefore, a nation has decided that a social activity needs governmental regulation, full responsibility should rest upon the government (the executive branch) as the decision-making body, and responsibility should not be shifted to interest groups by incorporating them into the administrative machinery.

The incorporation of interest groups into the administrative system may actually have the effect of weakening what some call mass participation but what is better designated as spontaneous responsiveness to political decisions. For when the interest groups become semipublic bodies, part and parcel of the state machine, their independence lost, spontaneous responsiveness to policy decisions is weakened. The social organization turns into bureaucratic, semistate structures, incapable of acting as critics of the state.

Thus the essence of the democratic political system does not lie in mass participation in political decisions, but in the making of politically responsible decisions. The sole criterion of the democratic character of an administration lies in the full political responsibility of the administrative chief, not to special interests, but to the electorate as a whole. The model of a democracy is not Rousseau's construct of an identity of rulers and ruled, but representation of an electorate by responsible representatives. Representation is not agency; the representative is not an agent, acting on behalf of another's rights and interests, but one who acts in his own right although in another's (the national) interest. Political action in a democracy is the free election of representatives and the preservation of spontaneous responsiveness to the decisions of the representatives. This, in turn, requires that social bodies such as political parties and trade unions remain free of the state, open, and subject to rank and file pressure; and that the electorate, if faced with serious problems, be capable of spontaneously organizing itself for their solution.

These are simple considerations—but they seem to be largely forgotten. Many of the suggested remedies against bureaucratic absolutism seem actually to strengthen antidemocratic tendencies. In short, only within a specific context is the growth of governmental bureaucratic structure a threat to democracy.

A further and deeper threat arises from the growing antagonism between the potentialities of our historical situation and their actual utilization. Technological progress (the *conditio sine qua non* of cultural progress) is used today largely for armaments. No threat to the political system of democracy can arise if the fruits of advancing technology are diverted from normal use for a relatively short period. But our historical experience tends to show that a long-range postponement of expectations is possible only in a wholly repressive system. It is difficult to be exact in determining either the time span or the intensity of the conflict between the potential and the actual. But the principle must be clearly seen; democracy is not simply a political system like any other; its essence consists in the execution of large-scale social changes maximizing the freedom of man.

Only in this way can democracy be integrated; its integrating element is a moral one, whether it be freedom or justice. This moral legitimation is perhaps most eloquently expressed in the Prometheus myth which Protagoras expounds to Socrates:

> After a while the desire of self-preservation gathered them into cities; but when they were gathered together, having no art of government, they evil entreated one another and were again in process of dispersion and destruction. Zeus feared that the entire race would be exterminated, and so he sent Hermes to them, bearing reverence and justice to be the ordering principles of cities and the bonds of friendship and conciliation. Hermes asked Zeus how

he should impart justice and reverence among man: Should he distribute them as the arts are distributed; that is to say, to a favored few only. . . . "To all," said Zeus, "I should like them all to have a share; for cities cannot exist, if only a few share in the virtues."[101]

But there is opposed to this a second integrating principle of a political system: fear of an enemy. Fascist political thought[102] asserts that the creation of a national community is conditioned by the existence of an enemy whom one must be willing to exterminate physically. Politics thus denotes not the construction of a good society but the annihilation of an enemy. Anything—religion, art, race, class antagonisms—may be or may become political.

If the concept "enemy" and "fear" do constitute the "energetic principles"[103] of politics, a democratic political system is impossible, whether the fear is produced from within or from without. Montesquieu correctly observed that fear is what makes and sustains dictatorships. If freedom is absence of restraints, the restraints to be removed today are many; the psychological restraint of fear ranks first.

It is the existence and manipulation of fear that transforms a people into a mob. The antidemocratic theories of de Maistre, Bonald, Donoso Cortès, Spengler, and a host of others assert that democracy must, by its inner logic, degenerate into mob rule. Such necessity is a myth, very often promoted by those who wish to demonstrate the superiority of dictatorship. But the transformation from democracy into dictatorship seems to arise when the political system discards its liberal element and attempts to impose a creed upon its members, ostracizing those who do not accept it. This will be successful if, in John Dewey's words, we attain the "stage of development in which a vague and mysterious feeling of uncertain terror seizes the populace."[104]

NOTES

1. This article is a continuation of my paper "Approaches to the Study of Political Power." A German version, in an abbreviated form, was published under the title "Zum Begriff der Politischen Freiheit," *Zeitschrift für die Gesamte Staatswissenschaft* 25 (1953). Parts of it were read as papers in Arthur W. Macmahon's Columbia University Seminar on The State and before the Twelfth Symposium on Science, Philosophy, and Religion, New York, 1953. The discussions provoked by the papers helped greatly in the clarification of my ideas.

2. The preceding paragraphs form the transition from my article "Approaches to the Study of Political Power."

3. See Wilhelm Humboldt, *Ideen zu einem Versuch die Grenzen der Wirksamkeit des Staates zu Bestimmen* (Leipzig, 1851), ch. 16.

4. On this see particularly Edward Corwin, *Liberty Against Government—The Rise, Flowering and Decline of a Famous Juridical Concept* (Baton Rouge, 1948).

5. Montesquieu's formula, however, has a certain ambiguity. See my "Montes-

quieu," in Franz L. Neumann, *The Democratic and Authoritarian State* (Glencoe, Ill.: Free Press, 1957).

6. See G. W. F. Hegel, *Philosophy of Right*, trans. T. M. Knox (Oxford, 1942), sec. 5 add.

7. This, most certainly, was not the view of Plato, at least not in the *Republic*. But in the Aristotelian political philosophy, as revealed in his discussion of the rule of law in his *Politics, Ethics, and Rhetoric,* the individualistic element begins to enter. Plato's architectonic or organic conception of justice meant that the individual can have no claim against the social whole. Aristotle, in contrast, defines justice as distributive, as the restoration of proportionate equality, and he is thus compelled to consider the claim of man against man as an individual. Aristotle anticipates an individualistic conception, but for him the criterion of justice is still the order of the *Polis*. The history of the growth of the competing anti-Platonic individualistic conception initiated by the Sophists, taken up by Epicurus and the Skeptics, and transformed by the Stoics, is too well known to deserve another treatment here (see Sabine, *A History of Political Thought*, ch. 8, rev. ed. 1950), but one may say that with Aristotle's death man's history as an individual begins. See Tarn, *Hellenistic Civilization* 69 (1927). Cicero's legal philosophy is probably the first full-fledged individualistic Stoic presentation of a natural law doctrine which, in Christianity, was extended and deepened as well as narrowed and diverted into the spiritual realm—the equality of souls before God.

8. This is obvious in the case of the individualistic-liberal theories, since they have been conceived with this aim in mind. But it applies equally to the individualistic-absolutist theories of Hobbes and Spinoza. Both assert that the individual, threatened in the state of nature, is driven by the law of self-preservation to organize a state to which he surrenders his natural freedom. Both writers, however, qualify their radicalism: Hobbes by constructing the social contract as a kind of business agreement obligating the sovereign to maintain peace, order, and security, the contract lapsing when the sovereign fails to carry out his duty; Spinoza by identifying right and might, a formula that permits every social group to transform itself from an *alienus iuris* into a *sui iuris* and thus to become sovereign.

9. See Fritz Kern, *Gottesgnadentum und Widerstandrecht im früheren Mittelalter* (Leipzig, 1914), pp. 161–284, 310–312, 367–371, 394–396, 412–415, 432–434. See also Magna Carta, ch. 61.

10. See on this my two papers "Types of Natural Law" and "On the Limits of Justifiable Disobedience," both in Neumann, *The Democratic and Authoritarian State*. For the sake of accuracy it may be wise to stress that civil liberties in Great Britain owe probably less to either the Thomistic or the Lockean system than to the common law conception of historic rights of the Englishman and the techniques and the skill of the common lawyers.

11. Plato, *Laws*, trans. Jowett (1871), pp. 713–715.

12. Aristotle, *Ethica Nicomachea*, trans. W. D. Ross (London, 1925), bk. 5, ch. 9, 1137b.

13. A detailed analysis of this problem appears in my dissertation "The Governance of the Rule of Law." [Reprinted in *The Rule of Law: Political Theory and the Legal System in Modern Society* (Dover, N.H.: Berg, 1986).]

14. See Raymond Carre de Malberg, *Contribution à la Théorie Générale de l'Etat* (Paris, 1920), p. 289.

15. J. J. Rousseau, *Contrat Social* (1672), bk. 2, ch. 6.

16. John Austin, *Lectures on Jurisprudence* (London, 1929), p. 94.

17. I am not concerned with the intellectual history of this theory from Plato and Aristotle to the Stoics, and to the Thomistic system, and from there to the Descartian-Newtonian philosophy, but rather with its actual functions.

18. As in England and France.

19. This is clearly demonstrated in the rider to the appropriation bill denying salaries to Lovett et al. See United States v. Lovett, 328 U.S. 303 (1946).

20. Despite their latinity, the rules were both only in the eighteenth century. See Hall, "Nulla Poena Sine Lege," *Yale Law Journal* 47 (1937): 165.

21. "Retroactivity is the greatest crime the law can commit; it is the tearing up of the social pact, the annullment of the condition by virtue of which society may demand obedience from the individual. . . . Retroactivity takes away from the law its character; the retroactive law is no law." With these words did one of the apostles of liberalism, Benjamin Constant, attach retroactivity. *Le Moniteur Universel*, June 1, 1821, p. 754, col. 3.

22. Today, the rule against retroactivity has virtually a meaning only in criminal law. On the American doctrine see Corwin, *Liberty Against Government*, pp. 60–61.

23. These principles are equally applicable to common law. I have attempted to show this in *The Rule of Law*. The *ratio decidendi* of the judicial decision fills the role of the code or statute; English judges deny that they create new law and assert that they merely apply to the general principle contained in the *ratio decidendi*. For important statements on this problem see Paul Vinogradoff, *Common Sense in Law*, 2d ed. (London, 1946); Goodhart, "Precedent in English and Continental Law," *Law Quarterly Review* 50 (1934): 4.

24. The following is based on my article "The Change in the Function of the Law" [reprinted above].

25. The one case that I could discover illustrates well the ethical significance of the general principle. In Rex v. Earl of Crewe (1910) 2 K.B. 576, approved in Sobhuza II v. Miller (1926) A.C. 518, 524 (P.C.), the court had to deal with the proclamation of a colonial high commissioner for detention of a native under an Order in Council based upon the Foreign Jurisdiction Act, 53 & 54 Vict., c. 37 (1890), by which the Habeas Corpus Act was suspended. Farwell, L. J., in giving the judgment, said: "The truth is that in countries inhabited by native tribes who largely outnumber the white population such acts, although bulwarks of liberty in the United Kingdom, might, if applied there, will prove the death warrant of the whites" (p. 65), thus admitting the legality of suspending the Habeas Corpus Act not only generally, but also "in respect of a particular individual" (p. 616); and Kennedy, L. J., adds that the proclamation is "'privilegium'—legislation directed against a particular person, and generally, as I hope and believe, such legislation commends itself as little to the British legislators as it did the legislators of ancient Rome" (p. 616), while Rowlatt, for the defense, pointed to the relationship between the proclamation and a bill of attainder (pp. 583–588).

The Supreme Court decisions United States v. Lovett, 328 U.S. 303 (1946), applies the very same principle not only to legislative deprivation of the freedom of named individuals but to deprivation of every right.

26. Cicero, "Pro Cluentio," in *The Speeches of Cicero*, trans. Hodge (1927), sec. 53, p. 146.

27. Voltaire, "Pensees sur le gouvernement," in *Oeuvres Completes*, ed. Garnier (Paris, 1879), vol. 23, p. 526.

28. See Max Weber, *Wirtschaft und Gesellschaft* (Tübingen, 1922), p. 174.

29. See Max Weber, *The Protestant Ethic and the Spirit of Capitalism*, 2d ed., trans. Talcott Parsons (London, 1950), p. 17.

30. See particularly Adam Smith, *A Theory of Moral Sentiments*, 5th ed. (1781), pt. 3, ch. 3.

31. See Roscoe Pound, *The Spirit of the Common Law* (Boston, 1921), p. 46.

32. The formula (according to Corwin, *Liberty Against Government*, p. 13) was coined by James Harrington, *The Oceana*, ed. John Toland (London, 1747), p. 37, who ascribes it to Aristotle and Livey. Cicero uses much the same term.

33. According to Rudolf Gneist the word *Rechtsstaat* has been coined by Robert von Mohl, *Die Geschichte und Literatur der Staatswissenschaften* (Erlangen, 1855), p. 296. On the difference between Germany and England see Burin, "The Rule of Law in German Constitutional Thought: A Study in Comparative Jurisprudence," unpublished thesis in Columbia University Library, 1953.

34. F. J. Stahl, *Rechts- und Staatslehre*, 3d ed. (1878), p. 137.

35. Robert von Mohl himself, however, did not accept the Stahl formula. To him, the character of a state as a *Rechtsstaat* is equally determined by the political and social goals expressed in the legal system. His view did not find acceptance.

36. A. V. Dicey, *Introduction to the Study of the Law of the Constitution*, 8th ed. (London, 1915), p. 402.

37. Thus Jeremy Bentham demanded a code because it

> would not require schools for its explanation, would not require casuists to unravel its subtleties. It would speak a language familiar to everybody; each one might consult it at his need. . . . Commentaries, if written, should not be cited. . . . If a judge or advocate thinks he sees an error or omission, let him certify his opinion to the Legislature.

"General View of Complete Code of Laws," in his *Works*, ed. John Bowring (Edinburgh, 1843), vol. 3, p. 210. What Bentham advocated the French carried out. See Francois Geny, *Méthode d'Interprétation et Sources du Droit Privé Positif*, 2d ed. (Paris, 1919), pp. 77, 84; and Malberg, *Contribution à la Théorie Générale de l'Etat*, p. 719. The French forbade the judges to interpret laws and created, in 1790, the *référé législatif*, a mandatory of the legislative power, to interpret ambiguous provision of law (abolished only 1828–1837). The "enlightened despots" Frederick II of Prussia and Joseph II of Austria flatly forbade legal interpretations of laws; a Bavarian instruction of 1813, probably drafted under the influence of Paul Johann Anselm Feuerbach, forbade officials and private scholars the writing of commentaries to the Bavarian penal code. See Gustav Radbruch, *Paul Johann Anselm Feuerbach, ein Juristenleben* (Vienna, 1934), p. 85. Savigny took the same line.

38. See *Table Talk of John Selden*, ed. Frederick Pollock (London, 1927), p. 43.

39. See *Bl. Comm.*, vol. 1, p. 62.

40. See Immanuel Kant, *Philosophy of Law*, trans W. Hastie (Edinburgh, 1887),

p. 51, where equity is defined as a "dumb goddess who cannot claim a hearing of right. Hence it follows that a Court of Equity, for the decision of disputed questions of right, would involve a contradiction."

41. Frederic Maitland, *Equity: A Course of Lectures*, ed. A. H. Chaylor and W. J. Whitaker (Cambridge, 1928).

42. Gee v. Pritchard, 2 Swan, Ch. 402, 414, 36 Eng. Rep. 670, 674 (1818).

43. But not only there. There is a second set of circumstances which I do not discuss here: the problem of colliding interest of equal value to society (e.g., divorce law).

44. Thus, correctly, Corwin, *Liberty Against Government*, p. 6.

45. Not quite happily, Professor Freund calls them "passive liberties." See Paul Freund, *On Understanding the Supreme Court* (Boston, 1949), p. 23.

46. U.S. Const. Amend. IV.

47. U.S. Const. Amend. II, VI.

48. U.S. Const. Amend. IV.

49. See the statement on principles by Justice Cardozo, Palko v. Connecticut, 302 U.S. 319 (1937).

50. In light of this the Rabinowitz decision, covering unreasonable searches and seizures, is very hard to take. United States v. Rabinowitz, 339 U.S. 56 (1950).

51. 336 U.S. 77 (1949).

52. 340 U.S. 315 (1951).

53. But for the United States, consider the more favorable decisions, Terminiello v. Chicago, 337 U.S. 1 (1949), and Thomas v. Collins, 323 U.S. 516 (1945), and the discussion in Zachariah Chafee, *Free Speech in the United States* (Cambridge, Mass., 1941), pp. 409–435.

54. Schenck v. United States, 249 U.S. 49 (1919).

55. See Riesman, "Civil Liberties in a Period of Transition," *Public Policy* 3 (1942): 33, 39.

56. 283 U.S. 697 (1931).

57. 319 U.S. 624 (1943).

58. 323 U.S. 516 (1945).

59. Dennis v. United States, 341 U.S. 494 (1951).

60. In Germany the famous Articles 10 and 17 of the Prussian General Code (*Allgemeines Landrecht*) gave almost complete discretionary power to the police, and the institution of "protective custody" rested on this provision. Legally the situation is similar in all countries. The differences between the various countries are thus caused by different attitudes of the courts and of the lawmakers, and not by the formulations.

61. Board of Education v. Barnette, 319 U.S. 624, 639–640 (1943).

62. See Rousseau, *Contrat Social*, bk. 2, ch. 6.

63. Dennis v. United States, 341 U.S. 494, 555 (1951).

64. Lucretius, *On the Nature of Things*, trans. H. A. J. Munroe (London, 1919), bk. 1, p. 6.

65. Plato, *Republic*, trans. F. M. Cornford (London, 1945), ch. 4.

66. Epicurus, *Epicurus, The Extant Remains*, ed. Cyril Bailey (Oxford, 1926), p. 97.

67. Epicurus, *Epicurus, The Extant Remains*, p. 107.
68. On the intellectual history of Epicureanism, see M. Guyau, *La Moral d'Epicure et ses Rapports avec les Doctrines Contemporains*, 3d ed. (Paris, 1886).
69. See David Bidney, *The Psychology and Ethics of Spinoza: A Study in the History and Logic of Ideas* (London, 1940), p. 372.
70. See Benedictus de Spinoza, *Ethics*, bk. 5, prop. 20 (1677).
71. See Sigmund Freud, *Civilization and Its Discontents*, trans. Jean Riviere (London, 1949).
72. See Sigmund Freud, *Group Psychology and the Analysis of the Ego*, trans. James Strachey (London, 1948).
73. See Soren Kierkegaard, *The Concept of Dread*, trans. Walter Lowrie (Princeton, 1944), pp. 37–38; Sigmund Freud, *Hemmung, Symptom, und Angst* (1926).
74. See Giambattista Vico, *The New Science of Giambattista Vico*, trans. Thomas Bergin and Max Fisch (Ithaca, 1948).
75. Vico, *The New Science*, bk. 1, nos. 132–143, pp. 56-57.
76. See Neumann, "Montesquieu," pp. xxxv–xxxix.
77. Although, of course, St. Augustine had a similar notion.
78. For the most recent philosophical discussion of the marxist conception, see Gustav Wetter, *Der Dialektische Materialismus, seine Geschichte und sein System in der Sowjetunion* (Vienna, 1953), pp. 403–406.
79. See Neumann, "Montesquieu," pp. xxxi–xxxii.
80. On this see my *Behemoth: The Structure and Practice of National Socialism* (New York: Harper & Row, 1944).
81. Whether state sovereignty in domestic and international politics fulfills or can fulfill today the same function is of no concern in this study.
82. Especially in Marx, "Ökonomisch-Philosophische Manuskripte" (1844) and "Die heilige Familie" in *Marx-Engels Gesamtausgabe, Erste Abteilung* (1932), vol. 3.
83. See Aristotle, *Oeconomica*, trans. Foster (1920), 1343a; Aristotle, *Politics of Aristotle*, trans. Ernest Barker (Oxford, 1946), 1255b and passim.
84. For a good survey see Bede Jarrett, *Social Theories of the Middle Ages, 1200–1500* (Boston, 1926), pp. 122–149.
85. The very good survey, Richard Schlatter, *Private Property: The History of an Idea* (London, 1951), unfortunately fails in this. An interesting theory, little known and appreciated in the Anglo-American world, is that by the late Austrian President Karl Renner, first published in 1911 and translated as *The Institution of Private Law and Their Social Functions*, trans. O. Kahn-Freund (London, 1949).
86. This was also Chief Justice Stone's position. See United States v. Carolene Products Co., 304 U.S. 144, 152 n.4 (1938); see also Schneider v. State, 308 U.S. 147, 161 (1939). Against this see particularly Justice Frankfurter in Board of Education v. Barnette, 319 U.S. 624, 646 (1943) (dissenting opinion).
87. It is impossible to define within the system of democracy specific institutions which are potentially superior to other institutions, notwithstanding the old tradition that within the democratic system certain institutional arrangements make for the better protection of freedom: the doctrines of mixed government, of separation of powers, and of federalism.

As to mixed government, Aristotle as well as Polybius, both advocates of the doctrine, never understood by it a mere constitutional arrangement, that is, the mixing of monarchic, aristocratic, and democratic elements. They correlated the constitutional distribution of power with the distribution of social power. Both had specific social goals in mind.

Montesquieu's doctrine of separate powers is equally correlated to the distribution of social power. Moreover, if we look into political reality we cannot discern a coherent pattern. The English system of parliamentary democracy, which knows no doctrine of separate powers (except for the uncontested and uncontestable doctrine of judicial separateness and independence) maximizes political freedom; the continental parliamentary democracies have failed in this task; while the United States, with her presidential democracy, has maximized freedom—at least in the past. As Bentham recognized in the Montesquieu critique, the division of state functions into legislative, executive, and judicial and the allocation to three separate constitutional organs can protect freedom only if different social groups control the three agencies, the division losing its protective value if the three agencies are controlled by the same social group. See Neumann, "Montesquieu."

There exists as little correlation between political freedom and federalism. Montesquieu, probably following Plato's conception that the size of the *Polis* is determined by the reach of the Herald's voice, believed that democracies could function only in small territories. See Montesquieu, *Considerations on the Causes of the Grandeur and Decadence of the Romans*, trans. Jehu Baker (New York, 1882); and Neumann, "Montesquieu," p. xliv. But since they may be threatened by external danger, confederation can give them external strength without jeopardizing the internal strength derived from their smallness. Montesquieu, *The Spirit of the Laws* (1748), bk. 9, sec. 2. Jefferson followed this reasoning, adding to it his view that an agrarian society is the most stable substratum of democracy. See Thomas Jefferson, *Commonplace Book*, ed. Gilbert Chinard (Baltimore, 1926); but see Alfred Griswold, *Farming and Democracy* (New Haven, 1948). None of these propositions holds up to a critical analysis. There is no discernible relation between the size of a territory and political liberty, and none between federalism and democracy. England and France are centralistic democracies; the United States a federalist democracy; Imperial Germany and many Latin American republics have or have had a federalism that served to strengthen authoritarian trends.

Such theories are expressive of what I call constitutional fetishism, the attribution of political functions to isolated constitutional arrangements which have meaning only in a total cultural, and particularly social, setting. In short, the sociocultural bases of a system of political freedom are far more important than the specific constitutional manifestations. This is today quite important because the various occupation powers in the Far East and Europe have tended to impose their specific political institutions upon the occupied countries because they attribute to bare constitutional arrangements political effects which they could not possibly exert.

The value of political democracy as a system preserving the rule of law, taking account of the increase of knowledge, and rationally changing society to keep up with knowledge, is not to be challenged; but within the system no specific institutions are, per se, more effective than others.

88. Aristotle, Politics, 1281b.

89. I take it that the freedom of the *Polis* is, simultaneously, that of her citizens. See on this Michael Foster, *The Political Philosophies of Plato and Hegel* (Oxford, 1935).

90. See Max Radin's delightful study, *Epicurus My Master* (Chapel Hill, 1949).

91. The extent to which the volitional element is based on the corresponding philosophical trends (culminating in Fichte's philosophy) need not be discussed here.

92. See Edward Carr, *Michael Bakunin* (London, 1937), particularly pp. 31–32.

93. This brief discussion does not intend to analyze the legality of the measure but merely to hint at their political relevance.

94. See Executive Order 9835, March 21, 1947, Fed. Reg. 1935 (1947).

95. Bailey v. Richardson, 182 F. 2d 46, 66 (D.C. Cir. 1950) (Edgerton, J., dissenting).

96. American Communications Association v. Douds, 339 U.S. 382 (1950).

97. See 61 Stat. 146 (1947), 29 U.S.C., sec. 159(h) (Supp. 1952).

98. 336 U.S. 77 (1949).

99. See also Robert MacIver, *The Web of Government* (New York, 1947).

100. On the dangers in Germany between 1919 and 1933 see my *Behemoth*, pp. 400–413.

101. Plato, "Protagoras," in *Dialogues*, trans. Benjamin Jowett (New York, 1871), p. 322.

102. See Carl Schmitt, *Der Begriff des Politischen*, 2d ed. (Munich, 1932).

103. See Jefferson, *Commonplace Book*, p. 259.

104. John Dewey, *Characters and Events* (New York, 1929), p. 819.

EIGHT

Labor Law in Modern Society[1]

Franz L. Neumann

As I begin my discussion of labor law in modern society, I am quite clear that I cannot say anything particularly novel. No country contributed as much to the development and study of labor law as Germany during the period of the Weimar Republic. No organization promoted labor law and its intellectual cultivation as decisively as the Weimar labor unions. When we criticize the Weimar Republic—and this we do far too rarely—we can exclude labor law and social policy from the scope of that self-critique. Both fields do honor to Weimar and the Weimar labor movement. The flaw of Weimar democracy lay not in its considerable achievements in these areas, but rather in the discrepancy between the overall political weakness of the workers' movement and the impressiveness of its attainments in the area of social policy. Because contemporary Germany is threatened by the danger of a loss of precisely those portions of its traditions that need to be preserved, I am concerned here with attempting to renew the tradition of Weimar labor law. I will simply try to point to the necessity of reformulating some features of Weimar labor law so that the legacy of Weimar democracy can be shown to have relevance for the imperatives of contemporary politics. Of course, I am well aware that I am not fully informed about conditions in Germany right now.

I

We are probably in agreement about the basic issue regarding labor law: dependent labor. The fact that labor is dependent makes the labor relationship different from all other legal relationships; it is unique. It is the

Editor's Note: Originally appeared in *Recht der Arbeit* 4, no. 1 (1951).

achievement of jurists such as Otto von Gierke, Philipp Lotmar, Carl Flesch, and Hugo Sinzheimer[2] to have grasped the special characteristics of this object in legal terms. What makes it unique? Surely not only in the fact that the worker is separated from the means of production, but also in that in his work he depends on the use of instruments owned by an "other." This "other" thus stands in a power relationship to the worker. This formulation already points to a dilemma that we perhaps did not adequately grasp before 1933. Influenced by collectivist conceptions of labor law, we permitted ourselves to make the mistake of believing that the nature of this "other" was essential to the individual worker as a worker. Is the question of who possesses this power decisive for someone subjected to this alien form of power? Whether this "other" is a single entrepreneur, a local or regional government, the state—either a public law proprietor or a civil law proprietor?

The collectivist theory of labor law was repeatedly expounded in this way: as soon as property is communally owned, it ceases to be an alien form of property. Then, the power of the proprietor is no longer an alien form of power, the worker becomes self-determining, and a perfect identity between rulers and the ruled results. True democracy is achieved. Fascism, National Socialism, and Bolshevism—by means of different formulations—argued in this fashion, and we led ourselves down a blind alley by means of this identitarian conception [*Identitätstheorie*]. We assumed—and perhaps there are many who still believe this—that the socialization of the means of production puts an end to domination of human beings over other human beings within the work place. Socialization solves many problems (although I do not want to discuss them here), but it certainly fails to provide a solution to this one: the relationship of the individual worker to the "concrete principal"—to use an expression of my teacher, Heinrich Titze, to describe those persons who exercise direct power within the work place on behalf of the juridical proprietor.

Regardless of whether property is public or private, this exercise of power remains. Work still has to be organized. The fundamental problems of modern industrial civilization still exist: the division of labor, the work regime, and workplace discipline. Whether the "abstract principal" is the state or some other public or quasipublic body, the concrete principal is still the group of human beings who runs the workplace and thus exercise power.

If you are willing to accept this view, then you should find yourself in agreement with my conclusions. The interests of the worker can never be made identical with the interests of the state. The worker's interests will inevitably involve the attempt to improve his material and legal status; he will always be forced to defend his rights—whether against a private or a public proprietor. In a socialist system, these interests will not be rendered null and void. They still exist. In fact, I would go so far as to maintain that they become even more important than they are in a capitalist society. The worker in a capitalist society is more willing to tolerate injustice; from the perspective of the worker, injustice is essential to the operation of the system. In a socialist system, injustice committed against the worker is a crime, especially when committed in the name of Socialism itself. This is undoubtedly why the Bolshevik system seems so immoral to us. Workers' rights are daily sacrificed there in the name of Socialism.

We need to draw two inferences from this insight: the existence of adequate legal guarantees for the individual worker and free labor unions are tremendously important. Regardless of the nature of the existing economic and social system, both remain central to labor law.

II

So let me discuss the first problem at hand: the role of labor law protections for the individual worker.

We undoubtedly neglected problems associated with the labor contract before 1933. But to determine the significance of labor law guarantees for the individual, we first have to reach some agreement about the juridical nature of the labor contract. First of all, the labor contract is surely an exchange contract [*Austauschvertrag*] in which a commodity (labor power) is exchanged for money. It is one of liberalism's achievements to have treated the labor contract as a contract based on reciprocal obligations [*Schuldvertrag*] and labor as a commodity; it is one of liberalism's demerits to have treated the labor contract as *nothing more than* a contract based on reciprocal obligations and labor *merely* as a commodity.

These two sentences contain the entire problematic of labor law. The labor contract is a contract that recognizes mutual obligations and thus belongs among the most fundamental categories of a rational system of law. Constitutionalism's world-historical contribution is to have developed rational law as an instrument for the protection of interests, and it is the great achievement of the Englishman Jeremy Bentham and the German Max Weber to have clearly grasped both the political and intellectual significance of the protective functions of rational law. Some have criticized this view by claiming that an analysis of the labor contract in terms of a contract based on reciprocal obligations is necessarily lacking in theoretical significance because it simply describes a concrete state of affairs without saying something novel about it. I cannot follow this line of argumentation. The construction of the labor contract in terms of a contract involving mutual obligations means that the services of the employer and the employee can be precisely defined and thus rendered absolutely calculable. Neither courts nor administrative bodies thus are permitted either to create additional legal claims for the relevant parties or to negate existing ones. This is an exceptionally progressive ideal.[3]

As you know, precisely this principle was undermined in the Weimar Republic by the influence of the Free Law School [Freirechtsschule].[4] Just recall the abuse with which theorists of the Free Law School showered the federal courts for acquitting someone accused of having stolen electric energy because electricity could not be considered an "object" as defined by paragraph 242 of the legal code. In reality, this ruling by the federal court reveals the progressive character of rational law: it has protective functions.

Unfortunately, the German courts after 1918 tended to forget its own principles and increasingly relied on the ambiguities of paragraph 242 as a cure-all for the civil law evils of Weimar.[5] "Good faith," "good customs"—and many other vague legal standards—began to replace rational legal relations between employers and employees. If we examine the functions of such amorphous legal clauses in the sphere of the labor contract, we can conclude that they possessed the following dual functions:

1. They worked to trim and sometimes even destroy workers' contractual rights (for example, judicial rulings concerning the Factory Safety Laws).[6]
2. They facilitated the juristic construction of new duties for workers that lacked any real basis in the labor relationship (for example, duties based on the idea of "good faith," or derived from the laws on unfair competition).[7]

But I have also just stated that the labor contract does not simply involve reciprocal obligations: it is a power relationship as well.[8] This is often deemed inaccurate because work relations allegedly should be conceived as having a "communal" character; only then allegedly is it possible to formulate socioethical maxims according to which labor relations could be effectively regulated. But I do not believe that the labor relationship offers a basis for deducing socioethical principles. The level of wages, the duration of vacations, the length of notice required before a worker can be dismissed—these depend on workers' overall status in society, not on the juridical nature of labor law. For this reason, the argument on behalf of a community-centered conception of the labor relationship is inconsiderable. More significantly, this view is wrong and downright dangerous: regardless of how beautiful it may sound, the concept of "community"—if one wants to be truly radical—should be driven from Germany. "Community" can only exist where there is an identity of interests: in the family or maybe in the labor union, but only to the extent that solidarity is genuine and experienced inwardly as such. Where there is no real identity of interests, the concept of the community can very easily become an ideological instrument of authoritarian domination, as happened in National Socialism. I do not want to tire you with a long-winded analysis of the origins and meaning of the concept of community. But let me just point to one example, which I can even draw from the history of democratic theory, in order to illustrate the dangers here. Rousseau is considered the prototypical defender of democracy, and for decades his *Social Contract* was considered the bible of democracy. Rousseau hoped to achieve a genuinely popular system of rule in which there would be neither rulers nor the ruled—in other words, where a perfect identity between the ruled and rulers would be found. This is a praiseworthy goal. But read the final chapter of the *Social Contract*, where the dangers of this type of theory become quite clear. Rousseau knew very well that such a perfect identity of interests as a rule does not exist, but since he wanted to achieve it anyhow, he needed to force it into existence. The last chapter of his work therefore contains the demand that all citizens should be obligated to a common civil religion, a community-based morality. Whoever refuses to accept the principles of this system of morality, Rousseau demands, should be expelled from the political community; whoever acknowledges the legitimacy of this system of morality but fails to live up to its demands should be punished with the death penalty. Terror is often the consequence of artificially forcing a community-centered theory upon an internally antagonistic society.

In the sphere of work relations, the community-centered view of labor law means the sacrifice of the worker's interests and rights to a collective interest, in most cases to be determined by those who exercise power within the factory. Again, this is the case whether the power holder is capitalist or socialist.

On the contrary: the labor relationship is based on reciprocal obligations *and* power: human beings stand in a relationship of domination with other human beings. This is the basis for the legal principle that those who possess this power (again, regardless of whether they are private capitalist or socialist in nature) are obligated to fulfill additional duties (social services)[9] in relation to the object of that domination, the worker. But this does not imply that the object of domination—as the community-based conception suggests—requires the worker to fulfill duties for the employer in addition to those outlined in the labor contract.

So let me summarize the results of my argument. More now than before 1933, the protection of the interests and rights of the individual worker in the face of (either a capitalist or socialist) employer should constitute the core of labor law. Every tendency to rely on vague legal standards or a community-centered conception of labor relations to justify trimming the worker's rights or burdening him with additional obligations needs to be attacked. If the protective functions of rational law are to be made fully effective, there is need for greater precision in legislation and within the formulation of contracts. Pursuing this agenda is more urgent than ever before: unless myriad pieces of evidence prove deceptive, antirational tendencies in German jurisprudence are gaining strong support today.

III

The defense of the worker's rights and interests is a task for the labor unions, works councils, and the government.

There is no time here for an adequate discussion of public obligations to the worker. In contrast to the situation in the United States, it is widely believed in Germany that the government owes many obligations to the worker. The importance of these responsibilities should not be minimized. The Weimar Republic guaranteed quick and inexpensive legal protections for the worker by means of a system of labor courts. The statute was good; perhaps it can even provide a model. But this is not the place to address the details of this issue.

As a labor unionist you know that the protection of individual rights for the worker does not merely depend on the quality of the court system and its procedural guarantees. Equally important, perhaps even more important, is whether the social organizations that aspire to protect the rights of the worker possess the power and will to do so. The best statute for labor courts can never succeed without effective labor unions.

But it is the peculiarity of German legal development that works councils function alongside labor unions as instruments for protecting workers' rights. There are a number of substantial problems with this set-up. Yet one thing is certain: the works councils cannot be wished away from labor law and social policy. Regardless of how their competences are defined, there is no doubt that the works councils in the Weimar Republic made an exceptional contribution to the democratic education of the workers. During precisely that period when voters were flocking to the National Socialists and Communists, works council elections produced defeats for both parties. The nonbureaucratic structure of the works councils, their proximity to the work place, and their close ties to the labor unions made the works councils effective instruments of political education.

Nonetheless, they may still have contained one basic flaw. The councils were supposed to undertake three different tasks: first, the protection of the rights of individual workers; second, the pursuit of the workers' collective interests; third, the defense of the factory's overall interests. Of course, defending all three of these interests at the same time is always quite difficult. It becomes even more difficult as emphasis is placed on the importance of the factory's collective interests, and less difficult when the emphasis on those interests is reduced.

In legal theory and practice, a community-centered category of labor law [emphasizing the idea of the "factory community" or *Betriebsgemeinschaft*] seems to have become dominant; under the National Socialists, it became the official theory. The factory was construed as an organism and thus—as is inevitable with every organic theory—encouraged a set of reactionary trends. The factory agreement (in other words, the contract) became nothing but a set of factory regulations standing above and beyond those parties involved. This development seems to have culminated in the total subordination of the interests of the individual worker to the interests of the "factory in itself."

Hence, one should consider differentiating legal regulations that protect the individual worker from unfair dismissals from the legal substructure of the works councils; such protections belong to that sphere of labor law explicitly concerned with assuring legal guarantees for the individual. Such a reform might bring about three changes: first, protection against unfair dismissals would be guaranteed to all workers and not just those having a factory council; second, the labor unions, which are further removed from the immediate scope of the workplace than are the factory council representatives, could more effectively help individual workers fight unfair firings; third, works councils could focus their energies on the defense of the collective interests of the employees by making sure that contractual agreements are being respected by the employer and by more effectively supervising the production process. As the underlying character of the economy becomes increasingly collective, such issues undoubtedly will take on ever increasing significance.

IV

Clearly, labor law does not simply defend the rights and interests of the individual worker: it is also a crucial component of the social order. As in the past, this social order today is determined by the existence of property in the means of production. Property influences three different markets—the labor market, the market in goods or commodities, and the "political market" (the state). According to German practice, in each one of these markets we find at least one type of independent organization. In the labor market, property organizes itself into entrepreneurs' associations (*Arbeitergeberverband*); in the commodity market, property is organized into cartels, concerns, and individual monopolies; in the political arena, business interests take the form of territorial organizations, industrial and trade chambers (*Kammern*), and sectoral associations (*Fachverbände*). These bodies interlock in many different ways. This is widely known and need not be discussed in greater detail here.

For the workers, only the labor unions—and to some extent the works councils—stand opposite these three forms of business organization. This suggests a serious sociological dilemma.

Organizations of the propertied are typically associations or federations consisting of relatively powerful individuals and groups. Organizations representative of wage labor are mass-based and composed of economically powerless individuals. But it is a sociological fact that small numbers have many advantages vis-à-vis large numbers in the political and economic arena. Max Weber even went so far as to speak of the principled superiority of small numbers. This superiority stems in part from the importance of secrecy in waging political struggles: strategic and tactical decisions must be kept secret if they are to prove politically successful. But it is evident that secrecy is better preserved in small groups than in large mass organizations. This dilemma is even more significant for mass-based organizations, like the German Trade Union Federation, that are no longer ideologically homogeneous;[10] this makes an open discussion of strategy and tactics even more difficult. This sociological fact results in the emergence of what often is described as the formation of labor union oligarchy or, in a deprecatory tone, "boss rule." Sociologists who study this problem have repeatedly argued that rule by such oligarchs is undemocratic.

But this view is at least somewhat one-sided. Leadership, and especially independent leadership, is a decisive element of democracy. It is therefore false to describe the leaders of mass-based organizations as oligarchs. They only become oligarchs when they are no longer selected in accordance with free elections and have managed to place themselves outside the scope of democratic controls. There are two reasons why this needs to be said: first, we need to criticize a misuse of the term oligarchy that misleadingly suggests that democracy and political leadership are incompatible; second, I want to encourage you to take the problem of securing genuinely free elections, and an authentic system of control over elected union leaders, much more seriously than labor unions have in the past. From the perspective of jurisprudence, this means that more attention should be focused on the internal legal structure of the labor union. To the credit of the German unions (and on the basis of studies of many other unions), I would like to emphasize that the German labor union movement suffers far less from oligarchical trends than do the labor movements of other countries.

V

But an even more serious political problem emerges alongside this sociological dilemma. The labor unions are outfitted with the task of factually opposing the three different types of market organizations that represent propertied interests. The key question is whether the unions can and should function effectively on all three fronts (the labor market, commodity market, and in the political arena). I cannot provide an adequate answer to this question here. But let me just try to hint at the problematic at hand.

The real domain of the labor union is the labor market; there the unions make use of the instruments of the strike and the collective agreement. The principles underlying the collective agreement were developed with such precision in the Weimar period by Hugo Sinzheimer, Kaskel, H. C. Nipperdey, and others that I do not believe that there is much more room left for juristic imagination in this area.

But we left two issues unanswered in 1933: the place of binding arbitration, and declarations of general applicability for a collective agreement.[11] I am against binding arbitration. It is immoral and incompatible with the existence of free labor unions. It permits parties to feign a willingness to fight and simultaneously heap abuse on the arbitration process when in reality they are quite happy to have the responsibility of waging labor disputes and securing labor peace taken off their hands. This becomes perfectly clear as soon as one examines the statistics on binding arbitration (like those gathered by W. Woytinsky). It is probably unnecessary to explain why binding arbitration is incompatible with the spirit of autonomous market organizations. If the state wants to intervene in labor disputes, it should do so directly and hence without relying on the mediation of independent organizations—and, naturally, only if such intervention is constitutionally permissible.

It is somewhat more difficult to evaluate the usefulness of attempts to make collective agreements universally valid. You will recall that this legal institution rests on a compromise. On the one hand, Lujo Brentano wanted to transform the labor unions and entrepreneurs' associations into compulsory bodies so that labor contracts would automatically cover all workers. The Allgemeine Deutsche Gewerkschaftsbund[12] and Sinzheimer militantly opposed this position; the legal institution of universally valid contracts was the result of a compromise between these two positions. But because it pays a premium to those forces hostile to autonomous organization and simultaneously gives the state too much influence over the labor unions, this compromise is unsatisfactory. Despite this, no responsible labor unionist can unconditionally oppose this institution. For that would mean leaving the unorganized to their own fate, and no one—rightly—wants to introduce the closed shop. Perhaps the solution to this problem lies in the initiation of a comprehensive system of state-backed minimum wages. I cannot say whether that is likely to be achieved in Germany today.

VI

The participation of labor unions in the commodity market and in the political sphere results in an even more serious set of problems. Despite the renaissance of the ideology of the free (or "social") market, the role of politics in the economy has grown and will continue to grow. More so now than ever before, the theory of laissez faire is an ideology that only can succeed with great effort in veiling the state's support for those who possess economic power. There are no longer any "purely economic" problems. The economy is political, just as politics now is inherently economic.[13]

Although we surely are in agreement on this point, it is still difficult to draw precise implications from it. As an umbrella organization, the German Labor Union Federation cannot legitimately line itself up with a particular political party.[14] The formula "political, but neutral in terms of party politics" nicely expresses the necessity for the unions to acknowledge the primacy of politics without abandoning neutrality in relation to individual political parties. This formula thus expresses two ideas: first, that the labor unions have a responsibility to take an independent position on all important political questions; and second, that they should use their social influence to act—as we Americans describe it—as a "pressure group" that influences those parties sympathetic to their political aims.

The German Labor Federation has also demanded the establishment of a system of worker codetermination. In other words, the unions hope to take part in the administration of the economy. I cannot discuss this agenda in detail here. Of course, the demand for worker codetermination highlights—there is little disagreement about this—a real dilemma: the need for the union to reach a balance between acting as an autonomous economic organization and exercising responsible authority as a partner in the organization of the economy. No one could possibly deny that reaching a balance between these two tasks is difficult. But a basic postulate should never be forgotten: labor unions must preserve their character as autonomous, independent private associations. The existence of independent labor unions is not only decisive for the unions themselves but, and even more so, for the future of German democracy.

Democracy cannot function without free, private associations and a flexible set of autonomous organizations. We live in a period of growing bureaucratization. Autonomous social organizations are the key to correcting this alarming trend, which may lead to social paralysis, the death of initiative, and then easily to a new authoritarianism. Let us not forget that the essence of the totalitarian state unveils itself most clearly in its treatment of the labor unions. The leader of the fascist unions, Edmondo Rossini, was defeated in his struggle on behalf of relative labor union autonomy by Mussolini: in 1928, Rossini disappeared and the last remnants of union autonomy were obliterated in Italy. Because he also tried to preserve some autonomy for the soviet labor unions in relation to the Communist Party, Tomsky met the same fate in 1929. During the purges, he disappeared and was driven to commit suicide.

In the interest of democracy, the labor unions in my view should pursue no policies that potentially decrease their autonomy, independence, and their private status. That is the most important standard to be taken into consideration during the discussion about worker codetermination.

I have a second point as well: if my thesis about the primacy of politics is accurate, and if it is also correct that autonomous labor unions are essential for the functioning of democracy, then it is equally important to insist on the necessity of democracy for the labor unions. A far more ambitious task than the mere defense of pay and work conditions follows from this for the unions. The labor unions must live up to the responsibilities of democracy: to the ideals of civil liberties, parliamentary sovereignty, and a democratic judiciary and system of administration.

(Translated by William E. Scheuerman)

NOTES

1. This essay is a revised version of a lecture presented for the Committee on Social Policy of the German Labor Union Confederation (Deutscher Gewerkschaftsbund) on September 8, 1950, in Düsseldorf. It includes some responses to the valuable criticism of the lecture raised at the meeting.

2. Editor's Note: Hugo Sinzheimer was the chief architect of German labor law and one of Neumann's main teachers. In recent years, his work has been the object of growing interest among critical-minded German jurists. See Hugo Sinzheimer, *Arbeitsrecht und Soziologie* (Frankfurt: EVA, 1976).

3. Editor's Note: For an elaboration on this argument see Franz L. Neumann, *Behemoth: The Structure and Practice of National Socialism* (New York: Harper & Row, 1944), pp. 419–422.

4. Editor's Note: For a discussion of the Free Law School, see "The Change in the Function of Law in Modern Society," reprinted above. For an accessible recent overview of its basic tenets see J. M. Kelly, *A Short History of Western Legal Theory* (Oxford: Clarendon Press, 1992), pp. 359–362.

5. Editor's Note: For a more detailed account of paragraph 242, see "The Change in the Function of Law in Modern Society," reprinted above.

6. Editor's Note: In an earlier essay, Neumann argued that the ambiguities of the Weimar Factory Risk Act tended to work to the benefit of business. See Franz L. Neumann, "Betriebsrisiko," *Arbeitsrechts-Praxis* 1, no. 10 (October 1928): 219–223.

7. Editor's Note: See "The Change in the Function of Law in Modern Society," reprinted above.

8. From the perspective of legal theory, it is impossible to construct the labor contract merely in terms of a contract involving reciprocal obligations; this position makes it impossible to resolve the problems associated with the acquisition of property by means of "working up" (*Verarbeitung*) (*Spezikation*). This interesting question has a long prehistory in social theory, but I cannot examine it here.

9. E. Bührig has pointed out that the term "social services" (*Fürsorgepflicht*) is

poorly chosen because it has the aroma of "social charity" or "welfare." A better term needs to be invented.

10. But I do not mean to be considered an opponent of centralized labor unions. On the contrary: I consider the unified and centralized character of the German unions a blessing.

11. Editor's Note: Under certain circumstances, a labor agreement may be declared to apply not only to those organizations that reached the agreement, but to all organizations and businesses within, for example, a particular industry or sector of the economy.

12. Editor's Note: This was the main pre-1933 labor union coalition.

13. Editor's Note: For an elaboration of this argument see Franz L. Neumann, "Economics and Politics in the Twentieth Century," in his *The Democratic and Authoritarian State: Essays in Political and Legal Theory* (Glencoe, Ill.: Free Press, 1964).

14. Editor's Note: Neumann is focusing on a number of issues of interest to German labor unions in the immediate postwar period. His comments arguably have somewhat broader significance as well: the legal problems discussed here remain central to labor unions and labor law in many parts of the world.

NINE

The *Rechtsstaat* as Magic Wall

Otto Kirchheimer

I

I shall begin with some remarks on the historical setting of the British Rule of Law and the German *Rechtsstaat*.[1] From there I shall proceed to show how these concepts have been transplanted and are still serviceable under conditions of present-day industrial society. Changes in the apparatus of government, and the substitution of executive and bureaucratic government for parliamentary government, bring about modifications of the rule of law without affecting the requirement that it serve the essential protective needs of the individual. The true yardsticks of legal devices, as of the regimes to which they belong, are their practices. It is the behavior of state officials, who along with their political elites are the creators and manipulators of institutions, that determines the effectiveness of available legal devices.

What types of claims is society willing to satisfy by putting legal machinery at everybody's disposal? How does society proceed when it is faced with the necessity of setting its course in uncharted or half-charted waters? What does it do with traditional formulas? Hide behind them, junk them, or try to adapt them to the purposes at hand?

"*Ein Schelm gibt mehr als er hat.*" Questions are cheap and answers may be long in coming.

The career of concepts resembles that of established trade names. The good will attached to them is too precious, too much in the nature of mental first-aid kits, to be cast aside lightly. What matters then is to hold the gloss added by successive generations against the original text, thus helping them to analyze and provide for their own situation. But is there an original

---

Editor's Note: Originally appeared in *The Critical Spirit: Essays in Honor of Herbert Marcuse*, ed. Kurt H. Wolff and Barrington Moore, Jr. (Boston: Beacon Press, 1967).

text in the concept of Rule of Law in Britain or the related German *Rechtsstaat*? I think that for all the differences in historical roots and particular legal traditions[2] their common denominator lies in the simple thought that the security of the individual is better served when specific claims can be addressed to institutions counting rules and permanency among their stock-in-trade than by reliance on transitory personal relations and situations. Beyond that, a good part of their common success probably lies in the mixture of implied promise and convenient vagueness. Who would not breathe more freely if told that the law can rule and that state and law may march hand in hand? Yet, rule may mean different things to different men. It may imply that the legal rule dominates the scene with a firm hand, but it may also mean an indefinite type of overlordship entrusting the actual running of things to those who minister to the needs of the customers. Such a state of affairs would leave the rules somehow in the position of the god of eighteenth-century deism, providing those in need with a certificate of correct origin, but little more. What is the nature of the law that rules or that, in the German version, enters into an indissoluble partnership with the state? What transformations does it experience in this union? If the state fathers the law, how and under what circumstances does it become a force of its own? Is it a center that directs or at least forms the conscience of the state? How much will rule-of-law concepts help us to answer these questions?

The British Rule of Law is a token of gratitude to a political success story. When formulated in 1885 by Dicey it connoted a safely established level of political civilization and a career of constitutionalism nearly 200 years old. Constitutional continuity is by no means tantamount to social continuity. But the fact that the political establishment did not snap out of order during the bitter years of post-Napoleonic starvation and repression or during the years of Chartist agitation lends some color to the asserted connection between the political success story and the constitutional underpinning. What Dicey did was to fuse the timeless elements of the story—the interest of all individuals to be hauled into court only for specific breaches of law established by general propositions (Parliament) and under regular procedure—with the particular concerns of a British Whig. Arbitrary power was thus not only the policeman's knock on the door but also what we might call the discretionary power of the administration to act in the interest of public welfare. Conferring of such powers should be maximally avoided and submitted to what Dicey, in a polemical way and with a side glance at the contemporary French situation, called "regular law courts."[3] Added to this was a somewhat myopic view of the meaning of equality before the law. It had nothing to do with the entry of new classes into the fold of the community but instead was another paean to the virtues of middle-class constitutionalism. The fact that a colonial governor, a secretary of state, or a military officer could be hailed into court like any ordinary citizen was for

Dicey both the necessary and sufficient content of legal equality. (This is not to deny that Dicey was on firm ground when he established "equality before the law" in the formal sense as an integral part of his Rule of Law. What later generations criticized was the absence of any thought that the formal concept of the Rule of Law would need to be supplemented by an ever increasing body of legislative and correlative administrative action.)

But where does this law come from? As common law it is the judge's and his predecessors' own creation. As statute law it originates in Parliament, formally omnipotent but which, as a corporate body, is thoroughly reasonable and "does not interfere with the course of the law."[4] Dicey's *fin de siècle* formula mirrors both the constitutional tradition and a social ambience. In the absence of a written constitution Parliament has a theoretical omnipotence which, given the careful doses of nineteenth-century enlargement of the franchise, raised few problems. To the extent that law was statute law, a "popularly revered judiciary,"[5] safely recruited from Oxbridge precincts, remained loyal to the emanations of Parliament. In case of need, however, the latter could be rendered harmless by a narrow interpretation of statutory intent.

In contrast to the placid career of the British Rule of Law throughout the nineteenth century, the German *Rechtsstaat* retained some elements of a snake charmer's performance, remaining an index of partly fulfilled and partly outstanding claims. How can a rising class, the bourgeoisie, gain entrance into the official setup without being able to make the requisite show of strength? In classical fashion, it will assert the universality of its demands. Thus, when the century was young, it protested against an eighteenth-century, police-state concept of individual freedom that would allow the state to busy itself with the personal happiness of the individual for which, according to Kant and Feuerbach, there was no general law. As long as the state apparatus was slated to stay in the hands of privileged groups, a *Rechtsstaat* concept featuring the state's limitation to legal purposes deriving from the moral freedom of the individual might provide the objective law that would miraculously bind ruler and ruled together in common observance. The *Rechtsstaat* idea might permeate the state apparatus and induce the state to observe as objective law what could not be postulated as subjective right.[6] A bureaucratic concept of duty might thus have to compensate for the absence of legally enforceable claims by individuals or groups. But what if the ruler were not willing to subscribe to the tenets of early constitutionalism? Kant could not find a right of revolution, though he would accommodate its results.[7]

When Bismarck undertook to fix the relations between army, bureaucracy, and bourgeoisie, he did not hand over full legislative power to the bourgeoisie but rather conceived it as a unifying bond between relevant social forces. For the administration, the legislative power circumscribed, as Gneist put it, the discretionary space within which it could continue to operate.[8] For the bourgeoisie it safeguarded its primordial role in the legislative machinery, jointly to be operated by the federal and state bureaucracies and itself. If Bismarck granted the bourgeoisie at best an indefinite share in what Gneist had called the Archimedean point of the *Rechtsstaat,* participation in local self-government,[9] he gave it its full share of legislative power. But at the same time he made the bourgeoisie uncomfortable by the introduction of universal suffrage which, in the words of its spokesman Gneist, "produces average opinions which cannot maintain the stability of legal principle."[10] The people at large, besides being admitted to the precincts of the Reichstag, became beneficiaries of a system of administration based on law (*Gesetzmässigkeit der Verwaltung*). Administrative action was subjected to legal scrutiny by courts, civil and administrative, whose members were somehow not completely integrated into either the bourgeoisie or the reigning regime but managed to maintain their own *esprit de corps.*

II

When the battle of concepts was again joined after the two world wars, the European political scene had changed. In the beginning of the century, practice had been concerned with supervision of a limited number of state functions and with the techniques of guaranteeing individual freedom and property. The more or less efficient carrying out of these tasks now made it quite evident that in a number of countries individual freedom was threatened more by those who controlled jobs and the necessities of life than by the official authorities of the day. Hence there arose increasing demands for positive governmental action, whether pertaining to town and country planning or health and welfare legislation.

These demands were facilitated by the fact that everywhere in the West the electoral franchise had become universal. The last remnants of more limited forms of representative government had by the end of World War I given way to political democracy. But the appearance on the parliamentary scene of mass parties committed to the speedy fulfillment of the abovementioned welfare demands raised a new problem: how to relate the rule of law to the new output of the legislative body. Since the beginning of the twentieth century a practice, recognizable enough in its outlines even if not always tidily followed, had developed, requiring that general rules for identical case situations were to be issued by parliamentary legislation. Individual cases were to be dealt with by the administrative services on the basis of these statutory rules. Such cases were to be reviewed, upon application, by courts of law which scanned both the legal basis and, at least to some extent, the limits of discretion applied in administrative action. The criminal case and the civil claim continued to enjoy the benefit of direct access to the courts without need of prior administrative decision. Could the same general scheme which applied to the granting of professional licenses, building permits, and so on, be transferred to the handling of an increasing body of legislation in the fields of city planning, health and welfare, agricultural subsidies, and so on, which either conferred benefits on the individual or made some of his activities dependent on administrative agreement?

Attacks were now forthcoming in force, alleging that the extension of state activities to such an ever increasing number of fields was not compatible with the rule of law and would destroy its protective character. It was intimated that special legislation introducing numerous new administrative jurisdictions in the interest of a great variety of social and professional categories was incompatible with a concept of equality of law, which rested essentially on the existence of a body of common law to be uniformly applied by the judiciary to all groups. The French jurist Ripert had blazed the trail, and Swiss, Austrian, and Italian lawyers, economists, and social scientists followed suit.

Is not, for instance, legislation allowing the government to take away land for a compensation, fixed at prices substantially inferior to those prevailing on the free market, a violation of the rule of law?[11] This idea that the rule of law requires the state to restrict its activities to whatever is compatible with formal guarantees of legal equality, thus necessarily excluding the legislator from the welfare field, is a theorem which does not become more tenable by endless repetition. On the contrary, a more far-reaching measure of social equality, exemplified by some types of land legislation, while not required by the equality postulate of the rule of law, is in no way contradictory to it. Nobody will doubt the immense importance of land-use planning in densely settled areas after World War II. The almost uniform failure of the French, German, and Italian governments to deal comprehensively with the immense surplus profits accruing to proprietors of development land, and the consequent impossibility for the overwhelming majority of the population to acquire land of their own, has become one of the social characteristics of post-war Europe. Could it be seriously argued that the accident of physical proximity of land to urban agglomerations vests in the proprietor a right, attributable to the rule-of-law concept, to benefits toward which he has contributed nothing? In such cases remedial legislation, without doing violence to the concept of formal equality before the law, supplements it with a concept of social equality.

It has also been argued that any policy carrying out the substantive ideals of distributive justice must inevitably lead to the destruction of the rule of law as the impact of decisions becomes incalculable. Yet it is not intelligible why social-security rules cannot be as carefully framed, and the community burdens as well calculated, as rules concerning damage claims deriving from negligence actions. As to the chances of the foreseeability of results in yesterday's and today's social system, one might safely ask a French peasant of the 1960s whether he prefers the old-age pensions and government-fixed wheat prices of today or his grandfather's competitive freedom under Méline.

Such arguments are quite dated by now. More far-reaching contentions are made to uphold the link between economic liberalism and the rule of law. Doubts have been raised whether the lawmaking process by central authorities and the core of the rule of law are mutually compatible. Downgrading the importance of central legislation, according to this opinion, is justified not only by the simultaneous prevalence of a free market economy and common law as the predominant source of law for private disputes in the nineteenth century, but also by the superiority of economic over political choice. At the basis of the whole argument is mistrust of unwelcome majority decisions and an attempt to seek refuge in the *fata morgana* of a society able to dispense with intermediary public organizations, those mediating between groups and between individuals and groups. A spontaneous lawmaking process through voluntary cooperation of individuals as loosely tied to each other as they were under the reign of the trusted nonexpert, the common-law judge, is recommended as an alternative. But this is at best romanticism, at worst sheer evasion of the administrative tasks to be faced in order to make the world a place worth living in for the majority of the population in our age. One does not wish away the reality of the administrative state in mass society by reminiscing on the judges' social role in bygone days.[12]

Economic liberalism's attacks on the compatibility of the rule of law and collectivist forms of society are rearguard skirmishes. The more intensively a particular state went through a period of massive economic and social dislocation and the resultant abandoning of constitutionalism, the more urgent thereafter the insistence that community planning for decent living not only has a political priority, but constitutes a task postulated by the very constitutional order. The *Rechtsstaat* is transformed into the *Sozialrechtsstaat*. What previously might have been stated in purely permissive terms may now become elevated to the dignity of a constitutionally prescribed mission for the whole community.[13] Thus legal protection is no longer only an appanage of conflicts concerning personal freedom and property titles. It becomes available for other claims to which the individual may be entitled in his various status capacities, whether this status derives from his own initiative or is a consequence of a merger of societal guidance and personal response. If social services may be produced for the purposes of mass consumption, the accompanying procedures guaranteeing these rights must be producible too.[14]

But the doubts expressed about the legislature's role in the rule-of-law scheme come not only from the ranks of those who deprecate the extension of community interest from commercial and penal codes to land speculation and social insurance. It is asserted that parliaments have for a long time been covering up for a job which in fact is being done by somebody else, namely the bureaucracy. Yet the relative weight given to the interest of the individuals in the forming of general rules does not depend on specific forms of representation. The individual's chances depend on organizational vigilance, multiplicity of points of access to respective decision makers, and, closely connected, the existence of some form of intrabureaucratic competition. Neither of these requirements is necessarily tied to the parliamentary institution, which, as experience has shown, is as prone to manipulation as any other body. Some of the rules formulated by the still powerful American legislature have been like bills of attainder, legislation as inequitable as decrees occasionally produced by de Gaulle's government.

There has been a merger of the authorities who make the general rules with those who apply them to the individual case. What about the possible dangers that application of rules may represent in the context of this administrative practice of post-parliamentary society? Is the individual ruling the citizen receives from an administrative office now more aleatory because the bureaucracy is likely to have had a decisive hand in forming the general rule thereafter applied to his case? Most countries provide a layer of isolation between the rulemaking activity and the decision of individual cases—possibly as much in the interest of the efficiency of the establishment as in the asserted welfare of the customer or in deference to the doctrinal claims of the constitutional lawyer. They cannot rearrange the applicable categories each time to fit the particular purposes of the case. Even de Gaulle experienced resistance when he repeatedly reshuffled extraordinary military courts in order to obtain desirable policy results.[15]

Moreover, the substantive ends of justice require that the individual be able to make effective use of its procedural weapons. This has recently led to a remarkable diffusion of an institutional device originally domiciled in northern European countries, the ombudsman. As supervisor-extraordinary in the interest of both the aggrieved citizen and administrative efficiency, he has been allowed to lift some of the veil of intrabureaucratic case handling[16] which a judge may only pierce with the heavy weapon of subpoena of documents and records. It may well be that the ombudsman—as a nonformalized half-insider able to penetrate somewhat further into the mysteries of administrative discretion that a court bound by strict rules of evidence—will become a blessing for the little, organizationally unattached fellow pursuing a pension claim or chasing after a change-of-residence indemnity. To that extent he fills in for the member of parliament of old. For the petitioner, the certainty of a thorough examination is enhanced by exchanging a high-level parliamentary letter-carrier for a semidetached bureaucratic representative, but the member of parliament by this token might lose his line of contact with the ordinary citizen.

Nevertheless the relative success of the ombudsman—relative because only isolated success stories have been reported on inquiries of a more complicated nature pertaining to disputes involving larger sociopolitical complexes—brings only into sharper relief a large additional problem area. This area is exemplified by pension or overtime claims of former employees where the social situation and the antecedent relations out of which the claim originated are relatively simple and clear-cut. This could explain why the rate of compliance with the respective judgments may be quite high, why in this type of case the legal determination of the claim and its realization (*Recht* and *Rechtsverwirklichung*) have a tendency to converge. The near certainty that many types of claims once established will in due course be satisfied makes it reasonable for many legal systems to take such great pains to build up foolproof procedures to establish claims. If adjudication of a claim is tantamount to final settlement, it is certainly worth the effort to equip the parties with the best available means to get to the decision stage. But does the assumption of a unity between law and its realization hold true in all cases? If it did, our job would be finished. For Rule of Law and *Rechtsstaat* would be truly identical with the availability of generous and impartial procedures for obtaining legal protection or pursuing legal claims. To what extent does this proposition hold true? Is the concept of the rule of law exhausted by the availability of legal redress?

III

In 1956, during the trial of the German Communist Party before the constitutional court, a discussion arose whether that party could claim a "right of resistance" against specific policies of the West German political leadership which in the Communist Party's opinion were violations of the Basic Law. In answering this line of argument, the reasoning of the court decision[17] insisted on the fundamental difference between what the court called an intact constitutional order, in which isolated violations of the Basic Law might happen, and an order in which the organs of the state show no respect at all for law and justice and therefore corrupt the constitution, the people, and the state as a whole. Only in the latter case, so argued the court, would legal remedies be of no use to the people, so that resistance might be justified.

From this dictum we might assume that a clear-cut dichotomy exists in the mind of the German court between good and bad regimes. The good ones would provide effective and honest procedures of legal redress for any and all parties that might feel their position threatened by an abuse of public power. There is an implied premise that well-functioning means of legal redress, part of what we have recognized as the traditional armor of the rule of law, will always guarantee a balance between individual and public authority, thus arresting trends in a process of deterioration that would land the state in the "bad" column.

Is there such an easy way to sort out the good from the bad state? How does the problem of the "good" and the "bad" state present itself to the *homme situé,* the man trying to exist within the confines of modern society? Generally speaking, the state, "good" or "bad," remains an abstraction. People think in terms of subdivisions: politicians, tax collectors, welfare officers. Only in periods of turmoil does the day-to-day confrontation recede behind the expectations and fears directed toward larger entities. How do the men who constitute the state behave in the most acute and not infrequent situation when a break of continuity occurs and a new regime takes over?

For the officials or other dignitaries of the establishment, continuity, with its double sense of legal and social continuity, is the password. The first is elliptic and contains an element of necessary self-deception. The official is at one and the same time the witness to and the creator of this continuity. As a contemporary he watches the transition, the mixture of accidental or contrived emergency, of coercion and formal correctness, in the course of which the requirements theoretically set by the antecedent regime's constitutional documents are fulfilled. The official's continuing performance in his job constitutes the major certificate desired by the new regime to show that the fact of transition had all the hallmarks of regularity. The new regime thus hopes to earn the first credit toward transforming a shaky legality into legitimacy. Thus continuation in his job, immensely valuable for the incoming regime, both registers and by the same token creates the legality of the formal takeover. Yet the very nature of this transition also contains the official's absolution for his mode of acquiescence: passivity. Frequently the official in the exercise of his duties need not concern himself with the question of the legality of the regime. If he stopped running the trains or delivering the mail when the regime changes, he would be dubbed a partisan rather than an official. Insulation in correct jurisdictional grooves avoids such difficulties; yet the victims of extralegal violence that may accompany the changeover might still appeal to judicial officialdom, as did the bedraggled Prussian government after its ejection from office in 1932. But this appeal only proved that this particular government was not prepared to fight for its life. What could a judge do for a party unwilling to incur any risks in the service of its own cause? Its attitude only indicated that the cause was beyond rescue even before the chain of legality had snapped completely and the case evaporated into thin air. Thus, when the chips are down, in the very process of maintaining or changing power the official must either join the fight, if there is anything or anybody to fight for, or, as he usually does, become a witness and passive but valuable co-creator of the new regime's legality.

But legality, whether representing true or barely contrived continuity, is a step, and no more than that, toward creating legitimacy. To behold legitimacy there must either be social continuity or the attractive promise of a new social system. This legitimacy is the business of the community as a whole, not only the official's. The official may have been instrumental in creating the penumbra of beneficial legality but, this job done, he steps back into the ranks and becomes a citizen, naive or skeptical, enthusiastic or matter-of-fact, reticent or correct, scheming against or joyfully participating in the regime. In contrast to the official, the citizen at large, unless he is one of the few declared partisans in politics, need not take a position at all, as nothing is asked of him but to continue to pay his taxes and give an occasional cheer from the sidelines. His act of registering events is steeped in ambiguity and less consequential than the official's behavior with its precedent-building quality. It is both these things at the same time, because the social continuity which the citizen's passivity helps to create could be endangered, lacerated, or cut through by many manifestly contrary acts.

If the regime engages in foreign wars and imperialist conquest, the legitimacy problem reaches new dimensions. The citizen's total identification with both internal and foreign policy, which hitherto might have been evaded, may now become inescapable. Unless the foe of the regime has made a clear-cut choice of rejecting the official ideology, the daily necessities that are seemingly unconnected with the larger purposes of the regime may take precedence. Alienated, he may continue the daily routine. Court opinions dealing with negative choices, naturally written only under a successor regime, are not a very reliable guide, especially if the judges themselves have to realign and rationalize their own record in this process. But at least they elucidate the dimensions of the problem and show that behind the neat differentiation between "good" and "bad" regimes there may lurk a number of additional problems. Complications arise from the fact that even "bad" regimes must run the mails and feed their citizens, in short, pursue the millions of transactions without which the civilized existence of millions of people would rapidly come to an end. The citizen who refuses to lend a hand separates himself not only from the regime, but perhaps also from his fellow citizens' intent to continue living as well.

Thus men's actions under any regime will have to be judged in the light of their own contribution. The record of the regime under which they serve establishes at best a rebuttable presumption as to their own behavior. There are few who will deny this truth when it concerns the record of what commonly is called a "bad" regime; indeed, much time has been spent in the courts of many a country to put the burden of a fallen regime on the broad shoulders of its principals if they are safely out of the way, thus by logical implication absolving all those acting in their and the regime's name. But the opposite contention is one which bears some additional inspection, that is, that a regime that has some well-established and well-safeguarded channels for setting up general rules and universally accessible procedures to redress injustice is a perfect rule-of-law candidate.

There is no hard and fast line of separation between the formal remedies and the substantive goals of a social order. The availability of legal remedies for the citizens and the implantation of legal duties for the official world may, under favorable circumstances, lead to the attainment of individual or community goals. Whether available procedures are put in motion and whether legal rulings once obtained will be enforced or complied with has to be investigated for each category of cases. Without making such an effort, a rule of law, resting only on the theoretical availability of legal remedies somehow resembles a modern house whose glass wall, the major attraction for all visitors, already stands, but whose wooden utility walls no one has so far bothered to build.

It is a big step from the fact that, in some cases, finding the law is almost tantamount to executing its mandate, to assuming that such a situation must invariably prevail. Let me develop a case whose interest centers not only on the psychology of the players but on the intermeshing of many levels of participants. Presumably all of them acted correctly within their understanding of the rules of the *Rechtsstaat* and yet never arrived at satisfactory results. What I have in mind are the antecedents of and the 1965 German debate leading up to what in effect amounted to a prorogation of the statute of limitations for National Socialist murders. Official statements, as well as the course of the public and parliamentary debate, have established beyond doubt that until more than eight years after the Federal Republic was established no one in a responsible official position took the initiative systematically to collect evidence and initiate proceedings against the multitude of Nazi murderers. This does not mean that no one against whom witnesses had preferred complaints, or whose anonymity was lifted by private or bureaucratic accident, was investigated and, if the evidence was sufficient, prosecuted by the competent local authorities. But, as an official German report puts it with unintentional irony—as if murder were something which is only followed up upon specific complaints—"the survivors were much too busy building up a new life to care to push criminal prosecutions in Germany."[18] As no agency coordinated these individual local efforts, collected evidence, or systematically searched through the mountains of documents dispersed over many places at home and abroad, the outcome of these chance proceedings was unsatisfactory. Of 12,882 persons indicted between May 8, 1945, and January 1, 1964, only 5,445 were convicted; 4,033 or 31.8 percent were acquitted, whereas the highest acquittal rate in German courts for all types of proceedings in the 1950s was 8.5 percent. The remaining persons were discharged without judicial proceedings.[19]

It is thus entirely clear that the German executive, administrative, and judicial authorities during the first decade of the new state did not perceive any connection between the *Rechtsstaat* concept and the need to look for ways of dealing effectively with the problem of the National Socialist murders. The relentless zeal that characterized the German federal government's handling of the reverse side of the Nazi criminal account, the energetic and successful pressure on the Western High Commissioners in 1951 for speedy release of war criminals sentenced by Western occupation courts, found no resonance in the field of settling accounts with Nazi murderers. It took eight years until in the wake of public pressure, following the revelations of the Ulm SS trial, the various federal and state administrations of justice founded an agency coordinating the collection of evidence and other documents. After another six years it became clear that the statute of limitations would run out before it became possible to start proceedings against all presumable participants in Nazi murder activities. Under the impact of new pressures from abroad, some of them mainly designed to embarrass the regime, the Bonn legislature then decided that the statute of limitations for murder, which had been presumed to have started running again in May 1945, would be deemed to have come into operation only in December 1949. Thus, sins of omission were followed by the sin of commission—depriving presumed, not yet adjudged, culprits of the mild type of protection that the statute of limitations furnishes against the abuse of bureaucratic routine and changing political pressures. Moreover, the new solution solves the problem as little as did the policy before 1958 of diffuse and hit-or-miss prosecution. Certainly the 750 proceedings presently pending, with more than 7000 defendants, which so far have not ripened into the trial stage, together with the new proceedings which may be opened in the next four years, would push the trials well into the 1970s. This not only would put a burden on the defendants called to task more than a quarter of a century after the incriminating acts but also raises the question with what yardstick a new generation of judges, jurors, and the public, acting in a totally changed political situation, should measure the deeds of a previous generation.

The whole episode shows that the *Rechtsstaat* concept can be honored by scrupulous observation of all prescribed forms and proceedings while its spirit is constantly violated by an unwillingness to initiate steps commensurate with the magnitude of the problem at hand. In terms of the official rule books, the Law on the Administration of Justice, and the Code of Criminal Procedure, every German authority was proceeding correctly within its own jurisdiction. Many minor impediments to action (initial remnants of the few Allied reservations on jurisdiction; partial unavailability of records; access to records only under conditions not in accord with the goals of inter-German or German foreign policy, etc.) were allowed to stand in the way of facing the problem squarely, allowing it to be downgraded in this process to a series of interminable individual cases. There is no discernible individual to whom responsibility can be assigned. Who is to be blamed? The German Parliament, which in the 1950s withstood right-wing pressures to issue blanket amnesties for National Socialist crimes but carefully refrained from checking up on the positive performance of the bureaucracies involved? The political and administrative heads of the federal and state ministries of justice who waited until 1958 to take the necessary coordinating steps? The untold numbers of individual prosecutors and judges who acted properly in terms of the cases before them but never transmitted doubts to their superiors nor aroused the public as to the spotty and unsatisfactory results obtained?[20] They all acted bureaucratically correctly in terms of their individual jobs and yet eluded their responsibility when the occasion arose for showing that mass murder could be prosecuted in an administratively and morally difficult situation, yet one well within the safety margin of the regime they were serving.

The example is instructive: not because it proves that the Federal Republic is not a *Rechtsstaat*—which obviously it does not—but rather because it shows that the implementation of the rule of law is a problematic affair and that the mere enumeration of available remedies and jurisdictions does not suffice. The case shows how compartmentalization of organizations, each of which acts correctly within its own jurisdiction, may lead to results which might satisfy the tactical needs of participants in the official game, but falls wide of the mark of what one might call a step toward solving the substantive problems involved. The German politicians, lawyers, and administrators must have been fully aware that buying four more years for initiating new criminal proceedings would take the spotlight off an unsatisfactory record while compounding old sins of omission by new iniquities. Quite probably a full parliamentary inquiry into the causes of failure, which, except for exculpatory arguments, were only evoked in the most cryptic terms, would have been more appropriate than the theorizing on the justifiability of proroguing the statute of limitations, a measure of which nobody knew the meaning in actual practice. An analysis of the shortcomings of case handling would have laid bare the need for a new approach to the problem of human dignity. Is the time of the subject at the unlimited disposal of the official, is it part of the suspect's preemptive punishment to be at the authority's disposal literally till his last judgment day? Or is an enforceable provision for "deliberate speed" part of the subject's inalienable legal rights? What comes to the fore, therefore, is the *Rechtsstaat*'s need to strive for the attainment of substantive justice through procedures that are not liable to negate the very goal of the *Rechtsstaat* itself. The admixture of complementary elements of mass democracy and bureaucracy may create distortions at both ends.

IV

It is the title to glory of the *Rechtsstaat* and of the Rule of Law that remedies for all claims are provided. Implicit in the rule-of-law concept is the calculation that the mere availability of remedies will settle most claims out of court or enhance the chance of voluntary observation of the law, even though only a fraction of the offenders can ever be pursued. We ask more rarely whether a claim is always recognized where injury has been inflicted. Suppose the injury has occurred in an area where the individual concerned has established no business or employment relations with the agency involved. The job holder who loses his employment through mistaken withdrawal of his security clearance may have avenues of redress, but the job seeker equipped with all necessary professional qualifications who for security reasons is not permitted to pass beyond the interview stage never has a chance to contest the report which deprives him of access to entire job categories.[21]

Would it help in this connection if we introduced a differentiation separating the roles of the rule of law in conflicts involving public law from those in private law? Recently an erstwhile official practitioner of international law has opined that the private sphere is eminently related to courts, whereas law as a system allocating public power is by no means the creation of judges and courts. If judges go beyond the limits in which they can effectively exercise power, the result will be evasion rather than vindication of legal authority.[22] The statement reflects experience in a field where the discrepancy between existing norms (above all, Article 2, paragraph 4, Article 51, and Article 53 of the United Nations Charter) and the unwillingness of the major powers to comply with these norms makes it problematic how far the rule of law extends into the field of major power relations. Increasingly we meet attempts to deny that the rules in question are legally applicable to a specific situation or to reconstruct the meaning of the concept of compliance. In the place of judging a state's willingness to comply with a legal norm, it is now proposed that we consider compliance as a "spectrum, . . . a matter of degree varying with the circumstances of the case."[23] But such an approach confounds the job of the lawyer with that of the sociologist. The latter may try to determine what circumstances a rule is enforced or meets with resistance. The lawyer, however, cannot turn doubts and considerations antedating his opinion into some sort of statement like the following: "Because of original doubts as to whether my country is acting in self-defense or committing an act of aggression, I am recommending the landing of a limited troop contingent only." Limited or unlimited troop commitment, either acting in self-defense or committing an act of aggression—if the problem is considered as a proposition of law, the action can only be classified as either aggression or self-defense, compliance with or violation of the rules of international law.

Insofar as the rule of law enters international relations, it exists only at the sufferance of the major power holders and to the extent that the latter find it advantageous to submit to its working. Given the ever increasing importance of interpersonal and interorganizational exchanges on an interstate level, the absence of enforceable rules governing the behavior of the most powerful territorial units is fraught with the danger of a constant spillover into other fields. But while the spillover from international relations into the domestic field may be a constant threat in our times, it has relatively little to do with a differentiation between an acceptable rule of law for private violations and its unacceptability for the public sector.

Our world knows no magic wall separating the structure of private from that of public law. Nonjusticiability in the one sphere can easily spill over into the other. Witness the situation already mentioned concerning the activities of agencies protecting the security of the state. If anyone is in public business, then these agencies are, yet they interfere with the chances for a private life of untold multitudes of people, or take the matter of race relations, where the finding of meaningful solutions has become a matter of critical public concern and where one of the major difficulties lies in the permanent intermingling of public objectives and private decisions. The effectiveness of new state or federal policies is frequently predicated on a great variety of attitudes of private persons: the behavior of labor unions toward opening equal employment opportunities, the reaction of real-estate interests and their customers to fair housing regulations, or the degree of willingness of negro parents to submit their children to the tormenting experience of serving as guinea pigs for integration. Are the busloads of SNCC students traveling south engaged in a private trip? What then about the reception they will receive from the local sheriff? Or do we have to await how the sheriff's actions will be characterized, first in the state courts and then in the federal courts? Semantics may help to rationalize a court decision one way or another, though to harmonize federal decisions and those of southern states is beyond human ingenuity. But one interesting observation can be made: the (until recently) official U.S. practitioner of international law would call "public" the area from which he wanted the courts to be excluded, whereas in the realm of race relations the argument would go the other way. The U.S. Supreme Court rationalizes the right to interfere with a certain institution by referring to its public character, while it calls private relations those areas in which it does not feel entitled to interfere. The private-public dichotomy is thus largely a matter of the different manipulative concerns of various agencies. It offers no clue to the problem of which relationships should be left to private arrangements and what form necessary cooperative arrangements should take.

One can hide the magnitude of the enforcement problem as one of the touchstones of the rule of law, as, for example, in Llewellyn's variant of legal realism. Only those legal rules may then be considered meaningful which involve solutions acceptable to major forces in the community. From this viewpoint, few enforcement problems are likely to arise. First, lawmakers are psychologically conditioned to issue norms compatible with the wishes of major clienteles; second, if the lawmakers have somehow failed to take such ground rules into account (the motto being "where reason stops, there stops the enacted rule"), the duty of restrictive interpretation takes over.[24] As Llewellyn puts it, "even the machinery of the rightest of right *jus* is subject to limitations of human inventiveness."[25] In other words, few occasions arise for conflict between the will of the legislator and grass-roots obedience to his mandate, because the intermediate level of interpreters takes care of accommodation and excludes what to the legal realist must be "meaningless" conflicts. No doubt this has happened often enough. One might even add the numerous cases where the legislator is of such uncertain or divided mind that the called-for interpreter, be he judge or, as is more frequent, administrative agency, will have full freedom to evolve substantive decisions of his own with only a minimum of legislative guidelines.[26]

Yet legislative efforts, sometimes braced up by the executive, are not always uncertain about what they want to achieve, nor do judges invariably function as harmonizers or eternalizers of the existing group equilibrium. In other words, there may be situations where the question of enforcement of a definite policy may be inescapable. This was the case, for instance, in the United States in World War II when the Office of Price Administration was set up to ration all scarce but essential commodities. They were to be distributed fairly among customers at prices within inflation-preventing ranges. The allocation part of the system somehow worked. The number of commodities available outside rationed channels was curtailed, but not to the extent that the ethically relevant part of the goal, equality of sacrifice, could be sufficiently realized. Enough commodities, like gasoline or meat, moving in parallel channels, remained available for those willing and able to pay. Yet, the risk of suspension orders, injunctions, civil-damage suits, and to a very minor degree fines was reflected in premiums of various sorts. Now one might say, in the fashion of legal realism, that the authorities had neglected to calculate the magnitude of organized pressures against the system, which were simply too great to allow for anything but hit-or-miss enforcement.[27] Thus, in the nature of things, people would understand that punishment, that is, prison sentences, remained mostly reserved for those in the business of counterfeiting ration coupons, while all other visitations by the authorities were simply reflected in the size of the risk premium.[28]

The OPA case shows that the enforcement of legal sanctions is anything but automatic, even though in contrast to the German case it involved routine problems of a continuing political and social order—sanctions destined to keep goods out of undesirable channels and to further a reasonable price level and patriotic morale. Yet, enforcement presented the difficulty that businessmen against whom measures were to be taken were organized, in close contact, and therefore never broke ranks to help the prosecution; moreover, the potentially much more numerous supporters of enforcement policy, the consumers at large, had neither an organization to speak of nor many voices to represent them in public. The outcome of the individual enforcement skirmishes may have been unpredictable. Trade associations, more often than not helped along by politicians, joined issue with the OPA staff. The latter was itself frequently split according to whether the division in question was more interested in the survival of the organization, with its important allocation function,[29] or in attempts to implement policies aimed at equality of sacrifice. If a conscious choice had ever been made, it would have been between symbolic enforcement as part of an educational bargaining drive and effective enforcement to obtain the goal of equality of sacrifice. Circumstances helped to avoid such a clear-cut choice. In essence, both sides, the government and the consumer, carried part of their points, because the concatenation of propaganda, compromise, and symbolic enforcement—and still more the reality of ample profits through a guaranteed mass market rather than through inflationary prices—kept price rises in bounds. And the chiseler won, in that attempts at enforcement, such as they were, were never able to stamp out the market in parallel-risk premiums. Seen from the viewpoint of legal organization and the rule of law, the outcome was at best dubious, for neither the substantive goal of equal sacrifice nor evenhandedness in enforcement procedure made a particularly strong showing. It demonstrates the difficulty of harnessing the legal system to the pursuit of nationally approved goals in the face of concerted resistance by major organizations in the establishment.

The situations in law enforcement are too multifarious for even a rudimentary attempt to catalog them. Visualized as a continuum, at one end there would be adjudicated individual claims for wages or damages—reinstatement claims of employees being quite a different matter—deriving from contractual relations. At the opposite end would lie situations such as that presented in Korematsu v. U.S., the case of Japanese exclusion during World War II.[30] Here the government, by expelling citizens from their homes and places of work and sending them into camps because of their Japanese ancestry, committed direct and acute injury, but the courts in trying to remedy the situation might have run head-on into difficulties in enforcing their judgment against the executive. They thus had to choose between covering up the impotence of the law by adducing a special war-time jurisdictional scheme allowing security questions to be decided by the military without outside interference and—as done in Justice Jackson's well-known dissent—establishing a dichotomy between the judicial power, which applies the law and the Constitution and must judge accordingly, and the military power, telling the people at the same time not to rely on the exercise of judicial power in such circumstances.

A judgment first and above all renders a decision on the concrete situation that has been presented. To that extent the administration as well as the private litigant must fashion their attitude so as to bring themselves into line with the specific order of the court. But higher courts do not make their decisions merely with regard to the particular case before them. They may want to give directives to future actors in only partly charted fields or to weed out malpractices not in conformity with their notions of applicable law or constitutional rule. To what extent will they succeed? A look at wiretapping, search and seizure, and utilization of illegally obtained confessions, gives rise to the following observations.

Courts have no direct supervisory power over the police—federal, state, or local—except in relation to the individual case under review. From the viewpoint of the administrator their decisions serve therefore primarily to introduce a new element of risk. Politicians can be expected to make declarations showing deference to the court, yet in the absence of continuous organized political pressure the situation in the case directly under review will differ from the sum total of the practice falling under related headings. In the particular case under review, the Supreme Court in nine cases out of ten may be able to see its mandate through, even if the instrument through which it has to work is as unpromising as a state court in the deep South. But in later cases the lower courts, if they feel the urge or are exposed to sufficient pressure, may exercise the fine art of distinguishing some elements justifying a different outcome and, at the very best, requiring time-consuming new litigation in the higher courts. On the other hand, however, lower courts may also get tired of shielding police practices against criticism by higher courts that might possibly reflect a large segment of public opinion. In any case, from then on the administrators will have to face increased risks against which even legislative support is not invariably a permanent help.

Conformity of administrative practices with rules emanating from lawmakers and bodies interpreting the law has not the same meaning for administrative and judicial organizations. For the administrative organization, conformity to the law is one factor among many in its calculations. To obtain such conformity is essential, however, for courts, whose very impact is predicated on the community's willingness to abide by the rules set by courts. On the other hand, the fact that the courts are outside bodies that do not stand to the administration in a relationship of hierarchical superiority enhances the numerous factors of uncertainty in their relations to each other.

The facile idea that the availability of procedure for making claims or upholding the public order is tantamount to guaranteeing that these rules are effectively observed or put to work has little to recommend itself. Wherein then lie the benefits derived from rule-of-law concepts and from the institutions to which they correspond? For both procedural and substantive goals, rule-of-law concepts are best understood as yardsticks for performance. They connote law as observed regularities. Where the route is charted, and only there, there is a great advantage to drawing up formulas to be applied to both the object and the subject of power situations. The sheer need to avoid the eruption of chaos among the ever increasing masses of population, as much as the unheard-of increase in the productive capacity of the advanced nations, puts a premium on satisfying the expanding needs of such multitudes. The efficient handling of the host of recurring problems that make up their daily existence, pertaining to job conditions, living quarters, health arrangements, and the easy translatability of such typical needs into corresponding money equivalents, makes the operations involved smooth and calculable—up to a point. To the extent that the rule of law furthers these ends, it contributes elements of personal security and even of substantive justice. It may well be, however, that the historian of the twentieth century will be less impressed by diverse propagandistic claims of various regimes as to the reign of law under their dominion than with the close cohabitation between wide stretches of certainty for mass man's daily living conditions with unheard-of areas of oppression, lawlessness, and rewards for maximum aggressiveness. A generation that has lived through Auschwitz and Hiroshima and was indifferent or powerless to prevent them, and which is prepared to see bigger Hiroshimas, has no cause for complacency about its preservation or even enlargement of some orderly forms of living. It may have forgotten the essential: there must be life for life to be worth living.

NOTES

1. Speaking of Western countries, I treat "rule of law" here as a generic proposition. Its specific cases of historical application include Germany's *Rechtsstaat* and the British Rule of Law, which will be capitalized.

2. These differences are sharply emphasized in Ernst Fraenkel, *Das amerikanische Regierungssystem* (Cologne and Opladen, 1960), pp. 196–200.

3. See A. V. Dicey, *Introduction to the Study of the Law of the Constitution*, 10th ed. (London, 1908), p. 198.

4. Dicey, *Introduction to the Study of the Law of the Constitution*, 10th ed., p. 415.

5. Dicey, *Introduction to the Study of the Law of the Constitution*, 7th ed., p. 398.

6. C. Welcker, *Letzte Gründe von Recht, Staat, und Strafe* (Giessen, 1813), p. 95. See also Leonard Krieger, *The German Idea of Freedom* (Boston, 1957), p. 255.

7. *Metaphysische Anfangsgründe der Rechtslehre*, para. 49a.

8. Rudolf von Gneist, *Der Rechtsstaat* (Berlin, 1873), p. 159.

9. Von Gneist, *Der Rechtsstaat*, p. 160.

10. Von Gneist, *Der Rechtsstaat*, p. 137.

11. See Bruno Leoni, *Freedom and the Law* (New York, 1961), p. 69.

12. R. Stevens, "Justiciability: The Restrictive Practices Court Reexamined," *Public Law* (1961): 265, reports the astonished reaction of English legal circles when judges were recently called upon to sit in implementation of the vague policy concepts of the 1956 Restrictive Trade Practices Act. Their attitudes belie continued reliance on the judges as experts in nonexpertise.

13. Konrad Hesse, "Der Rechtsstaat in der Verfassungsordnung des Grundgesetzes," in his *Staatsverfassung und Kirchenordnung. Festgabe fur Rudolf Smend* (Tübingen, 1962), p. 78.

14. H. W. Jones, "The Rule of Law and the Welfare State," *Columbia Law Review* 58 (1958): 155.

15. See *Conseil d'etat*, 19 octobre 1962, *Canal et autres*, and the remarks of Francois Mitterand in *Journal officiel* (Debats, Assemblee Nationale), 4 janvier 1963, p. 221.

16. The emphasis lies on "some." Intraoffice memos in preparation of a case, even in the country where the institution originated, became available to the ombudsman and his staff only after they had been placed into the permanent record, which is to say after the case had long been closed. C. F. Herlitz, "Publicity of Office Documents in Sweden," *Public Law* (1958): 50, 65.

17. Vol. 3, p. 737.

18. *Die Verfolgung Nationalsozialistischer Straftaten im Gebiet der Bundesrepublik Deutschland seit 1945* (Bonn, Bundesjustizministerium, 1965), p. 49.

19. *Die Verfolgung Nationalsozialistischer Straftaten im Gebiet der Bundesrepublik Deutschland*, p. 43.

20. Admittedly, however, the very change of role of the German judicial apparatus, from involvement in the legal politics of the national socialist regime to the handling of the latter's criminal legacy, made such an expectation largely illusory.

21. For the most recent discussion of this problem, see J. Rottmann's review of H. U. Evers, *Verfassungsschutz im Rechtsstaat* (Tübingen, 1961), in *Archiv für öffentliches Recht* 88 (1964): 227–244.

22. A. Chayes, "A Common Lawyer Looks at International Law," *Harvard Law Review* 78 (1965): 1396–1413.

23. L. Gross, "Problems of International Adjudication and Compliance with International Law," *American Journal of International Law* 59 (1965): 56.

24. See K. N. Llewellyn, *Jurisprudence* (Chicago, 1962), p. 228.

25. Llewellyn, *Jurisprudence*, p. 486.

26. M. Edelman, *The Symbolic Uses of Politics* (Urbana, 1964), ch. 3.

27. Whole regional production lines, like Del-Mar poultry or Southern lumber,

worked outside the system. See H. C. Mansfield, *A Short History of the OPA* (Washington, 1948), p. 257.

28. M. B. Clinard, *The Black Market* (New York, 1952), reports that 88 percent of a sample of businessmen in 1945 simply did not understand the difference between criminal fines and payments that had to be made as the result of triple damage suits (p. 235), and quite justifiably so, since this was all included in the same risk premium.

29. See V. A. Thompson, *The Regulatory Process in OPA Rationing* (New York, 1950).

30. 323 U.S. 214 (1944).

INDEX

Absolutism, 29, 45, 67, 102–104
Administration. *See* Bureaucracy
Adorno, Theodor, 2–3
Antiformal trends in law: in contemporary democracy, 4, 204–205, 246–249; in National Socialism, 11–16, 132–138, 144–146, 175–177, 233–234; in Weimar Republic, 35, 44–59, 125–132. *See also* Formal law; General law; Rule of law
Antisemitism, 40, 146, 159–160, 164, 177
Aquinas, Thomas, 105, 137
Aristotle, 199, 204, 214–215
Auschwitz, 261
Austin, John, 112, 199

Bentham, Jeremy, 1, 113–114, 233
Binding arbitration, 239. *See also* Labor law
Blackstone, William, 110, 112, 204
Brüning, Heinrich, 39–40, 49, 59
Bureaucracy: in contemporary democracy, 220–223, 240–241, 243; in National Socialism, 14, 155–157, 178–181, 185; in Weimar Republic, 6–9, 35–36, 44–59, 73, 124

Capitalism: and legal development, 12–13, 122–132, 143; and liberal rule of law, 109, 116–117, 201–202; and National Socialist legal order, 132–138, 143–144, 148, 157–158; and state intervention, 34, 204–205, 239–240; in Weimar Republic, 30, 38–43, 122–132

Caretaker government, 30–31
Codetermination, 220, 240–241. *See also* Economic democracy; Labor law
Collectivist democracy, 32–33, 123–124
Colonialism, 112, 201, 244
Common law, 199, 245
Communist Party: in postwar Germany, 250; suppression by Nazis, 41, 149–151, 154–155, 166; in Weimar Republic, 38–39, 53–56, 236
Concentration camps, 41, 153. *See also* National Socialism
Conceptual realism, 64
Conciliar political theory, 105–106
Constant, Benjamin, 113
Constitutionalism: in France, 46–47, 53–54; posttraditional type, 5–6, 10; in postwar Germany, 250; in United States, 72–73, 207–210, 217–219, 259–260; in welfare state, 5–6, 32–33, 209. *See also* Rule of law; Weimar Constitution
Corporatism, 18, 32–33, 122–124, 220–221
Courts. *See* Judiciary
Crimes of omission, 174–175
Criminal attempt, 149, 172
Criminal law, 13–15, 145–155, 172–186
Critical Legal Studies, 1–3, 15 n. 45

Death penalty, 147–148, 155, 166, 177, 182–184, 235
Decisionism, in law, 11–15, 104, 132–138
de Gaulle, Charles, 249

265

Democracy: defined, 65–67, 222; direct forms of, 5, 31, 82–87, 222; heterogeneity in, 9–10, 64–74; homogeneity in, 64–67, 219–220, 235; identitarian conception of, 197, 219–220, 222, 232–235; instrumental view of, 9, 68–70; in labor unions, 238; and political freedom, 215–217; and rule of law, 203–210
Democratic socialism, 10, 17, 80. *See also* Social democracy
Dewey, John, 223
Dicey, A. V., 119–120, 203, 244–245
Disenchantment, in modernity, 14, 70
Due process clause, 37, 72. *See also* Constitutionalism
Dworkin, Ronald, 15 n. 44

Ebert, Friedrich, 30, 40, 123
Economic democracy, 5, 32–34, 37–38, 57, 220, 236–237
Emergency rule, 35–36, 44–59, 73
Epicurus, 210–212, 215–216, 220
Equality before the law, classical liberal view of, 44, 106–118, 199–203. *See also* Formal law; General law; Rule of law
Equity, 111, 204–205
Executive-centered rule, 6–10, 35–36, 44–59, 73, 124, 243

Fear, and politics, 223
Fish, Stanley, 13 n. 35, 15 n. 45
Formal law: decay of, in contemporary democracy, 107, 204–205, 246–249; decay of, in Weimar Republic, 35, 78, 127–132; destruction of, by Nazis, 12–15, 132–138, 144, 172–186, 234; ethical function of, 117–118, 144, 201. *See also* General law; Rule of law
France: constitutionalism in, 46–47, 53–54; rule of law in, 111–115
Frank, Hans, 142
Frankfurt School, 2–4, 11, 15
Freedom: cognitive aspects of, 17, 210–215; contemporary threats to, 217–223; legal aspects of, 101–108, 197–210; volitional aspects of, 17, 215–217
Free law school, 36–37, 128–129, 234
Free speech, 65–66, 207–208
Freisler, Rudolf, 142, 150, 155, 172
French Revolution, 51, 68, 111–114
Freud, Sigmund, 211

General law: defined, 106–108, 199–200; spurious form of, 107. *See also* Formal law; Rule of law
German Federal Republic, 236–241, 250–256
Gierke, Otto von, 135, 137, 232
Groener, Wilhelm, 30, 55, 123

Hayek, Friedrich, 17–18
Hegel, G. W., 30, 108, 118, 133, 197, 212, 214
Heller, Hermann, 82 n. 73
Hindenburg, Paul, 35, 39, 123
Hiroshima, 261
Hobbes, Thomas: Epicureanism in, 211, 315; in law, 112–113; on liberty, 76, 108; on sovereignty, 102–104, 212–214
Homogeneity, 64–67, 219–220, 235
Horkheimer, Max, 2–3
Hugenberg, Alfred, 40–42

Individual measure, 106–107, 112, 116–118, 125–138, 204–205
Institute for Social Research. *See* Frankfurt School
International law, 213–214, 256–257

Jay, Martin, 3 n. 8
Judicial review, 36–37, 72–73, 115, 127–128
Judiciary: in classical liberal theory, 36, 107–108, 113–115, 118, 200–204; in Imperial Germany, 36–37, 120–121; in National Socialism, 14, 132–138, 142–155, 174–178; in Weimar Republic, 36–37, 44–59, 120–132; in welfare state, 204–205, 249
Jurisdictional state, 68, 72–73
Jury system, 153, 184–185

Kant, Immanuel, 30, 111, 118, 204, 206, 214, 245
Kelsen, Hans, 9, 66–67, 199
Kiel School of Criminal Law, 173–175
Koellreutter, Otto, 53–54

Labor law: collectivist theory of, 232; community-centered concept of, 56–58, 130–131, 234–237; in contemporary democracy, 231–241; in National Socialism, 135, 143, 160–164, 232, 234–237; in Weimar Republic, 56–58, 130–131, 231–237

Labor unions: in contemporary democracy, 236–241; destruction of, in National Socialism, 41–42, 160–161; in Weimar Republic, 31, 37–41, 122–124
Landowners, and Nazism, 30, 38–43, 143, 164–165, 175
Law: enforcement of, 256–261; and morality, 3, 14–15, 129–138, 143–144, 173–174, 186, 201; political concept of, 104–106, 138; rational concept of, 104–106. *See also* Constitutionalism; Formal law; General law; Rule of law
Legal analogy, 14–16, 146–147, 175–176
Legal institutionalism, 134–138
Legality: concept of, 44–50; disintegration of, 6–10, 44–59, 173–174; and legitimacy, 6–10, 44–59, 64–88, 173–174
Legal positivism, 7, 113, 121, 129, 137–138, 173
Legal realism, 258
Legal security, 117–118, 121, 142, 201, 244–250
Legitimism, 45 n. 1
Leoni, Bruno, 18
Liberalism: and class-divided society, 54; and Frankfurt School, 2–3, 16
Llewellyn, K. N., 258
Local government, 32, 37, 50–51, 158–159
Locke, John, 102–103, 197, 213–214
Lukacs, Georg, 16

Machiavelli, 196
Majority rule, 9, 49, 64–67
Mannheim, Karl, 69
Marcuse, Herbert, 2
Marsilius of Padua, 105–106, 212
Marxism, 12–13, 16, 68, 156, 212
Montesquieu, 31, 111, 113, 197, 212, 223

National Socialism: Carl Schmitt's role in, 40, 132–138, 142, 173, 223; concept of property in, 134–138, 158; on democracy, 68; legal system of, 132–138, 142–166, 172–186, 232–237; seizure of power by, 41–43, 155–157; social bases of, 30, 41–43, 132–138, 143, 157–158, 160; war crimes, 19, 253–256
Natural law, 14, 102–106, 121, 127–132, 144, 198–199
Nazism. *See* National Socialism
Neutrality, in liberal legal thought, 74, 124

Nietzsche, Friedrich, 172
Nominalism, 105–106
Nulla poena sine lege, 147, 173, 200

Ombudsman, 249–250

Parliamentarism: in contemporary democracy, 18, 220–222, 248–249; and direct democracy, 82–86, 222; Schmitt on, 82–84; in Weimar Republic, 4–10, 31–41, 44–45, 48–49, 58–59, 123–124. *See also* Democracy
Philosophical individualism, 197
Plato, 195, 199, 210, 215, 220
Plebiscitary rule, 9–10, 49, 68, 86–87
Political alienation, 19, 195–197, 215, 219–220
Political justice, 143–155, 253–256
Political participation, 19, 216–217, 220–223
Political power, 195–196
Polycracy, in Weimar Republic, 37
Popitz, Johannes, 37, 59
Pound, Roscoe, 202
Private property: classical views of, 214; National Socialist concept of, 134–138, 158; and power, 33–34, 232; and rule of law, 116–117, 142, 201–202. *See also* Capitalism
Proportional representation, 78–79, 85–87
Preuss, Hugo, 5
Public-private distinction, 256–258
Puritanism, 110, 202

Radbruch, Gustav, 35
Rational legality, 6, 44
Rawls, John, 1
Rechtsstaat. *See* Rule of law
Reichstag arson, 41, 147, 177, 200
Representation, 82–84, 86–87
Retroactivity of law: liberal view of, 106–108, 112–113, 116, 200; in National Socialism, 133, 144, 147, 173, 177, 200
Riesman, David, 207
Rights: categorization of, 65–66, 102, 108–109, 205–208; and general law, 108, 197–198; system of, in Weimar Republic, 5, 33–34, 124. *See also* Social rights
Right to resistance, 45–46, 105, 198
Robespierre, 114
Röhm execution, 156, 174

Roman law, 144, 148
Rousseau, Jean-Jacques: on homogeneity, 66–67, 220–222, 235; on rule of law, 106–107, 111, 117–118, 126, 199
Rule of law: in Britain, 109–116, 119–120, 243–245; and calculability, 116–118, 201–205; classical liberal view of, 101–122, 197–204; decline of, 2–4, 35, 122–132, 204–205, 246–249; destruction of, in National Socialism, 11–16, 132–138, 142–166, 172–186, 234; ethical function of, 13, 117–118, 144, 201; formal structure of, 122, 201–202; political function of, 115–116, 118–122, 202–203; Prussian *Rechtsstaat*, 111–116, 118–120, 202–203, 243–246; Schmitt on, 3, 8–9, 118, 125–138, 142; social function of, 201–202; and socialism, 126; and supremacy of legislature, 109–110, 115–116, 119–120, 201; in United States, 203; Weber on, 11–13, 129, 142, 233. *See also* Constitutionalism; Formal law; General law; Law

Savigny, Friedrich, 114–115
Schleicher, Kurt von, 39–40
Schmitt, Carl: on concept of the political, 223; on constitutional amendments, 75, 127–128; on democracy, 9–10, 64–70; on general law, 8–9, 125–127; on homogeneity, 9–10, 64–70; and National Socialist legal order, 11–16, 132–138, 142–143, 173; on parliamentarism, 82–87; on plebiscitary dictatorship, 8–10, 68, 86–87; on rights, 65–66; on rule of law, 3, 8–9, 118, 125–138, 142; theory of concrete orders, 137–138, 173; on Weimar Constitution, 7–10, 40, 64–88, 125–132
Separation of powers, 113–118, 134, 142–144, 200, 248–249

Sinzheimer, Hugo, 135, 232, 239
Situationsjurisprudenz, 15
Social contract, 106, 122–124
Social democracy, 30–34, 41, 53, 54, 123. *See also* Democratic socialism
Socialization, 33, 232
Social rights, 5, 18, 124, 219
Sovereignty, 101–106, 212–214
Sozialrechtsstaat, 248. *See also* Welfare state
Spinoza, Benedict, 103–104, 211–214
State of nature, 102–103

Technological development, and democracy, 19, 222

Unger, Roberto, 1

Vico, Giovanni, 211–212
Volitional theory of criminal law, 14, 148–149, 172–173
Voltaire, 75, 118, 201
von Papen, Franz, 39–40

Weber, Max: and advantage of small numbers in organization, 238; on Free Law School, 129; on rational legality, 6, 44; on rule of law, 11–13, 142, 233
Weimar Constitution: amendment procedures, 74–77, 84–85, 127–128; Article 48, 6–7, 33, 35, 44–59; basic structure of, 4–10, 31, 46–47, 124; material-legal clauses in, 5–10, 32–34, 47, 70–74, 80–82, 124; Schmitt on, 7–10, 40, 64–88, 125–132; social democratic elements in, 5, 8, 32–33
Welfare state: conservative critics of, 247–248; and rule of law, 13, 18, 204–205, 209–210, 246–249; in Weimar Republic, 5–6, 34

Designer:	UC Press Staff
Compositor:	Prestige Typography
Text:	10/12 Baskerville
Display:	Baskerville
Printer:	Braun-Brumfield, Inc.
Binder:	Braun-Brumfield, Inc.